THE PLACE OF MUSIC

Mappings: Society/Theory/Space
A Guilford Series

APPROACHING HUMAN GEOGRAPHY: An Introduction to Contemporary Theoretical Debates
Paul Cloke, Chris Philo, and David Sadler

THE POWER OF MAPS
Denis Wood (with John Fels)

POSTMODERN CONTENTIONS: Epochs, Politics, Space
John Paul Jones III, Wolfgang Natter, and Theodore R. Schatzki, Editors

TRAVEL, GENDER, AND IMPERIALISM: Mary Kingsley and West Africa
Alison Blunt

WRITING WOMEN AND SPACE: Colonial and Postcolonial Geographies
Alison Blunt and Gillian Rose, Editors

LAW, SPACE, AND THE GEOGRAPHIES OF POWER
Nicholas K. Blomley

GROUND TRUTH: The Social Implications of Geographic Information Systems
John Pickles, Editor

INDIFFERENT BOUNDARIES: Spatial Concepts of Human Subjectivity
Kathleen M. Kirby

LOGICS OF DISLOCATION: Models, Metaphors, and Meanings of Economic Space
Trevor J. Barnes

SPACE, TEXT, AND GENDER: An Anthropological Study of the Marakwet of Kenya
Henrietta L. Moore

EMANCIPATING SPACE: Geography, Architecture, and Urban Design
Ross King

THE PLACE OF MUSIC
Andrew Leyshon, David Matless, and George Revill, Editors

The Place of Music

Edited by
ANDREW LEYSHON
DAVID MATLESS
GEORGE REVILL

THE GUILFORD PRESS
New York   London

© 1998 The Guilford Press
A Division of Guilford Publications, Inc.
72 Spring Street, New York, NY 10012
http://www.guilford.com

All rights reserved

No part of this book may be reproduced, translated, stored in a retrieval system, or transmitted, in any form or by any means, electronic, mechanical, photocopying, microfilming, recording, or otherwise, without written permission from the Publisher.

Printed in the United States of America

This book is printed on acid-free paper.

Last digit is print number: 9 8 7 6 5 4 3 2 1

Library of Congress Cataloging-in-Publication Data

The place of music / edited by Andrew Leyshon, David Matless, George Revill.
    p. cm.—(Mappings)
  Includes bibliographical references and index.
  ISBN 1-57230-313-1 (hardcover).—ISBN 1-57230-314-X (pbk.)
  1. Music and geography. 2. Music and society. I. Leyshon, Andrew. II. Matless, David. III. Revill, George. IV. Series.
ML3795.P58 1998
780'.9—dc219   97-46480
                                                                                CIP
                                                                                MN

Contents

		Contributors	vii
		Preface	ix
		Introduction: Music, Space, and the Production of Place Andrew Leyshon, David Matless, and George Revill	1
Chapter	1	The Global Music Industry: Contradictions in the Commodification of the Sublime John Lovering	31
Chapter	2	The Early Days of the Gramophone Industry in India: Historical, Social, and Musical Perspectives Gerry Farrell	57
Chapter	3	Welcome to Dreamsville: A History and Geography of Northern Soul Joanne Hollows and Katie Milestone	83
Chapter	4	Victorian Brass Bands: Class, Taste, and Space Trevor Herbert	104
Chapter	5	Locating Listening: Technological Space, Popular Music, and Canadian Mediations Jody Berland	129
Chapter	6	Borderlines: Bilingual Terrain in Scottish Song Steve Sweeney-Turner	151
Chapter	7	England's Glory: Sensibilities of Place in English Music, 1900–1950 Robert Stradling	176

Chapter 8 Samuel Coleridge-Taylor's Geography of 197
Disappointment: Hybridity, Identity, and
Networks of Musical Meaning
George Revill

Chapter 9 Global Undergrounds: The Cultural Politics 222
of Sound and Light in Los Angeles, 1965–1975
Simon Rycroft

Chapter 10 From "Dust Storm Disaster" to "Pastures of Plenty": 249
Woody Guthrie and Landscapes
of the American Depression
John R. Gold

Chapter 11 Sounding Out the City: Music and the Sensuous 269
Production of Place
Sara Cohen

Chapter 12 Desire, Power, and the Sonoric Landscape: Early 291
Modernism and the Politics of Musical Privacy
Richard Leppert

Index 322

Contributors

JODY BERLAND, PhD, Department of Humanities, York University, Toronto, Ontario, Canada

SARA COHEN, PhD, Institute of Popular Music, University of Liverpool, Liverpool, United Kingdom

GERRY FARRELL, PhD, Department of Music, City University, London, United Kingdom

JOHN R. GOLD, PhD, Department of Geography, Oxford Brookes University, Oxford, United Kingdom

TREVOR HERBERT, PhD, The Open University in Wales, Cardiff, United Kingdom

JOANNE HOLLOWS, PhD, Department of English and Media Studies, Nottingham Trent University, United Kingdom

RICHARD LEPPERT, PhD, Department of Cultural Studies and Comparative Literature, University of Minnesota, Minneapolis, Minnesota

ANDREW LEYSHON, PhD, School of Geographical Sciences, University of Bristol, Bristol, United Kingdom

JOHN LOVERING, BA, Department of City and Regional Planning, University of Wales, Cardiff, United Kingdom

DAVID MATLESS, PhD, University of Nottingham, Nottingham, United Kingdom

KATIE MILESTONE, PhD, Manchester Institute for Popular Culture, Manchester Metropolitan University, Manchester, United Kingdom

GEORGE REVILL, PhD, Department of Geography, Oxford Brookes University, Oxford, United Kingdom

SIMON RYCROFT, PhD, School of Cultural and Community Studies, University of Sussex, Brighton, United Kingdom

ROBERT STRADLING, PhD, School of History and Archaeology, University of Wales, Cardiff, United Kingdom

STEVE SWEENEY-TURNER, PhD, Department of Music, University of Leeds, Leeds, United Kingdom

Preface

While this book aims for a transdisciplinary mode of inquiry, it has obscure subdisciplinary origins. An ad hoc evening meeting at an Institute of British Geographers annual conference, set up on the basis that there had never been a substantive critical engagement between geography and music, produced not only a high degree of entertainment as discussion veered between contributors' specialist interests—punk, disco, kazoo bands, popular organ music—but an organizing committee for a conference eventually held in September 1993 at University College London. "The Place of Music," held under the auspices of the Economic Geography Research Group, the Landscape Research Group, and the Social and Cultural Geography Research Group, brought together a mix of academics and practitioners, some from geography, some not. A number of the chapters in this collection were originally presented at the conference, others have been specially commissioned.

Since 1993 the specific disciplinary engagement between geography and music has continued to develop. There has been a theme issue of *Transactions of the Institute of British Geographers*, published in 1995,[1] as well as a growing number of review essays arguing that music should be considered as "integral to the geographical imagination."[2] As stated at the onset, however, this volume is not an exercise in internal disciplinary argument. Many of the contributors to this volume would not style themselves as geographers and may have been surprised to be approached by those who do. If this volume is about exercising a geographical imagination, then this is not in terms of one discipline colonizing others, but of considering how various senses of the geographical are present in the production, transmission, and consumption of that particular part of the soundscape designated music. The book, is, we hope, both a distinctive and an entertaining transdisciplinary exercise in spatial thought and is aimed at a readership that spans the humanities and social sciences.

One of the biggest dilemmas that faced us when putting this book together was agreeing upon a running order for the chapters. One option we considered was to group the contributions into sections that we might have labeled "theory," "history," and "the contemporary," for example. On reflection, we decided not to do this. We decided that such a demarcation would suggest difference between chapters that do not really exist. Therefore, in the end, we chose a far less rigid organizational structure. The chapters are not arranged in sections, although they are arranged in a particular order. Thus, at the front of the book, the chapters tend to focus more upon the political economy of music, whereas later chapters focus more upon cultural and aesthetic issues and themes. We hope that this way the continuities and similarities between all the chapters in the book will emerge more clearly.

A debt is owed to a number of people and organizations: our contributors for showing patience as the volume had progressed at varying speed; the speakers at the original conference whose papers for whatever reason do not appear here; Jacquie Burgess of the Department of Geography at University College London for her help in staging the conference; the Economic Geography Research Group, the Landscape Research Group, and the Social and Cultural Geography Research Group for their financial assistance; Stuart Corbridge and Gerry Kearns for their initial enthusiasm; Peter Wissoker at The Guilford Press for even more patience; the series editors, Michael Dear, Derek Gregory, and Nigel Thrift, for their encouragement when it was needed; and Kit Kelly, Liz Humphries, Hanne Page, and Anna Pasckowicz for secretarial help along the way.

NOTES

1. Hudson, R. (1995). Making music work?: Alternative regeneration strategies in a deindustrialised locality: The case of Derwentside. *Transactions of the Institute of British Geographers, 20,* 460–473. Kong, L. (1995). Music and cultural politics: Ideology and resistance in Singapore. *Transactions of the Institute of British Geographers, 20,* 447–459. Valentine, G. (1995). Creating transgressive space: The music of kd lang. *Transactions of the Institute of British Geographers, 20,* 474–486.

2. Smith, S. (1994). Soundscape. *Area, 26,* 232–240, especially 238. See also Kong, L. (1995). Popular music in geographical analyses. *Progress in Human Geography, 19,* 183–198. Nash, P., & Carney, G. (1996). The seven themes of music geography. *Canadian Geographer, 40,* 69–74.

INTRODUCTION

Music, Space, and the Production of Place

ANDREW LEYSHON
DAVID MATLESS
GEORGE REVILL

WHAT IS THE PLACE OF MUSIC?

More than colours and forms, it is sounds and their arrangements that fashion societies. With noise is born disorder and its opposite: the world. With music is born power and its opposite: subversion. In noise can be read the codes of life, the relations among men. Clamour, Melody, Dissonance, Harmony; when it is fashioned by man with specific tools, when it invades man's time, when it becomes sound, noise is the source of purpose and power, of the dream—Music. . . .

All music, any organization of sounds is then a tool for the creation or consolidation of a community, of a totality. It is what links a power center to its subjects, and thus, more generally, it is an attribute of power in all of its forms. Therefore, any theory of power today must include a theory of the localization of noise and its endowment with form.[1]

In typically extravagant style Jacques Attali boldly marks out a place for music at the center of the development of Western civilization since the Middle Ages. In *Noise: The Political Economy of Music,* Attali proposes that the economic, social, and political dynamics of Western society are both presaged by and encapsulated in the relations of musical production. While this thesis is simultaneously daring and highly contentious, we do not begin with it here as a formula for what follows. Rather, Attali's statement serves to indicate the multiple scales of the place of music, the potential scope of inquiry, and the range of social and political pertinence of music and noise. Originally published in 1977, well before the proliferation of interest in the social production of music, and translated into English in 1985, *Noise* resonates with current thinking in the social sciences and humanities, touching on processes central to contemporary theorizations of music and modernity.

For Attali, the political economy of music begins with the social distinction between nature and culture, continues through a set of processes localizing and commodifying sound, and results in the mobilization of particular sound as a universal globalizing aesthetic, political, and economic force. Music for Attali is a source of identification, a shared symbol of collectivity, and a means of generating and enforcing social conformity. The dynamics of musical production are inherently social and political, coercive and collaborative, concerned both with identity formation and the establishment and maintenance of social groupings. Making and consuming music are considered to be inseparable parts of musical production. Attali reminds us of the psychological potency of music, as well as its power as an economic commodity and its social and symbolic value. The mobility of music, its particular qualities that enable it to inhabit different times and places thanks to reproduction in performance, by recording, and through various forms of electronic transmission, raise issues of spatial scale and the role of music in mediating between "a power center and its subjects." The production of music, the creation of place and the deployment of music in the exercise of power lead Attali to a consideration of the practices by which something as local and particular as Western classical music can be mobilized as a universal discourse. Thus Attali concludes that "any theory of power today must include a theory of the localization of noise and its endowment with form." Here Attali has arrived at a focus for study that recognizes the simultaneously material and imaginal qualities of musical production, through processes that both localize and give form. It is a focus that gives a central role for the spatial processes by which sounds are differentiated, and through which the economic, social, and aesthetic geographies forged through musical practices are intimately bound up with the production of space and place.

By adopting the term "noise" as the central problematic for his study, Attali immediately recognizes the social role of music in the establishment and maintenance of binary opposites recognized as fundamental to the social construction of modern consciousness: order and chaos, human and nonhuman, civilization and barbarism, culture and nature. In the cultural politics of sound, deployment of the term "noise" to distinguish between music and nonmusic acts as a very powerful ideological signifier. For a sound to be classified as "noise" places it outside understanding and beyond culture in the realm of pure materiality, a world of sound waves and audio frequencies, pitch, and timbre. This is both the nonsignifying province of value free science and the primordial wilderness of raw nature, while as a counterhegemonic strategy the power of sound as "noise," to be disquieting, subversive, and antisocial, makes it a vehicle for critique and change. Attali suggests this with his claim "With noise is born power and its opposite: subversion." In such countercultural projects "noise" reenters the realm of signifying practices and sounds move back and forth across the social divide between music and nonmusic.

Particularly illustrative of this tension and opposition is a local battle drawn from the history of our own discipline of geography. Distinctions of music and noise, as well as contrasting visions of the local and the global, ran through a curious and furious exchange in 1973. Outlining his "Geography of the Future," radical geographer William Bunge offered a particular soundtrack for a new society:

> Clearly a world culture of international youth is arising. . . . It appears that from the younger generation everyone will speak English. . . . The world culture probably will be technologically Western European, heavily electronic with free electricity. It is less clear but likely that African music and dance forms will be the dominant world-wide forms . . . people the world around are voting with their feet, so to speak, for this dance and music.[2]

Bunge's celebration of a new global soundscape brought an angry reply from Donald Fryer:

> We are to move in a world of youth in which languages other than English have virtually ceased to exist . . . and sprawl around on the floor listening to "African" music [i.e., hard rock] amplified and distorted by a universal electronic agency. Nor shall we escape the electronic blare beyond our homes, where outside in the streets people will be dancing to the same cacophony. Bunge complains rightly of the noise pollution of our modern society, but shows no awareness that perhaps as much as one-third of our high school and junior high school population has already suffered serious auditory damage from listening to such overamplified electronic music, which many of us would already regard as one of the major noise pollutants of modern life.[3]

Two geographers diverge on what counts as music, and by implication what qualifies as culture. Bunge's soundworld is Fryer's nightmare: "if our younger generation prefers 'beat' to Bach . . . this reflects not so much an autonomous decision of our youth as the superior pressure exerted on them by record manufacturers, disc jockeys, and radio and TV stations for highly commercial purposes."[4] Fryer and Bunge offer different soundtracks for future geographies. Fryer laments cuts in musical education: "Nobody pushes Bach . . . Such material is . . . the first to be cut in times of real or imagined financial stringency, as indeed the Legislature of the State of Hawaii is doing to the Schools Symphony Concerts program as I write."[5] For Fryer, the environment of pop is an anti-culture, with universally commercialized African rhythm undermining the universal cultural standards of the classical Western canon. For Bunge, the new and global is to be celebrated because it is popular and young; Fryer chastises a "resurrection by a professed radical of the discredited economic doctrine of consumer sovereignty."[6] It is curious that Fryer, rather than the radical Bunge, echoes Theodor Adorno: "A critical sociology of music will have to find out in detail why today—unlike a hundred years ago—popular music is bad, bound to be bad, without exception."[7]

Bunge and Fryer begin to bring out some of the key issues addressed in this book: the nature of soundscapes, definitions of music and cultural value, the geographies of different musical genres, and the place of music in local, national, and global cultures. It is perhaps significant that such matters emerged only in a polemical exchange; geographical work on music has until very recently tended to restrict itself to mapping the diffusion of musical styles, or analyzing geographical imagery in lyrics, working with a deliberately restricted sense of geography, offering the geographer's angle on well-trodden ground rather than asking how a geographical approach might refigure that ground. In contrast we proceed from a sense that to inject geography into music might produce an effect analogous to that which David Harvey claims in relation to social theory: "The insertion of concepts of space into any social theory has a numbing effect upon that theory's central propositions."[8] *The Place of Music* presents space and place not simply as sites where or about which music happens to be made, or over which music has diffused; rather, here different spatialities are suggested as being formative of the sounding and resounding of music. Such a richer sense of geography highlights the spatiality of music, and the mutually generative relations of music and place. Space produces as space is produced. To consider the place of music is not to reduce music to its location, to ground it down into some geographical baseline, but to allow a purchase on the rich aesthetic, cultural, economic, and political geographies of musical language.

Introducing a collection such as this is rather tricky. The authors consider such various musical spatial practices as driving around a region in search of rare soul music, globally producing new musical technologies, singing on behalf of a nation, marking out spaces of rebellion in sound, using song to track migration, and listening to the radio while driving. The essays work through multiple spatial registers: the personal, wider collective social spaces, nations, empires, worlds. Rather than introducing the volume through some all-embracing summary of chapters, forcing them all into line, we offer here a particular route into the place of music by working through the dialectics of the universal and the particular that have informed both "classical" and "popular" musics in the West over past centuries. Our aim here has been to go beyond collections that focus on one particular genre of music, in part so as to bring out the distinctive spatialities constitutive of questions of genre. The labeling of music as "classical" as opposed to "popular," for example, has worked in part through a value system based on a geographical categorization, with classical music in conventional accounts contributing to the development of a progressive, abstract Western high culture—universal, self-justifying, ostensibly place-*less*—and popular music marked down as a "merely" local form, appealing to everyday emotions and particular circumstances and making no contribution to an autonomous realm of musical language. The distinctions between classical–pure and popular–worldly express a spatiality that assumes particular relationships of music, economy, and culture.

In one sense, however, this collection does have a rather limited geography, in that the contributions focus primarily on elements of Western music. We have not sought here to provide a representative map of the world's music; indeed, with one or two exceptions, the contributions do not proceed through cartographic or ethnographic investigation.[9] This Introduction also proceeds very much through Western examples, although we would argue that the kinds of questions raised here are by no means parochial. We have structured the Introduction around a dialectic of the universal and the particular, moving through the operation of categories of universal and particular in the production of spaces of classical music to the variegated spaces of contemporary pop culture. Our intention is not to reproduce distinctions of universal and particular but to question the socially constructed boundary between these spheres. We wish to highlight not only the many similar social and economic trajectories of genres such as "classical" and "popular," but also how the divide itself is negotiated and renegotiated. We conclude the introduction by considering another sense of music's spatiality, namely, the "environment of music." While the authors in this volume may not have had such frameworks in mind when they produced their chapters, we feel such questions fit the spirit in which their contributions work. The Introduction may not map the volume but it should at least provide a guiding thread.

UNIVERSAL MUSIC 1?: A CLASSICAL LANGUAGE

Since the mid-18th century classical genres have been defined by practitioners and musicologists as a transcendent language of individual self-expression, above concerns of economy, polity, and society.[10] Such a definition has its own historical geography, one linked to the rise of the nation-state and bourgeois society. The idea that sounds speak directly to us in an unmediated fashion found its philosophical grounding in German idealism,[11] with music "at once the most humanly-revealing form of art and the form most resistant to description or analysis in conceptual terms."[12]

Music has played its part in marking a nature–culture divide in Western thought since classical antiquity, turning on such issues as those debated by Rameau and Rousseau in the mid-18th century as to whether harmony was natural and thus subject to universal (mathematical) laws.[13] Throughout the Renaissance and into the Enlightenment music and mathematical science fused in theories of cosmic order and practical treatises on the rules of harmony and counterpoint. A particular conception of nature defined and rationalized culture, justifying particular structures of social and political authority.[14]

Processes of "naturalization" in music can also be traced through the spaces of practical performance. The arrangements of listening in the concert room, along with the separation of music from medieval ritual, the development of specialist musicianship, commercial publishing, and the invention of synoptic scores, enshrined the individual performer/performance as an unmediated, "natural," and "neutral" channel for the work of the composer.[15] The reversal of the medieval situation of musicians waiting on an audience produced "a gradual objectification of performance,"[16] while auditorium design eliminated variability in listening, giving the illusion of unmediated contact with the music through the performer.

Such spatial relationships coincided with the dominance in the late 18th century of sonata form, combining the tension between a binary harmonic structure and an overlaid ternary thematic structure. Dramatic structures of emotional tension, expectation, and resolution derived from the formal properties of the music itself, rather than from extramusical literary or narrative sources. Rosen[17] relates this development directly to the new requirements of the bourgeois concert room, where the sonata's symmetry and clarity could hold a large audience without the assistance of ornamental enhancement or instrumental or vocal elaboration. As the site of performance was regularized, so performance itself was placed under the full control of the composer. Individuality of performance was displaced into an interpretation of the heroic individual composer. In this context Beethoven emerged as the epitome of the composer genius, celebrating the universal values of the French Revolution with a mercurial individual masculinity speaking through the abstract logic of pure form.[18]

The separation of music from ritual and its emergence as a commodity associated with the bourgeois concert hall is linked to the commodification of musical knowledge.[19] The development of music colleges, professional qualifications, and theoretical treatises on form, harmony, and history during the 19th century gave music and musicians cultural distinction. John Shepherd argues forcefully that universal musical standards were defined through minority cultural practice: "Belief in the other-worldly nature of musical inspiration and the ability of only a minority to exploit it in turn leads to the concept of an objective aesthetic."[20] For Shepherd, the assumed fixed criteria against which all music can be judged are rooted in the musical languages of ruling groups privileging the "classical" over the "popular" and the "masculine" against the "feminine." Such cultural distinctions were brought to bear both within and beyond the West. Leppert and McClary show how such formulations have legitimized Western sophistication and complexity against the "primitive," and suggest that ethnomusicological questioning of music and society has been acceptable only when applied to other cultures: "Recognizing that other musics are bound up with social values does not necessarily lead to the conclusion that our music likewise might be: more often it simply results in the chauvinistic, ideological reaffirmation of the superiority of Western art, which is still widely held to be autonomous."[21] George Revill's chapter on Samuel Coleridge-Taylor in this volume (Chapter 8) shows how for a black composer in Edwardian London categories of the classical and the primitive could conspire to frustrate ambitions to enter such a space of musical autonomy. Revill combines notions of hybridity from postcolonial and actor–network theory to trace Coleridge-Taylor's movement through racial and gendered categorization in England to racial affirmation in the United States.

As Leppert discusses in his book *Music and Image*,[22] the apparent primitive directness, emotional transparency, and "naturalness" of musical expression has long presented difficulties for and generated contradictions within the attempted gendering of musical practices. His work on 18th-century musical education shows how music was represented as both an intellectual discipline, and therefore a suitable activity for young males, and as emotional and expressive, and therefore suitable only for females. Gender ambivalence relates closely to music's particular position between nature and culture and has often worked to marginalize and ghettoize women in many areas of musical practice since the Renaissance. The exotic otherness of classical dance, the romantic hysteria of the operatic heroine, no less than the heroic masculinity of the lead guitarist in a rock band or the Lawrentian attempts by early-20th-century folk theorists such as Rolf

Gardiner to reinvent folk dance as a masculine "priest's dance of ritual and discipline ... the remains of a purely masculine ceremonial, ... a ritual of discipline for war and sex expression"[23]—all have worked to carve out spaces for women within music that are malleable, supportive, and reactive rather than proactive and creative.[24]

PARTICULARIZING THE CLASSICAL

Music has always been implicated in the social and political world. Music's power to affect, disturb, rouse, and subdue has been used to great effect by monarchies, armies, and governments throughout history. In the 20th century alone art music has served imperialism, nationalism, and totalitarianism through the state's appropriation of such composers as Wagner in Germany, Shostakovich in the Soviet Union, and Elgar in Britain. As Edward Said suggests, "The closer one looks at the geography of Western culture and music's place in it, the more compromised, the more socially involved and active music seems."[25] As Trevor Herbert shows (Chapter 4, this volume) in relation to interrelationships of class, taste, and space in the history of the brass band movement, the definition of music as an art form that transcends particular circumstances itself has a key role to play in the specific location of its popular social reproduction. The "morally improving" embedded force of such music could be held to derive precisely from its supposedly transcendent aesthetic.

Designed to fit particular formal and ceremonial spaces, music at once defines and reinforces the disposition of power within those spaces and the authority represented by that space. Music's ability to carry ideologically explicit meanings yet remain open to various interpretations as a universal particular has made it a potent political force in the figuration of national and, as Herbert shows, subnational geographies. Music's apparent naturalism was important for 19th- and early-20th-century European nationalist composers such as Dvořák, Brahms, Vaughan Williams, Sibelius, Janáček, Bartók, and Kodály.[26] Such music combined a belief in the sovereign authority of the composer and the universality of musical forms with a faith in music's power to refer directly to everyday experience. The imitation of natural sounds, the quotation of folk songs and dances, and references to localities and regions could rhetorically tie music to the rhythmical structures of land, landscape, and language.[27] For example, in Smetena's depiction of the Czech lands *Ma Vlast* (My country), the story of the river Moldau flowing from its source through forest and plain offers national integration and reconciliation. Robert Stradling (Chapter 7, this volume) draws out a parallel English national musical symbolism around the River Severn in the work of self-styled "national" composers, who both worked out and worked up their pastoral Englishness through sensibilities of the particular. Vaughan Williams linked folk tunes to specific landscapes, presenting folk songs, "the natural development of excited speech," as founded on the rhythm and timbre of native language and expressive of a national essence.[28] Composition could become a form of national service: "We must cultivate a sense of musical citizenship. Why should not the musician be the servant of the state and build national monuments . . . ?"[29]

The categorization of composers as "universal" or "particularist" has its own history. Individuals have been placed in both groups at different or even the same times. While the early-20th-century atonal avant-garde valued J. S. Bach as a rational, mathematically precise composer of pure universal music, European nationalist composers promoted Bach as a provincial musician serving the needs of his home community, who was a countersymbol to a supposedly dehumanizing modernism.[30] Mach[31] similarly traces the redefinition of Chopin. At first seen as a late-19th-century symbol of an independent Poland's contribution to universal European culture, he was later transformed into a socialist hero, who adhered to his roots and refused to "conform to the bourgeois aesthetics of romanticism."[32]

The issues of musical universality and nationality raised here and in the preceding section have been most famously addressed by Adorno. For Adorno, art could show the liberating power of human creativity, as in the works of Beethoven where the ethos of liberal humanism found expression in every detail of the work's dynamic tonality and structural form. Modern "culture industries" had destroyed such potential, channeling utopian possibilities into passive consumption.[33] At the heart of Adorno's social criticism is a universalist ideal of western classical music whereby "good" music directs its developing autonomy toward social critique, questioning accepted aural structures and rejecting the ideologies and market mechanisms connecting music to bourgeois society. In this context Adorno privileges the atonal avant-garde, dismissing as "regressive" or "false" a countertradition following Berlioz, Rossini, Verdi, Elgar, Stravinsky, and the like, in part because of its social specificity.[34] For a sociology of music whose ultimate aim is social involvement, the result is a rejection of a certain form of musical sociospatiality. Adorno dismisses national musics, and all popular musics, because of their particular connections to place.

UNIVERSAL MUSIC 2?:
THE CONTEMPORARY MUSIC INDUSTRY

The making of music is not only a cultural and sociological process, it is also an economic process. However, to date, economic geography, perhaps because of a lingering productivist bias, has not undertaken a serious appraisal of the spatial dynamics of the music industry. In this volume (Chapter 1) John Lovering seeks to extend a political-economy approach to this cultural industry, tracing the production of new spaces of music via processes of globalization feeding off diversity. The global music industry emerges as a business needing to work through a limited voraciousness such that the spaces of emerging new musics can be monitored and tapped yet not stifled. As Gerry Farrell illustrates in his contribution (Chapter 2, this volume), the global ambitions of musical capital are almost as old as the industry itself. Farrell's study of the forays of London-based Gramophone and Typewriter Ltd. into India during the early 20th century shows an encounter with, and a marketing of, diversity. He reveals how a putative global industry effectively remade local spaces of production and consumption.

At the end of the 20th century, Western companies operating within the music industry continue to range across the global in search of markets, and do so now with the security afforded by an extraordinary level of market power. In 1992, the music industry generated worldwide sales of $29,000 million, in a market dominated by just five major global corporations: Warners, Bertlesmann Music Group, Polygram International Group, EMI–Virgin, and Sony. Seventy percent of world record sales were generated in just five national markets, each dominated by the "majors," which between them captured 73% of sales in the United States (31% of the global market), 60% of sales in Japan (15%), 90% of sales in Germany (9%), 73% of sales in the United Kingdom (7%), and 87% of sales in France (7%).[35]

If one looks beyond these indications of market power, then it is possible to discern a process of corporate restructuring that provides a fascinating case study of an industry being remade in line with corporate strategies which, informed by a discourse of globalization, seek to reap the benefits of mergers, acquisitions, and alliances on a global scale. The boundaries of the music industry have blurred as powerful corporate interests have acquired controlling stakes in record companies to exploit both horizontal and vertical integration processes.[36] Economies of scope are exploited via horizontal integration through "media synergy,"[37] linking musical output to other media such as movies or publishing to maximize corporate revenue. Thus the Warner record company is owned by U.S. media conglomerate Time–Warner, while German publishing company Bertlesmann AG has its own record division, Bertlesmann Music Group. Vertical integration has proceeded through the purchase of large record companies by manufacturers of audio reproduction equipment. Phillips Electronics controls Polygram International Group, while, until recently, Thorn EMI owned the EMI–Virgin record company. The fifth major, Sony, has pursued both horizontal and vertical strategies, buying into the record industry through its purchase of CBS Records, and moving into related forms of cultural production through the purchase of Hollywood film studios Columbia and Tristar.

Horizontal and vertical strategies are linked in the key role played by copyright legislation. Ownership of copyright confers the exclusive right to the income derived from the exploitation of cultural products,[38] enabling the synergetic exploitation of cultural products across a range of media, and playing a crucial role in the creation of new formats for the reproduction of recorded music. By purchasing record companies and their copyrights, manufacturers of audio equipment seek to safeguard their reproductive investments. Consumers will only buy new formats such at digital audio tape and digital compact cassettes if musical output can be played upon them. By owning copyrights, manufacturing companies ensure the availability of musical "software" for their musical "hardware."[39] Such questions of media synergy are again not entirely new. Trevor Herbert (Chapter 4, this volume) indicates how in the 19th century the operations of music publishers effected parallel controls over the production of music. The publisher Novello owned the *Musical Times,* a major opinion-forming voice in British music and a vehicle for promoting Novello's publications. The publishers Chappell and Novello both sponsored major concert series in late-19th-century London, while Chappell & Co were part owners along with another music publisher of St. James' Hall, London's premier concert venue between 1858 and 1905.[40]

The restructuring of the music industry is not only a tale of globalization. The majors are reliant on the global–local interplay of economic and cultural processes. Music is realized as a commodity through complex production filières that lock production into particular locations. The discovery, nurture, and recording of artistic talent is a transactional, information-rich, and highly discursive process. As a consequence, local social networks are critical to global success. Negus describes the key role of A&R (artist and repertoire) staff in fostering "a contact network covering a range of production companies, minor record labels, publishers, managers and lawyers.... So that what is happening across the country can be communicated to and assessed by the corporation." Such contacts seek a benefit in turn: "They might enthusiastically 'talk-up' certain artists. ... They will probe the large company for information about the type of acts and material being sought."[41] Such organizational characteristics place a premium on proximity. Thus the creative part of the music industry tends to be characterized by spatial agglomeration, concentrating in a handful of key centers, notably Los Angeles and London.[42] The five majors anchor the music business in these nodes, surrounded by a dense institutional matrix of smaller record companies and related businesses, some independent but others increasingly "affiliated" to the larger companies through a sometimes short-term equity, financial, or contractual relationship.[43] Smaller record companies tend to act almost as centers of research and development within the industry, spotting and cultivating new trends and musical styles (Figure I.1). Through such contractual relationships the majors are locked into particular musical economies. The globalized music industry is thus forever in motion, characterized by "continually shifting corporate constellations which are difficult to plot, as deals expire, new relationships are negotiated, new acquisitions made and joint ventures embarked upon.... The distinctions between an inside and outside, and between centre and margins, have given way to a web of mutually dependent work groupings radiating out from multiple centres."[44]

This interplay between institutions, actors, and their discursive practices has been important in the creation of musical places over a long period of time. Indeed, entrepreneurs, impresarios, and commissioning agents have played a key role in fashioning performers and performances, localizing musical practices, and commodifying and universalizing cultural values since the beginnings of commercial concert life. For example, impresarios such as the violinist John Bannister in the 1670s and Johann Peter Salomon, who persuaded Joseph Haydn to come to London in the 1790s, helped to make the city a unique center for professional commercial music making, substantially outside the control of church and state.[45]

The exchange of social and (sub-)cultural capital is important not only in the making of music, but also—indeed, perhaps even more so—in the consumption of music. According to Thornton,[46] there are many groups in possession of sufficient "subcultural capital" to be able to foster new musical genres and to help constitute new audiences for emerging styles of music: "DJs, club organisers, clothing designers, music and style journalists and various record industry professionals all make a living from their subcultural capital.... People in these professions often enjoy a lot of respect not only because of their high volume of subcultural capital, but also from their role in defining and creating it.[47] The relative importance of these different groups varies from time to time, from genre to genre, and from place to place. Within the genre of dance music, for example, DJs are especially important in helping to inscribe cultural value upon the records they play.[48] The ways in which a subculture can coalesce around particularly influential DJs is clearly illustrated in this volume in Hollows and Milestone's historical geography of northern soul (Chapter 3). They illustrate how, by emphasizing obscurity and rarity, the DJs reinscribed the cultural and economic value of the records they played, and in so doing became leading arbiters of "taste" within the scene.

One should be wary, however, of romanticizing spaces of consumption, or indeed of assuming that consumption is a responsive realm conforming

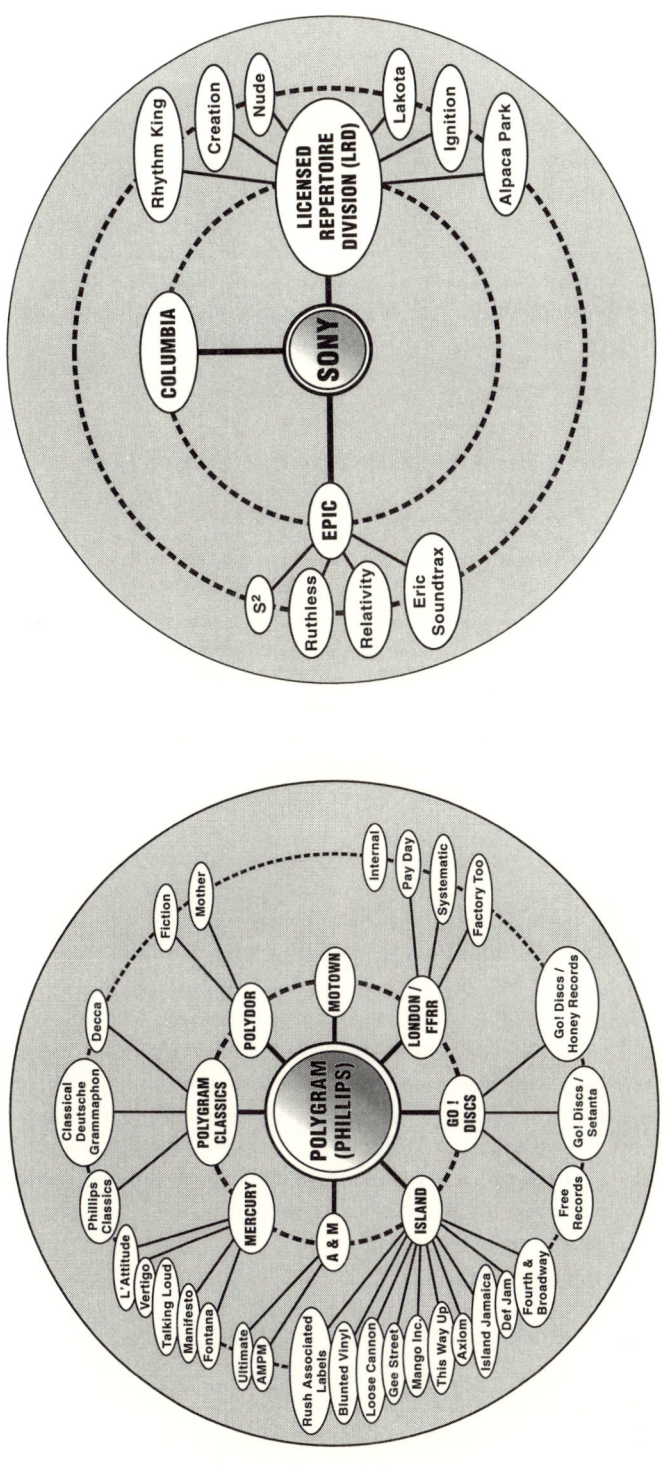

FIGURE I.1. Corporate networks in the music industry: Polygram and Sony. Adapted from Whom owes who II. (Researched by L. O'Brien). (1996, April). *Q*, pp. 41–46. Adapted by permission.

to or dissenting from already formed spaces of production. In common with many other industries,[49] the production process within the music industry is increasingly coming under the influence, of large retailers seeking to influence if not control, consumption. As du Gay and Negus argue:

> Retailers now occupy an increasingly influential position within the production/consumption relations of popular music. Whereas in the past, the record companies as "producers" or "manufacturers" tended to exert control over the retailers through "forward integration" and control of the product, today it is "backward integration" from the retailer which is shifting power relations within the industry.[50]

The power that the large music retailers possess, founded in their growing control of sales of recorded music, is increasingly being felt at the heart of the musical production process. The monopsonistic power of the retailers is exerted in several ways:

> The work of persuading buyers to stock recordings—the job of the record company sales force—has become harder. Sales staff are confronted by statistical histories of the sales of artists and genres of music. Not only are retailers less likely to take a risk with new artists and genres . . . , there are indications that retailers have begun making demands about the packaging or artists' products in their stores, and exerting a subtle (and occasionally not so subtle) influence over the image of the artists that will appear in the store.[51]

In the face of such developments it becomes ever more difficult to sustain the romantic myth of the struggle of the artist to carve out spaces of creativity by resisting the commercial impulses of a capitalist music industry. All acts of musical production are necessarily creative in one way or another; but if the artist wishes to continue working within the music industry, then his or her "product" must also be commercially successful in order to sustain the economic imperatives of the industry.[52] Thus, musical output flowing from the global music industry is necessarily both creative and commercial; whether a particular type of music is subsequently categorized as one or the other seems to depend much more on postproduction discursive struggles involving the record companies, the artists themselves, and the various agents of subcultural capital.

SOUNDS OF HETEROGENEITY

Whatever its global–local complexities, the emergence of a global capitalist music industry might be seen as confirming Adorno's worst predictions of commodified and commercialized culture, with differences flattened into global uniformity as a bad new Western pop universal supersedes Adorno's good classical version. For Negus, the "global production and consumption of popular music in the 1990s is defined by the North Atlantic Anglo-American cultural movements of sounds and images, and European, USA and Japanese dominance of finance capital and hardware."[53] Audiences and markets are constituted for cultural production on a global scale. A "global music" has emerged that sells across national and international cultural boundaries. Artists such as Madonna, Michael Jackson, U2, and the Rolling Stones may be products of Anglo-American culture, but in another sense they are almost placeless, their product endlessly circulating the globe via world tour or electronic media. Is Michael Jackson Adorno's nightmare made flesh?

Such a view of homogenized and commodified culture has been contested. Shuker, arguing for "oppositional popular possibilities," suggests that to consider the popular music audience as "a mass of passive recipients is totally at variance with contemporary audience studies."[54] Popular music is regarded as a potential site of resistance. Local live music, while not necessarily producing an alternative sound, may enable people to experience music in distinctive localized ways.[55] The audience for popular music is not uniform but instead characterized by fragmentation, division, and fracture. Some argue that far from being a homogenous cultural space, the terrain of popular music is pitted with alternative spaces of musical production and cultural resistance. Will Straw's discussion of the "alternative" rock scenes found in most North American cities traces infrastructures of performance, production, transmission and distribution developed as local punk scenes stabilized in the early 1980s, fostering a variety of musical styles self-consciously local and historical. Such alternative musical scenes were characterized by low turnover, and differed from their equivalents in the United Kingdom (considered below) in not necessarily judging success on their music's "capacity to register collective change within the larger cultural space in which it circulates."[56] The national musical space was sidestepped: "In their reliance on small-scale infrastructures of production and dissemination, these spaces are rooted deeply within local circumstances, a feature commonly invoked in claims as to their political significance."[57] Straw argues that a stress on locality is accompanied by a complex historicity: "A variety of different temporalities ... come to coexist within a bounded cultural space. There is often a distinctive density of historical time within the performance styles of alternative groups: most noticeably, an inflection of older, residual styles with a contemporary irony which itself evokes a bohemian heritage.... Temporal movement is transformed into cartographic density."[58] Straw interprets such scenes as sites of cultural resistance whereby relatively small, insular, and mainly white audiences assert their distinction from a hegemonic mainstream musical culture.

A parallel Canadian story emerges from Jody Berland's chapter in this volume (Chapter 5), which focuses less on spaces of production and performance than on methods of transmission. Berland shows how public radio as a particular kind of communication has acted as a space for the reproduction of musical values not always congruent with those of commerce. Certain forms of music cohabit the radio with other sounds—local news items, weather reports from around the country—to produce a cultural zone at odds with another North American soundscape of, Berland suggests, placeless music and talk. Just as in Britain listening to the radio shipping forecast can imply tuning into a certain space of public culture for the least nautical listener, so in Berland's story a litany of place-names reporting weather effects to locate the listener in a public soundspace. Berland's chapter in many ways follows John Lovering's distinction of the commercial–global and the resistant–local (Chapter 1, this volume). Other alternative spaces, similarly encompassing listening and driving but also collecting and dancing, are mapped by Joanne Hollows and Katie Milestone in their study of the British northern soul scene (Chapter 3, this volume). Their chapter is less concerned to set place against the placeless, the local against the global, than to see how a particular scene emerges out of a mix of international record exchange and regional club culture. Rare black U.S. soul records become the commodities to fuel a white musical culture in the English northwest setting itself against the musical prescriptions of London. A network of clubs linked by informal publications and a new regional motorway network are the focal spaces of Hollows and Milestone's "Dreamsville."

Arguments regarding audience fragmentation can be made for many musical genres; classical, jazz and folk have experienced a proliferation of subgenres in recent years, for example, in early music and authentic performance movements and in crossover and fusion styles. It is arguably too easy to view such pluralism in terms of localism and cultural resistance alone. The impetus for these forms of fragmentation lie not only in the dynamics of subcultural social groupings operating in both elite and popular culture but also depend on complimentary economic and technological dynamics. At a time when the service industries have made niche marketing into a fine art, it is often very difficult to determine where local "grassroots" cultural practice ends and commercial exploitation begins, or, in fact, the extent to which the two are mutually incompatible.[59] Are enthusiasms for "big band" music, traditional jazz, country and western, Celtic rock, or Breton folk music merely the musical equivalents of the heritage landscapes and eclectic postmodern nonplaces produced by the leisure industries? In the United Kingdom many of these musical subcultures appear to exhibit similar sociological characteristics to those suggested by Milestone and Hollows for northern soul, for example, informal news networks, ghettoized media coverage, and specialist record markets. These create an imagined community embedded in particular local social structures by geographical focus on a few key venues and festivals. Such sociospatial specificities help produce forms of self-consciously crafted regional identity. These often have some grounding in both place and practice, history and geography, as suggested by the stereotype of the East Anglian rural "cowboy" listening to Tammy Wynnette in his/her pickup truck, or the northern "folkie" with a penchant for real ale and a commitment to lost working-class community.

It is precisely these kinds of acts of local appropriation and adoption of cultural forms that are cited by critics of the cultural imperialism thesis. Although the music forms enjoyed by audiences may not be "authentic," in that they have not sprung organically from the communities in which they are celebrated, they are used and consumed in ways that are sufficiently outside the mainstream of cultural production that they become locally distinctive.

Similar arguments can be used to defuse a related critique of the "world music" phenomenon, which sees the commercial success of music recorded by artists from developing countries as due merely to the way in which this music provides "new sounds for a bored [Western] culture."[60] Moreover, critics such as Timothy Mitchell have argued that the Western consumption of music from the global periphery represents yet a further stage in the exploitation and plundering of developing countries by the populations of core capitalist countries:

> At the risk of over-simplifying the nature of the relationship between the West and "world musicians," it is too often reminiscent of colonial trade patterns. In a very real sense, the music of South America, African and Asia is being mined as a raw resource.... Locally recorded albums are pressed and packaged abroad, then exported back as the "refined" product in much the same way as the Gambia, a major exporter of ground nuts, imports tubs of peanut butter.[61]

However, as Mitchell goes on to argue, acts of cultural appropriation work both ways, so that it is probably safer to consider world music as part of a broader process of cultural circulation, rather than as a one-way process of musical extraction. Indeed, much of what circulates as world music in the West should be seen as a hybridized product of the mixing of local musical styles and genres with imported Western musical forms and musical instruments. Mitchell points to a musical "conversation," the origins of which are difficult to locate, and which has radically different political consequences than those alluded to by critics who sympathize with the cultural imperialism thesis. Responding to the comments of geographer

Peter Jackson,[62] who argues that when Western audiences listen to world music artists such as the Zimbabwean band the Bhundu Boys they engage in a form of "musical tourism," which continues the process by which black music has been exploited and appropriated by others, Mitchell argues that such musical exploitation and appropriation can also be viewed in a different, more positive light, one that sees benefits accrue to the producers of world music, such as the Bhundu Boys and others:

> The Bhundu Boys have adapted Anglo-American rock music forms and produced an open-tuned, distinctively African electric guitar idiom. This makes possible a cross-fertilization of Zimbabwean music with the range of popular dance musics in the Western world and paves the way for the mass marketing of other music from this source, such as the chimurenga ("music of the struggle") of the politically militant Zimbabwean musical mentor, Thomas Mapfuno. In 1989 Island's Mango label released Mapfuno's album *Corruption,* while in 1990 the Virgin Earthworks label released two volumes entitled *Zimbabwean Frontline,* featuring Mapfuno, the Four Brothers and a number of Zimbawean bands.[63]

Therefore, despite the commercial exploitation that inevitably follows from an engagement with the capitalist music industry, bands from developing countries are at least finding receptive audiences and markets in the West, with some economic spinoffs for themselves and, hopefully, for their home countries and communities. At the same time, and if nothing else, the circulation of these products at least provides a point of contact with social and political processes in developing countries for Western audiences.

We can trace similar arguments over the influences of the local, the authentic, the hybrid, and the mobile in accounts of rap and hip-hop, which has been frequently portrayed by practitioners, critics, and intellectuals as a counterhegemonic music with a distinct and significant history and geography. The "standard" narrative, written in the main by African-American intellectuals with background in journalism and cultural studies, places rap in a long line of black musical forms transported from Africa to America during slavery and based upon antiphony (call and response), and developing through a series of genres thereafter.[64] This narrative locates the time–space origins of rap in the South Bronx of New York of the late 1970s, and defines rap as a very local form of cultural expression[65] that was originally performed by artists concerned to "keep the music real" and who wrote lyrics that reflected the concerns of African-Americans living in inner-city New York. Rappers such as Melle Mell, KRS1, and Chuck D of Public Enemy were heralded as Gramscian "organic intellectuals," using their music to reflect upon and challenge social and economic decay, police oppression, and life in a drug-dominated social milieu.[66] Rap gained a still more heightened currency of "the real" with the emergence in Los Angeles in the mid-1980s of "gangsta rap," which was willfully nihilistic, often misogynistic, and claimed to articulate the gang conflict of South Central L.A.[67]

There is, however, a problem with the standard historical geography of rap, one common to many place-based accounts of music. The assumption that to place rap is to explain it risks denying the mobility, mutability, and global mediation of musical forms. Paul Gilroy[68] argues that rap is best seen as a hybrid cultural form, reflecting the increasingly migrant flows of musical influence and tradition,[69] and presents a different historical geography more sensitive to movement across space.[70] Gilroy emphasizes the role of Jamaican migration to New York in the 1970s, bringing to the South Bronx not only labor power but the reggae sound system. The emphasis that this Jamaican cultural form placed upon the DJ or the MC working over previously recorded music became a central component in rap, which then took off through innovations of scratching, mixing, and sampling. Gilroy questions the geographical and ethnic bounding of rap: "We have to ask how a form which flaunts and glories in its own malleability as well as its transnational character becomes interpreted as an expression of some authentic African-American essence? How can rap be discussed as if it sprang intact from the entrails of the blues?"[71]

GEOGRAPHICAL INTERVENTIONS

Rap and hip-hop show not only the complex geography of musical formations but also the explicit engagement of popular music with issues of place identity. We here expand on these geographical interventions through popular music's role in the production and subversion of national identities.

Just as classical composers have sought to produce a national music, so pop has played out versions of the nation, a theme easily demonstrated by the anti-national music of punk. From 1976 the music and style of London punk, focused upon the Sex Pistols and their mentor Malcolm MacLaren and inspired in part by the spatial politics of situationism,[72] sought to subvert through spectacle and excessive sound. Punk gained momentum into 1977, playing on and disrupting the ground of national identity in Queen Elizabeth II's Silver Jubilee Year.[73] The summer of 1977 brought an orgy of patriotic bunting, and a little cultural disrespect went a long way. At the end of May the Sex Pistols released "God Save the Queen," an anti-national anthem which, had it not been for some none-too-subtle chart doctoring, would have been the nation's number-one record during Jubilee week. The Jubilee celebrations marked the coming of age of a movement growing throughout the 1970s to "save" a particular elite version of English/British heritage.[74] The monarchy remained at that time the ultimate "enchanted glass"[75] for reflection upon British/Englishness. The year 1977 (official version) confirmed that a particular vision of the nation was still alive and street-partying in a time of economic crisis. The year 1977 (punk version) noted that "there's no future in England's dreaming" ("God Save the Queen"). In this Jubilee soundtrack current dreams were a head-in-the-sand fantasy doing nothing to forestall the arrival of a bleak future. The Sex Pistols' songs, like Derek Jarman's film *Jubilee,* inhabited, amplified, and parodied a Jubilee of "collective forelock-tugging,"[76] in part by setting up an alternative national heritage of anarchic protest, and more commonly by refusing any national symbolic coherence: "The very English phlegm which had served as a powerful physiological metaphor for denial and needless stoicism was now, literally, expelled in torrents."[77] As if to (not) top the charts with a different kind of anthem was not enough, on June 7 the Sex Pistols gave an alternative pageant, taking a boat, the "Queen Elizabeth," along the Thames from Charing Cross Pier. A streamer proclaimed to London that "Queen Elizabeth Welcomes Sex Pistols"; the evening trip acted as "a mocking precursor to the Queen's own river progress through London on the 9th."[78] An artery harnessed by the monarchy to confirm its own national place was given a rude transfusion. Arrests at the quayside completed the spatial theater, the floating of an anti-nation in the capital's heart.

While such sounds subverted the nation, in another sense punk involved the reassertion of placed identities. Where much white music of the mid-1970s had aimed to locate itself in mid-Atlantic, or in a mythic fantasy land, punk gave a different phrasing to pop, not simply, as Greil Marcus puts it, "the sound of the city collapsing,"[79] but a registering of music into other regions. Local scenes were fostered by new cultural and economic structures. The era witnessed creation of the national infrastructure of the socialist Rock against racism[80] and crucially the development of independent record labels. A particular form of economic organization became part of a cultural ethos of local control, producing and selling music beyond the rules of the international industry. In production and distribution the site of music was evident. Cities other than London, notably Manchester, emerged as alternative centers of production, although the tendency remained for major commercial success to involve gravitation to London. As noted earlier, many such labels have been gathered up in the majors' search for new spaces of alternative music.

The place of such music was also often evident in subject matter and accent. A preoccupation with place connected elements of punk to earlier British pop, though with a less homely geography. The punk equivalent for the urban pastorals of Ray Davies and the Kinks (much revisited today) was a counterpastoral city of violence, alienation, concrete, boredom, and so on. In Britain pop has often dealt with and appealed to its audience through a definite geography—urban, regional, rural, suburban—seeking to express place in the fabric of musical language. In Scotland and Wales music following in punk's footsteps has often sung from a strong and militant particular. In Scotland bands singing in Gaelic, Scots, or an accented English, and on specifically Scottish themes, have connected music with nationalist and/or regionalist campaigns. In this volume (Chapter 6) Steve Sweeny Turner traces a "bilingual terrain" in contemporary Scottish song, connecting language and politics to bring out different possible forms of Scottish identity ranging from a conservative nostalgia to a polyglossic affirmation of a "minor" language voicing its multiple alterity to dominant English.[81]

To draw attention to place in this fashion does not imply a revival of Vaughan Williams–style folk theories whereby music expresses a geographical essence evident in sound[82]—indeed such notions have themselves been satirized in pop. Glasgow-based Postcard Records' ironic touting in 1980 of Orange Juice as the "Sound of Young Scotland" played with such assumptions (Figure I.2); none of the classic codes for Scottishness were musically in evidence. In Wales in recent years a network of music sung in Welsh has simultaneously asserted and questioned senses of Welshness. At the "Place of Music" conference, Rhys Mwyn of Anhrefn showed a video of the band's situationist-inspired takeover of the summit of Snowdon. Anhrefn are based in Caernarfon, sing in Welsh, and perform their punk-derived music around Europe. In June 1990 they chartered the tourist train that runs up Mt. Snowdon and played in the restaurant on the summit: "For once Snowdon was overflowing with LOCAL people. The summit was DOMINATED by the noise of a Welsh band. The predominant spoken language was Welsh—for once the TOURIST had lost control."[83] The train had "in effect been hijacked": "The number of local people who took advantage of the event to gain cheap access to the summit (i.e., those who do not wish to/cannot walk) was significant." The video, excerpts of which were shown on S4C News that evening, showed bemused mountaineers wondering at the noise: "Their tranquillity shattered by the sound of angry pop songs." Anhrefn shattered the mountain's accepted soundtrack with a sound that they asserted as being more of the place than the National Parks–style quiet valued by the visitor.[84]

THE ENVIRONMENT OF MUSIC

This example of mountain pop, of a sound that for some is in place and that for others is out of place, points to another dimension of the place of music, namely, its role as a key component of broader spatial and environmental cultures. We conclude this Introduction by addressing this wider environment of music.

FIGURE I.2. "The Sound of Young Scotland," cover of Orange Juice single "Poor Old Soul," 1981. Reprinted with permission of Postcard Records.

For a rather obvious example of music's place in a broad spatial culture of movement, take the road song. The freedom and escape of the road song a as commercial popular genre is historically particular, driven by American youth, generally white and male, speeding in postwar affluence out of suburban confinement, modeling their movement in part on a hobo culture moving out of the necessities of poverty.[85] The road song shows not least how an analysis of music's power cannot remain with words. Greil Marcus provides a classic study of word and rhythm in discussing Jonathan Richman's "Road Runner,"[86] the song following and breaking a beat, describing a drive in the way that, say, a crayon describes a line, producing as it moves. The road song also has a geography in the sense of its ability or inability to travel across cultural boundaries. Can Route 66 find a British equivalent? Billy Bragg has satirized the movement of American mobility into English culture by translating "Get your kicks / on route 66" into "Go motoring / on the A13." The glamour of a transcontinental highway doesn't quite work in south Essex. A less upbeat tale of movement emerges in John Gold's study in this volume (Chapter 10) of the songs of Woody Guthrie, ostensibly documenting a landscape of dreams and desolation, and themselves becoming active players in debates over the peoples and environments of the Midwest and California. Gold's chapter acts as a counterpoint to Stradling's (Chapter 7), tracing the making of a consciously unofficial and alternative national song through the imagery of landscape.[87]

Music has often figured in the making of broader environmental cultures, both conservative—as in the English composers discussed in this volume by Stradling—and radical. The promotion of open-air music since the 1960s through a festival culture has often worked through a set of environmental values whereby culture and nature harmonize through music. In this volume (Chapter 9) Simon Rycroft maps the musical spaces of Los Angeles in the late 1960s, showing the ways in which different urban environments accrued different meaning and potential through the music happening there. For Rycroft the underground's cultural ecology is made through a spatial politics of sound and light.

Similar matters are addressed in a British context by George McKay in his study of cultures of resistance since the 1960s. McKay shows how such cultures have worked via "the construction of their own zones, their own spaces."[88] One form of spatial politics meets another as police and state seek to monitor and regulate free festivals, Albion Fairs, raves, and protests. Music is central to all of the spaces McKay considers—indeed, it is impossible to imagine any of these events and movements without music. And this is not an incidental soundtrack for other actions: rather, the texture of its sound is quite deliberately made for its particular spatial event. In the conflicts generated by such events music is an essential component for both sides. Both work through definitions of what is an appropriate soundscape for a pleasant rural environment.[89] Sound, like other senses, forms a part of environment's "moral geography,"[90] whereby certain forms of conduct belong and others do not.

Such debates have a long history, as shown in this volume (Chapter 12) in Richard Leppert's discussion of the "sonoric landscape" of 17th-century Holland. Through a close reading of a series of paintings Leppert addresses the place of music in the soundworld as a signifier of social distinction or a mark of low culture. Through its particular point of emanation and its transmission over air, music is seen and heard to articulate social hierarchies. Leppert shows how music could signify distinctions between leisure and work, languor and effort, sensual desire and social restraint, and serve to mark a socially constructed divide between civilization and nature. Leppert's discussion of the role of music in marking out polite spaces, in this case firmly tied to distinctions of the polite and the vulgar, points also to a broader question of the environment of music, namely, that of music which seeks to blend into rather than declare itself apart from an everyday soundworld. While much of the music we have addressed in this Introduction has been valued for its often violent distinction, there is a world of music valued precisely for its qualities of comfort, of familiarity, of consolation, although this is not to say that such music may be any less complex. As Gill Valentine points out in her study of kd lang, an acceptably pleasant sound can give a different kind of comfort to different listeners: "Playing lang's music in the parental home allows young lesbians to eke out an identity in a cultural and mental space that is often constraining and repressive."[91] In this volume Berland (Chapter 5), in her evocation of public radio, and Sara Cohen (Chapter 11), in her study of music, ethnicity, and community through the memories of one Liverpool man, likewise consider complex local aural ecologies where music does not necessarily declare itself in a fashion aiming to disturb the taken-for-granted and everyday. Cohen cites Ruth Finnegan's study of amateur music making in Milton Keynes,[92] in whose "variegated landscape" Colin Ward has discerned anarchist principles of mutual aid and a "remarkable social fact: that music-making is, more than anything else you can think of quickly, the cement of society."[93]

While the environment of music may act as a kind of cooperative social glue, its very importance as a carrier of values can also be seen in attempts at its regulation, as the work of McKay and others shows. Again such arguments have a long history, and have often worked through the labeling of certain sounds and musics as alien. For example, concerns over the preservation of landscape and the Englishness it symbolized were prominent in the 1930s, and involved attempts to regulate aural environmental cultures. Influential preservationist geographer Vaughan Cornish developed an aesthetic of sound as well as of vision: "The song of birds, the sounds of running water . . . are scenic amenities. Discordant noises are an offence against one of the amenities."[94] Planner Patrick Abercrombie expanded on Cornish's call for "harmonies of scenery": "There is a special note or tone in different countrysides. . . . The honk of the motor-car, the sound of the gramophone in the open, the whirr of the speed-boat on the lake, do not enter into the chord: their dissonance is seriously felt and of singular pervasiveness."[95] The everyday soundscape here becomes expressive of cultural values. A radio sound might fit in the city street, but intrude in the country lane. Those preserving rural England sought to keep out the "alien," and that included music. Cyril Joad heard something foreign to the Lake District: "The atmosphere vibrates to the sounds of negroid music. Girls with men are jazzing to gramophones in meadows."[96] The black and American are out of place, destroying the national heritage of quiet natural sound, and leading English girls with men astray.[97] As at a free festival, a rave, an Albion fair, music becomes a central element in environmental cultures.

NOTES

1. Attali, J. (1985). *Noise: The political economy of music.* Manchester, U.K.: Manchester University Press, p. 6. (Original work published 1977)
2. Bunge, W. W. (1973). The geography of human survival. *Annals, Association of American Geographers, 63,* 275-295, quotation from p. 289.
3. Fryer, D. W. (1974). A geographer's inhumanity to man. *Annals, Association of American Geographers, 64,* 479-482, quotation from p. 482.
4. Ibid., p. 482.
5. Ibid.
6. Ibid.
7. Adorno, T. (1976). *Introduction to the sociology of music.* New York: Seabury Press, p. 225. (Original work published 1962)

Fryer, now retired, has mainly produced work on the regional geography of Southeast Asia, but has continued to work on the geography of music. Our reference to his earlier paper in the special issue of the *Transactions of the Institute of British Geographers* brought a personal communication that revealed his continuing investigations into the development of symphony orchestras in places of Western colonization, as well as his continued concerns about the spread of popular culture, which has now infected the groves of academe with what he clearly considers to be lamentable consequences:

> In my department valedictory address I attempted a comparison of the representation of forested landscapes in painting and music, rather frustrating in view of my colleagues' limited acquaintance with classical music; nobody had ever heard From Nature's Realm, the Aplensinfonie or Tapiola, and only one knew Forest Murmurs. But all were well primed on Pop. No wonder Peter Gould asks why Geography has nothing to equal Simon Schama's magisterial "Citizens." (Fryer, personal communication, 1996)

8. Harvey, D. (1984). On the history and present condition of geography: An historical materialist manifesto. *Professional Geographer, 36,* 1-11, quotation from p. 8.
9. For the latter, see Stokes, M. (Ed.). (1994). *Ethnicity, identity, and music: The musical construction of place.* Oxford: Berg.
10. Leppert, R., & McClary, S. (Eds.). (1987). *Music and society: The politics of composition, performance, and reception.* Cambridge: Cambridge University Press. Said, E. (1992). *Musical elaborations.* Oxford: Oxford University Press.
11. Middleton, R. (1991). *Studying popular music.* Milton Keynes, U.K.: Open University Press, p. 106.
12. Norris, C. (1989). Utopian deconstruction: Ernst Bloch, Paul de Man, and

the politics of music. In C. Norris (Ed.), *Music and the politics of culture*. London: Lawrence and Wishart, p. 307.

13. Verba, C. (1993). *Music and the French Enlightenment: Reconstruction of a dialogue, 1750–1764*. Oxford: Clarendon Press, p. 5.

14. Koeiningsberger, D. (1979). *Renaissance man and creative thinking: A history of concepts of harmony, 1400–1700*. Brighton, U.K.: Harvester. Glacken, C. (1967). *Traces on the Rhodian shore: Nature and culture in Western thought from ancient times to the end of the eighteenth century*. Berkeley and Los Angeles: University of California Press, p. 17. Miller, S. (1993). Towards a hermeneutics of music. In S. Miller (Ed.), *The last post: Music after modernism* (pp. 5–27). Manchester, U.K.: Manchester University Press, pp. 6–9.

15. Durant, A. (1984). *Conditions of music*. London: Macmillan, p. 32. Chanan, M. (1994). *Musica practica: The social practice of Western music from Gregorian chant to postmodernism*. London: Verso, p. 157.

16. Durant, *Conditions of music*, p. 31.

17. Rosen, C. (1988). *Sonata form*. New York: Norton, pp. 11–12.

18. Revill, G. (1995). Hiawatha and Pan-Africanism: Samuel Coleridge-Taylor (1875–1912): A black composer in suburban London. *Ecumene*, 2(3) 247–266.

19. Attali, *Noise*.

20. Shepherd, J. (1991). *Music as social text*. Cambridge: Polity Press, p. 53.

21. Leppert & McClary, *Music and society*, p. xviii.

22. Leppert, R. (1988). *Music and image: Domesticity, ideology, and sociocultural formation in eighteenth-century England*. Cambridge: Cambridge University Press.

23. In Boyes, G. (1993). *The imagined village: Culture, ideology and the English folk revival*. Manchester, U.K.: Manchester University Press, p. 174.

24. Ibid. McClary, S. (1991). *Feminine endings: Music, gender, and sexuality*. Minneapolis: University of Minnesota Press. Citron, M. J. (1993). *Gender and the musical canon*. Cambridge: Cambridge University Press. Shepherd, *Music as social text*.

25. Said, *Musical elaborations*, p. 58

26. Longyear, R. M. (1973). *Nineteenth-century romanticism in music*. Englewood Cliffs, NJ: Prentice Hall. Dahlhaus, C. (1980). *Between romanticism and modernism: Four studies in the music of the later nineteenth century*. Berkeley and Los Angeles: University of California Press.

27. Dahlhaus, C. (1985). *Realism in nineteenth-century music*. Cambridge: Cambridge University Press.

28. Vaughan Williams, R. (1934). *National music*. Oxford: Oxford University Press. Revill, G. (1991). "The lark ascending": Vaughan Williams' monument to a radical pastoral. *Landscape Research*, 16(2), 25–30. Stradling, R., & Hughes, M. (1994). *The English musical renaissance, 1860–1940: Construction and deconstruction*. London: Routledge.

29. Vaughan Williams, *National music*, p. 10.

30. McClary, S. (1987). Talking politics during Bach year. In R. Leppert & S. McClary (Eds.), *Music and society* (pp. 13–62). Cambridge: Cambridge University Press. Revill, "The lark ascending."

31. Mach, Z. (1994). National anthems: The case of Chopin as a national

composer. In M. Stokes (Ed.), *Ethnicity, identity, and music* (pp. 61–70). Oxford: Berg.

32. Stokes, *Ethnicity, identity, and music*, p. 14.

33. Adorno, *Introduction to the sociology of music*. Norris, Utopian deconstruction. (1989). Chanan, *Musica practica*.

34. Middleton, *Studying popular music*, p. 36.

35. Monopolies and Mergers Commission. (1994). *The supply of recorded music: A report on the supply in the UK of pre-recorded compact discs, vinyl discs, and tapes containing music*. London: HMSO.

36. Burnett, R. (1996). *The global jukebox: The international music industry*. London: Routledge. Almost grown: A survey of the music business. (1991, December 21). *Economist*. Longhurst, B. (1995). *Popular music and society*. Cambridge: Polity Press. Negus, K. (1992). *Producing pop: Culture and conflict in the popular music industry*. London: Longman. Shuker, R. (1994). *Understanding popular music*. London: Routledge.

37. Negus, *Producing pop*, p. 5

38. Frith, S. (1987). Copyright and the music business. *Popular Music, 7*, 57–75.

39. Burnett, *The global jukebox*. Sadler, D. (1997). The global music industry as an information industry: Reinterpreting economies of culture. *Environment and Planning A, 29*, 1919–1936.

40. Ehrlich, C. (1985). *The music profession in Britain since the eighteenth century: A social history*. Oxford: Clarendon Press.

41. Negus, *Producing pop*, p. 47.

42. Cf. Amin, A., & Thrift, N. (1992). Neo-Marshallian nodes in global networks. *International Journal of Urban and Regional Research, 16*, 571–587.

43. Monopolies and Mergers Commission, *Supply of recorded music*.

44. Negus, *Producing pop*, p. 18; on agglomeration and subcontracting in the manufacturing side of the industry, see Monopolies and Merger Commission, *Supply of recorded music*.

45. Chanan, *Musica practica*, pp. 132–142. Weber, W. (1975). *Music and the middle class: The social structure of concert life in London, Paris, and Vienna*. London: Croom Helm. There are numerous other examples. Revill (Chapter 8, this volume) demonstrates the key role played by commissioning agents such as August Jaeger of the publisher Novello & Co. in fashioning reputations and constructing career prospects for classical musicians during the early 20th century. During the early years of this century Jaeger was reputedly among the most influential people in British music: his preferences and prejudices helped to shape the course of the English musical renaissance (Stradling & Hughes, *The English musical renaissance*). Gilmore's study of the economic, social, and organizational structure of classical concert life in New York (Gilmore, S. [1988]. Schools of activity and innovation. *Sociological Quarterly, 29*) recognizes three "relatively distinct" subworlds, each linked to and formed by a particular set of institutional and financial arrangements, distinctive social subcultures, and specific aesthetic values. Each subworld defines a particular set of universalized "classical" musical values through particular and localized musical practices. Largest and most visible is the "Midtown" concert organization dominated by high-profile performers playing the standard repertory

of pre-20th-century works in prestigious concert halls to large audiences. This world is most formally organized in terms of training and recruitment and there is little room here for aesthetic experimentation or financial risk. Gilmore demonstrates how these interests are represented in an academic "Uptown" subworld with a stress on innovative composition and performance practice within classical music and in a "Downtown" subworld characterized by its radical avant-garde, cultural crossover, and pluralism. In this latter subworld, "instrumentation, performer competence, even the definition of composition itself, are constantly open to challenge and debate; thus the socialisation of participants and the organisation of concerts is irregular and highly informal" (Martin, P. J. (1995). *Sounds and society: Themes in the sociology of music*. Manchester, U.K.: Manchester University Press, p. 189).

46. Thornton, S. (1995). *Club cultures: Music media and subcultural capital.* Cambridge: Polity Press.

47. Ibid., p. 12.

48. Ibid. Turnham, A. (1997). *An historical geography of "house."* Unpublished M.Sc. dissertation, Department of Geography, University of Bristol.

49. du Gay, P. (1996). *Consumption and identity at work.* London: Sage. Wrigley, N., & Lowe, M. (Eds.). (1996). *Retailing, consumption, and capital: Towards a new retail geography.* London: Sage.

50. du Gay, P., & Negus, K. (1995). The changing sites of sound: Music retailing and the composition of consumers. *Media, Culture, and Society, 16,* 395–413, quotation from p. 397.

51. Ibid., p. 403.

52. Negus, K. (1995). When the mystical meets the market: Creativity and consumption in the production of popular music. *Sociological Review, 43,* 316–341.

53. Negus, *Producing pop,* p. 14.

54. Shuker, *Understanding popular music,* p. 22.

55. Smith, S. (1994). Soundscape. *Area, 26,* 232–240. Street, J. (1993). Local differences: Popular music and the local state. *Popular Music, 12,* 43–55.

56. Straw, W. (1991). Systems of articulation, logics of change: Communities and scenes in popular music. *Cultural Studies, 6,* 368–388, quotation from p. 377.

57. Ibid., p. 378.

58. Ibid., pp. 380–381.

59. Cf. Frith, S. (1988). The industrialisation of music. In *Music for pleasure.* Cambridge: Polity Press.

60. Boyd, quoted in Mitchell, T. (1996). *Popular music and local identity: Rock, pop, and rap in Europe and Oceania.* Leicester: Leicester University Press, p. 74.

61. Glanvill, quoted in Mitchell, *Popular music,* p. 85.

62. Jackson, P. (1989). *Maps of meaning: An introduction to cultural geography.* London: Unwin Hyman.

63. Mitchell, *Popular music,* p. 60.

64. George, N. (1992). *Buppies, b-boys, baps, and bohos: Notes on post-soul black culture.* New York: HarperCollins.

65. Allinson, E. (1994). Music and the politics of race. *Cultural Studies, 8,* 438–456.

66. Berman, M. (1996). Justice/just-us: Rap and social justice in America. In

A. Merrifield & E. Swyngedouw (Eds.), *The urbanization of injustice:* London: Lawrence and Wishart. Lipsitz, G. (1994). *Dangerous crossroads: Popular music, postmodernism, and the poetics of place.* London: Verso.

67. de Genova, N. (1995). Gangster rap and nihilism in black America: Some questions of life and death. *Social Text, 43,* 89–132. See also Rose, T. (1994). *Black noise.* Middleton, Conn.: Weslyan University Press.

68. Gilroy, P. (1993). *The Black Atlantic: Modernity and double consciousness.* London: Verso.

69. Clifford, J. (1992). Travelling cultures. In L. Grossberg, C. Nelson, & P. Treichler (Eds.), *Cultural studies* (pp. 96–116). New York: Routledge.

70. Back, L. (1996). *New ethnicities and urban culture: Racisms and multiculture in young lives.* London: UCL Press.

71. Gilroy, *The Black Atlantic,* pp. 33–34.

72. Bonnett, A. (1989). Situationism, geography, and poststructuralism. *Environment and Planning D: Society and Space, 7,* 131–146. Marcus, G. (1989). *Lipstick traces: A secret history of the twentieth century.* London: Secker and Warburg.

73. Hebdige, D. (1979). *Subculture: The meaning of style.* London: Methuen. Savage, J. (1991). *Music as social text.* Cambridge: Polity Press.

74. Wright, P. (1985). *On living in an old country.* London: Verso.

75. Nairn, T. (1988). *The enchanted glass: Britain and its monarchy.* London: Radius.

76. Savage, *Music as social text,* p. 359.

77. Ibid., p. 373.

78. Ibid., p. 358.

79. Marcus, *Lipstick traces,* p. 8.

80. Savage, *Music as social text.*

81. See also Kane, P. (1992). *Tinsel show: Pop, politics, Scotland.* Edinburgh: Polygon.

82. Boyes, *The imagined village.*

83. Mwyn, R. (1993, September 13). *Taking Welsh culture out of the twentieth century.* Paper presented at The Place of Music Conference, University College, London.

84. The reaction at the conference to Mwyn's presentation is discussed by Shurmer-Smith and Hannam who recall a mixture of curiosity, condescension, opposition, and marginalization on the part of the academics (Shurmer-Smith, P., & Hannam, K. [1994]. *Worlds of desire, realms of power: A cultural geography.* London: Edward Arnold, p. 131).

85. Cresswell, T. (1993). Mobility as resistance: A geographical reading of Kerouac's *On the road. Transactions of the Institute of British Geographers, N.S., 18,* 249–262. Jarvis, B. (1985). The truth is only known by guttersnipes. In J. Burgess & J. Gold (Eds.), *Geography, the media, and popular culture* (pp. 96–122). London: Croom Helm.

86. Marcus, *Lipstick traces,* pp. 60–63.

87. Billy Bragg has recently been engaged in setting some of Guthrie's unpublished words to music, and has rewritten his song "This Land Is Our Land" for the British landscape with connection to debates over recent criminal justice legislation.

88. McKay, G. (1996). *Senseless acts of beauty: Cultures of resistance since the sixties.* London: Verso, p. 7.

89. Sibley, D. (1995). *Geographies of exclusion.* London: Routledge.

90. Matless, D. (1994). Moral geography in Broadland. *Ecumene, 1,* 127–156.

91. Valentine, G. (1995). Creating transgressive space: The music of kd lang. *Transactions of the Institute of British Geographers, 20,* 474–486, quotation from p. 481.

92. Finnegan, R. (1989). *The hidden musicians: Music-making in an English town.* Cambridge: Cambridge University Press.

93. Ward, C. (1992). Anarchy in Milton Keynes. *Raven, 18,* 116–131, quotation from p. 120; see also Russell, D. (1987). *Popular music in England, 1840–1914: A social history.* Manchester, U.K.: University of Manchester Press.

94. Cornish, V. (1934). The scenic amenity of Great Britain. *Geography, 19,* 195–202, quotation from p. 195.

95. Abercrombie, P. (1933). *Town and country planning.* London: Thornton Butterworth, pp. 243–244.

96. Joad, C. (1934). *A charter for ramblers.* London: Hutchinson, p. 171. Matless, D. (1995). The art of right living: Landscape and citizenship, 1918–1939. In S. Pile & N. Thrift (Eds.), *Mapping the subject.* London: Routledge.

97. As with much of the material discussed in this Introduction, the relationship of music and the body is a key issue in these environmental examples. Whether raving or jazzing in a meadow, it is the way music makes bodies move, or the way in which bodies focus musical performance, which in part causes the offense. The general geographies of music and the body is a topic beyond this Introduction, but the issue runs through a number of chapters in this volume.

1

THE GLOBAL MUSIC INDUSTRY

Contradictions in the Commodification of the Sublime

JOHN LOVERING

  This chapter offers a modest contribution to the small but growing literature on the political economy of music.[1] It begins with an outline of the development of the music industry as a capitalist business, then focuses on the implications of the current global restructuring of the industry, and it concludes with a discussion of the relationships between what are commonly but misleadingly described as the "local" and "global" levels.[2]
  The assumption here is that the political economy of music is not mere "background" (or base) to which the aesthetic character of music is "foreground" (or superstructure). Rather, it is implicated and indicated not only in the social context, but also in the sonic vocabulary and structures of contemporary musics. At the same time, the social significance of music cannot be reduced to an act of passive "consumption."[3] At the "street" level of listening and performing, music is much more than an "end result" of pregiven cultural or psychological traits, or of economic systems.[4] Music is not just a hobby indulged at the end of the working day, an aspect of "entertainment consumption," or even a personal door to the sublime—al-

though it can be all these things. It is often also a profound influence on the way we see our world(s) and situate ourselves in relation to others.[5]

Interpretations of music, especially pop music, have often been influenced by social theories of rather dubious kinds. Prominent among these have been various "economic explanations of culture" that have tended to marginalize pop music's social importance and to minimize its aesthetic value. On the left this dismal tradition was formalized by the Frankfurt school, which mobilized an impoverished version of Marxist economic theory to write off jazz and other popular forms as mere capitalist dope for the masses. Adorno had a lot of interesting things to say about musical structures, but his sociology of music was crude and reductionist; according to him, pop music is essentially a set of standardized noises calling forth a standardized reaction, providing profits for companies and "catharsis for the masses, but catharsis which keeps them all the more firmly in line."[6]

Not only does this view make untenable distinctions between classical and popular musics (much of Mozart and Beethoven is as formulaic and predictable as much of pop), but it also assumes that pop music is simply imposed from above, with "the masses" lacking the desire or ability to develop their own musical tastes and exert any influence over the kinds of music produced.[7] Adorno failed to recognize that artistic creativity can be applied to the making of and listening to all sorts of musical styles.[8]

A similar willful tendency to see pop music "consumers" as puppets has also been common on the political right.[9] A number of cultural Cassandras have blamed "the commercial machine" for forcing pop music, all the more loathsome because it is American in origin, into our homes.[10]

Academic cultural observers now stand well back from making any musical evaluations of this sort. Much of the recent academic literature on music, in the Anglo-Saxon world at least, has adopted the framework of cultural studies.[11] It is a sin in certain postmodern approaches to cultural studies to suggest that anything is "good" or "bad." They also give relatively little attention to economic influences. The resulting decontextualized studies of individual artists or groups of consumers[12] all too easily lead to a flat intellectual and political populism.[13] This style of academic writing has been joined lately by a new "serious pop criticism," that has emerged alongside the internationalization of the industry.[14]

The argument in this chapter is that the ways in which music is practiced (both while making it and while listening to it) are intimately bound up with the ways in which the industry is organized. The development of music at the end of the 20th century is profoundly influenced by the fact that it is now a commodity flowing through a small group of giant companies with "global reach." But this does not mean that those companies simply call the tune.

MUSIC AS A CAPITALIST INDUSTRY

The Economics of Music: Supply and Demand

Economists approach the music industry, like all industries, by looking separately at supply and demand.[15] The "supply side," the production and circulation of particular musical commodities, depends on investment. And investment decisions depend on considerations of costs and estimated future returns. However, contrary to the dictates of basic economics textbooks, these decisions are based as much on subjective assessments as on objective indicators. In fact, all economic actions are also social and cultural actions,[16] and in the music business the salience of this fact is heightened. Despite Adorno, the demand for a particular piece cannot easily be predicted, so investment is shaped by highly subjective corporate projections regarding future consumption patterns.

The "demand side" in its turn arises out of complex personal and social processes shaping the construction of musical tastes and spending behavior.[17] There is much more to all this than global corporations simply plugging Madonna or Michael Bolton, and fans lapping it up. Nor is it a matter of giant corporations on the one side pushing their products, and local musical heroes on the other side fighting for artistic authenticity.

Although it is largely a mystery how it happens, the production, consumption, and marketing of particular kinds of music in particular places clearly influences the development of musical tastes and subsequent musical creativity. There are innumerable examples of how generational and cultural changes have transformed new forms into standards.[18] This process is often accompanied by a reinvention of the past. For example, songs accompanied by acoustic guitars are now widely thought of as "folk music." But "folk" is really only a modern label for a modern kind of music, for the acoustic guitar is a recent innovation, or intrusion.[19] To cite a second example, African music would not be equated now with lyrical electric guitars had not African audiences been exposed since the 1960s to Western pop music. The "traditional" or "ethnic" identity of such musics, or of rhythm and blues (R&B), cool jazz, and so on is an aspect of current musical culture and marketing, rather than of history. These are aspects of the inescapable "reflexivity" of musical activity,[20] a reflexivity that corporations certainly influence, but just as certainly do not control.

Over the last century the development of music has been profoundly influenced by the development of capitalism. The two have become interwoven as a result of the social and geographical extension of commodity production. To become a commodity—a thing that is exchanged for money on a systematic basis—individual musical constructions must be capable of being parceled up in ways that allow mass production and mass sale.

Commodification has subjected music to tendencies that are particular to capitalism.

First and most obviously, access to financial resources is conditioned by profitability. Moreover, it is not enough just to make a profit. The market pitches companies into a competitive struggle in which maximizing profits is a requirement for survival. The music industry actually makes fairly unremarkable profits—around 6% of turnover in 1994.[21] Companies cannot risk too many unprofitable ventures, especially when, as at present, they are investing huge sums around the globe in order to remain in the game.

Second, like all capitalist businesses, the music industry is profoundly dependent on public systems of regulation. There is and can be no such thing as a completely "free market" in the real world, as opposed to the wonderland of college economics textbooks. For markets will only work if they are framed by laws, by routinized behaviors, and by industry "technology standards."[22] The introduction of a standard format for interactive CDs, for example, is currently creating a new market. The legal structure of regulation is particularly sensitive because most music industry assets are "intellectual property" rather than physical things. Perhaps a third of the income of the music industry derives from royalties for air-play and other public use of recorded material. The annual royalty income from broadcasting of artists and record companies in the European Union (EU) is over $400 million. Music royalties brought invisible earnings of over £140 million to Britain alone in 1993. The ownership of a song is a property right that can be bought and sold in the market.

Paul McCartney's ownership of the song "Unchained Melody" brought him £125,000 in two weeks when the (abysmal) Robson and Jerome version shot to the top of the British charts to become the biggest selling single of the first half of the 1990s. In 1985 Michael Jackson bought the Beatles' songs for $48 million. Together with almost 4,000 other song titles, these were merged with Sony Music's repertoire in 1995, earning Jackson $500 million. The resulting Sony Music/ATV company, the third largest music publisher in the world, was said to own "one of the greatest contemporary music catalogues there is."[23] The sums involved in royalties are the result of legal arrangements established between industry bodies and national governments (the main organizations in Britain and the United States emerged in 1915 and in the 1920s, respectively). The current policy debate concerning European integration, Western company access to Asian markets, and the playing of music on the Internet is primarily concerned with putting in place regulatory systems so that companies can be sure they will get their dues.[24]

Third, as Adorno correctly pointed out, commodification "makes art more like products." On the one hand, this has made it possible to walk into a shop in almost any (Western) town and buy a delicious diversity of well-recorded musical noises to be enjoyed in circumstances of one's choosing. On the other hand, it has undoubtedly encouraged the forgetting of past forms of musical activity and imposed a set of economic pressures that affect the resources available to different types of musics unevenly. Adorno expected the range of musical genres to diminish. The music industry will churn out intensely derivative garbage if it sells, and clearly it often does. Conversely, a particular type of music may be much loved and desired, but it won't be recorded unless those who love and desire it have enough money to sustain at least a modest market.

However, technological changes are potentially democratizing the market. In the past few years it has become possible to record and manufacture even very small batches of CDs at a viable cost. Potentially, minority musical tastes can be served as never before. Yet in a global perspective, the music industry remains biased toward the affluent. The industrial nations account for 96% of singles sales. The world's poor do not buy even cheap CDs. Despite the celebratory talk of cultural globalization,[25] a large part of the world's population is unable to come to the party (hopefully, they are at different ones).

The Commodification of the "Embodied Performance": Recorded Music and the Emphasis on the Individual Performer

In most industries firms try to differentiate their product from those of their competitors. Such product differentiation can be difficult: washing machines or tubes of toothpaste are fairly indistinguishable. But in the music industry product differentiation is unavoidable, for the "product" is intimately connected to the individual body (and social experience and milieu) of the performer. No two people sing or play in exactly the same way (Thank goodness!). The increased value attached to the individual performer/performance is connected to commodification and the parallel development of new recording and reproducing technologies. The introduction of tape and then the disc enabled the faithful and intimate reproduction "of details of voicing beyond merely those of pitch, knotted dynamic and phrasing, tracing articulatory or phonational attributes." Recorded music made possible the consumption at a distance (in time and space) not only of a tune, but of the particular way in which it is sung or played and arranged. This has enabled the realization of a musical ambition that seems to be as old as written music and the division between performers and audiences: the precise inscription of the human voice as melodic contour, as recitative.[26]

Today the musical commodity is generally a song (or an instrumental) as performed by a particular artist, often packaged together with particular visual images. The popularity of a particular song generally fades, and thousands are written every year, but a performer is unique and some few have careers that last for decades. By encouraging us to "linger on the singer at the expense of the song"[27] the industry can win itself a welcome degree of stability.

This emphasis on the specificity of performer and performance is new. Until midcentury, the essence of popular music was usually the song (or instrumental piece). The singer, arrangement, and performance were contingent upon local circumstances (theater, music hall, front parlor, pub, etc.). Sheet music sales were important until long after the introduction of the record player, which remained a luxury item until after World War II. The rise of stars like Bing Crosby and Frank Sinatra, closely associated with the spread of cinema, augured a new emphasis on the commodication of song, performance, arrangement, and so on, as a "package," an "embodied performance." However, even into the late 1960s many consumers in Britain were apparently happy to buy "cover versions" of hits, re-created by the likes of the Woolworth Beat Group. By the late 1970s this market had disappeared.

Interestingly, the "cover version" has reemerged lately in somewhat leaden ironic mode, on the live-music circuit (the Bootleg Beatles, the Australian Doors, a thousand Abba, Bowie, and Blues Brothers copyists, etc.). Apparently some of these acts emerged in areas where famous bands never toured (notably Australia).[28] They would seem to underline the historically new emphasis on the "embodied performance."

Music corporations devote most of their resources to constructing images designed to differentiate the embodied performances of one artist from those of another, and to making sure that the products are readily accessible to potential buyers. The music industry is inherently an advertising business, concerned with creating and marketing "branded products."[29] As it reaches global maturity, the industry's emphasis is shifting even more from music creation to asset-value realization. This "advertising" dimension is becoming increasingly important.

Yet There Is Always Some New Music

The main business of the big corporations (the majors) is marketing and advertising. They generally leave the real musical matters to subsidiaries or "independents." Many of the independent labels are set up by individual musicians or entrepreneurs, of which there is an almost endless supply, such is the passion to make music, or to get rich. Others are spawned by the majors. In 1995, for example, MCA formed the small label Endangered to act as "a breeding ground for baby bands."[30] In European countries hundreds if not thousands of small recording companies, especially new ones, rely on the majors to get their product into the shops (notably, in Britain, Pinnacle and APT). In effect, the development and marketing of new music is subcontracted to small companies or units set up within big ones "to look independent."[31] The result is a complex industrial structure in which the big corporations are like mother ships served by many smaller craft designed for specialized missions.[32] This plurality is intimately connected to the evolution of the musical product. It is well known that many of the innovations in popular music have been introduced by independent labels. The musical and commercial entrepreneurialism of the pioneers of rock 'n' roll has often been painted in glowing colors, to contrast with the grey-suited corporate era that allegedly followed.[33] In fact the relationship between the majors and the independents is a dynamic and inherently volatile one.[34] This means that it cannot be assumed that its musical impact must always be conservative.

However, if a new musical product turns out to be commercially promising, the larger corporations are generally better placed to benefit from this promise. The costs and risks of raising products to the world scale can be insurmountable for small companies, many of which collapse when their acts become sufficiently sales-worthy to be lured away by a major. A good part, probably the majority, of the repertoire of the Big Five corporations is made up of music that developed in independents. For example, when Factory Records, a prominent Manchester-based independent company, went bankrupt, its major "world act" (New Order) was acquired by Polygram.

But there is another side to this coin. Pop music folklore insists that good artists tend to lose their creative edge when they succumb to the corporate embrace. The musical "labor process" is hard to control, and artists may dry up, drug themselves insensible, become boring, or simply die before recording enough to realize the corporate investment. Pop does tend to eat itself.

Business Cycles, Industrial Restructuring, and Musical Mutations

Popular music as we know it is relatively new. The record player was invented a century ago. The recorded music industry grew hesitantly at first, suffering a severe recession in the 1920s in the United States. But as in other industries, gales of destruction had a creative edge. The recession spurred the more adventurous to seek out new products and new markets.[35] Forays into the urban and rural hinterlands of America led to the discovery of "new" genres, and of new potential consumers. By the time the postwar boom was in full swing, an elaborate infrastructure of music finding, recording, and marketing was in place. In 1948 the first vinyl album was introduced. New generations entered the shops with more disposable income than their predecessors. Supply and demand grew hand-in-hand. New cheap recording devices made possible the proliferation of local recording studios, and these in turn became the "nursery units" in which modern pop music developed.[36]

Companies expanded through "vertical integration" in order to impose a greater degree of order at three crucial points: control over "musical supply" (the most difficult to establish, given the unpredictable nature of creativity and consumer tastes); control over the media to secure exposure of the product (manifested most notoriously in the 1950s "Payola" scandal that revealed widespread bribing of disc jockeys[37]; and control over the channels of distribution.[38] As audiences expanded, the record companies grew from local or regional to national (U.S.) organizations. In the early 1960s many of the smaller labels were absorbed by the majors. In the later 1960s and 1970s U.S. (and British) music companies began to invest seriously abroad, adding the "world tour" to their marketing of performer and product.

In the mid-1970s the postwar boom came to an end. Since then economic growth rates have halved, unemployment has trebled, and inequality has widened throughout the advanced capitalist world.[39] The music market has been affected by conflicting and fluctuating pressures. Although disposable incomes among society's gainers have grown, the relative decline of incomes among young people has thinned out the teenage market. Overall the market for recorded music in Britain has been fairly flat (from a corporate point of view) since the 1980s.[40] This situation has spurred new efforts to revive sales, especially by shifting to new consumer technologies in old markets, while searching for new markets abroad.

The arrival of the CD format in 1983 helped to realize the first goal, and a major part of industry activity since then has been devoted to re-releasing old material in the new format (and in video). In America and Western Europe sales of CDs rapidly outstripped sales of all other forms by the mid-1980s. But cassettes and vinyl records remain the dominant carrier in Eastern Europe and Asia; indeed, China is the world's biggest market for vinyl records. Interactive CD and other computer-based forms are being developed to give the product market another boost in more affluent markets.

The changing geography of music companies has affected the nature of the music product itself. Until the 1970s the United States was culturally inward-looking to an unusual degree (economically it still is, trading less with the rest of the world than most other advanced capitalist economies). American pop music emerged out of indigenous forms, and was later exported, especially to postwar Europe, where American GIs formed a large youth market with high disposable incomes, served by specialist radio stations. This American presence in turn influenced the musical environment of young people in Europe. Liverpool is a famous case: one of the main European embarkation points for migrants, it had been aware of U.S. popular music currents for a century. From the 1940s Liverpool was temporary home to thousands of U.S. servicemen, and Toxteth enjoyed several black clubs where American pop music and jazz was played by "the original artists." During the 1950s the American presence was sustained by the giant Burtonwood airfield which remained a major U.S. cold war base. The Beatles could hardly have avoided American music if they had tried.

By the early 1960s such American "intrusions" had resulted in new musical synteses in European cities. Just as English could no longer be defined as the language of the English, so pop music derived from American roots ceased to be American.[41] The British "pop invasion" of the United States in the mid-1960s marked a turning point. The introduction of karaoke into the West in the 1980s, the first Japanese musical import, which rapidly became domesticated, surely signified a similar historical turning point (I have not come across any recognition of this in the cultural studies and pop music literature). A similar tendency for imported music to "go local," mutate, and bounce back to the West[42] is now becoming apparent in Pacific Asia.

Consumption

A concert or record will only sell if someone values it enough to pay for it. I suggested earlier that demand is highly unpredictable. This is because the subjective valuing of a piece of music may derive from a wide range of motives and influences. A record may give pleasure because it signals the owner's identity, that is, membership within a particular social group, subculture, or "tribe."[43] Or music may be sought for a private personal experience of the sublime (giving access to "authenticity" in an inauthentic world). Or a piece of music may be valued for its nonmusical connotations—a precious memory perhaps.

The motives for consumption may matter to the musician as artist.[44] But for the major companies, all that matters is that the personal attribution of value is translated into the exchange of money. As I noted above, record companies devote most of their efforts to constructing images that suggest that desirable states will follow from buying particular music products. The very diversity of motives for consuming music poses corporate challenges as well as opportunities.

MUSIC AS BIG BUSINESS: THE GLOBAL CONCENTRATION OF CAPITAL

Millions of musical performances or one sort of another take place everyday. But music at the grassroots level is increasingly affected by the corporate organization of the music industry on a worldwide scale. One facet has been the emergence of "concert-tourism," an industry dedicated to moving audiences to large concerts in central sites. What was once an elite phenomenon in Classical music (Bayreuth, etc.) has become a mass popular activity; for example, the audiences for Bob Dylan's Paris concert in 1992 were made up of people from all over Europe and beyond. The organization of festivals and large concerts, involving management, stage production, trucking, and much more, is dominated by a small set of international companies.

Concerts and media appearances are rarely put on as an end in themselves. Live performance is increasingly subordinate to promoting recorded product. The bulk of the income of the music industry comes from the sale of various sorts of sound carriers (CDs, cassettes, and vinyl records) and from royalties. Although a growing part of musical activity is directed to other segments of the entertainment industry (notably, movies and television), the bulk of output goes to individual consumers. Worldwide, over three billion sound-carrier units are sold every year. By far the greater part of sales fall in the popular music category (in the United Kingdom classical music accounts for around 9% of total sales).

World sales of recorded music in the mid-1990s are around $36 billion. Over three-quarters of this take falls to the Big Five corporations: EMI, Polygram, Sony Music Entertainment, Warners Music International, and Bertlesmann Music Group (BMG).[45] The annual spending on music CDs and videos in 1994 was £1.6 billion.[46] U.K. artists account for just under a fifth of world sales of recorded music. Britain enjoys a positive trade balance in recorded music, exporting around one-and-a-half times as much as it imports, leaving a net balance of payments gain of some £109m (in 1994). In addition, net earnings on music royalties contribute a further £123m.[47] Considering that Britain is net importer of musical equipment, this shows that the music industry is an outstanding example of a sector where the source of "value added" lies in cultural assets and business skills rather than natural resources. The industry's importance as an export earner for the U.K. economy has combined with the obsession within it with advertising and promotion to transform an incestuous annual trade event into a full-blown media spectacle: "The Brit Awards." This celebration of music sales has an established place in Britain's entertainment calendar and successfully draws to it a full retinue of performers, media stars, business moguls, and even politicians.

The total employment generated by the music industry is unknown. In Britain around 5,600 people are employed in sound-carrier manufacture, but the total appears to be falling. As for musicians, the 1991 population census recorded 11,000 "authors, composers, and own-account artists." There are 22,000 writer members of the Performing Rights Society (membership is obligatory to collect royalties on air-play) and a further 3,500 publishers and copyright owners, but many members are "sleepers" or no longer actively involved in the industry.[48] Some have guessed that the music industry accounts for up to 50,000 jobs in the United Kingdom,[49] but this seems excessive. The "cultural" sector as a whole is a major and growing area of employment in Britain, where it employs twice as many as the motor industry. Within this, the music industry is one of the most dynamic areas.

Nevertheless, "name" artists and performers are merely the sharp tip of a huge iceberg. In addition to performers, composers, and writers, the music industry creates some kind of work for battalions of specialists and generalists: for example, sound technicians, stage management firms, artists management firms, tour promotion and production companies, and a wide range of occupations associated with product manufacture and distribution (notably including recording producers and engineers, pressing/duplication engineers, manufacturing employees, marketing and distribution staffs). It also employs large numbers directly in administration, and indirectly in video, legal, and other business services functions, plus the rest of the media and advertising industries.

It is hard to know where employees end and enthusiasts begin. Only a small minority of those regularly engaged in music are employed full time and receive a regular income from it.[50] Many bands, systems, DJs, and other performers pay to play. But at the other extreme, established artists and senior corporate managers and owners are among the most highly paid people on the planet. Worldwide, the industry employs some 30,000 top executives. Some of these Cats are extraordinarily Fat. In terms of income, employment stability, and geography, the music industry is one of the most grotesquely polarized in the world. It shares with other entertainment industries (with which it is increasingly interwoven) the ability to extract modest amounts of money from vast numbers of people, aggregating to a major transfer of income from the poor to the rich. This is also a spatially uneven process. The future global development of the industry therefore has significant economic implications, as well as social and cultural ones.

Corporate Strategies: Globalization and Reorganization

Companies are currently responding to both push and pull influences: the push of recession in the West, the pull of the emergence of massive new wage-earning and spending classes in the East, and the commodification of cultural production and consumption all around the world.[51] Mature markets in Europe and the United States are unlikely to generate a significant growth in sales. In Britain, the steady growth in consumer spending on recorded music came to an abrupt end in 1989, when the Thatcher government's second recession began. Total spending on recorded music fell by 18% between 1989 and 1992.[52] The leading companies fixed their eyes firmly on markets overseas. Apart from the United States, the critical markets they and their rivals are targeting are in Pacific Asia. In the early 1990s it was expected that the combined markets of China, South Korea, India, and Japan would grow to the scale of the US market in 1991 (see Table 1.1). All market forecasts must be treated with caution, and in the music industry demand is particularly unpredictable. In the mid-1990s there was a general revival in consumer spending in the traditional markets.[53] Nevertheless, all the major music corporations continued to expect significant growth in the so-called new markets of Pacific Asia.

Music company market strategies are bringing them closer to companies working in other media. When the Murdoch group took over the Asian "Star" satellite, it negotiated an arrangement with Bertlesmann, EMI, Warner, and Sony to supply a replacement for MTV. In 1995 the Bertlesmann group formed a joint venture with Crescendo targeting the Indian market, which it sees "as a dynamic market for Western groups."[54]

A trend toward reorganization was also evident in Europe in the early 1990s. Thirty years earlier, CBS, WEA (Warner Electra Atlantic), and RCA

TABLE 1.1. Sound-Carrier Market: Forecasts

	1991	2000	Increase No.	%
United States	7,834	10,639	2,805	36
Japan	3,812	4,899	1,087	29
Germany	2,574	4,151	4,151	61
United Kingdom	2,312	3,470	1,158	50
France	1,632	2,978	1,346	82
Italy	696	783	87	13
Spain	680	870	190	28
Netherlands	600	723	123	21
Austria	289	476	187	65
Switzerland	369	584	215	58
Sweden	333	500	167	50
Belgium	337	462	125	37
China	261	1,027	766	293
India	233	730	497	213
Turkey	209	250	41	20
Finland	167	274	107	64
Norway	158	259	101	64
Denmark	94	154	60	64
Greece	83	99	16	19
Portugal	78	93	15	19
Ireland	37	44	7	19
Hungary	24	37	13	54
South Korea	272	956	684	251

Source: Data from MIRO (Music Industry Research Organisation Ltd.), various reports.

had opened European bases to sell U.S. product. In the 1980s they added the search for local artists both for local markets and, possibly, the U.S. market. Their successors (Sony, Warner Music, and BMG) extended their penetration of the music industries in the countries in which they were located. According to one commentator, 1992 was the year American companies "discovered the world" and began to give their non-U.S. affiliates the chance to "test their local hits in international markets."[55] EMI created a grading system in Europe, differentiating artists with "local-nation appeal" from those with appeal for a wider language group, and those with possible appeal to international audiences. Sony set up Sony Music Soho Square in 1991 with the explicit aim of scouring the whole of Europe for artists performing in English, to be "groomed for global impact."[56] Warner Music International set up the Magnet label, and BMG set up BMG International Marketing, with similar goals in mind. It is suggested that BMG may become the first world-scale music corporation to have a predominantly non-English-speaking repertoire.

In the past decade the music industry in established ("Western") markets has thus been transformed by the absorption of smaller companies, and the artists they have nurtured, into webs centered on the large corporations.[57] The trend toward concentration is also visible on Main Street and at the local shopping mall. The growth of chains of Main Street outlets and megastores is concentrating retailing into a small number of large companies (which are also extending their activities into telly-shopping). This trend is likely to reduce the openings available to small music-producing companies, enhancing the power of the majors.[58]

The reorganization of the music corporations is concentrating resources in a select group of strategically placed world centers.[59] The new European divisions of Sony, Warner, and MBG, for example, are all based in London, where the music producer services industry is most highly developed. In Britain, no less than 48% of those describing themselves in the 1991 census as "authors, composers, own-account artists" lived in Greater London.[60] "World cities" and regional centers elsewhere are attracting the music industry along with the other business service industries in which they enjoy a commanding position.[61]

Product Consolidation: A "World Artists'" Repertoire

The international development of the music industry is dominated by short- to medium-term considerations. The establishment of a global technological and legislative infrastructure is expensive and risky, reducing the resources available for the infinitely unpredictable business of developing potential new products.[62] The music industry shares in the "short-termism" that is endemic in a world economy beset by stagnant overall growth, intensifying competition, and hyperactive finance capital.[63] This means that of the three corporate goals noted earlier—seeking out artists, establishing control over media exposure, and establishing retail outlets—the first is the least pressing. Most effort is going to the second and third goals.

The internationalization of the music business is thus primarily driven by the wish to seek out larger markets in which to sell existing stock. In fact, many companies have pruned their repertoire in recent years, shedding younger or less "commercial" established artists, including some great ones. MCA, for example, cut its roster by 75% in 1994–1995.[64] The roster of "world artists" is fairly static, being made up of acts that have been around for 10, 20, or even 30 years (or more, e.g., the Rolling Stones). The only major newcomer in the 1990s to sell "tens of millions of records all over the world" is Mariah Carey. In five years Mariah became a multimillionaire. In the sixth she married the president of her record company, Sony.[65]

The intense corporate competition on the world scale is manifested in every music shop window by the massive (and massively repetitive) promotion of a tiny repertoire of world artists, plus some "regional" stars. Marx argued that capitalism would tend to favor dead labor over living workers. The music industry shows that he was dead right. New technologies have even solved the minor problem of mortality: from the grave Nat King Cole sings duets with his daughter, and John Lennon rejoins the Beatles. Many other artists in the world roster are only slightly more alive than these.

Corporate Visions of the Future: Music as a File under "Global Infotainment"?

The music industry is rapidly becoming part of a generic entertainment industry.[66] All the major corporations have been attempting to position themselves for an expected overlap of the markets for information, entertainment (especially through a screen), music listening, and music making.[67] With the rapid transformation of the personal computer, the telephone, and video into an integrated product, the equipment production side of the music business is entering a new and frenzied phase. And so has corporate restructuring.

The early 1990s saw a series of international megamergers. Matsushita (Japan) acquired MCA (United States), Sony (Japan) acquired Warner Music (United States), MBG (Germany) acquired RCA (United States), EMI (Great Britain) acquired Virgin (Great Britain). Japanese companies rose to an important position. But this did not create a stable structure. In the mid-1990s EMI prepared to de-merge its music business, and Sony was thought to be considering selling off its Sony Music.[68] Warner, the world's second largest music company after Sony, became part of the Time–Warner group, which itself is seeking to expand into mixed-media markets. In 1994

Disney decided to buy a music company, and the following year it acquired ABC in a $19 billion merger, creating what the *Financial Times* described as a "media behemoth," rivaling the global reach of Rupert Murdoch. The music industry, like many other industries, is subject to a gigantic and increasing concentration of capital, on a global scale.

These technological and organizational revolutions contrast with the incredibly conservative music strategies adopted by all the major companies. Sony's first interactive music CD features Bob Dylan's "Highway 61 Revisited," a recording that is twice the age of most singles' buyers, but presumably about right for the age group with enough money to buy the new equipment needed to play the Dylan CD.[69] In established markets, a major effect of the globalization of the music industry has been to change "not so much what we listen to, but how we listen to it."[70] The emphasis on selling (and reselling) rather than producing music is directly connected to the massive concentration of capital in the industry and the pressure to realize profits.

The associated fetish for new reproduction equipment is socially ambivalent. On the one hand, the real cost of musical reproduction is falling rapidly—look, for example, at the Walkman market. As I noted earlier, this development has not only enabled many to join the party as listeners, it has also opened up the possibility of putting into the market previously marginalized musics. Here capitalism still seems to have a progressive edge.

Yet at the same time, since corporate competition leads to an orientation toward affluent markets, there are forces working to reinstate social inequalities in access to music. In Great Britain up to a third of the population were worse off in 1994 than they were in 1979.[71] Many families cannot afford a personal computer (PC), the supposedly egalitarian instrument of the "infotainment age" (the cost of a basic unit having risen in real terms). Worldwide, four out of five families do not even have a telephone.[72] The music industry eloquently expresses contemporary capitalism's contradictions: stagnation alongside dynamism, personal freedom alongside social division, creativity shackled to conservatism. Somehow Phil Collins or Madonna seem to suggest themselves as symbols of these paradoxes.

THE GLOBAL IN THE LOCAL, AND VICE VERSA

The International Music Industry and Musical Diversity

Adorno assumed that capitalism would ravage and deplete the musical environment much as it does the natural environment. The current corporate restructuring may reduce diversity, indeed that is its point. But people are not mere cyphers to be written upon, or sung to. The social and musical outcomes are not predetermined.

It was suggested earlier that the audioscape of music products influences the dynamics of the creative social practice of music (as musicologists have stressed).[73] The growing availability of recorded music in mid century America, albeit selected by the companies, created new means of aural transmission. Together with the emphasis among popular musicians on "learning by copying"[74] this led to the development of distinct, recognizable commodities, genres such as country, delta blues, R&B, rock 'n' roll, and so on). This was associated with a rationalization and bureaucratization of musical forms—there were often 11 or 13 bars in early versions of the supposedly 12-bar blues, and notions of what it is to be "in tune" have only recently become standardized. But genres and timbres cross-fertilized each other and spawned wondrous new progeny (the 12-bar blues colliding with the 32-bar music hall tune, etc.).[75] None of this could have been predicted. Blur and Oasis could not have existed without punk and the Beatles, and the Beatles would not have existed without imported U.S. R&B and the music hall tradition, and so on.

Corporate internationalization is currently accompanied by attempts to hold this dynamic in check and promote the consumption of an extremely limited global repertoire. Whatever the musical merits of this repertoire, and much of it is great, it is unlikely to be unchallenged. New types of music continually emerge as a result of the opportunities for cross-fertilization created precisely by the efforts of the companies. In recent years techno and rave styles have moved from the bedrooms of musical obsessives to mass public appeal (again, the Orb could not have existed without Kraftwerk, who were influenced by Pink Floyd, etc.). While commodification may be responsible for the extermination of some older musical experiences, it also makes possible new ones. It creates new "spaces of the imaginary" with gloriously unpredictable effects.[76]

The *Financial Times* music industry correspondent Alice Rawsthorn recently commented on the "irony" that "at a time when the music business has become more international ... musical taste is increasingly parochial. The American charts are dominated by indigenous genres such as rap and grunge, Germany is awash with thrash metal bands, Britain has Britpop."[77] Some industry commentators believe the music industry will see "more of everything" in the late 1990s.[78] Others suggest that the shift away from familiar Anglo-American axis may be associated with the "rediscovery," or more accurately the invention, of a new "European musical space."[79] In the meantime, the question whether corporate restructuring fuels local diversity or crushes it is being answered, at least at the national level, and on one musical dimension.[80] The chairman of EMI recently commented that Pacific Asian "markets will always be mainly local in their musical tastes."[81]

The result is a shifting geography of musical production and consumption. U.S. artists accounted for 45% of global sales in the mid-1980s, but for only 35% a decade later.[82] The share of the world market taken by British acts is falling, from 20% in 1989 to 15% in 1993 (but this could be reversed by a major new act "breaking" in the United States).[83] In the mid-1980s non-American artists finally overtook Americans in the European market. Sales of English-language pop music declined sharply relative to local-language artists in Germany, Italy, France, and other countries. The other side of this coin is a globalization of new European musics. The commercial success of acts like Two-Unlimited, Black Box, Enigma, or the heavy metal band Scorpions suggests that new European artists can attract an international audience.[84] The geographies of music consumption are changing.

"Local Musical Spaces"

Music is a collective human activity. Forms of production and consumption constantly and intimately influence each other. This relationship is at its most obvious in live performances, where audience responses affect the playing, and vice versa. The growth of new music technologies related to the club dance scene seems to have extended this intimacy into the production of recorded music. Spatial proximity is a prerequisite for all sorts of creative musical activity. And it often seems to be a motor of inventiveness.[85] It is a joyous fact of musical life that different social groups in different locations tend to be associated with different mixes of music, despite the ubiquitous presence of world artists.[86]

A "local musical space" can be thought of as a territory in which a "community of musical taste" identifiable to its participants emerges and is sustained by an apparatus of creation, production, and consumption.[87] Supply and demand adapt to each other. As noted several times already, rock 'n' roll and pop developed out of local styles in white and black communities, mobilized by local entrepreneurs. The British pop explosion of the 1960s similarly grew from localized activities, most at the city scale, as did ska, reggae, and punk. So-called world music, a touristic label for a gorgeous diversity, grew out of ex-colonial communities in Europe's major cities (most notably Paris, but also Berlin and London). The emergence of new computer-based dance musics in Europe from the 1980s reflected both the availability of new music technologies and the emergence of new social milieu (raves).[88] The core geographical bases appear to be mainly a number of suburban locations around cities with good provision for nightlife, notably in Britain, Italy, and the Netherlands. But this musical space is not tightly bounded, extending to bedrooms and bars from Iceland to Sarajevo. The geographies of music are varied, uneven, and changing.[89]

The scale, social nature, and musical content of existing "local musical spaces" varies widely. In Scotland, Wales, Brittany, and Lapland, for example, a distinctive musical practice seems to reflect the revival of "non–nation–state" languages. In some cases, public policy has played an important role in establishing local recording facilities and sustaining artists.[90] In other cases, the territorial basis of a "musical space" is narrower, most notably a city-region (e.g., Manchester or the Balearics in the late 1980s). The importance of the urban scale in some cases has been enhanced by the growth of interest in promoting "cultural industries," primarily for employment reasons.[91] For all the talk of the globalization of culture, spatial proximity sometimes remains extremely important.[92]

Local Musical Spaces at the Beginning of the 21st Century

The promotion of "local musical spaces" is not part of the normal strategy of a global music corporation. The industry did little to nurture reggae in Jamaica, compared with its efforts to sell it to white buyers elsewhere. Similarly the "Merseybeat" phenomenon of the 1960s produced world artists (and fortunes), but did little for music or musicians in Liverpool. Music lingered in Liverpool despite, rather than because of, the corporate strata of the industry, thanks to a core of locally committed musicians, "bespoke" record companies and shops, and a relatively cooperative local musical culture.

It was noted earlier that the current tendency in the corporate music industry is to intensify the pressure on artists, or at least aspiring world artists, to migrate to established metropolitan and corporate centers. Whether this will be to the cost of other musical spaces depends on a number of imponderables. By way of conclusion, the remaining sections address these by considering two different scenarios.

First, the "Mariah Carey" scenario. The critical factor today is the massive expansion of the scale upon which corporate music companies now develop their strategies. This echoes on a global scale the expansion of the U.S. music industry three-quarters of a century ago. In the 1920s American record companies responded to recession and falling sales by finding both new artists and new audiences within the urban ghettos, rural hinterlands, and lower classes in the United States itself. On the global scale the response to recession in older markets is once again to seek out new ones, but this time primarily with a view to selling more of the existing stock. The midcentury emergence of American pop music was profoundly enriched by small localized entrepreneurial companies that acted, in retrospect, as "out runners" gathering local musics into corporate nets.[93] It seems unlikely that there are many equivalents today capable of nurturing and projecting musics local to the communities into which the global corporations are now plunging, especially as many of these countries were formerly state controlled and centralized.[94] The arrival of global companies in Eastern Europe, Pacific Asia, and elsewhere is much more abrupt and invasive than the gradual evolution of small labels into majors in 1920s and 1930s America.

Corporate globalization-regionalization, in a broadly neoliberal policy environment, is more likely to reinforce the centrality of the corporations, key locations, and existing decision makers, than to distribute new resources to the more "peripheral" musical spaces. The music industry serves, and exploits, a profound and wonderful human need, but does so only insofar as those needs are translated into market forces, via the production and consumption of commodities. The current global restructuring is bound up not only with increased affluence and musical enjoyment, but also with the exacerbation of economic inequality, social exclusion, and cultural attrition, on the world scale.

Let's end with the alternative scenario. Once the new global infrastructure of marketing and distribution is in place, the companies will be able to respond to distinctive taste patterns in the varied markets they cover. Despite life-after-death technologies, the existing corporate stock of music(ians) will become exhausted in the new century, forcing companies to pay more attention to indigenous and new musics in the markets they hope to develop. And in the meantime, the infusion of corporate product into local spaces will create unexpected new creative musical opportunities, as it has in the past. Not least, it will open up access to new cheap recording technologies, putting hitherto unrecorded musics, and musics yet to be created, on the shelves. Most of the huge investment by music companies is in marketing and distribution networks, and in buying world stars, not in musical creation. The real costs of setting up a studio, or radio station, are falling dramatically.

New musics just keep bubbling up. There seems to be something about the effects of the commodification of music that spurs a far more insistent and creative mixture of embrace, response, and resistance than that of soap powder.[95] This is no doubt linked to the fact that listening to music highlights the question of "who speaks for whom."[96] The dialectic through which new musical sounds influence the development of tastes, which feed back onto the development of new sounds, is vibrant and inherently unpredictable. This reflexivity is beyond the control of corporations, and it subverts the forecasts of market researchers. The internationalization of the music industry and the spread of new music making and reproducing technologies and social milieus will tend to intensify such reflexivity.[97] The pleasures of playing, dancing and listening are too Dionysian, too social, too easily adapted to new technological possibilities, to be entirely codified and commodified by monster entertainment corporations.

CONCLUSIONS

Musical taste and creativity defies any deterministic theory. Thankfully, musicians and dancers don't worry much about theory and just get on with it. Only later do academics slink into the back of the hall and start tapping their laptops. Music is a matter in which people can not only intervene theoretically, they do so practically all the time, with miraculous energy, learning to play, setting up venues, bands, systems, festivals, shops, and so on, all around the world, all the time, generation after generation. And all this is inherently social. Although most musical spaces are already deeply influenced, in terms of musical styles, timbres, and so on, by the rest of the world, this evidently allows huge variations in musical creativity and personal and social musical activity, as several chapters in this book show. New musical spaces are being born, crossing territories, transgressing organization all the time.

At a more obvious level, the companies do not have it all their own way. They have to make deals with governments to get their royalties. This regulatory imperative creates a bargaining space. "Cultural politics," linked to economic regulation and resource redistribution at appropriate spatial scales, can have a major influence on the development of music, and also thereby on the development of jobs and incomes.[98]

Which of these scenarios will be realized? Bits of both presumably. The tide of globalization-regionalization is already flooding the world with identical product. And this is already stimulating reactions. Different communities of taste (operating on a range of geographies) will influence both the spatial–economic and the sonic–auratic outcomes. The political economy of music is shaped not only by corporations and accountants, but also by shared desire, organization, and solidarity.

ACKNOWLEDGMENTS

This chapter began as an ESRC application (unsuccessful), and mutated after the Place of Music Conference at University College London in September 1993. Thanks for conversations to Sara Cohen, Phil Tagg, and Peter Wade, and to Andy Leyshon and Dave Matless for comments on an earlier and even cruder draft. And especially to Owen Hughes of Cob Records in Bangor.

NOTES

1. See esp., Negus, K. (1992). *Producing pop: Culture and conflict in the popular music industry.* London: Edward Arnold. Laing, D. (1992). "Sadeness," scorpions and single markets: National and international trends in European popular music. *Popular Music, 11,* 127–141.

2. For a discussion of the reasons why these terms are misleading, see Lovering, J. (1996). Global restructuring and local impact. In M. Pacione (Ed.), *Britain's cities: Geographies of division in urban Britain*. London: Routledge.

3. du Gay, P., & Negus, K. (1994). The changing site of sound: Music retailing and the composition of consumers. *Media, Culture and Society, 16,* 295-413.

4. Shepherd, J. (1991). *Music as social text*. Oxford: Polity Press.

5. Attali, J. (1985). *Noise: The political economy of music*. Minneapolis: University of Minnesota Press. Durant, A. (1984). *Conditions of music*. London: Macmillan.

6. Adorno, T. W. (1990). On popular music. In S. Frith & A. Goodwin (Eds.), *On record: Rock, pop, and the written word* (pp. 301-314). London: Routledge, quotation from p. 314.

7. Middleton, R. (1993). *Studying popular music*. Milton Keynes: Open University Press. Shuker, R. (1994). *Understanding popular music*. London: Routledge.

8. Not just any noise will do. Creativity is manifested in the feeling that a song provides "the 'only possible solution' to the projected temporal unfolding of the genre" (Born, G. [1993]. Afterword: Music policy, aesthetic and social difference. In T. Bennett, S. Frith, L. Grossberg, J. Shepherd, & G. Turner [Eds.], *Rock and popular music: Politics, policies, institutions* [pp. 266-292]. London: Routledge, quotation from p. 284.). As to why it feels so right, that's the big question.

9. Shepherd, *Music as social text*, p. 66.

10. See, e.g., Paul Johnson's English nationalist moanings (cited in Frith, S. [1991]. Anglo-America and its discontents. *Cultural Studies, 5,* 263-269. Strinati, D. [1995]. *Theories of popular culture*. London: Routledge, p. 14.).

11. Grossberg, L., Nelson, C., & Treichler, P. (1992). *Cultural studies: A reader*. New York: Routledge.

12. E.g., see the bulk of Grossberg, Nelson, & Treichler, *Cultural studies*.

13. For critiques, see McGuigan, J. (1992). *Cultural populism*. London: Routledge; Savage, J., & Frith, S. (1993). Pearls and swine: Against cultural populism. *New Left Review, 198,* 107-116. Born, Afterword.

14. Kane, P. (1995). Rock criticism in the music press. In B. Longhurst (Ed.), *Popular music and society* (pp. 79-81). Oxford: Polity Press. (Original work published 1993 in the *Guardian*)

15. Vogel, H. L. (1986). *Entertainment industry economics*. Cambridge: Cambridge University Press.

16. A neat summary of recent discussions on the cultural construction of economic behavior can be found in Thrift, N. (1994). On the social and cultural determinants of international financial centers: The case of the city of London. In S. Corbridge, R. Martin, & N. Thrift (Eds.), *Money, power, and space* (pp. 282-332). Oxford: Blackwell.

17. In my experience most musicians, and many listeners, subscribe to the romantic position that what they do and what they like is inexplicable except in terms of some primal musical drive. Observing children, most of whom seem to respond to music long before they respond to words, it is difficult not to believe that certain sorts of harmony or dissonance or rhythm touch us in some pre- or transcultural way. Premodern thinkers had no problem with this, assuming that the meaning of music was intrinsic, echoing the language of the cosmos. But social

scientists are so used to thinking in constructivist terms that even to pose the question of a neurophysiological "basis" for music is to risk being regarded as slightly mad.

18. Durant, *Conditions of music*. Charlton, K. (1993). *Rock music styles: A history*. Madison, Wis.: Brown and Benchmark.

19. Hatch, D., & Milward, S. (1986). *From blues to rock: An analytical history of pop music*. Manchester, U.K.: Manchester University Press.

20. Beck, U., Giddens, A., & Lash, S. (1994). *Reflexive modernisation*. Oxford: Polity Press.

21. The split between "capital" and "labor" in the music industry is disguised because many of the highest earners receive much of their income in the form of royalties, producers fees, transfer fees, and so on, rather than as a formal share of profit (although they also get some of this). "The old breed of record executives—Richard Branson of Virgin or Chris Blackwell of Island—made serious money by setting up labels and then selling them. These days it is almost as lucrative to collect a six-digit salary, bonus and stock options from a global entertainment group" (Rawsthorn, A. [1995, September 16]. Pop across the pond. *Financial Times*.

22. Hodgson, G. (1988). *Institutional economics*. Oxford: Oxford University Press.

23. Eade, C. (1995, November 18). Sony inks deal with ATV. *Music Week*, p. 3.

24. Corporate anxieties over the Internet point to a central contradiction in the capitalist recording business. On the one hand, companies devote enormous efforts to producing superb technologies for recording and reproduction of sounds. On the other, they try desperately to prevent them being used (except by themselves). As music technology has become cheaper, copying has become a major criminal industry, accounting for £38 million (4% of total sales) in the United Kingdom (Rawsthorn, A. [1995, August 24]. Raid nets biggest haul of bootleg CDs. *Financial Times*, p. 5.). Individuals take away an unknown further share of the market by copying from friends. The lack of control over the Internet poses this dilemma in sharpened form. The companies are seeking to ban "pirates" placing their products on Internet "jukeboxes."

25. Featherstone, M. (1995). *Undoing culture: Globalisation, postmodernism, and identity*. London: Sage.

26. Durant, *Conditions of music*, p. 179.

27. de Lisle, T. (1995). *Lives of the great songs*. Harmondsworth, U.K.: Penguin, quotation from p. viii.

28. Thanks to Andy Leyshon for pointing this out.

29. Lash, S., & Urry, J. (1994). *Economies of signs and space*. London: Sage, quotation from p. 132. Lury, C. (1993). *Cultural rights: Technology, legality, and personality*. London: Routledge.

30. Eade, C. (1995, October 14). Singles come-back helps MCA's bid to raise profile. *Music Week*, p. 1.

31. Longhurst, B. (1995). *Popular music and society*. Oxford: Polity Press, quotation from p. 36.

32. Lash & Urry, *Economies of signs and space*, suggest that this exemplifies the model of "flexible specialisation." This may have some validity as a description of the work tasks and enterprise structures of performers, niche businesses, and

corporate decision makers. But it should be remembered that the industry has been like this for some time. The suggestion that the music industry represents "post-Fordism" jars with the profoundly conservative nature of product strategies (unlike those allegedly characterizing the new "flexible firm"). It also ignores the fact that the majority of employees have routine jobs in mass production, distribution, retail, administration, and the like. The music industry is not a dynamic synergistic nexus of companies with enduring commitments to each other, and no major asymmetries of power. It has an extremely hierarchical structure based on dependence and conflict, broken by contingent interludes of harmonious cooperation.

Similar objections may be raised against attempts to grasp the industry in terms of the supposedly general logic of "informational industries" (see Sadler, D. [1997]. The global music business as an information industry: Reinterpreting economies of culture. *Environment and Planning A, 29*, 1919-1936). To treat music as an informational industry is to bypass the question of why certain cultural activities are constructed as "information" that is exploitable in the market, while others are not. It also gives inadequate attention to the role of capital as the exercise of power that is central to the turbulence of the music industry, the gross inequalities that it produces, and the fates of particular musics and musicians. These problems are not limited to studies of music but characterize many recent attempts to explain economic developments in terms of "information," as if the latter is something that can be isolated from political and other influences.

33. Gillett, C. (1983). *The sound of the city.* London: Souvenir.

34. Negus, *Producing pop,* p. 17.

35. Hatch & Milward, *From blues to rock.*

36. Vogel, *Entertainment industry economics.*

37. In my all-too-brief career as a rock megastar in the early 1980s, we were approached by small specialist companies (one I remember was called "Bullet") who guaranteed to get a single on the charts, or on a BBC playlist, for upwards of £5,000. Corruption has allegedly declined in recent years, but the industry is so structured that profitable schemes are always likely to be possible.

38. Peterson, R. A., & Berger, D. G. (1990). Cycles in symbol production: The case of popular music. In S. Frith & A. Goodwin (Eds.), *On record: Rock, pop, and the written word* (pp. 140-159). London: Routledge, p. 143.

39. Michie, J., & Smith, J. G. (Eds.). (1995). *Managing the global economy.* Oxford: Oxford University Press.

40. Employment in the cultural sector. (1996). *Cultural Trends, 25,* 87-97.

41. Charlton, *Rock music styles,* p. 301. Wallis, R., & Malm, K. (1990). Patterns of change. In S. Frith & A. Goodwin (Eds.), *On record: Rock, pop, and the written word* (pp. 160-180). London: Routledge.

42. Gilroy, P. (1993). *The black Atlantic: Modernity and double consciousness.* London: Verso.

43. See Frith, S. (1992). The cultural study of popular music. In L. Grossberg, C. Nelson, & P. Treichler (Eds.), *Cultural studies: A reader* (pp. 174-181). New York: Routledge. Street, J. (1986). *Rebel rock: The politics of popular music.* Oxford: Oxford University Press. See also Cohen (Chapter 11, this volume) and Hollows & Milestone (Chapter 3, this volume).

44. It is not uncommon for musicians to feel their audiences, or companies, are getting the wrong message. This category includes this writer, for whom a

contract with the world's second largest record company (Warners USA) marked the end of the fun. "Globalization" here meant the names of New York lawyers I had never met appearing under "Thank you" on the album cover.

45. Negus, *Producing pop*, p. 1.

46. Rawsthorn, A. (1995, June 17). Music takes more than pennies from heaven. *Financial Times*, p. 7. Employment in the cultural sector.

47. Employment in the cultural sector.

48. But you can continue to receive royalties for years, since small PRS (Performing Rights Society) distributions are based on an estimated share. My last check was for 0.7 pence.

49. Cohen, S. (1991a). *Music city report*. Liverpool, U.K.: Institute of Popular Music.

50. Ibid.

51. Morley, D., & Robins, K. (1993). *Spaces of identity: Global media, electronic landscapes, and cultural boundaries*. London: Routledge.

52. The music industry. (1993). *Cultural Trends, 19*, 45–66, p. 48.

53. Musical chairs. (1995, December 23–January 5). *Economist*, 95–96.

54. *Financial Times*, June 28.

55. Ochs, E. (1993). 1992, the year the US discovered the world. *Music Business International, 2*, 12.

56. Laing, *Sadness, scorpions and single markets*, p. 131.

57. Negus, *Producing pop*.

58. In Britain the bulk of sales are still made through small independent specialist shops. But their number has more than halved in the past decade to around 1,500. An independent Main Street record shop may deal with 15–20 distributors in any week and the choice of stock is up to the owner. Managers in chain stores have much less autonomy in selecting which product to sell or promote.

59. Bennett, T., Frith, S., Grossberg, L., Shepherd, J., & Turner, G. (Eds.). (1993). *Rock and popular music: Politics, policies, institutions*. London: Routledge.

60. Employment in the cultural sector.

61. Knox, P. L., & Taylor, P. J. (Eds.). (1995). *World cities in a world-system*. Cambridge: Cambridge University Press, pp. 232–248. Negus, K. (1993). Global harmonies and local discords: Transnational policies and practices in the European recording industry. *European Journal of Communications, 8*, 295–316, p. 307.

62. Musical chairs.

63. Michie & Smith, *Managing the global economy*.

64. Eade, *Singles come-back*.

65. Rawsthorn, A. (1995, September 23). Mall-girl made megastar. *Financial Times*, p. 7.

66. Morley & Robins, *Spaces of identity*.

67. Askoy, A., & Robins, K. (1992). Hollywood for the 21st century: Global competition for critical mass in image markets. *Cambridge Journal of Economics, 16*, 1–22.

68. Musical chairs.

69. As I write this, Time–Life is advertising on TV their CDs of 40-year-old

songs packaged as "the rock 'n' roll era." I never expected to be hearing in my late 40s the same music I loved in my teens.

70. Employment in the cultural sector.

71. Report on income and wealth. (1995). York, U.K.: Rownstree Commission.

72. Stallabrass, J. (1993). Empowering technology: The exploration of cyberspace. *New Left Review, 211,* 3–32, p. 11.

73. Durant, *Conditions of music.* Charlton, *Rock music styles.*

74. Frith, The cultural study of popular music, p. 175.

75. Durant, *Conditions of music.*

76. Chambers, I. (1992). Discussion. In L. Grossberg, C. Nelson, & P. Treichler (Eds.), *Cultural studies.* New York: Routledge, p. 183. Middleton, *Studying popular music.*

77. Rawsthorn, A. (1995, September 19). Music and the man who has climbed to the top. *Financial Times,* p. 9.

78. Ochs, 1992.

79. Frith, Anglo America. Laing, Sadeness. Robins, K. (1989). Reimagined communities: European image space beyond Fordism. *Cultural Studies, 3,* 2.

80. Adorno might object that this is to celebrate minute variations within a contracting number of genres.

81. Musical chairs.

82. Ibid.

83. Rawsthorn, Raid nets biggest haul.

84. Smith, G. (1993). Continental acts hit the road to single market. *Music Business International, 2,* 12. Laing, Sadeness.

85. Bennett et al., *Rock and popular music.*

86. It will be interesting to see whether the Internet gives rise to a "virtual musical space" with new musical ensembles and audiences, or whether it will be colonized by corporate music product, at a price.

87. See Cohen (Chapter 11, this volume); Hudson, R. (1995). Making music work? Alternative regeneration strategies in a deindustrialised locality: The case of Derwentside. *Transactions of the Institute of British Geographers, 30,* 460–473; and Hollows & Milestone (Chapter 3, this volume).

88. Tagg, P. (1993). *From refrain to rave: The decline of figure and the rise of ground* [mimeo]. Institute of Popular Music, University of Liverpool.

89. Leyshon, A., Matless, D., & Revill, G. (1995). The place of music. *Transactions of the Institute of British Geographers, 20,* 423–433.

90. Local intervention can be more musically and socially stultifying than capitalist corporations if it does not reflect the social reality of the "musical space" in question. Wales would seem to be an example, slightly overromanticized by Malm, K. & Wallis, R. (1992). *Media policy and music activity.* London: Routledge). The Welsh language is the mode of existence of most people in the rural North, but public funding to support the Welsh language through the arts has provided a platform for a middle-class cultural elite in the urban South. In the name of "Welsh culture," public funding has been used to present (especially on television) dire rock bands, stereotyped traditional music, and conventional elite classical forms (Williams, K. [1994]. Singing in the rain: Music making and the media. *Planet, 103,*

16–20.). Meanwhile, there is a vibrant living Welsh-language musical culture from within which other pop musicians have won local and international audiences—e.g., Catatonia, Super Furry Animals, or Gorky's Zygotic Mynci. This Welsh musical authenticity has gained little patronage from the official Welsh cultural apparatus. There seem to be some parallels with the position of music in state-capitalist/Stalinist countries (see Wicke, P., & Shepherd, J. [1993]. The cabaret is dead: Rock culture as state enterprise. In T. Bennett, S. Frith, L. Grossberg, J. Shepherd, & G. Turner [Eds.], *Rock and popular music: Politics, policies, institutions* [pp. 25–36]. London: Routledge.).

91. Griffiths, R. (1993). The politics of cultural policy in urban regeneration. *Policy and Politics, 21,* 39–46. Greater London Council. (1985). *London industrial strategy.* London: Author. Cohen, S. (1991). Popular music and urban regeneration: The music industries of Merseyside. *Cultural Studies, 5,* 332–346. Hudson, Making music work.

92. Bennett et al., *Rock and popular music.*
93. Negus, *Producing pop.*
94. See Wicke & Shepherd, The cabaret is dead.
95. Born, Afterword.
96. Morley & Robins, *Spaces of identity.*
97. Lash & Urry, *Economies of signs and space.*
98. Malm & Wallis, *Media policy and music activity.* Hudson, Making music work. Bennett et al., *Rock and popular music.*

2

THE EARLY DAYS OF THE GRAMOPHONE INDUSTRY IN INDIA

Historical, Social, and Musical Perspectives

GERRY FARRELL

THE SOCIAL BACKGROUND OF MUSIC AND MUSICIANS IN INDIA AT THE TIME OF GAISBERG'S FIRST RECORDING EXPEDITION

A woman stands cradling the gleaming horn of a gramophone. She is bedecked in her finery—silk, bangles, pearls, earrings—with the folds of her sari finely pressed. Closer inspection shows the garish polish on her nails. She gazes away from the camera, lending a stilted, almost wooden look to her posture. Clearly she has been told to stand this way. Is the gramophone or the woman the center, the focus of this image? The gramophone sits grandly on a table. Its horn and winding handle invoke none of the comical resonances that they would in the present day; this is not a clumsy contraption for the reproduction of crackly nostalgia. It is 1906 and this machine is the acme of Western inventiveness, the almost miraculous purveyor of sound on small black disks—a commodity loaded with potent cultural and technological power. The gramophone is a symbol of affluence, of the advent of the 20th century; preceding the cinema, radio, and TV, it is the first manifestation of musical mass media.

The woman is named Gauharjan. She was a *tawa'if* (courtesan) from Calcutta and a well-known exponent of classical and light classical Indian vocal music. She was also one of India's first major recording artists. At the turn of the century Gauharjan and other musicians like her found themselves at the intersection of two worlds, both musically and culturally. By the 20th century older forms of musical patronage by rajas and nawabs, which had been in decline throughout the 19th century, had all but disappeared. The demise of courtly benefaction was accompanied by the slow but inexorable drift of populations from the country to the city. The vast railway network built by the British also played its part in hastening demographic change and brought new mobility for musicians, leading to a greater mixing of regional styles and genres.

The new patrons of music were the urban middle classes. The locus of musical activity shifted from the princely courts to large urban centers such as Bombay, Delhi, Calcutta, and Madras. Within the span of one generation Indian musicians could look back to a vanishing world of princely patronage and forward to a new commercial environment fraught with economic and artistic uncertainty. The place of work was no longer the sumptuous and rarefied court, but the urban *koṭhā* (salon), theater, recording studio, concert stage, or one of the many European-style music schools that were being established at the time.

The early days of the gramophone industry in India marked a new phase in the interface between Indian music and the West. For the first time Indian musicians entered the world of Western media. In Western terms, Indian music and Indian musicians were no longer curiosities written about by a few 18th- and 19th-century enthusiasts who concentrated on ancient Sanskrit texts that had ceased to have any direct relevance to performing musicians. Nor was this a manifestation of early-20th-century ethnomusicological inquiry—the first Indian gramophone recordings may have been of interest to comparative musicologists of the time, but that was not the reason that the recording industry descended on India.

The twin mediums of photography and recorded sound turned Indian music and musicians into saleable commodities. Through the intervention of Western technology, the financial and economic potential of musicians within India changed radically. At the turn of the 20th century Indian music was still an untapped market, and the gramophone arrived in India only a few years after its invention in the West.[1] In the social realm recorded sound brought many forms of classical music out of the obscurity of performance milieus such as the *cakla* (courtesan's quarter) and onto the mass market. The gramophone, and later film and radio, all inventions of the West, irrevocably altered Indian music in the 20th century.

The first recordings of Indian music were made in London in 1899 at the Maiden Lane studios of Gramophone and Typewriter Ltd. (hereafter GTL). The artists were a Capt. Bholonath, & Dr. Harnamdas, and someone identified only as "Ahmed." These recordings included examples of singing and recitation.[2] Their commercial potential could not have been great.

The first commercial recordings of Indian music were made by Fred Gaisberg in 1902. Gaisberg had gone to India as a representative of GTL with Thomas Dowe Addis and George Dilnutt.[3] He had already made successful recording trips to Germany, Hungary, Spain, Italy, and Russia. For the India trip Gaisberg designed "portable" recording equipment that used a weight-driven motor.[4] His expedition was undertaken in response to the growing market for gramophones in India—it was a move by GTL to consolidate and expand its interests in Asia. Gaisberg later went on to make recordings in Japan and China. It is telling that these and subsequent recording trips in the early part of the century were known as "expeditions"—GTL was exploring a "dark continent" of music. Following the Anglo-Indian vogue for "Hindostanee airs" in the 18th century, and the attentions of Orientalists and comparative musicologists in the 19th, Indian music was being "discovered" once again, as it would continue to be rediscovered throughout the 20th century in ever-changing commercial and cultural contexts.

Correspondence in the EMI archive reveals the forward planning and logistical problems encountered during the period leading up to Gaisberg's first Indian recordings in 1902. GTL's agent in Calcutta was John Watson Hawd. Hawd was aware of the potential economic rewards to be derived from recording "native" musicians and he was constantly urging the London office to send out an "expedition." But Hawd was also aware that they would have to corner the market quickly, for rival operators were already importing gramophones and records into India.[5] In February 1902 Hawd wrote: "There will be a big business done here when we have goods enough and it is best to own the territory then we know it is well worked." But in April of the same year he cautioned: "The country is so large that it will take a long time to cover it and as yet we have no dealers to speak of." Indeed, much of the correspondence of 1902 is concerned with establishing markets, trademarks, and franchises by means of lawsuits. Hawd's interest in Indian music appeared to be purely on the level of business. As he blithely put it in June 1902, "The native music is to me worse than Turkish but as long as it suits them and sells well what do we care?"

But GTL did not send Gaisberg out to India as quickly as they might have wished. In January 1902 the London office had written to Hawd:

> I am planning to send out Gaisberg to you the first of February to make records in your vicinity.... I am going to have him make haste to go

there direct and do the work thoroughly and well, and I predict as a result getting a very large business. We will now take up the Indian business on thoroughly business lines and put it on a firm and good foundation.

But by June of the same year Gaisberg had still not set out, and Hawd wrote in exasperation:

> Is he [Gaisberg] really coming? ... of course I don't care only I had made arrangements with artists which are now cancelled and I am not going to trouble again and until he has really landed for by the time be arrives the pooja will have commenced and nothing can be done till after December.

Hawd also adds, darkly: "About 12 to 14000 are dying in this territory weekly now of plague." Perhaps not the best circumstances in which to launch a recording industry!

Hawd's letters provide us with hints about how artists were recruited for recordings, and the nascent status of the gramophone among the Indian upper classes:

> We are arranging for a room for record making and if it is possible, but as this pooja lasts for two months, yet we are not sure we will be able to succeed. We have several wealthy rajas who are interested in the gramophone that have volunteered to help us in every way possible.

The expedition finally arrived in Calcutta at the end of October 1902.[6] Gaisberg himself describes their arrival and the first recordings they made in India in *Music on Record* (1942), which consists largely of entries from his diaries. His account gives a sense of the complex logistics involved as well as the culture shock of the experience[7]:

> It took three days to unload our thirty heavy cases and pass the customs officers. Our agent, Jack Hawd had arranged a collection of artists, who watched us curiously as we prepared our studio for recording. It was the first time the talking machine had come into their lives and they regarded it with awe and wonderment.

It was also the first time Indian music had come into Gaisberg's life, and it seemed to be no less awesome and traumatic to him than the effects of the gramophone on the Indians[8]:

> We entered a new world of musical and artistic values. One had to erase all memories of the music of European opera houses and concert halls: the very foundations of my musical training were undermined.

The first musicians Gaisberg recorded were enlisted by Hawd with the help of two "fixers" from local theaters, Amanendra Nath Dutt and Jamshedi Framji Madan.[9] Since the Westerners knew nothing about Indian music or its musical genres, they had to take what was on offer. In this sense the early recordings were musically arbitrary—everything from classical vocal music to "Bengali Comic Talk."[10] The first recordings of Indian musicians, made on Saturday, November 8, 1902, were of two *nautch* (dancing) girls called Soshi Mukhi and Fani Bala from the Classic Theatre. They sang extracts from popular theater shows of the time such as *Sri Krishna, Dole Lila, Pramode Ranjan,* and *Alibaba*.[11] According to Gaisberg, they had "miserable voices."[12] Elsewhere he describes his general dismay at the theater music he heard[13]:

> Our first visit was to a native "Classic Theatre" where a performance of Romeo and Juliet in a most unconventional form was being given. Quite arbitrarily, there was introduced a chorus of young nautch girls heavily bleached with rice powder and dressed in transparent gauze. They sang "And Her Golden Hair Was Hanging Down Her Back" accompanied by fourteen brass instruments all playing in unison. I had yet to learn that the oriental ear was unappreciative of chords and harmonic treatment, and only demanded the rhythmic beat of the accompaniment of the drums. At this point we left.

This paragraph encapsulates a wealth of misconceptions about Indian music held by Westerners and of Western music held by Indians. Undoubtedly the rendition of the ballad "And Her Golden Hair Was Hanging Down Her Back" with brass accompaniment was prepared especially to please the Western visitors. But the two musical cultures failed to connect on every level. Expecting Indian music, Gaisberg heard a bad arrangement of a Western song. The Indian band did not know how to score for brass. This concert and Gaisberg's reaction was an example of cross-cultural misfirings on every level. Above all, Gaisberg had no idea what he was looking for in Indian music, and was doubtless at the mercy of local "fixers" anxious to exploit the rich Westerners and their lucrative new talking machine.

Further evidence of the Westerners' confusion is found in the lists of the music recorded in those first sessions. often unclear from the titles whether the referent is a genre of music, as *khyāl* or *ṭhumrī*, or the name of a *rāg* (melodic form) or of a *tāl* (meter). In later recording expeditions such information became more accurate.

However, following hard upon his experience at the Classic Theatre, Gaisberg was ushered into a different world of Indian music. He was taken to the home of a "wealthy babu," where he heard, among others, Gauharjan the vocalist: "an Armenian Jewess who could sing in twenty languages and dialects."[14] Gaisberg had come into contact with the mainstream of classical and light classical music performance in India, but not in surroundings he would have been familiar with from classical music in Europe or America[15]:

> We elbowed our way through an unsavoury alley jostled by fakirs and unwholesome sacred cows, to a pretentious entrance.... No native women were present excepting the Nautch girls, who had lost caste.

That Gaisberg found the subsequent performance "long and boring"[16] and was offended by the betel-stained teeth of the musicians did not blunt his business acumen. Gauharjan was clearly a find. No doubt her rendition that evening of "Silver Threads among the Gold" was intended especially for the ears of the wealthy Western visitors. So at the end of "an unsavoury alley" Gaisberg stumbled upon the source for the 20th century's first commercial recordings of Indian classical music.

Gauharjan (ca. 1875–1930), koṭhās doyenne of the Calcutta *koṭhās* would become GTL's first major Indian recording artist. She recorded scores of songs, many of which were still on GTL's lists long after her death. Through the medium of the gramophone she became an immensely popular artist, so popular that she later appeared in silent movies miming to her own recordings–foreshadowing "playback" singers later in the century.[17] Gauharjan was an appropriate figure to play a role that bridged tradition and modernity, India and the West. She was born to Western parents,[18] but brought up in Banares by her mother who had converted to Islam after the breakup of her marriage.[19] Gauharjan was multilingual, glamorous, flamboyant, and fully aware of the commercial potential of the new medium.

In coming into contact with Gauharjan, Gaisberg entered a different musical world from that of the nautch girls at the Classic Theatre. Gauharjan was a trained singer of khyāl, ṭhumrī, and other vocal forms; she is also reported to have performed *dhrupad* and *sādrā*.[20] She was the student of Bhaya Saheb (1852–1920). This gave her a direct link to the world of courtly patronage, as Bhaya Saheb was the son of the maharaja of Gwalior. He learned singing from his mother, the maharaja's mistress. At the turn of the century Bhaya Saheb was considered a leading exponent of the light classical vocal form ṭhumrī, and taught many other well-known singers of the time, including Malkajan and Ghafur Khan.[21]

Gauharjan was clearly an imposing figure. She was not intimidated by Western technology or by the commercial wheeling and dealing associated with it. As Gaisberg noted[22]:

> When she came to record, her suite of musicians and attendants appeared even more imposing than those used to accompany Melba and Calvé

[contemporary opera singers]. As the proud heiress of immemorial folk she bore herself with becoming dignity. She knew her own market value, as we found to our cost when we negotiated with her.

Gauharjan's almost legendary status is underlined by the curious story that Gaisberg relates[23] about her throwing a party for her cat that cost 20,000 rupees! It seems that such tall tales, her extravagant and provocative appearance—she dressed in "delicate black gauze draperies embroidered with real gold lace, arranged so as to present a tempting view of a bare leg and a naked navel"[24]—and her habit of riding through Calcutta in a carriage and pair, created an ambience that made it easier for her to "sting" Gaisberg when it came to fees.

Gauharjan quickly became a "gramophone celebrity," appearing in numerous catalogues peering demurely into the camera or cradling the gramophone horn to her bosom. In her first recordings for Gaisberg Gauharjan recorded songs in Hindustani, English, Arabic, Kutchi, Turkish, Sanskrit, Bengali, and Pushtu. This body of work covers many of the vocal styles current in India at that time: *thumrī*, *dādrā ghazal*, and *khyāl*, as well as compositions in a variety of *rāgs* usually associated with lighter classical forms: *Pīlū*, *Jhiñjhoṭī*, *Bhūpālī*, *Kāfī*, *Khamāj*, and *Gārā*. However, among her first recordings are also examples of more serious *rāgs* such as *Malhar*, and rarer ones like *Dhānī* and *Janglā*.[25] But even though Gauharjan was a musician with a large repertoire of traditional compositions, the novelty value of the gramophone did not escape her notice.

One of her 1902 recordings is an English-language version of "My Love Is Like a Little Bird." The extant disk of this songs seems to have been recorded too slow, adding a curious high-pitched edge to Gauharjan's voice which exaggerates the nursery-rhyme quality of the lyrics:

> My love is like a little bird
> That flies from tree to tree.

The accompanying musicians carry on regardless of the curious musical setting they find themselves in, adjusting the Indian *tāl kaharvā* and the mellifluous flow of the *sārangī* to fit the four-square melody. When, midway through, Gauharjan suddenly forgets the lyrics, no one is disconcerted and the rhythm is picked up again when she restarts!

At the time of Gauharjan, Indian classical music and the musicians who performed it occupied an ambiguous place in Indian society. At the turn of the 20th century, performing classical music in India was regarded as a low-status activity (despite the Hindu revivalism of the 19th century) and had yet to attain its later image, in the West or in India, as a quintessential symbol of Indian high culture. For women, performing such music was considered a particularly disreputable profession, only one step away from undisguised prostitution. Musical activity in the cities centered on the koṭhās, situated in caklās where tawa'ifs performed music and danced for an audience comprised of musical afficionados and pleasure-seekers. The male accompanists, particularly players of the sāraṅgī, had the reputation, whether deserved or not as procurers or pimps.[26]

Such venues were connected in the minds of the Indian bourgeoisie with the loose and degenerate living previously associated with the courts. But it was also within this milieu that many of the stylistic innovations of 20th-century classical music took place. Male professional musicians frequented the salons and were influenced stylistically by the women performers, a dimension of Indian music history that has only recently been acknowledged.[27] Gaisberg himself noted that the first two male singers he recorded in India had "high-pitched effeminate voices," perhaps a result of female musical influences.[28] Lal Chand (L. C.) Boral, a particularly popular artist in the early days of recording, has a notably high-pitched vocal delivery. Manuel[29] also notes how some of the greatest male vocalists of the century, for example, Faiyaz Khan, emulated the performance practices of tawa'ifs.[30] Clearly, female musicians had great significance in India at the turn of the century, yet a photograph of a gathering of musicians at a conference in Nepal in about 1900 shows not a single woman.[31] It is perhaps necessary at this point to clarify the meaning of the term "courtesan" in relation to Indian women musicians and dancers. In former times the term referred specifically to women who performed music and dance at the courts of nawabs and maharajas. However, as this milieu of music patronage declined in the 20th century, the musical skills of the courtesans transferred to the urban centers and the salons. For example, even though she was apparently attached to the court of the maharaja of Darbhanga at one point in her life,[32] it is not strictly accurate to term Gauharjan a courtesan, or even less a "dancing girl" as Gaisberg describes her, with all the pejorative connotations that such a title carries in India. She was certainly the heir to that tradition, but she performed primarily in contexts that succeeded the courts. The musical and dancing skills she had acquired were those of the courtesan, but she represented a different and emerging stratum of professional urban musicians in India at the turn of the century.

The entertainment in the salons was a mixture of music, dance, and sensual indulgence. The koṭhā was not merely a brothel but also a venue where highly skilled musicians and dancers performed, a place of relaxation, gossip, and musical appreciation as well as of venery. Gaisberg notes that the women who performed were "from the caste of public women, and in those days it was practically impossible to record the voice of a respectable woman."[33] McMunn gives further background to the social status of the 20th-century courtesan[34]:

The mass of them come from the lowest of the depressed classes and untouchables and from outcast tribes.... The dancers have matriarchal descent for many generations perhaps, for though all dancers are courtesans, not all courtesans are dancers. The recruiting of the dancer class comes also from one more source, the unwanted daughter. The unwanted daughter may be sold, given to, or stolen by a gipsy tribe and sold on to some duenna of dancing girls, herself retired from the craft of keeping houses of ill fame.

Kidnapping as a form of "recruitment" to the salons may also have effected an intermingling of musical styles at this time, as some girls were brought from outside India.[35]

The courtesan-musicians constituted a distinct strata of Indian society. Their names often included a distinctive suffix, $b\overline{ai}$, a practice that apparently dates back to the time of the Moghul emperor Aurangzeb, who ruled from 1658 to 1707.[36] The term "$b\overline{ai}$" (dame, lady) has many connotations, being simultaneously honorific ($b\overline{ai}j\overline{i}$) and stigmatizing: honorific because it acknowledges the artistic achievements of the woman so named but stigmatizing because it links her directly to the courtesan tradition.[37] Some of the most famous vocalists of the 20th century, many of whom were recorded in the early part of the century, had names that incorporated the suffix, including Jankibai, Zohrabai, Hirabai Barodekar, and Kesarbai Kerkar, to name but a few.

In the courtesan's performance, dance was clearly as important as music. It is apparent that the two skills were closely integrated, with the performer singing and dancing simultaneously on some occasions, a style of performance known as *abhinaya*.[38] McMunn, despite his exoticism and romanticism, laced with a typical Western prurience regarding toward the mysterious East, nevertheless gives an interesting description of what actually took place musically during a performance at Hamesha Behar's koṭhā:

> From the large chamber within the darkened lattices there comes the luring throb of the little drum.... Within one of the inner rooms where the velvety cushions are super-velvety, Azizun the dancer taps the floor quietly with her embroidered crimson and green shoe to supple the sinews ... you can see every muscle under the soft olive skin of the bare abdomens and the transparent muslin of the dancers ... ankle and bosoms moving to the pipe, now in softness, now in frenzy.

Judging by the importance of the ankle bells worn by the dancers, the dance form was *kathak*, a sophisticated mixture of dance and mime, involving hand, foot, head, and eye movements matched to complex rhythmic patterns—a dance form at once theatrical, melodramatic, and abstract. The ankle bells worn by a kathak dancer, which accentuate the rhythms of the footwork, are considered sacred by the dancers and are an indispensable part of the performance. The accompanying instruments in McMunn's description are *tablā* (drums), *śahnāī* (a double-reed wind instrument) and "zithar"—probably a *tānpūrā* (plucked lute).[39]

Dance forms such as kathak and vocal genres like ṭhumrī are now accepted as vital elements of the mainstream of Indian classical culture. In Gaisberg's and McMunn's time, however, "outside police circles they would [have been] unknown to the Western world in India."[40] The music and dance of the koṭhā would also have been unfamiliar to the majority of the Indian population. With the first recordings, the music of the koṭhā was to move from a world of obscurity and social stigma into the mass media. Unknowingly Gaisberg was preserving via sound recording a crucial era in the history of Indian music, as well as examples of a unique women's stratum of music making.

From then on, tawa'ifs could be listened to in the respectable surroundings of middle-class Indian homes. On disks women often had "amateur" printed after their names to indicate that they were not professional performers, and were therefore respectable despite their musical accomplishments. They were in fact professionals but did not wish to make the fact public for reasons of propriety.

"THE MARVEL OF THE 20TH CENTURY"[41]: THE MARKETING OF THE GRAMOPHONE IN INDIA

The executives of GTL quickly realized that in India they were sitting on a potentially huge market for their new product. In 1903 Thomas Addis took over from Hawd as the firm's agent. He was an energetic and tireless promoter of GTL's Indian market, including the "native" or "vernacular" lists. Hawd went off to freelance in the Indian gramophone market, and became something of a thorn in the flesh of his previous employers—but that is another story. Correspondence for the years 1903–1905 shows not only the growth of the Indian market, but also some of the difficulties Addis encountered trying to convince his bosses back home about the commercial potential of local recordings, and the complexity of selling their product in India. In December 1903, one year after Gaisberg's first recording expedition, Addis wrote to London analyzing the market for recordings of Indian music and making some shrewd observations:

> India is a peculiar country in regard to language as if you go 300 miles out of Calcutta you would find a different dialect altogether which would not be understood here and so on through every state and presidency.

Each district has its local and popular singers whose records would sell freely. Now its this class of work that the better and middle class natives, who have the money enquire for and we are creditably informed the present sales are largely due to the excellent results obtained from the instruments [gramophones] alone, and that it is not the records themselves that are inducing the public to buy instruments.

Addis was making a point that gives us an important historical window on the meaning of the gramophone in Indian society in the first years of the 20th century. For the Indian middle classes who could afford it, the gramophone was a technological novelty and status symbol in itself, whatever the music being played on it—a concept that would be exploited in later publicity material. But Addis was also astute about the potential of regional language–based musics as part of GTL's marketing strategy. Two years later, however, he was still trying to convince London of the importance of linguistic diversity in the music market. He had done his research to back up this point[42]:

We have taken records in various vernaculars, but we have not, in my opinion, gone far enough into this matter. Permit me to fall back on figures to show the immense field there is to be developed in India:
India. Total population (1901) 287,000,000
There are 147 vernaculars of extraordinary variety . . . :
Hindi spoken by 60,000,000
Bengali do 44,000,000
Bihari do 47,000,000
Telegu do 20,000,000
Mahrati do 18,000,000
after which come Rajastani, Kanarese, Gujarati, Oriya, Burmese, Tamil, Malayalam, Pustu, pure Urdu etc., etc. The above figures convey, no doubt the enormous diversity hidden under the name "India."

When arrangements were made for the next recording expedition, the regional diversity of India was duly targeted. The London office instructed Addis to extend the catalogue by about 2,500 records, broken down by language[43]:

Bengali 300, Hindustani 500, Gujarati 300, Mahratti 150, Tamil 300, Telugu 250, Canarese 200, Cingalese 200, Bhutian Nepaulese Thibetan 120, Sanscrit, Persian 120, Beluchi 60.

Curiously, perhaps, such regional diversity in the Indian popular music industry would never be reflected again until a new recording technology, the cassette, broke the hegemony of the GTL and the Hindi language fīlmi song in the late 1970s.[44]

The fact that there was no record-pressing plant in India was also giving Addis problems. He was continually running out of stocks of Indian records and had to fight an ongoing battle to convince the London office to send more copies and dispatch another recording expedition to increase the list and record more and better artists. In September 1903 he wrote:

> We are rather dissappointed [sic] at the native records coming through so slowly especially when you consider that you have had the original records made here since the beginning of January last. . . . We have only a few Bengali records and people are beginning to lose faith saying that they do not believe they are coming at all. The same thing will happen regarding Japanese Chinese and other records . . . it will be quite another year before we shall be in a position to make a big move in the "Eastern Trade."

On 8 June 1905 Addis notes that all 300 copies of L. C. Boral's recordings were sold "within half an hour of the time they were opened."

Another major headache for Addis was the piracy by other Indian dealers of GTL trademarks, notably the famous "His Master's Voice" picture showing a dog listening to a gramophone, and the term "gramophone" itself. The *Morning Post* of February 1903 contained an advertisement for a Calcutta firm, the "International Gramophone Depot" of Dhurumtolla Street, that reproduced a picture of the music-loving dog to sell a variety of imported gramophones and accessories "All at American prices." Such infringements led to many lawsuits, through which GTL eventually established sole ownership of the now world-famous image.[45] In 1906 GTL catalogues were offering "Genuine Gramophone Needles in coloured boxes bearing our famous Copyright Picture 'His Master's Voice.' "

During the first five years of the century GTL's "native" list began to take shape, reflecting the regional and linguistic heterogeneity of India. The catalogues were published in all the major languages of the area such as Punjabi, Urdu, Hindi, Bengali, Tamil, Telegu, and Malayalam. The list had also increased owing to a second more extensive recording expedition in 1904. During this tour, led by William Sinkler Darby, recordings were made throughout India rather than just in Calcutta.[46]

As the list increased, the question of publicity was of utmost importance. There were teething troubles with the first catalogues, mainly due to the number of scripts and languages being employed.[47] But pointing to the sales figures, Addis noted the positive effect good sales would have: "what can and will be done when proper catalogues are printed." Photographs in early catalogues showed the big-selling gramophone celebrities such as Gauharjan and Malkajan. It is to the specially commissioned images for gramophone catalogues that I will now turn, however, as they incorporate the history, religion, mythology, and social mores of Indian life in a striking manner.

The question of images for GTL's catalogues is first raised by Addis in a letter to the London office dated January 19, 1905. Apparently he had a small picture, "painted by a local artist here, and which we propose to use on the cover of our new Indian catalogue"; but a Mr. Wortman who had been visiting had taken the picture away with him by mistake. The picture in question was in three separate colors. It had to be on a catalogue of 10-inch recordings in "100,000 lots." The latter figure indicates the way in which the trade was increasing and the urgent demand for publicity employing suitable images. It is difficult to ascertain exactly which picture Addis's letter refers to, but several interesting images from local artists appear in catalogues during the years 1906–1907. Addis could be referring to the colored image entitled "The Gramophone in the Court of Jahangier the Magnificent" by one Fred C. Rogers. This curious concoction of past and present is discussed in detail below. Or perhaps it is the image of the goddess Sarasvatī complete with gramophone, by G. N. Mukherji, which appears on the cover of a 1906 catalogue. These and other images show the way in which GTL tried to target its Indian customers by mixing ancient and modern, projecting the talking machine as an almost miraculous phenomenon worthy of taking its place next to emperors and goddesses, or as an essential adjunct to social status and progress. In a 1907 catalogue the ubiquitous "His Master's Voice" [HMV] hound is pictured sitting in front of the new gramophone in a comfortable middle-class Indian household (Figure 2.1). The text is Bengali but the decor of the room and the dress of the inhabitants are a mix of Western and Indian. The gramophone is the focus of attention, the centerpiece of the room. The status of the gramophone is reflected by the man of the house who stands with arm outstretched, presumably extolling the wonders and virtues of the new technology and presenting it proudly to his family and relatives. His wife stands at the other side of the table; she is clearly delighted with this latest addition to the household. The couple's two children, a boy and a girl, listen attentively, with the boy leaning forward eagerly to catch the sounds from the wondrous machine. An elderly man, the grandfather perhaps, listens with a younger relative or friend. There is also a servant who has been invited in to listen. The latter, wearing only a dhoti, crouches on the floor. The HMV dog sits beneath the gramophone, implanted out of context, a corporate trademark come to life in an Indian domestic scene. (Paradoxically, dogs are considered unclean in India and are rarely kept as domestic pets, except in upper-class Westernized households.)

This image is packed with social and cultural messages. The gramophone is an object, a possession, that represents a bridge between two cultural domains, the West and India, and as such it is a symbol of the

FIGURE 2.1. His Master's Voice.

aspirations of the burgeoning Indian middle class at the turn of the century. The gramophone is also a technological innovation that crosses generations. The pride of the up-and-coming young couple in their new acquisition is evident. Their son, leaning forward, is moving toward a mass-mediated future. The grandfather spans the generations and has lived to see the world change through the medium of recorded sound; his face is creased in amusement, perhaps at the younger ones and their fascination with this new toy. But relative status is intact in the presence of the servant, who sits on the floor while everyone else sits in chairs, who is half-dressed, whose skin is of a noticeably darker hue, and whose back is to the viewer. Technology democratizes, but not completely.

The inextricable link in India between religion and everyday life also did not escape the eye of the publicists. In one particularly striking image from 1906 (Figure 2.2) Sarasvatī, the Hindu goddess of arts and learning, is depicted in a rural idyll, perched on a lotus in the middle of a lake. On her knees is a *vīṇā*, a traditional stringed instrument, but rising from the water next to her and balanced on another huge lotus is a gramophone. She rests one hand on the frets of her instrument, and she uses her other hand to place the needle on the disk with the other. Nearby flowers contain neat piles of discs ready to be selected and played. Fishes, crocodiles, frogs, tortoises, serpents, and a beautiful swan also seem to listen to the gramophone.

FIGURE 2.2. Sarasvati, The Hindu goddess of arts and learning.

This image deftly incorporates the gramophone into a panoply of ancient symbols associated with Sarasvatī. Sarasvatī is the consort of Brahma and the "goddess of wisdom, knowledge, science, art, learning and eloquence, the patroness of music and inventor of the Sanskrit language and Devanagari letters."[48]

She is also closely associated with the concept of flowing water (the River Sarasvatī is in Uttar Pradesh). She is traditionally depicted as fair-skinned, four-limbed, often holding a stringed instrument, or a drum, and a book of palm leaves to symbolize her love of knowledge. Her vehicle is a swan, a symbol of "the whiteness or purity of learning and the power of discrimination, which is the essential quality for the acquisition of saving knowledge."[49] Sarasvatī usually appears in a vernal scene due to her associations with the beginning of spring. But Sarasvatī also has a particular relationship with sound and hearing. One mythological account has a special resonance for the coming of the gramophone[50]:

> In the Santiparva it is related that when the Brahmarshis were performing austerities, prior to the creation of the universe, "a voice derived from Brahma *entered into the ears of them all* [italics added]; the celestial Sarasvati was then produced from the heavens."

And so the gramophone enters the aural universe of Indian mythology, bringing music to the masses of India—or at least that part of the masses that could afford it, at anything up to 250 rupees a machine.

Sarasvatī was not the only goddess featured in the catalogues. An image from 1907 shows the goddess Durgā surrounded by wild beasts—tigers, lions, and pythons—that have been subdued by the music of the gramophone (Figure 2.3). Durgā, the consort of Śiva, is a terrifying figure in the Hindu pantheon, often depicted as the goddess of destruction in her incarnation as Kālī. The image of Kālī was also used as a ferocious symbol of religious nationalism during the first decades of the 20th century.[51]

But Durgā also has a virtuous side which is on display here in the company of the gramophone. The many beasts that surround her appear tamed by the sound of the gramophone. The lion is traditionally the *vāhana* (vehicle) of Durgā and symbolizes her strength in the continuing battle between good and evil. The tiger is associated with the goddess Kātyāyanī, and the deer with Vāyu, the wind god.[52] Durgā leans her arm on a serpent showing that she is impervious to this powerful and dangerous beast.

A similar traditional image appears in the iconography of Indian music associated with the *rāgmālā* (miniature painting) depicting the *rasa* (mood) of the *rāginī* Toḍī, who through her beauty and skill on the *vīṇā* has charmed the animals out of the forest to listen. The deer is always

FIGURE 2.3. Durgā, the consort of Śiva.

prominent in this representation.⁵³ This timeless image is cleverly transposed to suit the new technology of the gramophone.

Sometimes the publicity images for GTL move into the realm of the surreal. A truly curious example of this appears in the 1905 catalogue with the heading "The Gramophone in the Court of Jahangier the Magnificent" (Figure 2.4). The Moghul emperor Jahangier reigned between 1605 and 1627, a period when European contact with India was on the increase. This image shows the splendor of the Moghul court complete with attendants and concubines enraptured by the presence of a gramophone. The meeting has the look of a darbar or official gathering in the presence of the emperor. Such events were noted for their lavish and luxurious show of wealth. But who has presented this wonderful gift for the delectation of the monarch? There is no supplicant visible, only an armed guard who stands grimly by the machine. It would appear that the gramophone has arrived of its own volition—it is not only a talking machine, but also a time machine.

In this image the marvelous nature of the gramophone allows it to skip centuries into a dimension where Indian history is penetrated by Western technology. The message is clear: if these machines had been around in his time even Jahangier would have wanted one. Curiously, perhaps, Jahangier is credited with being the first Indian emperor to have a Western instrument at his court. In 1616 he received a virginal as a gift from King James I of

FIGURE 2.4. The gramophone in the court of Jahangier the Magnificent.

England. It is doubtful whether the 1905 image is a direct reference to that incident; rather, it is an odd coincidence. However, it is also recorded that Jahangier soon became bored with the virginal.[54] Would the same fate have awaited the time-traveling gramophone?

By the end of the decade, GTL had established a pressing plant in Calcutta, and was on the way to becoming the dominant recording company in the Indian subcontinent until well into the middle of the 20th century. The correspondence and publicity from those first years offer a rare glimpse into the logistics and cultural complexities involved in the gestation of a mass medium.

But what of Indian music and the new technology? How did the constraints of technology affect the style and structure of the music recorded? It is to this dimension of the gramophone in India that I finally turn.

MUSICAL FORM ON EARLY INDIAN RECORDINGS

Writing in 1942 Fred Gaisberg observed[55]:

> Thirty years have elapsed since my first visit to India. We found music there static and after a few years there was very little traditional music left to record. Songs for festivals and weddings were already in our catalogue and new artists were learning their repertoire from gramophone records.

No doubt Gaisberg had little appreciation or understanding of Indian music to back up his claim that the music was "static," but his final comment is more intriguing. As a way of disseminating musical material the gramophone was unprecedented, and it was inevitable that artists would copy songs from records.

Indeed, recording was a perfect tool for such endeavors. A record could be played repeatedly and mimicked without recourse to a teacher or notation. But what was being copied in terms of musical form, and how did recorded versions of khyāl, ṭhumrī, and other traditional genres relate to live performances? Were the records in fact "constructions" rather than "reproductions" of Indian music? To put it another way, was the music that appeared on disks the creature of recording technology rather than a representation of a genuine performance?

Manuel his noted that throughout the history of recording in India certain forms of music have been neglected because of their length. He cites genres such as Braj *dholā* and Budelkhandi *ālhā*, whose extended ballad forms were unsuitable for recording.[56] But many of the forms that did appear in the early recordings of Indian music were also unsuitable for rendition in two or three minutes, notably the vocal genre khyāl, of which Gauharjan recorded several examples.

Today a performance of khyāl is likely to involve extensive and elaborate improvisation. There is little evidence to suggest that live performance practices of khyāl and other genres including ṭhumrī differed greatly (at least in terms of duration) at the turn of the century. It is reported[57] that performances of *batānā*—a mixture of singing (usually ṭhumrī) and dance performed by courtesans—could last for up to three hours for a single piece! Although this is perhaps exaggerated, Gauharjan is nevertheless credited with giving extensive live performances of ṭhumrī and khyāl.[58]

Following the first recordings, Indian music performance existed in two worlds: the extended live performance and the two- or three-minute duration of the disk. It has been suggested that this represented a further split between the performance practices of the courts and those of the urban milieu of musical entertainment.[59] However, that the short duration of disks did cause problems is indicated by the fact that in the early days many great performers of Indian music refused to be recorded because they found recording to be contrary to the spirit of their art.[60] Feedback from the audience is also an important ingredient of Indian music performances. As the performance unfolds, the audience interjects exclamations of approval and astonishment at virtuoso passages. Such crucial interplay was absent from the recording situation, so that an important source of musical inspiration and affirmation was denied the performers.[61]

In one sense the early recordings are no more than snapshots of particular genres and styles of performance. But the recordings also give us clues as to how musicians dealt with the short amount of time available on disk as well as provide us with insights into the nature of Indian musical form and its flexible structure. On disk, time constraints throw the essential structural features of the music into sharp relief. Musical devices that usually enjoy detailed extemporization and exploration in live performance are compressed to short gestures on disc. In this way features of Indian musical form are poured through the sieve of recording technology and time limitation until only the essentials remain.

In order to illustrate some of the features of this process, let us look in more detail at a khyāl by Gauharjan from 1907, "Etane Yauban Daman Na Kariye" (I can no longer contain my youthful exuberance), in the penatonic rāg *Bhūpālī*. On this recording Gauharjan was accompanied by a bowed instrument, the sāraṅgī, and the tablā drums. The sāraṅgī has an important role in khyāl as a support to the vocal line, shadowing every subtle nuance and inflection of the voice.

In general terms khyāl is considered to be a more abstract and classical genre than ṭhumrī, although the latter also shows influence from the former.[62] In khyāl the sound and syllables of words are used as vehicles for abstract vocalizing; the literal meaning of the text, which is usually on a romantic or religious theme, is of secondary importance. The lyrics in a khyāl are usually only heard once in their complete form before becoming the source of improvisation. This contrasts with ṭhumrī where the lyrics are of greater importance. This is not to say that no improvisation with syllables takes place in ṭhumrī—this is an important element of the form—but there is more emphasis on the meaning of the words rather than on the musical sound.

The term *khyāl* comes from the Urdu word meaning "thought" or "imagination." By the turn of the 20th century khyāl had become the most widely performed classical genre of vocal music in northern India, supplanting the older austere vocal form called dhrupad. Khyāl is thought to be a synthesis of other vocal forms such as dhrupad and qavvāli, a type of Muslim religious song.[63] The form developed into a distinctive genre characterized by virtuosic vocal extemporization and dramatic bravura passages.

A live performance of khyāl falls into several sections: a slow composition known as *baṛā* (large) khyāl and a faster composition called *choṭā* (small) khyāl. The compositions can be set to various tāls, but a common format is: slow—*ektāl* (12 beats), followed by fast—*tīntāl* (16 beats). In khyāl there are no extended *ālāps* (slow unmetered preludes) as in dhrupad or instrumental music, although detailed ālāp-like improvisation takes place at the beginning of the baṛā khyāl composition, with tāl. This is often set to a very slow (*ati-vilambit*) basic beat. The performance opens with a few phrases of the rāg sung in ālāp style, then moves directly into the composition. Extemporization takes the form of slow explorations of the syllables of the words and faster melodic passages known as *tāns*, using either *sargam* (the pitch names *sā, re, ga,* etc.) or *ākār* (singing to the vocable *ā*). There is also much cross-rhythmic interplay (*laykārī*). An extended performance of khyāl is open-ended in duration.

How is it possible to perform a music such as khyāl in three minutes? Gauharjan's recording gives some insight. "Etane Yauban Daman Na Kariye" lasts for 2 minutes 14 seconds. The performance comprises:

1. A brief nonmetrical opening (ālāp), which leads into the refrain (*mukhṛā*) of the composition;
2. The composition itself (*cīz* or *bandis'*), with tāl. The composition is in two sections, *sthāyī* (which includes the refrain as its first phrase) and *antarā*, and forms the "fixed" part of the performance;
3. Sections of improvisation based on the sthāyī section of the composition.

Breaking down "Etane Yauban Daman Na Kariye" into composed and "improvised" sections shows the way in which Gauharjan uses the time available within the terms of Indian musical form:

"Etane Yauban Daman Na Kariye" Duration:	2′ 14″
Musical Feature:	Time:*
Ālāp/introduction	11″
Sthāyī x3	30″
Antarā x1	7″
Sthāyī x1	9″
Improvisation 1	17″
" " 2	17″
" " 3	11″
" " 4	8″
" " 5	10″
Sthāyī x1½	14″

* all timings to the nearest second

There is a clear sense of balance and shape in the way in which Gauharjan fits the form of khyāl into the short time span of this disk. The ālāp is reduced to a single sounding of the SA, or tonic note, followed by the refrain, the mukhṛā, of the sthāyī. The sthāyī is the most important part of the composition as it delineates the meter and mode of the piece and forms the basis for subsequent improvisations.

Gauharjan sings the sthāyī three times, then gives a brief rendition of the antarā, once only, before repeating the sthāyī again. In total the fixed composition, with sthāyī and antarā sections, takes up one minute, or almost half the total recording time.

The "improvisations" take the form of tāns (sweeping melodic phrases), with a return to the mukhṛā at the end of the phrase. In Gauharjan's recording the longest improvised break spans two cycles of 16 beats, returning to a compressed version of the mukhṛā. After two such improvisations at the central part of the recording, the improvisations shorten to one cycle before returning to the sthāyī.

It seems, however, that time finally caught up with Gauharjan on this particular recording, as she ends half way through a cycle, rather than on the first beat as would be typical in Indian music, leaving her a few seconds to announce (in English with a flirtatious flair) "My name is Gauharjan." Such announcements are a feature of many early recordings. It has been suggested that this practice was purely for reasons of novelty,[64] but it seems it may also have been a form of advertising. The announcements are not always in English, and on one recording by Malkajan of Agra she announces not only her name but also her address!

How is the form of Indian music reconciled to this recording? Within its own terms it is a perfectly balanced performance giving equal weight, in time, to the fixed and improvised parts of the performance. However, the time demands unbalance the traditional performance practices associated with khyāl. Rendition of the sthāyī and the antarā would never take up half of an extended performance of khyāl. Indeed, they may be sung in their complete form only one or twice in an extended performance. Extemporization of various kinds would take up something like 90% of the performance time.

The analysis of performance in terms of the proportions of composed to improvised sections is particularly valid in the context of recording, where the musician has to decide what to include and what to leave out. Such decisions have a different meaning in the unfolding of a temporally open-ended live performance. Although I do not wish to generalize too far from one example, I suggest that one possible effect of the limited duration of early recordings was to lead artists to give greater weight to the composed or fixed parts of the performances than they would normally have done in live recitals. This is particularly true of forms like the khyāl. To verify this point, however, requires further research with a larger sample.

The flexibility of Indian musical form undoubtedly helped in its transition to the medium of recording. However, early recordings of instrumental music do sound rather fragmented in a way that vocal recordings do not. For example, the 1904 recordings of the great sitarist Imdad Khan obviously suffer from his time restraints; we are left with mere tantalizing glimpses of complete sitar performances, sectionalized and taken out of context—an ālāp, a *joṛ*, but without the overarching coherence of a complete performance. In this case the recording ethic does not fit the form.

Later, especially in recordings of instrumental music, Indian musicians found ways to work round the time constraints in keeping with Indian musical form, especially after the introduction of two-sided disks. For example, sitar players performed ālāp with *surbahār* (bass-sitār) on one side of the disk and a *gat* (a fixed composition) with sitar on the flip side. But even though this pointed up the different movements of the rāg, there was still not enough there to give a detailed rendition.

Much research remains to be done on the formal effects of recording on Indian music performances, but general observations suggest that Indian musicians adapt their recorded performances readily as the technology changed. The advent of LPs in the 1960s led to longer performances, and now it is not uncommon to hear an extended performance of one rāg for 70 minutes or more on a compact disk.

CONCLUSION

In this chapter I have discussed various apects of the gramophone in India at the turn of the century. This is a fascinating and important era in the history of Indian music, but it has received little attention in the literature of ethnomusicolgy. Not only is there a wealth of historical and cultural material to be explored and analyzed, but also a large body of extant recordings by some of India's most prominent musicians. This period is unique in that it represents a musical culture in transition crossing over from a world of patronage to a world of global mass media. That moment in time is captured in sound by the early recordings of GTL, recordings that mark the beginnings of one of the largest recording industries in the world. From then on records would be used for a variety of purposes, from entertainment to the mass dissemination of information on health and hygiene, and in politics as part of the Swadeshi movement during the struggle for independence from Britain. The advent of the recording industry in India proved to be a musical and social phenomenon of enormous significance.

It seems appropriate to end with one final image from those early days (Figure 2.5). In a 1907 catalogue the HMV hound tilts his head in that quizzical way of his as two Indian dancers complete with ankle bells emerge from the horn of a gramophone to spin on the rotating disk. Surely there could be no more fitting symbol of Indian music's emergence into the 20th century through the medium of recorded sound.

ACKNOWLEDGMENTS

This research would not have been possible without the help, assistance, and advice of Ruth Edge, Sarah Hobbs, and Jenny Keen at the EMI archives. Special thanks to Michael Kinnear for generously sharing with me his encyclopedic knowledge of Indian recordings. Also thanks to Professor Cyril Ehrlich for his advice and criticism of various aspects of this research, and to Amaresh Chakrovarty who translated the lyrics of the Gauharjan example ("I can no longer contain my youthful exuberance"). My thanks to Norman McBeath who took the photographs of the EMI archive images. This chapter originally appeared in *British Journal of Ethnomusicology*, 1993, 2, 31–53. Copyright 1993 by International Council for Traditional Music (U.K. Chapter). Reprinted by permission.

EMI ARCHIVES:
Vernacular Catalogues and Publicity Material 1902–1910; Recordings 1902–1910; Correspondence 1902–1905; Reproduced by courtesy of EMI Music Archives, Hayes.

FIGURE 2.5. HMV hound and Indian dancers.

NOTES

1. Manuel, P. (1993). *Cassette culture.* Chicago: University of Chicago Press, p. 37.
2. Kinnear, M. (1994). *The gramophone company's first Indian recordings, 1899–1908.* Bombay: Popular Prakashan, pp. 73–74.
3. Ibid., p. 11.
4. Gaisberg, F. W. (1942). *Music on record.* London: Robert Hale, p. 52.
5. Kinnear, *The gramophone company's,* p. 9.
6. Ibid., p. 11.
7. Gaisberg, *Music on record,* p. 54.
8. Ibid., p. 54.
9. Kinnear, *The gramophone company's,* p. 11.

10. EMI Archives, *Catalogues for India,* 1902.
11. Kinnear, *The gramophone company's,* pp. 11–12.
12. Ibid., p. 11.
13. Gaisberg, *Music on record,* pp. 54–55.
14. Ibid., p. 55.
15. Ibid.
16. Ibid.
17. Kinnear, personal communication, 1992.
18. According to Misra, Gauharjan's parents were Robert Yoeward, "an engineer ... in Calcutta," and Allen Victoria Hemming. Although they were obviously Western, Misra does not state their nationalities (Misra, S. [1990]. *Some immortals of Hindustani music.* New Dehli: Harman.).
19. Ibid., p. 97.
20. Ibid., p. 96.
21. Manuel, P. (1989). *Thumri in historical and stylistic perspectives.* Delhi: Motilal Banarsidass, p. 75.
22. Gaisberg, *Music on record,* p. 56.
23. Ibid.
24. Ibid.
25. See Kaufmann, W. (1984). *The ragas of north India.* New York: Da Capo Press; and Manuel, *Thumri,* for details of these rāgs.
26. Sorrell, N., & Narayan, R. (1980). *Indian music in performance.* Manchester, U.K.: Manchester University Press, p. 65.
27. E.g., at the "Women Music Makers of India" conference held in New Delhi in 1984.
28. Gaisberg, *Music on record,* p. 56.
29. Manuel, *Thumri.*
30. Khan, M. H. (1988). *Music and its study.* New Delhi: Sterling, p. 81.
31. Neuman, D. M. (1990). *The life of music in north India.* Chicago: University of Chicago Press, p. 19.
32. Misra, *Some immortals,* p. 97.
33. Gaisberg, *Music on record,* pp. 56–57.
34. McMunn, Sir George. (1931). *The underworld of India.* Chicago: University of Chicago Press, pp. 80–81.
35. D. Neuman, personal communication, 1984.
36. Manuel, *Thumri,* pp. 49–50.
37. See also Neuman, *Life of music,* p. 100.
38. Manuel, *Thumri,* p. 65.
39. McMunn, *Underworld of India,* pp. 83–89.
40. Ibid., p. 82.
41. Advertisement for Gramophone and Typewriter Ltd., 1902.
42. EMI archive correspondence, 23.xi.1905.
43. Ibid., 6.xi.1904.
44. Manuel, *Cassette culture.*
45. EMI archive correspondence, 9.v.1904.
46. Kinnear, *The gramophone company's,* pp. 21–25.

47. EMI archive correspondence, 7–9.xii.1905.

48. Garrett, J. (1990). *A classical dictionary of India*. Delhi: Low Price Publications, p. 559.

49. Morgan, K. (1987). *The religion of the Hindus*. Delhi: Motilal Banarsidass, p. 106.

50. Garrett, *Classical dictionary*, p. 559; emphasis added.

51. Heehs, P. (1993, January). Religion and revolt: Bengal under the Raj. *History Today*, 43, 29–36.

52. Morgan, *Religion of the Hindus*, pp. 104–105.

53. Deneck, M. M. (1977). *Indian art*. London: Hamlyn, p. 39.

54. Foster, W. (Ed.). (1926). *The embassy of Sir Thomas Roe to India, 1615–19*. London, pp. 48, 76.

55. Gaisberg, *Music on record*, p. 58.

56. Manuel, *Cassette culture*, p. 39.

57. Misra, *Some immortals*, p. 98.

58. Ibid., pp. 99–100.

59. Michael Kinnear, personal communication, 1992.

60. Kinnear, *The gramophone company's*, p. 28.

61. Manuel notes how canned exclamations such as "Wah! Wah!" are dubbed onto present-day recordings of popular ghazals, to reproduce the excitement and immediacy of live performances (*Cassette culture*, p. 98).

62. Manuel, *Thumri*, pp. 142–143.

63. Wade, B. (1979). *Music in India: The classical traditions*. Englewood Cliffs, N.J.: Prentice-Hall, p. 169.

64. Joshi, G. N. (1988). A concise history of the phonograph industry in India. *Popular Music*, 7(2), pp. 147–156, p. 148.

3

WELCOME TO DREAMSVILLE[1]

A History and Geography of Northern Soul

JOANNE HOLLOWS
KATIE MILESTONE

The northern soul scene in Britain is a regionally based dance and club network that centers around "rare" soul records from the 1960s and 1970s. With its roots in the soul clubs of the mid-1960s, northern soul is still alive today. Northern soul events are primarily held in the North and Midlands of England, although they exist on a lesser scale in different parts of Britain. Despite the distinctiveness and longevity of this largely "underground" scene, northern soul has attracted little attention in cultural analysis. With the notable exception of Stuart Cosgrove's "Long after Tonight Is All Over,"[2] northern soul has tended to remain hidden in the footnotes of academic accounts of musical cultures and subcultures. In this chapter we aim to open up a space for talking about northern soul rather than offering any definitive account of it.[3]

In this chapter, we hope not only to raise the profile of this marginalized scene within popular music criticism, but also to show how the case of northern soul raises more general questions about the cultural study of music. In particular, the chapter addresses debates about place and identity and the relationship between local musical scenes and global musical cultures. The analysis is organized around four main concerns: the "northernness" of northern soul; rarity, exclusivity, and commodity exchange; the relationships between contexts of production and consumption; and the importance of place and pilgrimage within the northern soul scene. In negotiating these issues, we hope to highlight how the northern soul scene produces a sense of identity and belonging. In doing so, we hope to offer a different way of conceptualizing identity and the production of "community" in musical cultures from that offered by subcultural theory. In the process, questions about conceptions of musical value and commodity exchange within musical cultures will be highlighted.

The marginalization of northern soul in the cultural study of music is, at least in part, a product of both the predominance of subcultural theory[4] in analyzing musical cultures and the preoccupations of subcultural theorists. While Cosgrove's subcultural analysis of northern soul is informative, and we draw on his insights, the northern soul scene highlights the limitations of subcultural theory. Richard Middleton has noted that subcultural theorists were ill equipped to deal with cases such as northern soul where "subcultural identity is centrally focused on music" because they were more concerned with "music as symbol" than "music as music."[5] Furthermore, the romance and radicalism attributed to youth subcultures was compounded by the way in which subcultural theorists privileged notions of progress, change, and the new, never quite freeing themselves from the association between "youth" and "the future." It is partly for these reasons that, as Gary Clarke has noted, subcultural theory focused on the "innovatory moment" of subcultures, so they seem to exist in a "synthetic moment of frozen historical time."[6] The longevity of musical cultures such as northern soul and the scene's fascination with music from a bygone era (the U.S. soul music of the 1960s and early 1970s) meant that it failed to meet the theoretical requirements of subcultural theory.

The lack of attention paid to northern soul was also compounded by the fact that, until recently, scenes centering around discos and clubs have been marginalized from pop history.[7] The "authentic" subcultures of subcultural theory were usually located on the streets. The street operated as a sign of "authenticity" because not only has it traditionally been a site that is difficult to regulate but also because, unlike the club, the street is supposedly distanced from the world of commerce which, for subcultural theorists, is identified with ideological incorporation. By positioning the radicalism of subcultures against the ideological pull of capitalist commerce, subcultural theorists not only ignored more commercial scenes but also overlooked the intersections between the subcultures they studied and commercial activity.[8] If, in considering northern soul, we hope to open up one part of a hidden history of club culture, then we also wish to argue that a consideration of commercial activities within musical scenes should be central to cultural analysis. The case of northern soul highlights the ways in which the value of commodities such as records is not simply a product of processes of production or consumption but also a product of processes of exchange that need to be understood as meaningful cultural activities.

If northern soul has remained hidden from academic histories of pop, it is also a scene in which history and tradition are central values. This "soul underground" privileges a knowledge of musical histories and traditions that also inform the value of "rarity" within the scene. It is in relation to the values of history, tradition, and rarity that distinctions between the "authentic" and the "inauthentic" are constructed within northern soul. This is not to argue that northern soul is an "authentic" culture because it values "authenticity" but to consider how notions of "authenticity" are produced in different ways in different musical cultures. On one level, notions of "authenticity" and northern soul seem incompatible: as we have already noted, northern soul did not fit the criteria of authenticity fixed by subcultural theorists. Furthermore, musical cultures that are primarily organized around recorded music[9] are often seen as "inauthentic" in a folk discourse that privileges "live" music that is produced and consumed by "active" members of a "community."[10] Folk discourse, like subcultural theory, is suspicious of the commercial intervention of the cultural industries between producers in privileging the "authentic" as a sign of cultural value. For example, northern soul is based on a rejection of commercially successful records and, as we go on to argue, privileges a sense of "roots" by stressing the importance of the sociological and musical origins of northern soul records within local musical cultures.[11]

If subcultural frameworks can provide only a limited understanding of northern soul, Schmalenbach's concept of the *Bund* makes it possible to think of the relationships between place and identity and to conceive of the northern soul scene as an "elective, unstable, effectual form of sociation."[12] Unlike conceptions of "community" in which a sense of belonging is based on ascriptive social relations, geographical proximity, and tradition, social relations in *Bunde* are elective and based on sentiment, although, as we shall argue in the case of northern soul, they may aspire to produce their own traditions. In order to be sustained, the *Bund* must produce "a code of practices and symbols which serve as the basis for identification" and also produce a sense of belonging.[13] In the following discussion, we consider the practices and symbols that form the basis for identification in northern soul and highlight the ways in which these are bound up with the centrality of place within the scene.

A BRIEF HISTORY OF NORTHERN SOUL

The rare or northern scene has its roots in the early 1960s. As Stuart Cosgrove has argued, the first wave of soul imports was favored by people who sought to distinguish themselves from "popular taste," "those content with the formulaic records on the BBC playlist."[14] A "rare" or "underground" soul scene emerged in the mid-1960s out of both the Mod scene and the rhythm and blues clubs of the north. This scene tended to reject "popular" Motown sounds in favor of undiscovered, and hence "rare" or "underground" Detroit labels.[15] At this point in the scene's history, there was still an emphasis on new or relatively new tracks. The tracks were less specifically dance-orientated tracks but instead, as DJ Richard Searling puts it, records that people liked so much that they made them want to dance.[16] At this time, the scene was associated with clubs such as the Mojo in Sheffield, the Wheel in Manchester, and the Catacombs in Wolverhampton.

In the early to mid-1970s the rare or northern soul scene underwent some changes. Also at this time the northern soul scene received some media attention, and as a consequence discussions of northern soul have often been "fixed" around this era. At this point the scene shifted to become a distinctive "rare" soul scene based around obscure old records by maintaining an emphasis on 1960s soul. There was also some shift of pace to fast up-tempo stompers and a corresponding shift in the speed and frenzy of dance, aided by the consumption of "speed."[17] Richard Searling has noted that black participants tended to drift away from the scene as the pace of the music accelerated.[18] After the Torch in Tunstall (Stoke-on-Trent) closed, Wigan Casino all-nighters acted as a focal point for the scene from 1973, distinguished by high-speed soul that was suited to its cavernous interior. Wigan Casino, like the Torch before it, was also, crucially, well placed for motorway links.[19] Because Wigan became the focus for media attention, "northern soul" became equated with Wigan Casino, although it was only one of many clubs that held northern soul nights.

The 1970s not only saw a shift from slower to faster soul, but also the emergence of a schism within the scene between those who wanted to retain an emphasis on old soul and those who wanted to include new tracks. Furthermore, the increased publicity and popularity that the scene was receiving was seen as a danger to what was perceived as an underground movement that had made a cult out of obscurity. The media attention, along with the new/old split, threw the scene into crisis in the mid-1970s. Furthermore, although the scene valued "authentic" old soul, it demanded a constant supply of unheard "rare" records. But, the stocks of undiscovered up-tempo U.S. soul records were diminishing. The scene had to evolve and was faced with two options: either it could stick with tradition, play "authentic" oldies, and end up with a stagnant playlist, or it could maintain the rarity and obscurity of the scene by shifting to new "rare" soul.[20] This second option could be achieved in two ways: first, through the production of custom-made northern soul tracks geared to the dance floor which tried to keep some fidelity to the production values of 1960s soul; and second, by feeding into a living Afro-American dance music tradition by absorbing new black musics. Both options were taken up by Ian Levine, a DJ from the Blackpool Mecca. Levine went to the United States to try and produce new northern soul sounds and raise the quality of custom-made new tracks.[21] He also began to introduce new dance music which would eventually lead some people away from northern soul into nights organized around 1970s Philadelphia dance music (the basis for the 1980s "rare groove" scene) and others into an emergent jazz-funk scene.[22]

After the closing of Wigan Casino in 1981, the northern soul scene shifted pace again, often moving into smaller venues and centering around slower tracks from the 1960s and early 1970s. Obscure up-tempo tracks might have been used up, but there was still a ready supply of slower tracks, and, although rarities are once more getting hard to come by, new disks still occasionally emerge. The scene is also sustained through small-scale media such as DJ Richard Searling's show on the northern radio station JFM and music papers such as *Black Echoes, Soul Underground,* and *Blues and Soul.* Despite the occasional "discovery" of northern soul by the southern taste-making, "style" magazines such as *The Face* and *I-d*, contemporary northern soul is no youth culture, with the average age of participants at today's events pushing 40. Indeed, increasingly, the northern soul scene revolves around memory and familiarity, rather than rarity. As Cosgrove argues, legends and memories have always played an important part in the scene as well as being an important theme within the lyrics of many northern soul tracks.[23] Northern soul not only places value on a musical tradition but also on the scene's own traditions.

THE "NORTHERNNESS" OF NORTHERN SOUL

The term "northern soul" was coined by Dave Godin of *Blues and Soul* magazine after a visit to an all-nighter at the Twisted Wheel in 1970 to describe a distinctive soul scene that existed north of Watford, and mainly in the North and the Midlands. However, in order to understand the "northernness" of the scene, it is also necessary to place it in relation to the "regionally-based 'supremacy' " of the southeast.[24] In the late 1960s and early to mid-1970s—the time of the scenes heyday—soul was generally unfashionable among white audiences. The northern soul scene, which valued unfashionable musical traditions, was seen as backward and risible. Despite a few notable exceptions to the rule (Merseybeat, for example), until the 1980s the provinces in Britain were seen as places where people indulged in watered-down versions of what London was doing years ago, a form of geographical "trickle-down" thesis, although more appropriately in this case a "trickle-up" thesis.

As Bourdieu argues, forms of cultural capital are not only unequally distributed between classes, but are also unequally distributed in a "socially ranked geographical space."[25] The literal "cultural capital" of Britain, London, has the power to make distinctions between the legitimate and the illegitimate, in both traditional and newer cultural forms, and thus to distinguish between what is "in" and what is "out" or unfashionable. If forms of cultural capital are not simply distributed in social space but also in geographical space, it is important to note that distinctions between the legitimate and the illegitimate aren't simply distinctions between "high" and "popular" culture but are even made *within* popular culture, including youth culture.[26]

If the distribution of cultural capital in geographical space, cross-cut by the unequal distribution of cultural capital in social space, leads to London's superiority as a national center of economic, social, and cultural capital, then this is also based on a refusal of, and distinctiveness from, the regions as "culturally deprived" and "backward." Northern soul might best be thought of as a refusal of this refusal—that is, as a refusal of the South's claims to legitimacy and distinction.[27] The northern soul scene was not simply a watered-down version of a southern scene but was instead "produced" within the North. Because the scene was organized around old American records, it didn't need London's economic and cultural power in order to survive. In this way, as both a provincial and basically a working-class form, northern soul rejects the legitimacy of more powerful taste formations within the United Kingdom (while also being unable to displace them).[28]

RARITY, EXCLUSIVITY, AND COMMODITY EXCHANGE

If music is central to the northern soul scene for dancing, it is also crucial as a rare commodity. Northern soul nights are the site not only for dance but also for the exchange of records. The club is also a marketplace.[29] While the emphasis on rarity and obscurity has led some people to dismiss northern soul as elitist, this misses the point that strategies of distinction operate in all aspects of popular music.[30] Furthermore, the investment in particular forms of cultural capital that are recognized within the field of northern soul can not only be used to create a profit in cultural distinction but can also be converted into economic capital. Northern soul records can exchange hands for hundreds, and sometimes thousands, of pounds.[31] This not only highlights the centrality of commercial activity in many youth cultures—a fact ignored when authenticity is defined against the commercial—but also points to the importance of the processes of exchange and consumption as a source of both the cultural and the economic value of music. This challenges two dominant arguments to be found in music criticism, both of which privilege production as the source of value. The first argument, heavily reliant on folk discourse, claims that musical values are homologous with the values of the community in which the music is produced. The second, not unrelated, argument, draws on Marxist economics to argue that the cultural, and economic value of music is fixed in the production process. Instead, the case of northern soul illustrates that value is not only determined by the logic of production but that economic, cultural and symbolic value are produced through exchange and consumption practices in different cultural contexts.[32]

Records are not only bearers of musical meaning but are also material objects and commodities. Appadurai's work on the "social lives of things" is useful in thinking about the "conditions in which economic objects circulate in different 'regimes of value' in time and space."[33] For Appadurai, "Demand, desire, reciprocal sacrifice and power interact to create social value in specific social situations."[34] It is in this context that records can be seen to have value both as commodities and as bearers of musical meaning, and why these factors need to be thought together. As Will Straw argues, different musical cultures have their own logic which is a product of how value is constructed: "Cultural commodities may themselves pass through a number of distinct markets and populations in the course of their lifecycle. Throughout this passage, the markers of their distinctiveness and their bases of value may undergo significant shifts."[35] Furthermore, the practices and processes of exchange need to be understood as social activities that help to create and sustain northern soul.

Northern soul can be used to challenge the production-dominated Marxist view of the music industry and folk notions of musical communities because it highlights the "commodity candidacy" of records that had moved out of the commodity state.[36] The "socially regulated paths"[37] that these 1960s soul records on minor labels were doomed to follow was, if they were lucky, a six-month shelf life. Many didn't even make it to the commodity state in the first place and remained unreleased. However, as they moved into a different "regime of value"—the northern soul scene that valued obscurity—the commodity candidacy of these records was highlighted. In this way the northern soul scene worked with an opposite set of values to the record industry (and very similar values to music critics): it was the unpopularity and lack of commercial success of these records that made them so highly prized and gave them the mark of authenticity.

Appadurai argues that diversions from the socially regulated paths of commodities are always competitively inspired.[38] In the northern soul scene, it is DJs and dealers who make these diversions and who stand to make both a profit in cultural distinction and an economic profit from rare records. As Will Straw argues, DJs act as "intellectuals within a given musical terrain" and are "engaged in struggles for prestige and status."[39] The ability of DJs to act as intellectuals comes from the high amounts of cultural capital they possess within this particular musical terrain or cultural field. In the northern soul scene, as in contemporary dance-music cultures in the United Kingdom, it is the DJs who are as much stars of the scene as recording artists, and it is their names that are used to sell events. However, although DJs define the value of records, they also need records to define their own value.[40]

Northern soul events can be thought of as "tournaments of value," "complex periodic events which are removed in a culturally well-defined way from the routines of economic life."[41] For Appadurai, tournaments of value are status competitions between people in power, in this case DJs. Success in these competitions, argues Appadurai, is partly measured by the skill through which commodity paths are diverted or subverted.[42] One of the main ways in which DJs in the northern soul scene hype up the records' rarity value and their own prestige is through the use of white labels. By sticking white labels over the original labels and retitling them, DJs increase the exclusivity of records. The previous history of the commodity is temporarily eradicated in the process.[43] As DJ Richard Searling points out, this is also a source of entertainment within the scene.[44] Furthermore, as he also acknowledges, it is a means of transforming cultural capital into economic profit. The other function of white labels is to discourage bootlegging, the illegal copying of rare records which often occurred, especially in the scene's heyday.[45] Bootlegging undermined the values of authenticity and rarity that were central to the northern soul scene. Whereas bootlegs in some musical cultures are valued because of their rarity, within northern soul bootlegs lack the life history necessary to be valued. As with religious relics, verifying the object's history is central to its value.[46] By temporarily disguising the origins of records through the use of white labels, DJs prevented bootleggers from identifying the heritage of the music and thus from authenticating the fabricated.[47]

URBAN NORTH UNITED KINGDOM TO URBAN NORTH UNITED STATES

Thus the value of records that originally were the product of black America in the 1960s changed as they moved from one regime of value to another. However, this does not mean that continuities between the original context of production and the northern soul scene should be ignored. If northern soul refuses the authority of the "the South" of England, it allies itself with the American North, in particular with cities such as Detroit. Iain Chambers has commented on the appeal of what he calls "the sweet promise of the neon-streaked streets of American nights and pleasures."[48] On one level, then, northern soul is yet another example of the ways in which British working-class culture has produced an "imaginary" identification with America as an "escape" from native cultural traditions, an identification which offered a more "extensive ... sense of the possible."[49] The identification with "America" is, however, contradictory. On the one hand, both the authentication of old disks as U.S. products and the association of these disks as the product of particular places in the United States is important within northern soul. On the other hand, the "America" that is consumed is the "pop cultural myth" of America rather than the "USA as a real place."[50]

If the northern soul scene attempts to build a regionally based culture by bypassing and rejecting the limitations of the national, it does so by positioning itself in relation to global relations. However, to claim that northern soul represents a local appropriation of global cultural flows is insufficient because the music used to "produce" the northern soul scene is not drawn from a "globalized" international culture. This is not to argue that northern soul exists "outside" of global capitalism nor to argue that the independent labels on which northern soul was originally released were somehow "independent" of the agendas of the global music industry in general and thus were more "authentic," although this attitude may well exist within the scene. Rather, we wish to stress that northern soul's privileging of a regional identity, based on the rejection of the national, needs to be understood as based on interregional affiliations at a global level. The sense of regionality in northern soul is produced out of material circumstances—the clubs, the fans, and so on—but also depends on other regional "references groups," and "on ideas and fantasies that are themselves mediated globally" through international flows of images.[51]

The regional base of northern soul—England's North and Midlands—is not of course a region in which northern soul is the only musical scene. Indeed, as Will Straw argues, what is more interesting is the diversity of musical practices within localities.[52] Instead, northern soul's interregional association with Detroit, and other Rust Belt cities to a lesser extent, directs us to the "ways in which the making and remaking of alliances between communities are the crucial political processes within popular music."[53] Northern soul also highlights the ways in which the politics of identity associated with processes of globalization and localization, which are taken as products of post-Fordism and postmodernization and are often associated with the impact of new communication technologies, are not in fact novel but have a long history within diasporic musical cultures.

The value of the records used within northern soul is not only their "Americanness" but more specifically an identification with black urban America (a point that has been made about a range of postwar British youth subcultures).[54] As Cosgrove has argued, not only is "the single most important feature of Northern Soul its respect for the music of Black America," but the scene also "tries to relive and imitate the imagery" of African-American culture.[55] As has already been noted, the northern soul scene respects history rather than novelty, and this attitude corresponds with the wider claims about the importance of history in black musics. For example, Gilroy has argued that "black music has ... only partially obeyed the rules of reification and planned obsolescence. Its users have sometimes managed to combine the strongest possible sense of fashion with a respectful, even reverent, approach to the historical status of their musical culture which values its longevity and its capacity to connect them to their historical roots."[56] Of course, for white northern soul fans, the relationship to black America is "imagined." On the one hand, musically and lyrically the tracks offer a sense of history, but on the other, they make connections with, and fetishize, the history of the "Other." Thus while attempting to draw connections between the urban American North and the urban English North, we are not seeking to equate the experience of white British and black Americans. Indeed, the fetishization of black musical cultures by white Britain needs to be understood in relation to "an exotic fantasy, not the reality of living under [specific forms of] oppression."[57]

However, just because the relationship to black urban America is "imagined," this does not diminish its power and significance within the northern south scene. To ignore different engagements with musical forms by distinguishing "true" soul fans from "false" soul fans reproduces the politics of exclusion and inclusion inherent in subcultural theory and accentuated in cases of white fans of music identified as "black."[58] Gilroy suggests that thinking of musical cultures in terms of Edward Said's concept of an "interpretive community" might be more profitable.[59] In this way, it is possible to think of an interpretive community of soul fans that extends from the streets of Detroit through the northern soul scene and into the bedrooms of young women lip synching to Diana Ross records. These fans are linked by certain possibilities within soul music and the discourses within which the meaning of soul is produced. As Shepherd has argued, while musical meaning is neither immanent in the sound nor in the lyrics, "the sounds of music restrict significantly the range of affective states and meanings that can be invested in them. For that reason, the sounds of a particular musical event will always be likely to encourage the investment of certain traces and resonances."[60]

As we have already argued, the respect for history and tradition within black musics is present in northern soul's sounds and words. The ways in which soul privileges "ecstasy" and "solidarity"[61] is built on in the dance-floor culture of northern soul. Furthermore, the way in which vocals tend to follow the beat in many northern soul tracks produces a sense of urgency and movement, creating a music for socializing and dancing.[62] There are also lyrical possibilities in the music of the northern soul scene that become meaningful in the context of the urban British North. For Cosgrove, the appeal of soul in the British North lies in its attempts to deal with the pain of city living.[63] Although these songs deal with images of poverty, suffering, and "life in the backstreets," they also at both lyrical and musical levels offer some attempt to temporarily transcend problems. This is partly a result of the gospel heritage of soul. The imagery of a desolate northern landscape is central to many northern soul tracks.[64] For British soul fans, it is this identification with an imaginary American urban landscape that allows the daytime's urban decay to be produced as the nighttime's glamour. In a global culture, "mediascapes," "images of the world created by the media," blur the lines between "realistic" and "fictional" landscapes.[65] Therefore, although there are various possibilities already in the sounds and imagery of northern soul, this doesn't determine consumption. As Shepherd argues, "Affect and meaning have to be created anew in the specific social and historical circumstances of each instance of music's creation and use."[66]

The importance of the sounds of the Rust Belt in the northern soul scene also needs to be understood in relation to Fordist production methods. Soul not only emphasizes suffering and redemption, it also celebrates leisure time as the time free from industrial processes and reclaims the body from the world of work as an instrument of pleasure.[67] Although many northern soul songs are love songs, this format can be used to explore emotional exploitation and male rationality which can also offer a critique of industrial exploitation. For example, Eloise Laws's "Love Factory" uses industrial metaphors to demonstrate how the rationality of Fordist production methods has invaded the "private" sphere of the emotions.[68]

To conclude this section, in understanding the ways in which records, and as we shall see, places, are used within the northern soul scene, it is therefore necessary to combine the analysis of meanings located in the musical text with meanings that become attached and embedded in the music through use. As we have seen, in northern soul, the meaning of the music and the meaning of records as material objects are both important and interrelated because they help to sustain a sense of identity and belonging within the scene. Furthermore, as we have argued, northern soul values music that is not only unpopular in the present but was often condemned to oblivion at the time it was produced. It is the significance that accrues to northern soul music through use that adds to its value. It is through becoming integrated into the northern soul scene that these records acquire a new "reality." One of the clearest illustrations of this point is to be found in Henry Jenkins's work on fan cultures, in which he quotes a children's story that tells the tale of how toys are made "real": "Real isn't how you are made. It's a thing that happens to you. When a child loves you for a long, long time, not just to play with, but REALLY loves you, then you become real."[69]

PLACE, PILGRIMAGE, AND IDENTITY

The relationship between place and identity in northern soul is, as we have already seen, based on a regional rejection of the south of England and an affiliation with the black north of America. However, this far from exhausts the significance of place in northern soul. The sense of "community" within northern soul is not one based on locality or neighborhood but instead is "produced" through travel and an attachment to the spaces that are usually considered mundane but that acquire an "aura" as sacred places because they are central to the scene. In this last section, we explore the ways in which travel, place, and identity are interrelated in the production of the northern soul scene.

Members of the northern soul scene would, and still do, travel hundreds of miles to attend a particular event.[70] Travel within the scene both reproduces and subverts aspects of traditional daytripping. Northern soul events are associated with the weekend and with special bank-holiday events. In some ways, this draws on the older notion of the "dance train" of the early 1930s that carried single, working-class youths from Manchester and Salford to Saturday night dances at Blackpool's Tower Ballroom.[71] With some of the key sites in the northern soul geography located in seaside resorts—for example, Blackpool, Morcambe, and Cleethorpes—the scene reproduces traditional working-class leisure patterns. This integration of older working-class cultural practices into the scene again reinforces the value of tradition within northern soul. As Rob Shields has argued, the "liminal 'time-out'" offered by daytrips and holidays is "partly accomplished by a movement out of the neighbourhoods of 'everyday life' to specific resort towns."[72] Travel to these sites then reproduces older working-class leisure patterns in which trips are tied to a move from "production spaces" to "consumption spaces,"[73] drawing on the place-image of seaside resorts as sites of "liminality."

However, the northern soul scene both uses and subverts aspects of traditional daytripping. Although it subverts the idea of daytripping by "night-tripping," it is also based on organized bus trips and train travel that integrate the act of travel into the collective practices of the scene. Members can also collect sew-on embroidered patches from these sites which can be sewn on to the hold-alls[74] associated with the scene.[75] If the practice of clubbing and traveling "produced" this scene out of dispersed members, then columns in magazines also worked to produce a sense of "community" by giving details of such events as northern soul marriages and meetings between characters on the scene.[76] This sense of a dispersed community and the scene as a migrant scene also connects with the importance of displacement and migration in many northern soul songs.

If travel to seaside resorts can be explained in terms of traditional working-class leisure practices, what is less easy to explain is why fans traveled to places like Wigan and Tunstall which are mundane "production spaces" rather than "consumption spaces." On one level, it is the very act of travel that is crucial to the scene, building on the ritualistic pleasure of "going out" which can be seen in more recent club cultures. Furthermore, as Hetherington argues in his work on New Age travelers, an act of pilgrimage allows both for identity renewal and a symbolic escape from everyday life.[77] The specific sites that motivated travel, and that changed over time (often due to attempts to regulate nightclubs) were not specific towns so much as specific clubs. As Shields has argued, certain sites when appropriated "become socially important not only for their empirical facilities but for their qualities as what William Whyte called 'schmoozing' spaces which support personal and group identification."[78] The centrality of particular clubs to the scene, enshrined in treasured embroidered patches, operates in a similar way to the centrality of the music. Through acts of consumption, these sites become "re-enchanted," acquiring "an aura of symbolic values."[79]

The collective practices through which mundane urban sites become "re-enchanted" are integrated with identity formation within the northern soul scene. As we have already noted, Hetherington has drawn on Schmalenbach's concept of the *Bund* as "an intense form of affectual solidarity, that is inherently unstable and liable to break down very rapidly unless it is consciously maintained through the symbolically mediated interactions of its members."[80] Furthermore, the *Bund* requires "self-conscious, ritualised and symbolic practices of group maintenance."[81] The activity of travel and the use of "sacred places" such as the Torch and Wigan Casino as sites of "social centrality" need to be understood, alongside other ritualized practices within the scene discussed earlier, as practices that help to maintain the dispersed community of northern soul fans. The emphasis on tradition and legend within the scene, which we have noted throughout, is a mechanism through which the scene both produces and reproduces a collective history in which place-images are central.[82] Stories, legends, and traditions are important mechanisms for maintaining a club scene through the times it is suspended and relatively inactive, nurtured only through infrequent fanzines, radio shows, and listening to the music at home.[83]

By thinking about identity formation in the northern soul scene with reference to the concept of the *Bund*, it is possible to solve some of the problems in thinking about identity in relation to musical cultures. One of the major problems with subcultural theory was its emphasis on a "subcultural identity" which while arising out of structural positions also seemed to transcend all other identities that members of subcultures could inhabit. As Angela McRobbie puts it, "Few writers seemed interested in what happened when a mod went home after a weekend on speed."[84] Members of musical scenes are not simply "teds," "mods," "punks" or "northern soulies," but also mothers, sons, husbands, and workers. Furthermore, they may also, for example, be fans of "Coronation Street" or the Stoke City football club. As Rob Shields argues, we often claim that " 'we wear many hats.' ... Each momentary identification corresponds to a role in a given social 'scene'—a scene dominated by a group and the group ethos."[85] It is through specific consumption practices attached to travel and to particular sites that a sense of collectively and "affectual solidarity"[86] is produced and reproduced within northern soul. It is through these practices that the *Bund* can be maintained despite being unstable and despite the fact that members have a diverse range of identifications.

Writing this piece, it became clear that religious associations continually reoccur in our discussions of the northern soul scene. On the one hand, this association is clearly evident in the nature of soul with the strong relationships between many soul performers and the church, its gospel roots, and the sense of ecstasy and transcendence that most soul offers, however secularized. On the other hand, the sense of a religious fervor also comes out of our discussion of the practices associated with the scene whether in phrases like "Keep the faith" or in the sense of "possession" in northern soul dancing or even in the status of records as relics, clubs as sacred places or shrines, and travel as pilgrimage. The emotional attachments that are central to affective "communities" or *Bunde* have been downplayed in subcultural accounts of musical cultures, quite possibly because of the "feminine" association of these qualities. Yet the desire for a sense of attachment, of belonging and of having "a place," are central to the northern soul scene, in both the music and the practices associated with it. This sense of tradition and faith in the production of the northern soul "community" offers a different way of understanding musical cultures to the portraits of innovatory subcultural moments. Although northern soul puts far more emphasis on place than most musical cultures, it also provides a signpost toward other popular music cultures that are increasingly spread across generations and divorced from a simple association with youth.

If, as we have noted throughout, the attachment to place in the northern soul scene is complex, the scene also begins to challenge some of the assumptions embedded in the current theoretical popularity of notions of "liminal spaces." Both Shields's and Foucault's concepts have useful applications, but neither can, nor should, be applied too liberally. While northern soul draws on the liminal status of seaside resorts in some of its central sites, it is rather difficult to conceive of Wigan and Tunstall as "liminal spaces." Certainly, both towns are "places on the margins" of the centers of economic and cultural power. Their landscapes share many aspects of industrial and deindustrial urban centers but lack the cultural infrastructure of the city. In this sense, they are "liminal." However, they lack the place-image of pleasure that Shields attributes to seaside resorts.

While the clubs involved may operate as consumption spaces, many of these are far from "glamorous" in any normal sense of the word. Yet within the northern soul scene, they are sites that motivate pilgrimage and memorabilia. If northern soul draws on a preconstructed "place-myth"[87] of Detroit, then the myths attached to places such as the Torch are a product of the scene alone. The value of these sites is not just a product of the DJs associated with them, the sound quality, and so on—although these are important—but their importance as sites of social centrality within the scene and the histories constructed by the scene. It is through these processes that a weekend in Wigan or Stoke becomes a meaningful experience, just as value is added to the music through processes of consumption. To return to this story of how toys become real, "Once you are Real, you can't be ugly, except to people who don't understand."[88]

By using the work of Schmalenbach and Hetherington to think about how the production of a sense of belonging and identity in northern soul is also bound up with the production of sites of social centrality and a sense of place, we hope to offer an alternative way of thinking about the relationships between musical cultures, identity, and place. Furthermore, the case of northern soul highlights the complexity of the relations between space, power, and musical cultures. Northern soul also highlights the importance of understanding how musical cultures are not only conscious productions but must be consciously reproduced, reworked, and maintained in order to sustain a scene.

ACKNOWLEDGMENTS

Thanks to Kevin Hetherington, Mark Jancovich, and Martin Parker for their help and comments.

NOTES

1. Ambrose, S. (1965). Welcome to dreamsville. Originally released on Musicor in the United States and on Stateside in the United Kingdom. Reissued on *Up all night, Vol. 2: Thirty hits from the original soul underground,* Charly, 1993.

2. Cosgrove, S. (1982). Long after tonight is all over. *Collusion,* no. 2, pp. 38–41. Since this chapter was written, there have been some publications that extend some of the debates we touch on. On northern soul, see Milestone, K. (1997). Love factory: The sites, practices, and media relationships of northern soul. In S. Redhead et al. (Eds.), *The club cultures reader: Readings in popular cultural studies* (pp. 152–167). Oxford: Blackwell. Also of interest is Frith, S., & Gillett, C. (Eds.). (1996). *The beat goes on: The rock file reader.* London: Pluto. It is also important to note that many of the debates we engage with in this article have also been developed in more depth in Thornton, S. (1995). *Club cultures: Music, media, and subcultural capital.* Cambridge: Polity Press.

3. In particular, although we provide a "reading" of northern soul, there is obviously a need for some ethnographic work on the scene.

4. See, e.g., Hall, S., & Jefferson, T. (Eds.). (1976). *Resistance through rituals.* London: Hutchinson; and Hebdige, D. (1979). *Subculture: The meaning of style.* London: Methuen.

5. Middleton, R. (1990). *Studying popular music.* Milton Keynes, U.K.: Open University Press, p. 166.

6. Clark, G. (1990). Defending ski-jumpers: A critique of theories of youth subcultures. In S. Frith & A. Goodwin (Eds.), *On record: Rock, pop, and the written word.* London: Routledge, p. 83.

7. Thornton, S. (1990). Strategies for reconstructing the popular past. *Popular Music, 9*(1), 87–95.

8. See, e.g., McRobbie, A. (1989). Second-hand dresses and the role of ragmarket. In A. McRobbie (Ed.), *Zoot suits and second-hand dresses.* Basingstoke, U.K.: Macmillan; Middleton, R. (1990). *Studying popular music.* Milton Keynes, U.K.: Open University Press; Shepherd, J. (1993). Value and power in music: An English–Canadian perspective. In V. Blundell et al. (Eds.), *Relocating cultural studies: Developments in theory and research.* London: Routledge.

9. However, this is not to neglect the importance of "live" acts during the late 1960s and the 1970s; see, e.g., The Torch Story, *Blues and Soul,* no. 103, pp. 12–14.

10. Frith, S. (1986). Art versus technology: The strange case of popular music. *Media, Culture, and Society, 8,* 263–279.

11. Redhead, S., & Street, J. (1989). Have I the right?: Legitimacy, authenticity, and community in folk's politics. *Popular Music, 8*(2), 177–183.

12. Hetherington, K. (1994). The contemporary significance of Schmalenbach's concept of the Bund. *Sociological Review, 42*(1), p. 16. As Hetherington points out, Schmalenbach's concept has been used as a way out of Tönnies's opposition between *Gemeinschaft* and *Gesellschaft. Bunde* are neither inspired by the unconscious sense of belonging in traditional ascriptive "communities" nor by rationality, but instead are an "intentional" and "conscious phenomenon derived from mutual sentiment and feeling" (p. 9). As Freund puts it, the *Bund* "would be a place for the expression of enthusiasms, of ferment, and of unusual doings" (cited, p. 6).

13. Ibid. As Hetherington points out, similar ideas have emerged more recently in Maffesoli's conception of the "neotribe" in which forms of solidarity are "elective and affectual" rather than ascriptive as they are in older notions of the tribe (p. 14).

14. Cosgrove, Long after tonight, p. 39.

15. Although as Cosgrove has argued, Detroit is "the mythical capital of the scene" (Long after tonight, p. 40), rare soul would also be taken from other minor labels operating out of cities such as Chicago and Philadelphia. Some slower tracks would also be taken from "deeper" soul sounds of the South.

16. Taken from authors' interview with Richard Searling, December 1992.

17. As Cosgrove argues, "amphetamines and rare soul have a history together" dating back to the Mod scene in the 1960s and institutionalized in the first all-nighters in the mid-1960s. (Long after tonight, p. 39). Although not everyone at an all-nighter would take drugs, speed did play an important part in producing the scene, in a similar way to the centrality of ecstasy in rave cultures. In dance cultures, speed is not only valued for its energizing effects but the rituals of acquiring and taking speed have a symbolic role in producing the event of clubbing.

18. From interview material; see Note 16.

19. Torch story.

20. See Cosgrove, Long after tonight, p. 41.

21. For a fuller discussion of the problem of custom-made northern soul and the production of a new-release scene, see Cummings, T. (1975, November). Northern soul: After the goldrush. *Black Music*, pp. 8–14.

22. Cosgrove, Long after tonight, p. 41.

23. Ibid., p. 38.

24. Massey, D. (1994). *Space, place, and gender.* Cambridge: Polity Press, p. 109.

25. Bourdieu, P. (1984). *Distinction.* London: Routledge, p. 124.

26. Thornton, S. (1994). Moral panic, the media, and British rave culture. In A. Ross & T. Rose (Eds.), *Microphone fiends: Youth music and youth culture.* New York: Routledge, p. 188.

27. Even in more sympathetic accounts of the South, it is claimed that the southern soul scene lacked the institutional framework (clubs and record shops) that enabled the appreciation of rare soul and thus is seen as "deprived." See, e.g., Elson, F. Check out the North, *Blues and Soul,* no. 120.

28. E.g., in an interview with Dave Godin, soul journalist Neil Rushton claimed that "when the current disco bubble bursts, it will be of the upmost [sic] importance that somewhere there is a continuing audience for good music, and it happened before when the South, and London in particular, abandoned soul in favour of more fickle idols, no doubt the North will continue to carry the torch and the banner regardless. I think it's safe to say that the North is the only part of Britain where soul has ever approached anything like being an 'in' trend and it will always continue to draw a certain amount of strength and force from that region" (*Blues and Soul,* no. 200, July 6, 1976, p. 11).

29. This also draws on older working-class leisure traditions in the North. This argument is expanded in Hollows, J., & Milestone, K. (1995, April). *Inter-city soul.* Paper presented at the British Sociological Association annual conference Contested Cities, University of Leicester.

30. Thornton, Moral panics; Vulliamy, G. (1977). Music and mass culture debate. In J. Shepherd et al. (Eds.), *Whose music?: A sociology of musical languages*. London: Latimer Press.

31. E.g., Frank Wilson's "Do I Love You," which was released on a Motown subsidiary label on Christmas Day 1966 and immediately withdrawn. Only one copy of this record is known to exist and the record is valued at £5,000 ("Antique Records Road Show," BBC Radio 1, September 1992.).

32. See, e.g., Poster, M. (Ed.). (1988). *Jean Baudrillard: Selected writings*. Cambridge: Polity Press.

33. Appadurai, A. (1986). Introduction: Commodities and the politics of value. In A. Appadurai (Ed.), *The social life of things: Commodities in cultural perspective*. Cambridge: Cambridge University Press, p. 4.

34. Ibid.

35. Straw, W. (1991). Systems of articulation, logics of change: Communities and scenes in popular music. *Cultural Studies*, 5(3), 374.

36. Appadurai, Introduction, p. 13.

37. Ibid., p. 17.

38. Ibid.

39. Straw, Systems of articulation, p. 375.

40. This draws on Appadurai's analysis of the kula system of the Western Pacific. Appadurai cites Munn's observation on kula exchange in Gawa that "Although men appear to be agents in defining shell value, in fact, without shells, men cannot define their own value; in this respect, shells and men are reciprocally agents of each other's value definition" (Appadurai, Introduction, p. 20)

41. Ibid., p. 21.

42. Ibid.

43. Paul Gilroy has argued that in the sound systems of the 1960s and 1970s, the reliance on imported music and the removal of labels should be understood as a critique of commercialization and as subverting "the emphasis on acquisition and individual ownership which the markers of black music cultures identified as an unacceptable feature of black culture" (Gilroy, P. [1987]. *There ain't no black in the Union Jack*. London: Hutchinson, p. 167.). While not wishing to generalize to other musical cultures from northern soul, Gilroy's argument depends on searching out anti-capitalist elements as signs of resistance in black music cultures, a romantic view that may ignore the calculative and profit-motivated dimensions in these cultures.

44. From interview with authors.

45. Cosgrove, Long after tonight, p. 40.

46. Appadurai, Introduction, p. 23.

47. When northern soul gained increased popularity in the mid-1970s, authenticity and rarity were not only threatened by bootleggers but by rereleases. As Idris Walters observed in 1975, northern soul fans "would prefer to have to pay £2.50 for a single as long as it's going to stay rare, but, more and more, they are in danger of shelling out £5.00 for something that they aren't told will be on general release at 60p in the time it takes to get changed. The vigilance of the bootleggers and the legitimate record companies have combined to produce a new regime— overprovision, Northern soul for idiots, trans-Atlantic high finance" (Walters, I.,

[1995]. Is northern soul dying on its feet? Republished in H. Kureshi & J. Savage (Eds.), *The Faber book of pop*. London: Faber, p. 454.).

48. Chambers, I. (1985). *Urban rhythms*, London: Macmillan.

49. Chambers, I. (1990). *Border dialogues: Journeys in postmodernity*. London: Routledge. There are numerous accounts of the appeal of "America" to the British working classes. See, e.g., Chambers, I. (1966). *Popular culture: The metropolitan experience*. London: Methuen; Miles, P., & Smith, M. (1987). *Cinema, literature and society*. London: Croom Helm.

50. Frith, S. (1991). Anglo-America and its discontents. *Cultural Studies*, 5(3), 266.

51. Ibid.

52. Straw, Systems of articulation, p. 368.

53. Ibid., p. 370.

54. See, e.g., Hebdige, *Subculture*.

55. Cosgrove, Long after tonight, p. 39.

56. Gilroy, P. (1993). *Small acts: Thoughts on the politics of black cultures*. London: Serpents Tail, pp. 238–239.

57. Walkerdine, V. (1990). *Schoolgirl fictions*. London: Verso, p. 209. For the difficulty of talking about "black cultures," see Hall, S. (1992). What is this "black" in black popular culture? In G. Dent (Ed.), *Black popular culture*. Seattle: Bay Press.

58. This can also result in some essentialist tendencies. For a review of this debate, see, e.g., Gilroy, P. (1991). Sounds authentic: Black music, ethnicity, and the challenge of a changing same. *Black Music Research Journal*, 11(2), 110–136.

59. Gilroy, *There ain't no black*, p. 187.

60. Shepherd, Value and power in music, p. 198.

61. Middleton, R. (1972). *Pop music and the blues*. London: Victor Gollancz, p. 218.

62. Ibid., p. 220.

63. Cosgrove, S. (1991, January). *Living in the city: A soul essay*. Paper delivered at the Unit for Law and Popular Culture, Manchester Polytechnic.

64. Cosgrove, Long after tonight.

65. Appadurai, A. (1990). Disjuncture and difference in the global cultural economy. *Theory Culture and Society*, 7, 299.

66. Shepherd, Value and power in music, p. 188.

67. Gilroy, *There ain't no black in the Union Jack*, p. 202. While it is understood that the critique of productivism and reclaiming the body has additional meanings associated with slavery in African-American culture, this doesn't mean that the critique of productivism and celebration of leisure is in any way meaningless to the white British working class.

68. Laws, E. (1970). Love factory. Sequel. Of course, Fordist production methods have also been closely associated with the production of Detroit soul, most notably in the case of Berry Gordy's Motown. Gordy, it is often claimed, drew on his experiences of working in the car industry at Motown, introducing rigorous quality control, a workshop of songwriters, and the repeated use of the same formula. More recently, a more sympathetic account of Motown production has been developed that challenges some previous assumptions. See Fitzgerald, J. (1995).

Motown crossover hits 1963–1966 and the creative process. *Popular Music, 14*(1), 1–11.

69. Blanco, M. W. *The velveteen rabbit or how toys become real.* Cited in Jenkins, H. (1992). *Textual poachers: Television fans and participatory culture.* New York: Routledge, p. 50.

70. Despite the scene being associated with the north and Midlands of England, there were in fact many Scottish northern soul fans who would make regular trips across the border. There were also a few northern soul venues scattered around the South.

71. Davies, A. (1992). *Leisure, gender, and poverty: Working-class culture in Salford and Manchester, 1930–39.* Milton Keynes, U.K.: Open University Press, p. 90.

72. Shields, R. (1991). *Places on the margin: Alternative geographies of modernity.* London: Routledge, p. 85.

73. Ibid., p. 111.

74. As well as becoming part of the northern soul style, the hold-alls had a practical function. Sweaty from dancing, people would often change clothes during the course of a night.

75. One outlet for these badges was the International Soul Club which distributed sew-on patches and car stickers which included "Forever the Torch" and "Keep the Faith The Catacombs." Operating out of Newcastle-under-Lyme (Stoke-on-Trent), the International Soul Club boasted 30,000 members in 1973. For 10 pence a year membership, the club offered details of club dates and all-nighters as well as selling northern soul merchandise.

76. E.g., Frank Elson's "Check Out the North" column in *Blues and Soul.* More recently, another means through which the northern soul scene is sustained is through the internet. See Milestone, K. (1997). *From Detroit to Manchester to Berlin.* 9th Conference of the International Association for the Study of Popular Music, Kanazawa, Japan. Examples of websites include: http://www.nittygritty.fe/.

77. Hetherington, K. (1994, April). *New age travellers: Heterotopic places and heteroclite identities.* Unpublished paper presented at the Alternative Political Imaginations Conference, Goldsmiths College, University of London; forthcoming in *Theory, Culture, and Society.*

78. Shields, R. (1992). Spaces for the subject of consumption. In R. Shields (Ed.), *Lifestyle shopping: The subject of consumption.* London; Routledge, p. 16.

79. Shields, R. (1992). The individual, consumption cultures, and the fate of community. In Shields, *Lifestyle shopping,* p. 99.

80. Hetherington, K. (1992). Stonehenge and its festival: Spaces of consumption. In R. Shields (Ed.), *Lifestyle shopping,* p. 93.

81. Ibid., p. 95.

82. Revill, G. (1993). Reading Rosehill. In M. Keith & S. Pile (Eds.), *Place and the politics of identity.* London: Routledge.

83. There are currently numerous northern soul compilations available on CD on which the liner notes emphasize "histories" of both disks and clubs. This is emphasized by the ways in which some compilations stress the "place of origin" of the disks—e.g., "The Sound of Detroit"—or the place in which they were consumed—e.g., "The Golden Torch Story."

84. See McRobbie, A. (1990). Settling account with subcultures: A feminist critique. In S. Frith & A. Goodwin (Eds.), *On record,* pp. 68–69. While on the subject of this chapter, we are aware of the gender blindness displayed here. However, it is worth noting that the ways in which we have conceptualized members of the northern soul scene does not presume a masculine identity in the same way as is evident in much subcultural theory. Indeed, activities such as dancing and listening to love songs are often demarcated as "feminine." Positions of power within the scene, however, are almost exclusively occupied by men. There has been little research into the ways in which forms of "cultural" and "subcultural" capital are not only distributed between classes but are also gendered, but this may offer a partial explanation of the predominance of men as DJs and record traders within musical scenes. See Thornton, *Club cultures.*

85. Shields, The individual, p. 107.
86. Hetherington, Stonehenge and its festival, p. 93.
87. Shields, *Places on the margin.*
88. Cited in H. Jenkins, *Textual poachers,* p. 51.

4

VICTORIAN BRASS BANDS

Class, Taste, and Space

TREVOR HERBERT

The most quoted description of musical life in Victorian Britain was *Das Land ohne Musik* (The land without music). Few can still take this phrase seriously. There has been no period in British history when so many were actively musical, and it is doubtful whether the people of any other country, in the same proportion, matched the British level of musical consumption. Britain did not have a Schubert, a Brahms, or a Wagner. Arthur Sullivan, the closest England had to a great composer, seemed a modest talent in comparison to his foreign counterparts. But the sphere of musical life with which most Victorians were involved was unquestionably healthy, and throughout the period its dynamic was one of growth.

In this chapter I examine one part of this activity: the brass band movement. The chapter's subtitle—"Class, Taste and Space"—provides certain thematic continuities rather than a structure. My intention is to say something about why and how brass bands developed, to give an impression of their distribution and the extent and nature of their impact, and to outline the changes that were experienced in their first half-century, the most important period of their existence.

It is worth stressing that brass bands, which, in the late 20th century are often associated with nostalgic visions of class, time, and region, were a product of Victorian modernity. They came into being because of the coincidence of a number of social, economic, technological, and musical factors that provided a hospitable environment for their growth. But the most obvious and immediate reason for their emergence during this period is the instruments themselves, which, with a single exception (the trombone), were invented during Victoria's lifetime. They possessed capabilities never before available on brass instruments, and the social and musical consequences of these developments were wide ranging.

Brass bands were not, of course, the only new leisure activity to emerge in the Victorian period; indeed, they were only part of the massive growth of popular music. Social and economic conditions fostered the birth of new means of music making and the expansion of older ones. Choral societies, concertina bands, wind instrument groups, string orchestras, and a range of other formations appeared as urbanization developed and new communities emerged. All of this took place while the British music industry expanded on an unprecedented scale. Professional music making and the production of published music, instruments, concert and music halls, and other music paraphernalia touched the lives of ordinary people for the first time. All this occurred with the approval of moral reformers, whose zealous support of healthy, respectable, "rational" recreations was fired by their perception of a changing society in which many long-held values and the social structures that bound them were in the process of terminal erosion.

Brass bands have a special place within this context. As I explain below, the main achievement of the brass band movement was that it represented the first engagement of working-class people with virtuoso instrumental art music as practitioners. Furthermore, it was as responsible as any other agency for disseminating art music to new audiences on a massive scale.

The process that led to the establishment of brass bands as a defining feature of musical life in Victorian Britain is an interesting one, in that it seems to have been spurred on by a number of different influences. In offering a description of this process, I suggest that the pattern of development occurred both on a national and on a regional level. For reasons that are not always clear, the brass band movement developed at different speeds and different levels of intensity in different regions. But equally evident is the sense of commonly held musical values following a single, national vision. This cohesion of shared musical tastes, which far outweigh local diversities, formed the basis of what musicians recognize as the idiom of the brass band.

By the 1880s, perhaps even a little earlier, the idiom of the brass band was fixed. That idiom has changed little since then, even though almost all developments in the repertory have emerged since World War I. In the late 20th century brass bands are dispersed across Britain. In the 19th century they were primarily, but not exclusively, a northern phenomenon, but they were not, as is often assumed, inner-city organizations. Most brass bands, particularly the best ones, were founded in small towns in which there was a single major employer. This too has changed in the 20th century. Bands now carry the names of sponsors, with good old-fashioned names like "Park and Dare Colliery Band," or "Munn and Feltons Footwear Band" giving way to "National Smokeless Fuels Band" and "Rigid Containers plc Band," respectively. One band, perhaps the greatest of them all, the Black Dyke Mills Band of Queensbury, Yorkshire, has not changed its name since it started in 1855, but by 1986 not a single employee of John Foster and Sons Black Dyke [textiles] Mills played for the band, and few lived within an hour's drive of their rehearsal room. In 1880 the only person allowed in the rehearsal room who was not an employee was the professional conductor, and every man, woman, and child in Queensbury lived within earshot of the sound of the band practicing.

IMAGES OF VICTORIAN BRASS BANDS

At the beginning of the 19th century anyone with the ability to read staff notation fluently, who had some knowledge of the canon of Western art music and the capacity to exercise virtuosity in it, and who possessed a nurtured, educated musicality in instrumental music but made no living from it, was almost certainly a talented aristocrat or a wealthy bourgeois. Yet by the 1880s these qualities were found in thousands of players in working-class brass bands. This phenomenon represents one of the most remarkable shifts that has occurred in the sociology of music. Yet until recently it has been largely ignored.

There are few references to brass bands in the literature of British music history.[1] This is because, historically, brass bands have occupied an uneasy cultural position between art music and popular music. Few would link them with the progress of mainstream, "great" music. But brass bands in the Victorian period are worthy of more than passing attention. The British brass band movement probably represents the first engagement of masses of working-class people with instrumental art music as practitioners. Also, more than any other agency, it was responsible for the dissemination of instrumental art music to working-class audiences.

There have been few attempts to understand the brass band and its repertory in formalist terms, but there is no such hesitation about slipping into the easy alternative of referentialism. Referentialists argue that musical communication can be explained by the extramusical associations, or references, it summons. This approach, of course, is not just apt but inevitable for a large part of the Western repertory. Even music that is not programmatic stimulates evocations, because most tonal composers have assimilated cultural symbols into their compositional processes. Also, some evocations take root because of chronic association with a particular subject, symbol, or ancestry: horns and the hunt, trumpets and the military, castanets and Spain, and so on. In the modern world it is all too easy for a musical phrase or even a sound color to become inseparable from an image; it was this phenomenon that Leonard Bernstein had in mind when he observed that the true formalist musician is one who can listen to Rossini's *William Tell* overture without thinking of the Lone Ranger![2]

The references and associations that we derive from the sound of a brass band are immediate, compelling, and apparently fixed. They have been widely utilized in 20th-century media culture. Two illustrations from 1980s–1990s British TV commercials provide appropriate evidence of this truth. One is a long running advertisement for Hovis, the well-established brand-name for a type of wholewheat bread. The promoters, with great effect, present Hovis as a traditional product, as full of homely goodness in the late 20th century as it was 100 years earlier. The advertisement portrays an idealized representation of 19th-century working-class boyhood. A cloth-capped lad pushes a baker's bike up a cobbled hill, as a brittle, northernish voice intones the merits of the old days and how the highest standards of honest, homely integrity remain intact inside every loaf of Hovis. In another advertisement, for the private health conglomerate BUPA, kindly doctors are shown making *ordinary* people better extremely quickly in luxurious comfort. The message conveyed here is that private medical care is affordable: it isn't just for the wealthy.

The common feature in both is the background music: it is played by a brass band. Hovis has the slow movement of the *New World Symphony,* BUPA has something similar: a softly articulated cornet melody floating over a warm, homogeneous sonority with a hint of an euphonium descant. The music provides immediate and potent references to places and times. It also carries a message about class. The image is set firmly because the sound is unique. It occurs in no other music culture except where the British brass band sound is purposely imitated. The idea or reference it summons is, of course, a stereotype. Like all stereotypes, it has its origins in real experience, but equally, like other stereotypes, it gnaws at and camouflages the truth so that the root identity of its subject becomes obscured, or even lost.

Brass bands have become a cliché for a place, a time, and a class—instant Victoriana. What is the true story? The terms "working class" and "northern" provide a convenient and, to an extent, accurate description of the phenomenon, but it is not as simple as that. Brass bands could not have existed without the communities in which they grew. These communities were different, and consequently, emerging brass bands did not follow a single, monotonous pattern. The brass band movement is a useful model for investigating the interaction of music and people.

BRASS PLAYING BEFORE THE 19TH CENTURY

It is important to emphasize that brass instruments and brass instrument playing changed dramatically in the 19th century. Up to that time, players in Britain were mainly professionals, and were usually involved in mainstream art music. There were some amateur "choir bands" associated with rural churches and also some tiny military bands that were funded and kept by commanding officers. Neither type played written, *virtuoso* music, and in any case, brass instruments were not prominent in them.

At the start of the 19th century few people outside London and the main provincial centers had any experience of hearing brass instruments. Indeed, there was a less continuous tradition of their use in Britain than in other parts of Europe. A striking illustration for this is the case of the trombone. The trombone is the only brass instrument to have existed with all its major features unchanged since it was invented in the 15th century. It was a popular professional instrument in England up to the end of Charles II's reign, but with changing musical fashions it became obsolete. There were, *literally,* no British trombone players in the 18th century. The instrument was so unfamiliar in England in the 1780s that even Charles Burney, the most important English music historian of his time, seemed unsure what the word "trombone" meant.

Up to the 19th century brass instruments (with the exception of trombones) had technical limitations that restricted the number of notes their players could sound. Brass players have two means for playing different notes. One is to extend or contract the length of the tubing through which they blow—the ingenious telescopic "U"-shaped slide of the trombone provides players of that instrument with this facility. The other is to increase, or decrease, the speed at which their lips vibrate so as to obtain the naturally occurring series of partials, known as the harmonic series. Trumpets and horns were made from fixed lengths of tubing. Consequently, they were restricted to the notes of the one harmonic series that that length of tubing could produce. Those with a knowledge of physics or music will know that there are gaps in the harmonic series, so not all of the notes between the lowest and the highest can be sounded. This means that the higher brass instruments—so-called natural trumpets and horns—were restricted to the pattern of notes, and consequently, the habitually predictable types of tune, that characterize the repertory of the military bugle.

Many people, even music enthusiasts, are oblivious to these limitations, because works such as Bach's *Brandenburg Concerti,* the Mozart *Horn Concerti,* and the Haydn *Trumpet Concerto,* all written before 1800, sound so unambiguously tuneful. The reason for this is that the techniques used by Bach's and Mozart's players were virtuoso and professional. Even among professional players the *clarino* technique—the ability to play continuously in the upper partials of the harmonic series—was rare. It was the existence of clarino experts that made Bach's writing possible. Mozart's concerto horn players used "hand-stopping" and crooking, both effective but cumbersome ways of obtaining chromaticism.[3] Haydn's *Trumpet Concerto,* on the other hand, was written for an instrument called the *Klappentrompete,* or keyed trumpet. This was a newly invented, experimental instrument, an attempt to cope with the limited chromaticism of "natural" instruments. Keyed instruments are often thought of as one of the transitional phases between "natural" and valve instruments. They were widely available but were never mass-produced. Only skilled craftsmen could execute their manufacture; consequently, they were relatively expensive. They had another disadvantage compared to the valve instruments that succeeded them: the mechanics of keyed instruments made them difficult to master, particularly in the early stages of learning.

TECHNOLOGICAL CHANGES AND COMMERCIALIZATION

The invention that revolutionized brass instrument playing was the piston valve, which was first applied to musical instruments in the 1820s. The earliest inventions were only partially successful, but by the 1840s, a Belgian, Adolphe Sax, had perfected a system that could produce good intonation and an even tone across the entire chromatic range of each instrument. Furthermore, the basic geometry of the design could be applied to most tube lengths.[4] Thus, it was possible to produce brass instruments at various pitches, giving rise to a family of instruments with homogeneous and complementary timbres. Only three valves were needed to create the entire chromatic spectrum on any instrument, and these three valves were operated by the three most dexterous fingers of the right hand. A novice with average aptitude could master a basic scale within minutes of holding an instrument for the first time.

The invention of brass instrument valves was one of the most momentous in the history of music. It meant that, for the first time, entirely chromatic brass instruments could be made for treble, bass, and intermediate pitches. Suddenly brass instruments possessed a new musical facility, and potentially a new social identity. It was a time when idioms and practices were redefined.

Though valve instruments were available in Britain from the 1820s, the major expansion started after 1844 when The Distin Family, a family group of brass virtuosos who toured concert and music halls, met Adolphe Sax in Paris. The Distins, who also had notable entrepreneurial flare, took the franchise to promote his instrument designs in the United Kingdom.[5] From that time British firms mass-produced instruments that loosely cloned the Sax system. The instruments were widely promoted in magazines, in newspapers, and on the covers of cheap domestic music editions.

This was not the only musical activity to undergo expansion at this time. The Victorian period witnessed a stunning development of, and a widening franchise for, participative music. As with other musical activities, brass bands benefited from the congruence of many factors that provided a hospitable environment for these developments.[6] British industry showed an impressive capacity to produce new brass instruments because, to a large extent, they were made by modern, mass-production engineering methods, and not by slow craft work. This feature was new in the production of brass instruments and it occurred at the same time as a more general and dramatic expansion in the U.K. music industry. Because instruments were produced in large quantities, cost per unit benefited from economies of scale. This, together with other economic factors, made the real price of brass instruments fall dramatically over the second half of the century (see Figure 4.1). The advent of hire-purchase (installment plan) schemes—a phenomenon that one contemporary commentator characterized as "the very basis of the brass band"—was yet another element that made brass instrument playing accessible to working-class people.[7]

Because the instruments were relatively easy to learn, they could be taught by the self-styled "professors of music" who proliferated at the time. These professors, with unfailing self-confidence, found that their own frequent inability to play brass instruments was not an obstacle to teaching other people how to play them. It is likely, however, that the main function of these ambitious pedagogues was to teach staff and stave literacy.[8] Almost certainly, the most effective teachers of brass instruments in the early days of brass bands were local players who were self-taught from primers. Much of the teaching must have taken place within families. It is no accident that, over the length and breadth of the country, there were bands in which many players had the same surnames. The existence of dynasties of players has been one of the more striking features of the brass band movement.

FIGURE 4.1. Price list and general catalogue for the Manchester-based firm Joseph Higham, January 1887.

MORAL CONCERNS AND RATIONAL RECREATIONS

It would be naive to presume that the brass band movement could have gained any momentum without the condescension and concurrence of the middle and upper classes. Brass band instruments, music, and other paraphernalia that bandsmen purchased were elements in a vastly expanding capitalist economy. Also, music was highly regarded by the dominant class, who saw it as a panacea for temptations that seductively beckoned the lower orders. Music was seen as a "rational recreation" by the upper classes who encouraged working people to engage in an activity that they considered improving and uplifting—certainly a better alternative than other, more dubious temptations for a population which, for the first time, had some, if only a little, disposable wealth and leisure time.

This preoccupation was constant in the mid-Victorian period. A writer in *Leisure Hour—A Family Journal of Instruction and Recreation* summed it up succinctly: "The leisure time of the English people is greater now than it ever was before. I think I know the British artisan nearly as well as any other man; and when I think of his having eight hours for play, my instinctive inquiry is, What will he do with it?"[9] Though there are conflicting views as to the reasons why the dominant class went to such lengths to promote rational recreations, there is no doubt that it did, and that its support of certain types of activity was consistent. The growth in amateur, organized, instrumental music making took place in a period when, as the economic historian Cyril Ehrlich put it, "the flood" of a new age of commercial exploitation of music was at its zenith.[10] Instruments, sheet music, and other music goods were widely promoted in magazines and newspapers. Those whose wealth or influence made them capable of giving important encouragement to musical activity were under pressure to do so. This was an important reason why musical recreation (if it involved art music) was also *rational* recreation. But there appear to have been other reasons too.

Eric Mackerness has suggested that any form of communal activity which, by its very nature, fostered "harmony" and cooperation, was seen as worthwhile. This seems unconvincing in the light of other, more radical forms of behavior for which working-class people congregated and cooperated.[11] A more likely explanation is that music making, and playing in a brass band in particular, appealed simultaneously to a number of higher class prejudices. The routine nature of brass band activity was unthreatening. It fitted well into the rhythm of the work-time/leisure-time relationship. The fact that so many bands took a workplace as the name of their band further emphasized this. Also, the ease with which the instruments were learned made it eminently possible for a band to sound more than acceptable within a reasonably short time after its foundation. This must have provided impressive evidence of the potential of working people.

But for the high-minded, music held other, almost spiritual, powers. The Rev. H. R. Haweis's book *Music and Morals* (1871) rehearsed a thesis in which every aspect of music was held as having almost mystic powers to promote virtue.[12] Absurd as his ideas were, the book was reprinted 21 times by 1906. Other writers put forward more measured views than Haweis, but all recognized the *respectability* of musical activity. Also influential were journalists such as George Hogarth (whose daughter married Charles Dickens) who, in a number of magazines and journals, extolled the potency of music on the working classes.

> The tendency of music is to soften and purify the mind.... The cultivation of a musical taste furnishes for the rich a refined and intellectual pursuit. [For the lower classes, music offers] a relaxation from toil more attractive than the haunts of intemperance [and in] densely populated manufacturing districts of Yorkshire, Lancashire and Derbyshire, music is cultivated among the working classes to an extent unparalleled in any other part of the kingdom.[13]

This uncomplicated philosophy was shared by intellectual leaders too. Matthew Arnold might well have approved of brass bands—or at least, of the idea of them. The repertory that bands played was, in the main, derived from mainstream art music. Thus, the engagement of working people in an activity that the higher classes regarded as culturally refined—even for their own consumption—seemed unambiguously beneficial. Moral reformers, and some cultural hierarchists, believed that they were harmoniously sharing a cultural middle ground with working-class musicians.

ESTABLISHING BANDS

It is often assumed (following the stereotype) that brass bands were exclusively a north-of-England phenomenon and that they owed their existence to material philanthropy from an enlightened, entrepreneurial middle class. In fact, brass bands were founded in all parts of the country and their formation did not follow a standard pattern. However, almost all brass bands that had any sort of celebrity were found in places that had been touched by industrialization. Broadly speaking, there were four different ways by which a brass band came into being.

    1. Some bands owed their origins to the benevolence of a single industrial sponsor, such as a mill or factory owner. These "works bands" did exist, but there were comparatively few of them. Entrepreneurs seldom gave out large sums of money for no financial return. The famous Black Dyke Mills Band founded in the West Riding of Yorkshire in 1855, by the mill owner John Foster, is a rare example of such a phenomenon. But even in this case the formation of the band was part of a much grander plan that sought to establish a town of "improving" character around Foster's mill—the sole industry of the town. This process involved, among other things, changing the name of the town from Queenshead, the name of the ancient village pub, to Queensbury, a name invented by Foster.

2. Much more common were bands that, though they may have carried the name of an industrial concern, were, in fact, subscription bands supported by the wider community. Subscription bands often used the name of the main local employer as the guarantor for a loan to buy instruments. This practice was so common that brass band magazines and manuals started publishing model letters, with suitable blanks, for working-class petitioners to use when approaching their employers.

> Dear Sirs,
> We, the undersigned, being desirous of employing our leisure time in practising music, request your permission to form a brass band in connection with this [factory or other workplace]. We shall feel honoured if [the name of the most influential person] will consent to become President of the Band. Unfortunately, we are unable at the beginning to defray the entire cost of purchase of the instruments. [Here put the name of the supplier] are prepared to sell us the brass instruments required, provided that the firm, whose name we should like to take, will act as surety for the deferred payments
> We are, dear sir, yours respectfully etc.[14]

3. Some bands were town bands which, from the start, were supported by communities with no help from major industrial sponsors. It was not uncommon for civic authorities to take the initiative to set up such bands from scratch. This happened most often, but not exclusively, in small market towns without a major manufacturing industry. In East Anglia handbills and posters entreated local people to attend public meetings "to take into consideration the propriety of forming a saxhorn band.... The attendance of all persons favourably disposed towards such an object among the working class of society is respectfully invited."[15] Similarly, the records of the Llanelly Band in southwest Wales show it to have been formed and to have survived exclusively through public subscriptions and fundraising events.

Some historians have used evidence that shows the setting up of bands in places with some earlier form of wind music making to extrapolate a link between the brass band movement and the ancient tradition of the "waits."[16] Waits were town musicians who, from the Middle Ages, performed at civic functions and kept the watch. They were broadly similar to the German *Stadpfeifer*, who were professional town musicians. But the idea that brass bands were descended from waits is spurious. Brass bands, though occasionally evolving from the more rustic bands that immediately preceded them, were new in the 19th century, and owed little to any deep historical precedent.

4. Another stimulus to the amateur brass band movement was unwittingly provided by the War Office. By the late 1850s Parliament had

developed a near manic fear that Britain might be invaded. The French posed a threat, and because the greatest part of the British army was abroad defending and extending the empire, it was widely believed that the country was vulnerable. In May 1859 the secretary of state for war sent a letter to the lord lieutenants of all counties instructing them to set up a volunteer force. Within a year volunteering was being promoted as a rational recreation in its own right. Brass bands were often enlisted into corps en bloc. Bands, playing martial music, provided an authenticating, military image. The arrangement was profitable from the bands' point of view, too. They received free uniforms, pay for their bandmaster, and use of a drill hall for practice.

The original terms under which volunteer corps were set up made no provision for the funding of bands. In fact, it appears that spending on them was specifically forbidden. However, it was apparent to many, including correspondents to *The Times*—which ran regular columns on volunteering activities—that much of the funding of the volunteer force was spent on bands. This was confirmed in evidence to successive government commissions on the state of the volunteer force. Commanding officers regarded bands as an important element in their corps but found that the only way that they could be enlisted was by paying them. The lists of itemized expenditure given in these reports show that the practice was widespread. A casual glance at the titles of contesting bands between 1860 and 1870 illustrates the emergence of many carrying the name of a volunteer corps.[17] At least 10 of the entrants at the 1861 Crystal Palace National Contest had the words "Rifle Volunteer Corps" in their title.[18]

It is doubtful whether patriotism was the principal motive for bands who took up the volunteer cause. Indeed, many bands were reluctant to accept any form of military discipline. The problems this caused were often reported in the national press. Newspaper reports often cited bands as the primary cause of indiscipline in the force. A commissioned officer in the volunteer force who, having shared a railway compartment with a group of volunteer bandsmen who were "too drunk to stand" and had challenged fellow passengers to a fight, made his views clear to *The Volunteer Service Gazette*: "I think this incident shows that it is from the bandsmen of some corps that the volunteers get into disrepute. They are notorious for ... [showing] no sort of constraint and acknowledging no authority whatsoever."[19]

Some commentators have been amused by the ease with which bands drifted in and out of the volunteer movement and by their maverick disregard for military authority.[20] Many bands simply changed their name in order to become a volunteer band, then changed it back again when it suited them. In fact, such incidents demonstrate an important point about the social infrastructure of bands. By 1859 many brass bands had assumed something approaching institutional status. They had their own spheres of authority and sense of purpose. Not even the landed classes in uniform could usurp the independence that they, as a coherent group of musicians, felt they possessed. There existed a shared understanding between band members of the position they held in their communities. Often, this understanding was rigorously enshrined in rules and regulations that were formally drawn up by solicitors, and it was common for punitive measures to be taken against members who committed some form of transgression.[21]

REPERTORIES AND MUSICAL IDENTITIES

While it is possible to examine brass bands from a variety of perspectives, the most revealing types of source, those that inform our understanding of the individuality of bands, are those that shed light on their musical identity. Among such sources the most important are those concerning the repertory they performed. Bands played from handwritten and printed music. To the music historian, handwritten parts have a higher authority than printed music. This is because printed music, unless it is corroborated by other evidence—such as programs or other documents—shows only that the music was owned by the band, not that it was actually played. Many pieces must have been bought by bands, which subsequently found they either couldn't or didn't want to play them. But handwritten music, particularly when, as is usually the case, it is part of a cumulative sequence in band part books, shows what a band was playing, when it was playing it, and, consequently, how well it could play. It would make no sense for an arranger (usually the bandmaster) to arrange music that his players were incapable of performing.[22]

From the 1840s a number of publishers brought out journals for a variety of instrument combinations. The journals business was not restricted to brass band music: military bands, concertina bands, string bands, and fife bands, for example, had their own journals. Often the same pieces were published for these different combinations but they were suitably tailored for the idiom of the instruments. The journals were monthly publications containing about three pieces of music. The arrangements were so ordered that it was possible for the parts to be performed on a variety of compatible instruments. So, for example, the same music was available for a band of 6 or 10 players, and so on.

The music that made up the repertories of bands (and here I refer to both printed and handwritten music) can be roughly classified into three types: functional music such as marches; anthems and hymn tunes; and local-interest pieces—arrangements of folk tunes and so on. Dance music, particularly polkas, was often used as a subject for variations to make brilliant, solo, virtuoso works, together with transcriptions of art music—in particular, Italian opera selections. Though pieces by earlier composers such as Mozart, Handel, and Beethoven are quite common, the most popular composers were contemporary. The speed at which new works were transcribed for brass band is impressive. For example, Verdi's opera *La Forza del Destino* was first performed in St. Petersburg in October 1860. By January 1861 selections from it were widely available as brass band transcriptions in the United Kingdom. This is an important point that the brass band stereotype disguises, and it is equally applicable to dance music. Brass bands in the 19th century were, to a large extent, purveyors of *contemporary* music. This feature is further emphasized by the fact that, in the last decades of the century, the music of radical "modernists" such as Richard Wagner was transcribed with as much relish as that of Verdi.

The balance of these different types of music within the repertory of any one band varies according to the type, status, competence, and, to an extent, location of the band.[23] Bands reflected the circumstances in which they found themselves. Most molded themselves a style that was satisfying to them and recognizable to their community. The most distinguishing features of individual bands were their musical competence, the instrumentation they used, and their repertories. However, by the 1860s there is evidence of bands being aware that they were part of a wider, national activity. It is difficult to identify the first use of the term "brass band *movement*," but the suggestion in this phrase—that brass banding was thought of as organic, that it was spreading and developing—is hard to ignore. This was sufficiently true to ensure that, when a brass band press—the most long-standing organ of which is *The British Bandsman*—began to flourish in the 1880s, it could confidently address a single "movement" with a commonly understood vocabulary and value system.

UNIFORMITY, DIVERSITY, AND SPATIAL PATTERNS

As the brass band world developed, a number of tensions emerged concerning the social function and musical identity of individual bands. Most bands that had their origins in a particular locality and continued to serve that locality—often depending on local inhabitants for financial support—were also drawn toward the standards, values, and priorities of the brass band movement as a whole. In the 20th century this tension has been resolved, in that brass bands recognize themselves primarily as subscribers to a set of values, rules, and obligations that are determined almost entirely within the brass band movement itself. It is an esoteric, self-contained, self-conscious world.[24]

Such a resolution did not become absolute in the 19th century, but progress towards self-determination was always evident. It almost certainly began when the best brass band players acquired an appreciation of their own musical worth. This tension between uniformity and diversity is one of the most interesting features of the development of Victorian brass bands. As far as the idiom was concerned, almost all of the forces made for uniformity. The major differences between bands concerned the quality of their playing, and, as a consequence of this, the question of whether a band saw itself assuming a purely local role or pursuing a more ambitious quest for national or regional celebrity. While I do not wish to claim that the overview that follows in this part of my chapter is any substitute for the systematic research that the subject deserves, it may suggest avenues for further inquiry.

It is important to define a period of time when the brass band movement can be said to have started and had its strongest impact. As I have already stated, I hold the view that brass banding was a radically new phenomenon in the 19th century. It was only a development from earlier forms of communal instrumental music making in the broadest sense. The birth of the brass band movement followed rapidly upon the adoption of the Distin franchise in 1844. Between the mid-1840s and about 1880 all of its vital features emerged. As far as the number of participants was concerned, the movement reached its high point at the end of the century, but declined thereafter. Interestingly, however, most of the main developments in the repertory occurred in the 20th century. By the 1880s brass bands were a common feature of the cultural landscape of Britain. Brass banding was a mature, well-ordered activity with a national infrastructure largely, but not entirely, self-governed.

In the last 20 years of the century a loose pattern emerged. Bands fitted into three very broad divisions or groups, according to their musical competence. I am not referring here to the more formal divisions—or "sections"—that emerged later, which allowed bands of comparable ability to compete against each other, but rather to a simpler pattern. There were bands that were exceptional and that were often conducted by one of an élite group of professional conductors, others that were eminently competent, and a residue that were much less able and seemed content with that condition. The musical features and values of the bands within these groups were distinctive.

The evidence for these categorizations is necessarily impressionistic. The most competent bands—those that fit into my first two categories—entered contests, and while comparatively few collections of contest application forms and adjudications survive, their names were recorded in contest results and posters. After 1880 it became common for brass band magazines to report on contests and occasionally to compose summary pictures of results over a year (see Table 4.1). Smaller bands seem not to have entered contests, and left fewer traces of their existence and practices. However, evidence does survive for such bands; some photographs, newspaper references, and general commentaries in magazines and books of the time support the view of Ord Hume, who believed that the contesting bands were probably outnumbered by many examples of what he called "the remote village band which is generally composed of an unlimited number from ten upwards."[25]

The first group was the most influential. It contained the most famous and best bands. It is they who were the focus of the brass band movement, and who established its standards and style. They were fiercely competitive, virtuoso, ambitious, and thoroughly organized. They played the latest music, in bespoke (custom-made) arrangements, done for them by skilled professional bandmasters, who were the most influential figures in the formation of the brass band idiom. They were big bands with 20 or more players. Their instrumentations followed a similar pattern. Indeed, as the century progressed, this similarity developed into exact uniformity: each band had exactly 24 players who were allocated precise instrumental dispositions.[26] These bands were found primarily in the Nottinghamshire and Derbyshire coalfields, the Lancashire and Yorkshire coalfields and textile districts, and—a little later in the century—in the Durham and Northumberland coalfields. Yorkshire and Lancashire bands were highly prevalent in this category. Of the Belle Vue contests held between 1853 and 1914, 21 winners came from Yorkshire, 15 from Lancashire. In other years the prizes were evenly distributed, with no other county contributing more than 5 victors.[27]

As far as their quality is concerned, the second group is really a subset of the first. Within this group are some very fine bands; indeed some may have had a brief period of stunning success. They were of slightly lesser ability, but were nonetheless ambitious and well organized. Many of these bands were in the same districts and in the shadow of bands in my first category, but they also proliferated in Cumberland, the West Midlands, and Northamptonshire (the shoe towns spawned the best of them), as well as isolated patches further south. The South Wales coalfield and some areas of Scotland also had bands of this type.

Bands in my third category were less distinguished and unashamedly so. They too overlap the first two areas but they proliferated in the south of England, in Wales above the southern conurbation, and in parts of Scotland. They had fewer players, usually less than 12. They were less ambitious and competitive, and they played from printed journal music or simple arrangements. But they too were part of the national movement. They were aware of the standards and progress that was prevalent in the rest of the country. Though they were less able and could not, realistically,

TABLE 4.1. Summary List of Bands That Competed in 1893

Prize Bands of 1893.

WITH LIST OF PRIZES WON.

The following is a list of prizes won by each contesting Band in 1893. We are afraid that in some cases the figures are slightly incorrect, but we have done our best to be accurate. In this list divides count as wins for both bands.

	1st.	2nd.	3rd.	4th.	5th.	6th.
Aberavon Temperance	0	0	3	0	0	0
Aberaman	0	1	0	0	0	0
Acomb	0	0	0	0	1	0
Acomb Rifles	1	0	0	0	0	0
Aitkenhead	1	0	0	1	1	0
Alva Rifles	2	0	0	0	0	0
Alloa	4	3	0	1	0	1
Ashington Duke	1	1	0	0	0	0
Ashington Silver	0	0	0	1	1	0
Ashton Cave-Brown	0	0	0	1	0	0
Ashton Temp.	0	1	0	0	0	0
Aspatria	0	3	1	0	0	0
Atherton Public	0	1	0	0	0	0
Backworth	0	1	1	0	0	0
Bacup Change	0	1	3	2	0	1
Banks Rechabite	1	0	0	0	0	0
Barton Model	0	0	1	0	0	0
Barnsley Rifles	2	2	1	1	0	0
Barrow Iron & Steel Works	2	1	1	0	0	0
Barrow Wire Works	0	0	1	0	0	0
Batley Old	2	1	0	2	1	0
Bedford Wesleyan	0	0	1	0	0	0
Beith	0	0	0	0	1	0
Belper United	2	0	0	0	0	0
Besses	10	1	3	0	0	0
Birkenshaw	1	0	0	0	0	0
Boarshurst	0	0	1	0	0	0
Bonnybridge	1	2	1	3	0	1
Black Dike	7	3	1	1	0	0
Blaina	2	3	1	0	0	0
Bradford (Manchester)	4	3	1	1	0	1
Briercliffe	0	0	0	0	1	0
Broughton Rechabites	1	0	0	0	0	0
Bucknall	0	1	0	0	0	0
Burbage	0	1	1	0	0	0
Burslem Town	1	0	0	0	0	0
Burton Latimer	0	2	0	2	0	0
Cadishead	0	0	0	1	0	0
Cambusbarron	0	0	1	1	0	1
Cambuslang	0	1	0	0	0	0
Carlisle Artillery	0	0	2	0	0	0
Carriden	1	1	2	0	2	0
Castle Eden	1	0	0	0	0	0
Chadderton	1	0	0	0	0	0
Cheetham Hill P	0	0	0	0	1	0
Church Gresley	1	2	0	1	0	0
Churwell	1	0	0	0	0	0
Cleckheaton	2	1	1	0	0	0
Cleland	0	1	0	2	0	0
Clitheroe Boro'	0	1	1	1	0	0
Cliviger	0	0	0	0	0	1
Clydebank	1	0	1	0	2	0
Coatbridge	0	0	0	1	0	0
Cockerton	0	0	1	0	0	0
Consett	0	0	1	0	0	0
Copley Mills	0	0	0	1	0	0
Cornholme	3	3	1	0	0	0
Coseley	0	1	0	0	0	0
Crosley Villa	0	1	0	0	0	0
Dalmellington	0	0	0	1	0	0
Darlington Temp	1	0	0	1	0	0
Denby Dale	0	0	1	2	0	0
Denton	3	2	0	4	1	0
Denny	0	1	0	0	0	0
Derby Sax Tuba	0	0	1	0	0	0
Derby United	1	2	1	0	0	0
Derby Victoria	0	2	0	0	0	0
Derwent Iron & Steel Works	1	2	2	0	0	0
Dorking Town	0	0	0	1	0	0
Dowlais	0	1	0	0	0	0
Droylsden A.M.T.	0	1	0	0	0	0
Earby	2	1	0	0	1	0
Eagley	0	0	1	0	1	0
Earls Barton Old	1	1	2	0	0	0
Earlstown	0	1	1	0	1	0
Eccles Borough	4	2	5	1	0	0
Enderby	1	0	0	0	0	0
Eston Miners	0	0	1	0	0	0
Farnley Temp	0	1	0	0	0	0
Ferndale	0	0	1	0	0	0
Fochriw	0	2	0	0	0	0
Formby	0	0	0	0	1	0
Gainsborough	4	2	0	1	0	0
Galashiels	0	0	1	0	0	0
Glossop	0	0	2	2	0	1
Glossop Old	0	0	1	0	0	0
Golds Hill Subscription	0	1	0	0	0	0
Gorebridge	0	0	0	1	0	0
Gorton M.S. & L	0	0	0	1	3	0
Goodshaw	0	3	0	0	1	1
Greenfield R.G	2	0	0	1	0	0
Great Harwood	1	0	0	1	0	0
Gretton	0	1	0	0	0	0
Gresley Town	0	0	0	1	0	0
Haltwhistle Rifles	1	2	0	0	0	0
Hanley Amateur	0	0	0	1	0	0
Hanley Excelsior	0	0	1	0	0	0
Hanley Town	0	1	2	0	0	0
Harpurhey Mission	0	0	1	0	0	0
Hartlepool Recreation	0	1	0	0	0	0
Haslingden Temp	0	0	2	1	0	0
Hathern	0	0	1	0	0	0
Haverigg	1	1	1	0	0	0
Haverigg (St. Luke's)	0	1	0	0	0	0
Hawick	1	2	0	1	0	0
Heanor Temp	0	0	1	1	1	0
Hebburn Colliery	0	2	0	0	1	0
Heptonstall	0	1	0	0	0	0
Hetton Rechabites	1	0	1	1	0	0
Heywood Old	0	1	0	0	0	0
High Crompton	0	0	1	0	0	0
Hill Top, West Bromwich	0	1	0	0	0	0
Holbeach	1	0	0	0	0	0
Holborn Hill	7	1	0	0	0	0
Hollinwood	0	0	0	1	0	0
Honley	0	1	0	0	0	0
Horbury	2	2	0	0	0	0
Howden-le-Wear	0	1	0	0	0	0
Hucknall Excelsior	0	0	1	1	0	0
Hucknall Temp	2	1	1	0	0	0
Hugglescote	1	1	0	1	0	0
Hull Waterloo	0	1	0	0	0	0
Ibstock Excelsior	0	0	1	1	0	0
Irwell Bank	1	0	1	2	0	0
Kelty	0	1	0	0	0	0
Kettering Rifles	10	1	0	0	0	0
Kettering Town	0	5	1	0	1	1
Kilsyth	0	0	0	0	1	0
Kingston Mills	7	0	3	0	0	1
Kirbymoorside	0	1	0	0	0	0
Kirkcaldy	5	3	2	1	0	0
Lassodie	2	1	2	0	0	0
Lea Mills	0	1	0	0	0	0
Leyland	0	1	1	1	0	0
Leeds City	0	0	0	0	1	0
Leeds Engineers	2	1	1	1	0	0
Leek Temp	0	0	0	2	0	0
Lincoln Excelsior	0	0	1	0	0	0

(cont.)

TABLE 4.1. (cont.)

PRIZE BANDS OF 1893 (Continued.)

Band	Results
Lincoln Iron Wks.	0 ... 1 ... 0 ... 1 ... 0 ... 0
Lindley	1 ... 2 ... 0 ... 0 ... 0 ... 0
Linthwaite	2 ... 0 ... 0 ... 1 ... 0 ... 0
Llanelly	7 ... 0 ... 0 ... 1 ... 1 ... 0
Llan Festiniog	2 ... 0 ... 0 ... 0 ... 0 ... 0
Long Buckby	2 ... 0 ... 0 ... 0 ... 0 ... 0
Luton Red Cross	3 ... 0 ... 0 ... 1 ... 0 ... 0
Marley Hill	0 ... 0 ... 0 ... 1 ... 0 ... 0
Marsden Moor	0 ... 0 ... 0 ... 0 ... 0 ... 0
Methilbill	1 ... 1 ... 2 ... 0 ... 0 ... 0
Milburn's Model	0 ... 0 ... 1 ... 0 ... 0 ... 0
Millgate Temp.	0 ... 0 ... 1 ... 0 ... 0 ... 0
Millom Wesleyan	0 ... 1 ... 0 ... 1 ... 0 ... 0
Mirfield Rifles	0 ... 1 ... 0 ... 0 ... 0 ... 0
Morley	0 ... 0 ... 1 ... 0 ... 0 ... 0
Morriston	0 ... 1 ... 0 ... 1 ... 0 ... 0
Mosley	0 ... 1 ... 0 ... 0 ... 0 ... 1
Murton Colliery	1 ... 2 ... 0 ... 0 ... 0 ... 0
Musselburgh	0 ... 0 ... 1 ... 0 ... 0 ... 0
N.E.S. Ry. S., Hull	1 ... 0 ... 0 ... 0 ... 0 ... 0
Nantlle Vale	1 ... 0 ... 0 ... 0 ... 0 ... 0
Newhalley Temp.	1 ... 2 ... 0 ... 0 ... 0 ... 0
New Shildon	5 ... 5 ... 1 ... 1 ... 0 ... 0
Newton Heath Waggon Wks.	0 ... 0 ... 1 ... 0 ... 0 ... 0
Newbrough	2 ... 0 ... 0 ... 0 ... 0 ... 0
Newtown	1 ... 1 ... 0 ... 0 ... 0 ... 0
Niddrie	0 ... 0 ... 1 ... 0 ... 1 ... 0
Norland	0 ... 0 ... 1 ... 0 ... 0 ... 0
North Ashton	0 ... 0 ... 0 ... 0 ... 1 ... 0
Northampton Temperance	0 ... 0 ... 0 ... 0 ... 1 ... 0
Nottingham Borough	0 ... 0 ... 0 ... 0 ... 0 ... 1
Oldham Rifles	0 ... 1 ... 2 ... 1 ... 1 ... 1
Oldham Temp.	0 ... 0 ... 1 ... 0 ... 0 ... 0
Old Silkstone	2 ... 1 ... 0 ... 0 ... 0 ... 0
Olney Town	0 ... 1 ... 0 ... 0 ... 0 ... 0
Onward Temp.	1 ... 1 ... 0 ... 0 ... 0 ... 0
Ormskirk Rifles	1 ... 0 ... 0 ... 0 ... 0 ... 0
Ossett	0 ... 1 ... 0 ... 0 ... 0 ... 0
Pemberton Old	4 ... 1 ... 1 ... 2 ... 0 ... 1
Pendleton Old	0 ... 0 ... 2 ... 1 ... 2 ... 0
Percy Artillery	1 ... 0 ... 1 ... 0 ... 0 ... 0
Peterborough Borough	2 ... 1 ... 0 ... 0 ... 0 ... 0
Peterborough Excelsior	0 ... 0 ... 0 ... 0 ... 0 ... 0
Pickup Bank	1 ... 1 ... 1 ... 2 ... 1 ... 0
Platt Bridge	4 ... 3 ... 1 ... 2 ... 1 ... 0
Pessley Colliery	0 ... 0 ... 0 ... 1 ... 0 ... 0
Polesworth	0 ... 0 ... 1 ... 0 ... 0 ... 0
Pontlottyn	0 ... 1 ... 0 ... 0 ... 0 ... 0
Pontardawe	1 ... 0 ... 1 ... 0 ... 0 ... 0
Pontyberen St. James	0 ... 0 ... 0 ... 1 ... 0 ... 0
Portmadoc	1 ... 0 ... 0 ... 0 ... 0 ... 0
Portobello	0 ... 0 ... 0 ... 1 ... 1 ... 0
Pwllheli	1 ... 0 ... 0 ... 0 ... 0 ... 0
Radcliffe Old	0 ... 1 ... 0 ... 1 ... 0 ... 0
Radcliffe Public	2 ... 1 ... 3 ... 1 ... 2 ... 0
Raunds Temp	0 ... 1 ... 1 ... 0 ... 0 ... 0
Rawtenstall Boro'	0 ... 1 ... 0 ... 0 ... 0 ... 0
Reading Temp	1 ... 0 ... 0 ... 0 ... 0 ... 0
Redhill Town	0 ... 1 ... 0 ... 0 ... 0 ... 0
Rhyl Town	1 ... 0 ... 0 ... 0 ... 0 ... 0
Rishworth	0 ... 0 ... 1 ... 0 ... 0 ... 0
Rochdale Old	0 ... 0 ... 1 ... 0 ... 1 ... 0
Rochdale Public	0 ... 1 ... 0 ... 0 ... 0 ... 0
Rotherham Old B.	1 ... 1 ... 0 ... 0 ... 0 ... 0
Rotherham Temperance	4 ... 2 ... 4 ... 0 ... 0 ... 0
Rothwell Albion	0 ... 0 ... 2 ... 0 ... 0 ... 0
Rothwell Temp.	2 ... 0 ... 1 ... 1 ... 0 ... 0
Rothwell Town	0 ... 0 ... 1 ... 0 ... 0 ... 0
Rushden National	1 ... 0 ... 2 ... 3 ... 0 ... 0
Rushden Temp.	1 ... 3 ... 1 ... 1 ... 0 ... 0
Scunthorpe Vol	1 ... 0 ... 0 ... 0 ... 0 ... 0
Sguborwen Temp	0 ... 0 ... 2 ... 1 ... 0 ... 0
Sheffield Temp.	0 ... 0 ... 0 ... 1 ... 1 ... 0
Shelley	0 ... 0 ... 1 ... 0 ... 0 ... 0
Shields Harmonic	0 ... 0 ... 1 ... 1 ... 0 ... 1
Shildon Temp.	2 ... 4 ... 1 ... 1 ... 0 ... 0
Sheffield Dannemora	0 ... 2 ... 0 ... 0 ... 0 ... 0
Silverdale Town	1 ... 3 ... 0 ... 1 ... 0 ... 0
Skelmersdale Old	0 ... 0 ... 0 ... 1 ... 0 ... 0
Skelmersdale Temperance	3 ... 2 ... 0 ... 0 ... 2 ... 1
Skelton	1 ... 0 ... 0 ... 0 ... 0 ... 0
Skipton	1 ... 1 ... 0 ... 0 ... 0 ... 0
South Derwent	12 ... 2 ... 5 ... 1 ... 2 ... 0
South Notts	0 ... 1 ... 1 ... 0 ... 0 ... 0
Sowerby Bridge	0 ... 1 ... 0 ... 0 ... 0 ... 0
Standish	0 ... 0 ... 1 ... 0 ... 0 ... 0
Stanningley Old	0 ... 0 ... 1 ... 0 ... 0 ... 0
Steyning	0 ... 0 ... 1 ... 0 ... 0 ... 0
Stockton Boro'	0 ... 0 ... 1 ... 0 ... 0 ... 0
Stocksbridge Amateurs	0 ... 2 ... 0 ... 0 ... 0 ... 0
St. James', Gorton	0 ... 1 ... 0 ... 0 ... 0 ... 0
Tanfield Lea	0 ... 2 ... 0 ... 0 ... 0 ... 0
Thurlstone	1 ... 1 ... 1 ... 0 ... 0 ... 0
Tillery	0 ... 0 ... 1 ... 0 ... 0 ... 0
Tipton Prince's End	0 ... 1 ... 0 ... 0 ... 0 ... 0
Tipton Temp.	0 ... 0 ... 1 ... 0 ... 0 ... 0
Todmorden Old	0 ... 0 ... 0 ... 0 ... 1 ... 0
Tonyrefail	1 ... 0 ... 0 ... 0 ... 0 ... 0
Tranmere Temp.	1 ... 0 ... 0 ... 0 ... 0 ... 0
Trawden	0 ... 0 ... 0 ... 0 ... 1 ... 0
Trebanos	0 ... 1 ... 0 ... 0 ... 0 ... 0
Tyldesley Old	0 ... 0 ... 0 ... 0 ... 1 ... 0
Verdin Adelaide	0 ... 1 ... 0 ... 0 ... 1 ... 0
Warrington Boro'	1 ... 0 ... 0 ... 0 ... 0 ... 0
Weardale	0 ... 1 ... 1 ... 0 ... 0 ... 0
Wednesbury C.T.W.	0 ... 0 ... 1 ... 0 ... 0 ... 0
Wednesbury G.T.W.	1 ... 0 ... 0 ... 0 ... 0 ... 0
Wednesbury Temperance	0 ... 1 ... 0 ... 1 ... 0 ... 0
Wellington St. George's	0 ... 1 ... 0 ... 1 ... 0 ... 0
West Hartlepool Borough	0 ... 2 ... 1 ... 2 ... 1 ... 0
West Hartlepool Old Operatic	3 ... 5 ... 1 ... 1 ... 0 ... 0
Westhoughton Old	1 ... 1 ... 2 ... 2 ... 0 ... 0
West Pelton	0 ... 0 ... 2 ... 2 ... 0 ... 0
Whalley	0 ... 0 ... 1 ... 0 ... 0 ... 0
Wharncliffe Silkstone	1 ... 1 ... 3 ... 1 ... 0 ... 0
Whitewell Vale	1 ... 1 ... 1 ... 1 ... 2 ... 1
Whitworth	0 ... 1 ... 1 ... 1 ... 0 ... 0
Whitworth Vale	0 ... 1 ... 0 ... 0 ... 0 ... 0
Widnes (Gossage's)	2 ... 2 ... 1 ... 1 ... 0 ... 0
Widnes Subscription	1 ... 0 ... 0 ... 1 ... 1 ... 0
Wigan Rifles	0 ... 0 ... 1 ... 0 ... 1 ... 0
Willenhall Temp	7 ... 0 ... 1 ... 1 ... 0 ... 0
Wingates Temp.	2 ... 5 ... 1 ... 1 ... 1 ... 0
Wishaw	0 ... 0 ... 1 ... 0 ... 0 ... 0
Wokingham Town	0 ... 0 ... 0 ... 0 ... 1 ... 0
Workington Artillery	1 ... 0 ... 0 ... 0 ... 0 ... 0
Workington St. J.	0 ... 0 ... 1 ... 0 ... 0 ... 0
Woodcock Wells	0 ... 0 ... 1 ... 0 ... 0 ... 0
Wrawby	0 ... 1 ... 0 ... 0 ... 0 ... 0
Wrexham Boro'	2 ... 0 ... 0 ... 0 ... 0 ... 0
Wright Memorial	0 ... 0 ... 0 ... 1 ... 0 ... 0
Wyke Temperance	7 ... 7 ... 3 ... 0 ... 0 ... 0
Yeadon Old	0 ... 0 ... 1 ... 0 ... 0 ... 0
Ystalyfera	0 ... 1 ... 0 ... 0 ... 0 ... 0

Note. This list was printed in *The Brass Band Annual* of 1894. Most of the statistical summaries given in sources such as this should be treated with caution. As the prefatory remarks to the list hint, the publishers did not approach their task scientifically. The list of contesting bands is unlikely to be comprehensive, and the data on those that are included cannot be relied upon.

aspire to better standards, they imitated the style, sound, and other idiomatic features of bands in the first two categories.

A number of forces made for uniformity, or nationalism, across these three categories and groups of regions. The central commercial forces that controlled the production of sheet music and instruments was an important factor. Notions of what constituted a balanced sonority of low, middle, and high parts were established by the need for bands to have instruments that could play the basic versions of journal music. Also, in time, a standard pitch for brass band instruments was set.[28] But probably the most potent factor in promoting uniformity was brass band contesting. Brass band contests were promoted and managed by entrepreneurs. By far the most important of these entrepreneurs was Enderby Jackson (1827–1903), who is credited, probably correctly, with being the founder of the brass band contest as it is known today.[29] Jackson went to some lengths to ensure that the musical base for these contests was properly organized, establishing special rail excursions to carry contestants and audiences. They were presented as part of "day out" events at which other attractions such as balloon ascents were featured, and they became a hugely successful part of the entertainment industry. Even moderately sized competitions attracted audiences of 10,000 people. Hundreds of local and national contests were held each year throughout the country. The most important contests were those held at the Belle Vue Gardens in Manchester from 1853. A Crystal Palace "National" contest was spectacularly successful for a short time in the early 1860s, but was then dropped until the end of the century.

Contesting was important for many reasons. It gave rise to a common understanding of musical idioms, and promoted standards and standardization. It was the means by which the top bands acquired prestige and local pride. For the top bands, contests were also economically important. Contest prizes were high. For example, Besses o' th' Barn won a total of £742 in 1892, and Meltham Mills Band won £44,000 between 1871 and 1883. There were also other prizes of instruments, libraries of music, and other accruements. Major championship winners achieved great celebrity and undertook mammoth concert tours, both in the United Kingdom and overseas.[30]

Though it is often assumed that the great industrial towns of the north of England were the home of the best brass bands, this is not strictly true. Few of the best bands came from large cities or towns. They were often in the north but almost always in small industrialized settlements with, perhaps, one major industry such as a mine or textile factory. Some bands—like Black Dyke Mills in Queensbury— had consistent success. Others—the Meltham Mills Band, for example—fell on hard times after a period of great celebrity. Such decline often followed the decline of local industry, the economic collapse of a band, or the loss of key individual players. Smaller bands were particularly vulnerable because of their limited resources. The main reason for the success of small-town bands was that there was little local commercial music entertainment to compete with them for attention. The converse of this is also the reason why there were no great inner-city bands. For instance, in London, where professional entertainment was more widely available, there were few bands. However, this is a trend rather than an absolute rule, since Leeds, for example, which had many successful music halls, also had brass bands. In the south there was a much higher profile for professional military bands.[31]

A common feature of 19th-century British brass bands, with the exception of those in the Salvation Army, was that they seem to have been exclusively male.[32] Salvation Army bands remained separate from the brass band movement because of a series of measures initiated by William Booth, who saw dangers in bands behaving as discrete organizational units within the Army. These measures included a stipulation that the members of all bands must also be members of the Army, and that no member of a Salvationist band would have authority over ranked members of the Army. Booth was also directly responsible for the active recruitment of women for bands. He believed that women provided a good example for men when they came up against drunks and other abusers on their campaigns. "The women," he wrote, "can usually be reckoned on to stick to their guns, even if the men quit their posts."[33] Another reason why he was anxious to enlist women may have been to distinguish them from the all-male secular bands. The Army's attempts to draw this distinction were far-reaching. They set up their own publishing business, and in 1889 extended this enterprise to include the manufacture, sale, and repair of all Salvationist brass band instruments.[34]

MEDIATORS OF TASTE

It was in the north that the brass band movement had its greatest and earliest impact. The great Open contest, which became a mecca for bands, was always held in Manchester. When the Crystal Palace National contest had its brief existence in the early 1860s it attracted many major northern bands, but top prizes were won by bands from Blandford Forum in Dorset and Merthyr Tydfil in south Wales. However, both of these bands were exceptional. Little is known about the Blandford Band; unfortunately, its repertory, the key to its musical identity, is lost. The Cyfarthfa Band from Merthyr Tydfil, on the other hand, was probably the greatest band of the early 19th century. However, it was unique because it was always retained as a private band by the industrialist Robert Thompson Crawshay.[35] Thus it shared few of the ideals and characteristics that typified town or works bands.

The strongest musical influence on bands was exercised by a small number of individuals who were either based in the north, or London-based but with the north as their focus. Enderby Jackson, the biggest contest promoter, was based in north Yorkshire but still exerted a huge influence on contesting. More influential still were three conductors: John Gladney, Edwin Swift, and Alexander Owen. These three controlled the best bands for most of the last 30 years of the century. Fourteen of the eighteen bands who entered the top contest at Belle Vue in 1894 were conducted by one of them. Between 1873 and 1914 only one of the Open contests was won by a band that was not conducted by one of these three. It was the instrumental lineups formulated by Swift, Gladney, and Owen that became the standard brass band formation. They conducted bands between Cambridge and Cumbria, but mainly those around the Pennines where they lived. Their protégés were influential too. Almost all of the southern bands that made an impact—Luton Red Cross, Olney Town, and the St. Albans City, for example—were conducted by northerners at some time or other.

Influence was also exerted by professional, military bandmasters based in London who formed an intimate and often corrupt cartel with music publishers and instrument manufacturers. All the brass band journals were edited by professional military bandmasters. The father and son both called Charles Godfrey, and both members of a well-established dynasty of musicians, were particularly influential. Between 1871 and 1921 bands had to play the same piece—the test piece for that year—in the Open and National contests. In fifty-one of the sixty-one years in this period, the arrangement used as the test piece was by one of the two Godfreys.

CHANGE AND CONTINUITY

Vic and Sheila Gammon, in an important contribution to the literature of this subject, have argued that the change from the old vernacular, plebeian tradition to the modern, virtuoso-led, text-based, organized brass band movement was not a fracturing of older traditions, as is often assumed.[36] This is compatible with my own view of the relationship of brass bands to established musical and social structures. There was a time when older vernacular traditions coexisted with newer forms of music making. It is true, for instance, that in southern England the size of bands, the music they played, the means by which they learned, their function and the musical, social, and economic support they attracted owes something to the continuum from the old church band culture. There were hundreds, perhaps even thousands of southern bands that were smaller and less ambitious than those in the north, but which were, nevertheless, important focuses for community music making. They too were purveyors of art music, through journal editions. Ord Hume observed in 1900 that the "crack" bands should not obscure the efforts of the thousands of smaller bands in every part of the country, which still played from the old journal music and—as he put it—had enough of it to paper their walls with.[37]

These smaller bands were infused with many of the features of the wider movement. The impact they had on their communities was probably no weaker than that of the best bands on theirs. Bands had different levels of eloquence, but eloquence they all, almost certainly, had. The musical change fashioned by them was far-reaching and sophisticated. Through brass band transcriptions, instrumental art music was accessed by vast numbers of people who had no access to it in commercial concert halls. The fact that music of such good taste was transmitted by performers of their own class and communities must have been striking. This is probably the most important achievement of the brass band movement—but it is not the only one. The movement also established a tradition of brass playing in Britain that had a major impact on mainstream art music.

Dave Russell has wrestled with figures that might suggest the total number of bands that existed by the 1890s and has come to no firm conclusion.[38] I agree with his impression, though, that there may have been 30,000 of them. As far as the number of participants is concerned, the 20th century has been a period of decline. Bands still have a healthy survival but they now reside in a cultural ghetto, stereotyped by their history. Part of that stereotype is of the brass band world's own making. The competitive ethos has remained central in the brass band world and this has tended to ossify style, repertory, and practices. It is true that some established composers have written works for brass band (e.g., Elgar, Vaughan Williams, and Holst)—including some radical modernists (e.g., Henze and Birtwhistle). But the staple and popular diet of brass bands remains a tonally secure, familiar repertory, in which the technical demands are often appreciated as much as the musical, artistic values.

Brass bands were encouraged in Victorian Britain because they were a means of spiritual and moral elevation for working-class people. But at the height of their popularity, a refashioning of cultural values was taking place. The historians Terence Ranger and Eric Hobsbawm have observed the relocating of certain types of activities with social and class groups.[39] In this process brass bands became linked with May Day parades, miners' galas, contests, trades union demonstrations, and similar events. Thus, by the beginning of this century, the brass band, which had been promoted as a means by which the lower orders could acquire good musical taste, had become synonymous in the minds of the musical élite with bad musical taste. As such, it became one of the features that caricatured working-class behavior.

NOTES

1. See Herbert, T. (Ed.). (1991). *Bands: The brass band movement in the 19th and 20th centuries*. Milton Keynes, U.K.: Open University; Taylor, A. R. (1983). *Labour and love: An oral history of the brass band movement*. London: Elm Tree Books; Russell, J. F., & Elliot, J. H. (1936). *The brass band movement*. London: J. M. Dent.

2. See Bernstein, L. (1976). *The unanswered question: Six talks at Harvard*. Cambridge, Mass.: Harvard University Press.

3. For a description of crooking, hand stopping, and other transitionary techniques by which horn players obtained a diatonic or chromatic compass, see Morley-Pegge, R. (1973). *The French horn* (2nd ed.). London: Benn.

4. See Horwood, W. (1983). *Adolphe Sax, 1814–1894: His life and legacy*. Baldock, Hertfordshire, U.K.: Egon. Also, for a technical description of Sax patents, see Myers, A. (1991). Instruments and instrumentation in British brass bands. In Herbert, *Bands*, Appendix 1, pp. 169–195.

5. For The Distin family, see Horwood, *Adolphe Sax*, Chapter 4.

6. See Ehrlich, C. (1985). *The music profession in Britain since the eighteenth century*. Oxford: Clarendon Press, Chapter 5.

7. For a detailed overview of these developments, see Herbert, *Bands*, passim.

8. For musical education, see Ehrlich, *The music profession*, Chapter 4, and Rainbow, B. (1967). *The land without music: Musical education in England 1800–1860 and its continental antecedents*. London: Novello & Company.

9. Author not attributed (1872, August 3). A Midland town—Wolverhampton. *The Leisure Hour—A Family Journal of Instruction and Recreation*, p. 494.

10. See Ehrlich, *The music profession*, Chapter 5.

11. See Mackerness, E. D. (1964). *A social history of English music*. London: Routledge & Kegan Paul, p. 164.

12. Haweis, H. R. (1871). *Music and morals*. London: Strahan & Co.

13. *Musical Herald*, August 28, 1846, p. 40.

14. Rose, A. (1895). *Talks with bandsmen*. London: W. Rider & Son, p. 305.

15. Handbills at the Lynn Museum, Norfolk, U.K.

16. See, e.g., *The new Grove dictionary of music and musicians*. London: Macmillan, s.v. "Brass band"; and Russell & Elliot, *The brass band movement*, Chapter 1.

17. For an overview of the development of the volunteer movement, see Beckett, I. F. W. (1982). *Riflemen form: A study of the rifle volunteer movement, 1859–1908*. Aldershot, U.K.: Ogilby Trusts. For information on brass bands and the volunteer movement, see Herbert, *Bands*, pp. 25–30.

18. The Crystal Palace Contests were organized by Enderby Jackson. They were advertised as "National Contests" and ran between 1860 and 1864. For an overview of music at the Crystal Palace, see Musgrave, M. (1995). *The musical life of the Crystal Palace*. Cambridge: Cambridge University Press.

19. *The Volunteer Service Gazette*, July 25, 1868, p. 531.

20. See, e.g., Livings, H. (1975). *That the medals and the baton be put on view: The story of a village band, 1875–1975*. Newton Abbot, U.K.: David & Charles, p. 15.

21. E.g., the Minute Book of W. L. Marriner's Caminando Band (currently kept at the University of Leeds Brotherton Library) states in Rule 7 of its regulations: "For every oath or angry expression a penalty of three shillings." Further examples of such ordinances are quoted in Herbert, *Bands,* pp. 33-37.

22. The largest known collection of handwritten band music is that of the Cyfarthfa Band. See Herbert, T. (1990, January). The repertory of a Victorian provincial brass band. *Popular Music, 9*(1), 117-132.

23. Comparatively little work has been done on the repertories of 19th-century brass bands. Surviving but uncatalogued collections include those of the Black Dyke Mills Band and the Besses o' th' Barn Band. However, the catalogue of the repertory of the first virtuoso brass band, the Cyfarthfa Band, is given in Herbert, Repertory of a Victorian provincial brass band.

24. See Finnegan, R. (1989). *The hidden musicians: Music making in an English town.* Cambridge: Cambridge University Press.

25. See Ord Hume, J. (1900). *Chats on amateur bands.* London: (publisher not known). Chapter 1, passim; and Herbert, *Bands,* Chapter 1.

26. For the standard instrumental lineup of a brass band, see *The new Grove dictionary,* s.v. "Brass band."

27. See Herbert, *Bands;* Appendix 3, prepared by Clifford Bevan, contains a list of all winners of Open and National contests.

28. The pitch of a band or group is an agreed frequency to which all performers play. For example, the standard pitch today, which is recognized internationally, is A = 440 vibrations a second. Pitch was a controversial issue in the 19th century. There was no standard pitch for brass bands until late in the century. There is some evidence that it suited manufacturers to have several pitches operating simultaneously, because of the increased likelihood that bands would make purchases of complete sets of instruments more often. Professional military bandmasters used to express a preference for a particular maker's instruments in order to stimulate a new sale. See Herbert, *Bands,* pp. 44-46.

29. An autobiographical account of Jackson's brass band contests is given in Jackson, E. (1896). The origin and promotion of brass band contests. *Musical Opinion and Music Trades Review* (serialized).

30. Besses o' th' Barn and the Black Dyke Mills Band were the most traveled. For a history of the former, see Hampson, J. (ca. 1893). *The origin, history and achievements of the Besses o' th' Barn Band.* (Place of publication not given; almost certainly published privately.)

31. For an excellent overview of the issues discussed here and the broader context for music making in this period, see Russell, D. (1987). *Popular music in England, 1840-1914: A social history.* Manchester, U.K.: Manchester University Press. See also Lomas, M. J. (1990). *Amateur brass and wind bands in Southern England between the late eighteenth century and c. 1900.* Unpublished Ph.D. dissertation, The Open University, Milton Keynes, United Kingdom.

32. There were few professional women brass players in England at this time. However, it was common for American bands to include, or even to be entirely made up of, women players. Indeed, one of the great American cornet virtuosi of the late 19th century was a woman, Alice Raymonde, who was often billed as "the world's greatest lady cornetist." See Hazen, M. H., & Hazen, R. M. (1987). *The*

music men: An illustrated history of brass bands in America, 1800–1920. Washington, DC: Smithsonian Institution Press, passim.

33. *The Officer,* January 1895, p. 27.

34. See Boon, B. (1978). *Play the music, play! The story of Salvation Army bands.* London: Salvationist Publishing and Supplies; and Herbert, *Bands,* pp. 47–49.

35. See Herbert, T. (1988, August). The Virtuosi of Merthyr. *Llafur: Journal of Welsh Labour History,* pp. 60–69.

36. Gammon, V., & Gammon, S. (1991). From "Repeat and Twiddle" to "Precision and Snap": The musical revolution of the mid-nineteenth century. In Herbert, *Bands,* pp. 120–144.

37. Ord Hume, *Chats on amateur bands,* Chapter 1.

38. See Russell, *Popular music,* pp. 162–198.

39. See Hobsbawm, E., & Ranger, T. (Eds.). (1983). *The invention of tradition.* Cambridge: Cambridge University Press.

5

LOCATING LISTENING

Technological Space, Popular Music, and Canadian Mediations

JODY BERLAND

MAKING SENSE OF SPACE

The electronic media establish a space between the origin of a sound and its listener. That space is not linear, as the crow flies; the new space/relationship is not a unified or simple one. The electronic media, designed to conquer space, transform its very nature. Their accelerating conquest of space is inseparable from the increasing complexity of our place in it, our relationship to place itself. One result of this new reality is that music, indeed any mode of address in sound, seems to articulate time, which we then notice all the more, but not space, which nonetheless shapes both the music and its meanings in our lives.

This displacement is particularly evident in radio, which organizes our sense of morning, of activity, of the discipline of time. The temporal seems to dominate its activities. It's like the experience of driving a car along a familiar road at high speed—something I used to do each week between Peterborough and Toronto. On the road, it seems to be me that remains still, and everything around the car that rushes past me, into the past. In fact, it is the landscape that stays still and it is me, locked in a body in the driver's seat, that rushes across the space. But this factual observation doesn't account for the conceptualization of movement that comes with driving. It doesn't feel like space that interrupts the affinity between me and my destination, but rather time, punctuated by landmarks and musical endings, which together signal the episodic triumph of individual movement over the density of landscape, of time over space. This is a conceptual (mis)apprehension, since ultimately it is space—or the drive to expand or conquer space—that dominates the action, and time that is suppressed. This is what makes driving such a quintessentially modern activity.

This misapprehension preserves the location of experience in the singular. My perception does not extend outward to a topography with roads, electric wires, fields and houses, and little steel boxes rushing across it, but rather contains me within one steel box. With electronic media, listening to music comes to represent the same necessary (mis)apprehension. We objectify location as the space that contains our individual means of reception: the car, bedroom, or bar where the music is heard, the physical site within which one's body is surrounded by sound. At the same time, we subjectify the source of sound, hearing it only as a speaking subject: someone is being creative, or is dull, is making an event, or is reminding you of one. The source is not a place or a spatial economy but a singer, who creates an emotional state in which one is touched by sounds. We don't place ourselves and the sounds in a spatially conceived map of synchronic and diachronic movement, evaluate from whence we are addressed, or consider how we are positioned by the instruments that bring that touching address to our ears. Thus we fail to apprehend the places we inhabit, not as visible points in physical space, but as the product of diverse and complex forces. Lefebvre touches on this idea when he writes:

> Our illusion of transparency goes hand in hand with a view of space as innocent, as free of traps or secret places.... Closely bound up with Western "culture," this ideology stresses speech, and overemphasizes the written word, to the detriment of a social practice which it is indeed designed to conceal.... Such are the assumptions of an ideology which, in positing the transparency of space, identifies knowledge, information and communication.[1]

This misapprehension of spatial relationships may be common, in other words, but it is not silent. Indeed, it is tied to a proliferation of texts, which tumble into our ears at the flick of a hand. This apprehension is audible in the discourse of sound that penetrates space while ignoring its otherness: call it aggressive expressionism, call it "We Are the World." In this musical imagination, everyone is together in the same place. It's probably California. There is also a kind of sound in which you can lose yourself, a music that succeeds for a moment in lifting you outside of place altogether, as much New Age music seeks to do. Listening to the sounds of these despatialized vocabularies can make you feel as though you are everywhere, a universal self, an American; as if you might be sunning in California (but probably no such luck), or as if your happiest state might be floating nowhere in particular. A popular variation of these codes places you somewhere familiarly exotic like Jamaica or Africa.[2] Each of these imaginary spaces offers its own type of pleasure: not least the pleasure of categorical familiarity. Alternatively, you may suddenly find yourself listening from the vantage point of a particular place—a Toronto suburb, the car en route to work, a fishing town facing extinction, the gay village facing another death—where (you and the rest of) the girls are. Wherever it locates you, the music reminds you of your place. It speaks to the heart of where you are, and tells you something about what it means to live there. And then you, the listener, might begin to hear the ongoing flow of music and noise differently, as something that both celebrates and evaporates the colonizing of that place. With this mode of listening, space and location become explicit; then space is recognized as a social construction, outside of nature, and music as one of its codes.[3]

LOCATING THE QUESTION

"The experience of pop music," Simon Frith writes, "is an experience of placing: in responding to a song, we are drawn, haphazardly, into affective and emotional alliances with the performers and with the performers' other fans."[4] Obviously we do not have to be in physical proximity to the performers and other fans for this to occur. Music creates an embodied but imaginary space that mediates our feelings, our dreams, and our desires—our internal space—with the social, with external space. In this way music gives each of us a sense of place, sometimes in connection with coherent spaces, sometimes in their place. Once music travels, the external space/community may have little to do with the placement of bodies gathered together. Just as music mediates our feelings with the social, so reproductive technologies mediate music with an ever wider range of personal and public spaces. CDs, boomboxes, and car radios enable music to mediate personal and public space in a kind of third space, connecting us to something outside the actuality of physical space. And just as cultural technologies like radio mediate between the production of music and the production of us as audiences, so this "third space" that radio produces mediates between us and the diverse spaces we inhabit. "Our epoch," Foucault claims, "is one in which space takes for us the form of relations among sites."[5] We need to study these cultural technologies to learn how these "relations among sites"—these *spaces*—are produced.

Music has a special role in this process, for it enables listeners to find a sense of belonging in the midst of the most fragmentary mobilizations. Theorists have suggested that as soon as music is approached in terms of its technological mediation, the analysis of musical reception becomes more clearly decisive. As music comes to depend more on sound recording, broadcasting, and other technological mediations, so we must increasingly depend on understanding the practices and structures of listening to determine what and how the music means. In other words, music's context becomes both more powerful and more flexible. Thus John Mowitt, in his incisive discussion of music and electronic reproduction, proposes that the greater the technological mediation, the more reception precedes and structures production itself:

> If recording organizes the experience of reception by conditioning its present scale and establishing its qualitative norms for musicians and listeners alike, then the conditions of reception actually *precede* the moment of production. It is not, therefore, sufficient merely to state that considerations of reception influence music production and thus deserve attention in musical analysis. Rather, the social analysis of musical experience has to take account of the radical priority of reception, and thus it must shift its focus away from a notion of agency that, by privileging the moment of production, preserves the autonomy of the subject.[6]

In pointing to the "radical priority of reception," Mowitt reminds us that we cannot determine what music "means" by deciphering musical texts or the intentions of the musical artist—the ostensibly autonomous subject—because the ongoing expansion of technological reproduction into homes, cars, gyms, and countries around the world encourages the proliferation of different meanings. Such meanings are not contained by the boundaried spaces in which reception occurs, though, for the musical experience mediates between global and local, public and private, and other spaces that cultural technologies at the same time contribute to producing. For both cultural and commercial reasons, listening is part of this mediation. Listeners' tastes are increasingly taken into account during the recording and programming of popular music, whose producers are united by "the permanent and organized quest for what holds meaning for the public."[7] As with television and film, music is shaped by what I have elsewhere summarized as "the insertion of a targeted public into the heart of the production of popular music."[8]

Mowitt's argument is relevant to the question of location for several reasons. The cultural and geographic expansion of audiences is necessary for the economic expansion of the cultural industries. Just as the acquisition of international markets enables American television to employ deficit financing and thus to dump its products in other countries, so the expansion of musical markets enables global corporate hegemony for the "Big Six" in the music industry, transforming local cultures into markets for globally distributed music commodities and cultivating local musicians who can produce such commodities for an international marketplace. The social and industrial imperative to make music marketable internationally enters music making itself; composing, playing, and recording music are all shaped by how musicians absorb and respond to the dynamics of popular desire and/or commercial markets. In this context, the changing reception of popular music is crucial to the musical and commercial discourse within which it emerges.

This is not to suggest that the moment of reception—the act of tuning in, listening, buying—is itself freely formed. Mowitt argues that listening itself is mediated by commercial processes that deeply shape the listener's memory, desire, and experience.[9] These subjective attributes, along with her purchasing habits and technological horizons, and other aspects of her life situation—her class, place of work, style/formation, and so forth—are all implicated and made meaningful in the formation and reformation of (her) cultural location through changing structures of listening. As Paul Theberge puts it, "Specific activities related to making or consuming music result in differently structured listening habits. . . . Listening [is then] both context and effect."[10]

The increasing mobility of music technologies, and the seemingly paradoxical emphasis on identity that surrounds analysis of music consumption today, reveal how much the ongoing (re)shaping of listening habits is tied to our changing sense of location: where we are, where the music can take us, where we *belong*. At the simplest level, the link between listening and location arises from the "schizophonic"[11] movement of electronically reproduced messages across space, whereby sound is split from source, and image from sound. Listening practices are continuously transformed by technical innovations in music reproduction: the long-playing album, the transistor radio, and the Walkman have each successively shaped and mobilized our listening practices, enabling us to carry music "belonging" to one location or spatial scale into other places. At a second level we find social meanings in the sounds themselves, meanings that are continuously shifting, being recycled and rearticulated in the music as well as in its technical mediation. Composers, performers, sound mixers, producers, DJs, jingle writers, and radio programmers—all affect our listening practices by shaping the sounds we hear. Through diverse strategies they fundamentally shape the music's perceived meanings and uses. And finally there is a broad discourse *about* sound, in market research or in cultural and communication policy, for instance, which negotiates the constitution and deployment of collective musical subjectivity. These musical discourses and practices all contribute to shaping our habits and expectations as listeners. Since music plays so strong a role in "the cultural placing of the individual in the social,"[12] tracing these multiple mediations helps to identify processes through which the listener's sense of location can be continuously defined and redefined.

LOCATING CANADA

Listening, and its animation of our sense of location, occurs within, materializes, and challenges a range of structural constraints. In Canada these constraints have been organized into two broad institutional categories, publicly and commercially financed modes of cultural production, which work to organize the activities of musicians, producers, and broadcasters. Each institutional context situates music and metamusical meanings in different locational trajectories. In other words cultural technologies like public and commercial radio produce specific but diverse spatial meanings, a realization that for various reasons has emerged with particular clarity in the production of cultural space(s) within Canada.

To explore how listening to music in Canada contributes to the "cultural placing of the individual in the social," we need to join together several critical trajectories: Anglo-American cultural studies work on audiences and modes of reception, and the study of policy and media in Canadian communication theory. The difficulty of this encounter is a secondary theme of this discussion. Canadian theorists, living in a technologically advanced but economically underdeveloped, and culturally diverse but politically colonized, nation, tend to approach cultural politics with an ambivalence that coexists uneasily with Anglo-American cultural studies. While the latter usefully encourage us to investigate how people listen to, interpret, and use the music they hear, I don't believe, no matter what such listeners (including ourselves, at least while we are listening) may believe, that we freely choose among cultural resources and identities. Instead, I am obliged to remember the context in which this music comes to me. Consequently I see every moment of cultural connection as both a positive constitution of identity and a negation, a *displacement*: a contradictory process bound up with an imperial dynamic that produces both sameness and difference, belonging and displacement, in its drive for profit and power.

Listening to music illustrates this duality of belonging and displacement very well. The blend of selections flowing from commercial radio positions listeners in an abstract and/or American imaginary, drawing us into a cultural horizon that is semantically elsewhere or without any perceptible signification of place. Such music enters our media landscape and blends forcefully into our lives, mediated by our tastes and dispositions, the cultural technologies of our everyday lives, and various local or regional articulations—all of which are further mediated by commercial ratings. The more seamlessly the musical landscape joins together these diverse places, the more it approximates placelessness; like money, music that works anywhere can help create what Lefebvre calls abstract space. But this process never fully succeeds at the level of meaning, where inevitably the "escape" alluded to by Harvey and Lefebvre[13] originates. Understanding this "escape" takes us beyond positing disparate interpretations of a specifically musical landscape.

Canada was defined historically as a collective space through a continuous and overtly political mediation of the media. Consequently its media critics find it difficult to accept the North American musical mainstream on its own terms. Jon Crane exemplifies the American disposition when he maintains that the Top 40 vindicates the pleasures and rights of its listeners, demonstrating a populist logic responsive to and parallel with a social logic of pluralist flux. He thus views every popular hit as a "floating totem of public pleasure."[14] And certainly listening to music can perpetuate and invigorate this feeling, for each station chooses and combines music to draw its listeners into a pleasurably coherent and affirmative imaginary space. In rationalizing musical selection, radio rationalizes pleasure as well as numbers.

Like Manifest Destiny, though, Crane's view holds limited credibility in a context where economic logic so often prevents populist sentiment from achieving material form.[15] For as soon as we stop listening and start to read, our reception fractures into warring positions. We confront a kind of "crack" in meaning, which opens up a potential space for other practices and meanings and more generally points to possible limits to the hegemonic production of space. We learn that popular views on policy often fail to find expression in government action, and that popular sentiments about culture often fail to find expression in the mediascape of popular music. We realize that we rarely hear "Canadian culture" when we listen to commercial radio, and we rarely hear—unless we are very adept listeners—distinctly "Canadian" sounds in the Canadian music we do hear. Why is this? Should we care? Does it matter? What is a distinctive Canadian sound, anyway? I'll have more to say about this once I've more clearly established the geopolitical context of Canadian listening practices.

THE MUSICAL APPARATUS

Canadians rate as the second highest (after the Dutch) consumers in the world in terms of per capita expenditures on recorded music. The total annual revenue of the Canadian music industry, including concerts, sheet music, musical performance, and reproduction, is now over one and a half billion dollars. The largest record companies in Canada are foreign-owned; more than 85% of revenues from the Canadian domestic market goes to multinationals. Hundreds of millions of dollars leave the country each year as a consequence of our music consumption, with only a very small portion of revenue reinvested in Canadian music. The multinationals' interest in Canadian music is restricted to recordings that can be marketed across the continent (or, in the case of French language recordings, abroad).

Canadian record companies and studios produce most Canadian-content recordings, thus bearing the creative and economic risk of making music within the country. But Canadian musicians are largely denied access to the Canadian record buying public. Because record distribution is also owned and controlled by the multinationals, most records manufactured and sold within Canada (nearly 90%) are made from imported master tapes. As with television, it costs ten times more to produce an indigenous product than to import a similar product from the United States. Thus a recording artist usually needs to succeed in the U.S. to be heard in Canada. The predominance of cheap imports, and the cartography of music programming in commercial radio, tilt the balance of record production and sales contents heavily toward Top 40 releases.[16]

Whether marginal or indistinguishable, Canadian music's relationship to its listeners is established within this context and shaped by it. But this profile is not yet complete. While local music is "marginalized" from Liverpool to Los Angeles, marginality in Canada is shaped by a public discourse that positions it within the political problematic of Canada itself. Historically, communication technologies from radio onward were received and modified at an institutional level by policies and regulations influenced by widespread anti-continentalism and anti-commercialism. In the early 1930s Parliament concurred with public opinion that communication technologies were a necessary instrument for the development of a national public and that their content should be qualitatively different from that engendered by American commerce. Canada's broadcasting system was formed with the ostensible mandate to create national community, to resist foreign hegemony, and to advance public interest in contradistinction to commercial (American) media. With its nomination of a marginalized national space, not only radio but the whole field of culture was thereafter inflected with anxiety about cultural and economic sovereignty.

For diverse reasons radio acquired a privileged place in negotiations of commerce, culture and cultural sovereignty. As a result of Canadian content quotas and other interventions, the bond between music and listeners became linked metonymically to government cultural policy (or the lack thereof), and our attitudes toward this bond cannot escape association with such intervention.[17] Canadians, unlike their American neighbors, endowed the state with the right and responsibility to intervene in culture. But the state's actions have been quite contradictory. Government agencies defend "Canadian culture" by means of protective regulations such as Canadian content quotas for broadcasters, while simultaneously colluding in the foreign capitalization of Canada's economy and culture, not only in the expansion of commercial broadcasting but more broadly in the cultural industries of sound recording, publishing, and film.[18] While popular sentiment remains consistently in favor of public support for Canadian culture, the success of government protection becomes more and more elusive, because the market ascendancy of the commercial sector reinforces listening and viewing patterns that effectively counteract the nationalist objectives espoused by these same listeners and viewers.

This does not mean that government is absent in the commercial sphere. In the 1970s the public sector joined with commercial broadcasters to fund production of recordings that could fulfill Canadian content quotas for radio. Preoccupation with the continental cultural market for recorded music became explicit in the administrative design of the Sound Recording Development Program founded in 1986. This program subsidizes recording projects by musicians with demonstrated commercial viability, suggests that applicants pretest proposals by considering their suitability for commercial airplay, shapes musical criteria toward mainstream commercial radio formats, and subsidizes international music tours but not domestic ones.[19] The program thus assists the Canadian music industry to export recordings by deepening and extending the means whereby internal manufacture complements and serves the international industry. By seeking to reconcile citizenship and consumption in a mutual enterprise of privatization and delocalization, the state demonstrates its complicity in the ongoing capitalization of national space.

Both economic forces and the legislative and fiscal practices of the state thus push contemporary musicians and listeners (who are already quite advanced in this respect) toward a musical language that, whether celebrating global or local vernaculars, can succeed equally in Vancouver or New Jersey. The privileging of mobile musical meanings creates for us, as diverse listeners and subjects, the same double bind that structured the country's development. We are implicated in a visible process of nation building, through which the state legitimates itself by valorizing modes of cultural production that are appropriate to the formation of national subjects. At the same time we see (and hear) this same state submitting strategically—in our name as producers and consumers of culture—to the operations and artifacts of multinational capital. Thus government participates in the simultaneous creation of sameness and difference, while cultural consumption registers or seeks to reconcile the ambivalence of its subjects. From this compromise arises the structural paradox of our cultural technologies, which is reproduced in, and reinforced by, the ways Canadians think or talk about, watch or listen to film, television, radio, and music.

STRUCTURING SOUNDS

"Music's social significance," writes John Mowitt, "derives from ... how it articulates and consolidates structurally necessary practices of listening. By sanctioning specific technical mediation of listening as subjectively normative, musical reception supplies the social order sponsoring such mediation with an experiential confirmation."[20] Our task now is to follow these narratives into a closer look at the structuring of listening practices in connection with organized mediations of music, sound, and location. Many topics here invite our attention, from policy studies and listener ethnographies to the semiotics of musical sound. I want to focus on how such mediations work to organize musical flow, and thus the listening experience, in space and time.[21] With this focus we can begin to see how musical sounds, radio practices, social institutions, and listeners collaborate in "placing" listeners in their affective and topographic worlds.

In the current musical topography, "Africanness" is culturally and musically intelligible. We hear "African" music and organize a system of reception into which that music finds a place. Country music has also experienced what we could call, following Shklovsky, "the canonization of the junior branch," assuming we can still attribute privileged status to the industrial mechanisms of popular music.[22] (This is not an unreasonable assumption, since it is these mechanisms, rather than any qualities in the music itself, that justify the populist optimism of cultural studies today.) Canada's history has not produced this kind of intelligibility, and its popular musicians are rarely canonized on the basis of their perceived contributions to a distinctive Canadian culture. A record not aimed at export often fails to gain commercial distribution within the country: the canonization process is short-circuited because the junior branch is being turned into lumber before it has a chance to grow leaves.

While Canadian media like to celebrate the success of Canadian musicians, they ordinarily cannot themselves produce or claim credit for that success. This incapacity stands in contrast to broadcasting systems in other countries, not only the United States, but also, in a different way, Britain; as Frith has shown, "It was because of the BBC's public service attitude to youth programming that there were specifically British pop sounds and attitudes in place to inflect the meaning of 1960s rock.... The importance of public service broadcasting for the 'indie' British scene is apparent in the continuing role of the John Peel show." In other words, "market forces are not the only ones in play, [for] the meaning of popular music this century is inseparable from its use by the other mass media."[23] As we have seen, Canada's media are constrained by a transnational industrial structure perpetuating interdependent economies and mediations within a geography of symbolic (as well as economic) uneven development.

This is a tangible reality for Canadian songwriters who are compelled to record songs with lyrics about dying in Texas or mornings in Minnesota (rather than Manitoba)—or in another context, lyrics in English—as long as the industry forces a dependency on the American market.[24] Americans are well protected from exposure to foreign influences! Texas, Nashville, and Georgia thereby become doubly or triply coded signs; for most listeners, their use evokes an intertextual history of signs and genres rather than an experience of place. This semiotic depletion of meaning from place suggests an analogy between the mode of address in popular music, and that which has been so extensively described in cinematic enunciation, which does not "normally identify itself as proceeding from anywhere in particular: a film seems simply to be 'there' as it unfolds before our eyes."[25]

The musical flow in commercial radio offers a similar mode of enunciation. Critics have observed that local commercial radio programming has less and less to do with local music or cultural life outside of the advertising of local merchants, along with traffic and weather reports.[26] Music programming evolves through a blend of market research, industrial rationalization, government regulation, and global industry trends, which together work to eradicate or to codify traces of the "local" in the music itself.[27] The emancipation of the music experience/commodity from the semiotics of local experience is not the only way this programming works to produce a dispersed musical space. Stations compete with one another for listeners by means of playlists with a calculated blend of currency, genre, and musical temporality, based on the perceived dispositions of targeted listeners. Each blend patterns time in terms of transience and the poignancy of individual (but demographically calculated) memory. The flow of four-minute segments, moving calculatedly from new to old and back again, weaves a container of music and talk that seeks to meet each listener's musical biography and predisposition, temporal habits and perceptions, and—lest we forget—working needs.

Each radio station, hoping to enter and to join (but without drawing critical attention to) their listeners' homes, cars, or places of work, uses a specific temporally organized music discourse to create a sociomusical "third space" that can draw listeners into its fragmentary temporal flow and simultaneously disperse them into productivity. The passion of music alternates with the pragmatism of talk and advertising; the music is both there and not there, even while it's playing, allowing listeners to be also there/not there, suspended between actual and possible space. Listeners are thus brought together-in-time-outside-of-space, which is both conquered and removed from perception; not the space of radio but the space such radio helps to produce: the space that listeners simultaneously (and thereby more productively) inhabit. Such radio is for people who need to like and forget where they are: working, driving, washing dishes, waiting. The music connects them to fantasy, pleasure, and an ever-elusive future without separating them from the rhythms of everyday life.

In contrast, the rhetoric of public radio is one of direct address in the shared pursuit of public interest. The soundscape is meant to incorporate the listener into this pursuit and to unify both with physical and political space; to join *listening* (which is ostensibly elevated from the commercial work-discipline of mere *hearing* by complex artistic and narrative demands) to the project and territoriality of citizenship. The producers of soundtracks for radio documentaries, dramas, and sound art conventionally forefront the aural tangibility of location in their soundscape. The rhetorical synthesis of technology and presence signals that the vehicle is public (Canadian) culture, and therefore both oppositional and inhabitable. We are joined across an ascribed space and brought together in time, like the national subjects narratavized in Anderson's *Imagined Communities*.[28] The Canadian Broadcasting Corporation (CBC) speaks to us as members of a public that hears itself as from a long way off, communing among ourselves as citizens—insofar as we are listening. The contradictions of technological nationalism[29] find eloquent expression in this convention.

Public broadcasting's use of music correspondingly differs in (relationship to) time and space. CBC programs are indexed by musical signatures that become, over 10, 20, or 30 years, as familiar as the voices of a neighborhood or extended family. Framing these arbitrarily meaningful musical fragments we hear the mantras of place: a voice ceremonially mapping today's weather for Pentatanguishene, Kapuskasing, Sault St.-Marie, Timiskaming, Superior, and Thunder Bay provides word-signs that "anchor" the music we hear. Over time we learn to associate musical motifs with a constellation of places; when we travel within the country we hear other place-names, but the same music, and know we have not left our citizenship behind. On CBC Radio 1 in contradistinction to the blandly homogeneous classical music on Radio 2,[30] the music is somewhat diverse; people are joined to one another not by specific musical tastes (the AM network is adept at blending and defining a likeable, consensual musical horizon for its conversation), but by a broader disposition toward "public" space.

Differently again, community radio forefronts diverse local musics and nurtures a sense of difference-within-place through an interweaving of musical genres and talk. Community programmers become conduits between listeners, performers, and local sites; they tie listeners to location by chatting about—and to—local clubs and performances, controversies and events, to which listeners are incited to attend. Music programs are generically diverse and represent, at different times of the day, ethnically and culturally diverse communities. In community radio, in contrast to commercial and public radio, the boundary between programmers and listeners is fluid and dynamic. Because different communities take the air at different times, listeners must either browse the ethnomusical soundscape or learn the schedules. Either way, community radio refuses to become homogeneous or habitual. It demarcates and stands back from radio as an "acoustic wallpaper," as Crisell calls popular radio, or "a music while you work service riddled with commercialism," as Local Radio Workshop calls "local" radio in England.[31] Crucially, this is not simply a matter of what occurs within the acoustic space defined by listening. As with all such mediated spaces, we are here concerned less with "What kind of space is it?" than with "What kind of space does it help produce?"[32]

Listening to community radio means engaging with the production of multiple interconnected communities in an actual space, the city, rather than entering into a hyperorchestrated musical surround that simultaneously incites and disperses its listeners. In its interweaving of music, talk, and actuality, community is both named and mobilized as process. By seeking a more activist, informed, and diverse listening audience, community radio reduces the distance between the public and the private meanings of the music.

Canadian aural culture has produced a creative aural vocabulary privileging a sense of shared space. While music is an important part of this vocabulary, few would claim that they can hear a coherent grammar of *musical* difference. There are important exceptions to this oft-perceived absence: the musics of Quebec and Newfoundland; singer-songwriters like Leonard Cohen, Joni Mitchell, Neil Young, and Sarah McLachlan; the new urban country music of kd lang, Blue Rodeo, Cowboy Junkies, Spirit of the West; and so forth. Still, it isn't often one can hear a new piece of music and know that it comes from (English) Canada, unless one knows it already; then such recognition, and any emotional claim that might ensue, comes after the fact. At that point your listening brain has to work to compute the audible traces; it's not necessarily musical, per se, but you know you are hearing something ... a different grain of the voice, perhaps; an empathic, less driven sense of time, more literate and imaginative lyrics; a nostalgic but unsentimental violin; more complex acoustic textures; a sense of space....

But this is English music, actually *white* English music I am describing. What about the others? Is hip-hop or reggae less authentically "Canadian"? As ethnomusicologists of the Americas have realized, residents in the New World are "people whose ways of being share [only] the common quality of a foreign past ... and the long heritage of colonial rule."[33] Our musical landscape can tell us about that past, those migrations, this colonial rule, but only if we know how to listen. We don't know yet whether this makes an audibly "Canadian" sound.

Again: Should we care? If so, why? In her essay "Lesbians and Popular

Music: Does It Matter Who Is Singing?", Barbara Bradby looks to feminist literary theory to explore the question of lesbian identification in popular music. "In the area of popular music," she explains, "it seems that everyday listening practices raise similar puzzles around the performer explores a similar question about of a song as are raised around the author of a text."[34] It's not just that listeners don't "know" automatically whether a singer is or isn't one of them. In the very act of posing the question, they experience, like thoughtful readers of "women's writing," a contradiction between history and desire, between the intellectual recognition that the category "lesbian" is historically constructed and arbitrary, and the emotional need for a "dream of a lesbian nation, even as we recognize its fictionality." Listeners can realize the social nature of mythmaking, Bradby suggests, and still seek an "interplay between personal identity and the identity of a performer, a process which is socially mediated through the everyday practices of the lesbian 'community.'"[35]

We are talking here about another kind of location, but what could be more arbitrarily constructed than Canada? Its music has over time evoked a similar challenge: how to construct both difference and a sense of community in the face of topographically oblivious but still locally compelling globalizing imperatives. While some musicians attribute their sense of difference to the uniqueness of Canadian values, identities, or landscapes, others seek to *produce* difference through interactions between authorship, identity, and community.[36] For these performers and fans, "Such meanings are not simply inherent in musical or song texts, but . . . are embodied in material practices such as the exchange of cassette tapes, deejays' promotion of certain music, dancing at discos."[37] In other words, they identify Canada (and thus themselves) not as a "natural" space with a singular identity, but as intentional or (to return to the language of Lefebvre) as *produced* space, the result of a *project* involving distinct activities and values with respect to location, publics, scale, and community. Because this space is not "naturalized" in terms of history or ethnicity, we do not expect a common identity, a common sound. But this does not prevent us from demanding access to the means to express and communicate.

SPEAKING OF SPACE

This is why radio has been such an important site of musical practice. Its soundscapes teach us not only how to listen (or just as easily how *not* to listen), but also how to use music to make sense of our personal and social locations. Each kind of radio situates listeners and music differently in time and space. For Crane, as we have seen, popular hits act as a "floating totem of public pleasure"; he argues that rock radio's blending of old and new serves as a "continual reminder of one's place in the present state [of rock history]."[38] Its musical flow reminds us of "one's place" in culture through the temporal memory bank of the playlist. The reiteration of musical oldies patterns time in terms of transience and the poignancy of individual memory. Space is simultaneously gathered and fractured, conquered and removed from perception. We forget all this when we listen to music, but remember it when we think about politics. Our "identities" reside somewhere in the movement between this pleasure and this knowledge.[39]

Commercial radio offers currency and nostalgia, opposing sides of the same driven temporality, as a template to organize and mediate our search for place and belonging in the broader cosmology of pop culture. But other types of empowerment can be totemized in sound. Community radio creates pleasure/identity by locating listeners not (only) in relational (present) time, but also in relational (social) space. Radio whose musical flow emphasizes the passing of time via the playlist or hit parade alternately eludes, frustrates, and consoles us through its transitory cycles of currency and memory. Such radio processes space as an abstraction, increasingly so as programs and audiences are rationalized by satellite, syndication, and computerization. Conversely, radio that emphasizes space through its references to/constructions of regional, spatial, and political entities, emphasizes the interconnectedness of cultural location over time, and permits us to speak and know ourselves differently. It's a way of asserting the local "as a space of engagement and affective alliance for musical practice"; as Fenster reminds us, "The local is a critical site for the making and re-making of the social in musical practice."[40]

There are exceptions that confound this otherwise romantic image, of course; leftist songwriters who sing about Nicaragua but not about Canada, or "local" bands that perpetuate racism and misogyny. And attempts to evoke local culture may face opposition from unexpected quarters: kd lang sang bluntly critical neocountry songs about meat, farming, and sexual politics until members of the Alberta legislature, prodded by powerful cattle ranchers and homophobia, sabotaged her local career. Her next album won an award for best female "adult contemporary music" at the U.S. Grammy Awards. Eventually we do bump up somehow against the limits of the "local." For the sense of cultural belonging we draw from local cultures can as easily separate us from as join us to the discourses and entitlements of citizenship and political life.

SCHIZOPHONICS

In Canada, we occupy two dreams simultaneously. One is the dream that we are American; the other is the dream that we are not. The contradiction between the two dreams, lived simultaneously, like a split screen or half-awake hangover, has a definite material form in the structure of cultural production. It's not just that years of negotiation have divided broadcasting and the cultural industries economically and legislatively between the private and the public sectors, unequal partners in a national "single system." In addition, the compromises responsible for this arrangement, like the wizard technology propelling the entire system toward continentalism, speak to us simultaneously as significant achievements of the Canadian nation (and necessary to its survival) in the discourse of politics, and as the triumph of American culture in the discourse of entertainment.

Each of these two dreams has been actualized in a complex technological, economic, and symbolic apparatus whose components all work to reproduce themselves. Because of this dual apparatus our relationship to popular music is ambiguous. Situated in many places at once, tuned in, hooked up, wired into, we see ourselves as part of a global culture, and boundarylessness as the essence of who we are. Thus the frequent gender analogies for Canada in relation to the United States: in feminist analysis, woman is always "Other" to a dominant power in relation to whom she gains (momentary) advantage through submission, becoming consequently untidy in establishing clear boundaries to her self. It is a state that is intimately related to resentment and to silence, and that tends to be articulated, if at all, in a discourse of absence. Thus Canadian culture, manifested in much spoken and unspoken *ressentiment,* is a revenge against the present that preserves its own absence by denying its rage.[41] But of course women have a great deal to say, especially about speaking....

Sound erects few audible boundaries at or around the 49th Parallel, except, for Francophones, the boundary of language. The dream of universal comprehension accompanies corporate expansion, which succeeds on the basis of our pleasure in its beneficent hospitality. Listening to pop music radio means learning to separate our rational concerns about cultural politics from our pleasurable, visceral responses to popular music. Our economy of affections reproduces the identification of popular music with specific notions of fun and pleasure, and the inseparability of these from the American Dream. Yet Canadians believe they are different from Americans in some unclear but important way and wish to maintain that difference. Listening to music reiterates this contradiction, positioning us simultaneously in different, even opposing, sociomusico-mediated spaces.

The paradoxical nature of the cultural apparatus finds its analogue, then, in the paradoxical subjectivity with which we respond to music. The concept of "cultural technologies" requires us to pose the analogue more forcefully. Listeners, musical texts, and mediating institutions like radio form a complex structure of mutually determining practices. Tensions between international capital and nation states are not abstractions divorced from processes of cultural formation or deformation. Aside from their economic materiality and their consequences for everyday life, each of these powers employs its own means to elicit our desire, to win our allegiance to its myths and pleasures. The multiplicity of our musical subjectivity locates us as subjects of both capital and state, and of the contest between them. Fluctuating daily, hourly, between the uplifting seductions of Crane's "Tower of Babel," the earnest diversities of local invention, and the articulate dialogues of the CBC, we reproduce the historic double bind of our national construction. The only way to resolve this contradictory state is to engage in transformative practices, devising other strategies of electronic reproduction, making music, and engaging in broader discourses about sound. The goal of musical "authenticity" refers no longer to a point of origin (for this is no longer possible) but to a site of reflexivity in action.

LOCATING LISTENING

"That is why this apparently modest notion (*listening* does not figure in the encyclopedias of the past, it belongs to no acknowledged discipline) is finally like a little theatre on whose stage those two modern deities, one bad and one good, confront each other: power and desire."[42]

A theory of the contradictory nature of location as both context and effect of cultural consumption is crucially important. Otherwise no account of the role of popular culture in modernization, no recognition of the diverse roles of nation-states, and no analysis of the complex interaction between popular culture and imperialism is possible. This does not mean we can identify a coherent listening audience in terms of geographical, national, or any other location. Only commercial demographers, commercial broadcasters, and the CBC do that.[43] The coherence represented by any one of these constructions is tenuous indeed. To the extent that their purpose is to represent collective identity as a unified totality, each construction is a work of ideology, continuously disassembled by the famous creative disloyalty of listeners, for whom "freedom of listening is as necessary as freedom of speech."[44]

But the conflicts thereby disguised are not random, arbitrary ones. The tensions between local and/or national identities and the structured discourses of international entertainment represent a pivotal and quite tangible site of conflict in the context of contemporary cultural politics. For some, the presence of Canadian music—whether white, Native, African or Afro-American, or many others—on radio or television becomes the electronic equivalent of land claims on the ground. The issue is not musical "quality," antipathy to mainstream music, or nationalism. It concerns rather the question of whether place, location, the local, however musical communities choose to define that place, are to be valorized as sources for language. To the extent that they are not, the issue of territory is erased, made abstract; Lefebvre calls this the production of reproducible space. Reproducible space is continuously made abstract in accordance with the laws of capital, which, seeking to render ever more spaces interchangeable, seeks to dominate modes of consumption and production and to render other spaces devoid of agency.[45] To the extent that location is not valorized as a site or subject of language, entertainment reproduces itself in a condition of reification, for pleasure then defines itself as the exclusion of everything but itself, a privileged discursive feature of both patriarchy and imperialism.

NOTES

1. Lefebvre, H. (1991). *The production of space* (D. Nicholson-Smith, Trans.). Oxford: Basil Blackwell, pp. 28–29. I take up this theme at greater length in my forthcoming book, *Cultural technologies and the production of space*. Minneapolis: University of Minnesota Press.

2. "As music is colonized by the commodity form—its use becomes the exchangeability of its uses—listeners regress to the point where they will not listen to that which is not recognizable without first protecting themselves with an inoculation for the exotic" (Mowitt, J. [1987]. The sound of music in the era of its electronic reproducibility. In R. Leppert & S. McClary [Eds.], *Music and society: The politics of composition, performance and reception*. New York: Cambridge University Press, p. 187.).

3. My use of the terms "space" and "place" follows David Harvey, who argues that power derives from the ability to turn space into place. This is part of the enormous power that music has for us today. However much it generally accomplishes this end in a more fundamental sense, we westerners invest it with high emotional stakes because we need its help to do this. For Harvey, "space . . . is a metaphor for a site or container of power which usually constrains but sometimes liberates processes of *Becoming*" *(The condition of postmodernity.* [1989]. Oxford: Basil Blackwell, p. 213.). Lefebvre reiterates this when he writes: "In addition to being a means of production [space] is also a means of control, and hence of domination, of power; yet that, as such, it escapes in part from those who would make use of it" (Lefebvre, *The production of space*, p. 26).

4. Frith, S. (1988). *Music for pleasure*. New York: Routledge, p. 139.

5. Foucault, M. (1986). Of other spaces. *Diacritics, 16*(1), 22–27, quotation from p. 23.

6. Mowitt, The work of music in the age of electronic reproduction. In R. Leppert & S. McClary (Eds.), *Music and society: The politics of composition, performance, and reception*, pp. 176–177.

7. Hennion, A., & Meadel, C. (1986). Programming music: Radio as mediator. *Media, Culture, and Society, 8,* 281–303, quotation from p. 186.

8. Berland, J. (1992). Angels dancing: Cultural technologies and the production of space. In L. Grossberg, C. Nelson, & P. Treichler (Eds.), *Cultural studies.* New York: Routledge, p. 40.

9. It is not clear here how much Mowitt understands "technological" and "commercial" as identical, interchangeable, or interdependent forces, a point I would like to take up here but must leave aside for another occasion.

10. Theberge, P. (1995). What's that sound? Listening to popular music, revisited. In W. Straw, S. Johnson, R. Sullivan, & P. Friedlander (Eds.), *Popular music: Style and identity.* Montreal: Centre for Research on Canadian Cultural Industries and Institutions, McGill University, p. 276.

11. Murray Schafer uses the term "schizophonia" to describe the separation of sound from its source, and its effects (Schafer, R. M. [1986]. *The thinking ear.* Toronto: Arcana Editions, p. 139.).

12. Frith, S. (1987). Towards an aesthetic of popular music. In R. Leppert & S. McClary (Eds.), *Music and society: The politics of composition, performance, and reception.* New York: Cambridge University Press, p. 139.

13. Frith, *Music for pleasure.*

14. Crane, J. (1986). Mainstream music and the masses. *Journal of Communication Inquiry, 10*(3), 66–70.

15. See, e.g., Bashevkin, who shows that "a majority of the Canadian public, particularly since the mid-1960s, have supported the culturally nationalist positions of federal royal commissions," but that "American dominance in the areas of publishing and film has been only marginally challenged by federal government policy even though successive ministers of communications have promised more assertive nationalist regulations" (Bashevkin, S. [1986]. Does public opinion matter?: The adoption of federal royal commission and task force recommendations on the national question, 1951–1987. *Canadian Public Administration, 31*[1], 390–407, quotation from pp. 399–400.).

16. Audley, P. (1984). *Canada's cultural industries.* Toronto: Lorimer. Canada Department of Communications. (1987). *Vital links: Canadian cultural industries.* Ottawa: Supply and Services. Berland, J., & Straw, W. (1988). Report on the Canadian music industry (a). Summary of interviews (Windsor, Ontario) (b). International Communications and Youth Culture Consortium, 1987. Summarized in E. Buck, M. Cuthbert, & D. Robinson, *Music at the margins: Popular music and national cultures.* Newbury Park, Calif.: Sage. (Original work published 1987). Straw, W. (1993). The English Canadian recording industry since 1970. In T. Bennett, S. Frith, L. Grossberg, J. Shepherd, & G. Turner (Eds.), *Rock and popular music: Politics, policies, and institutions.* London: Routledge. Straw offers a useful portrait of Canada's recording industry; as he observes, "While record distribution has emerged, over the last twenty years, as the activity through which oligopolistic control is most effectively ensured, particularities of the Canadian situation have magnified its importance. The geographical expanse of Canada and the existence of two distinct linguistic communities has encouraged the development of distribution operations which are either regional in scope (such as those operating within Quebec), or directed towards dispersed, international markets (such as those for

dance music recordings). Most Canadian-owned distributors have confined themselves to such markets, leaving pan-national distribution as the province of multinational firms operating in Canada" (Straw, The English Canadian recording industry, p. 58).

17. Straw comments that "just as until recently government regulators have used the broadcasting system as the exclusive channel through which support for Canadian recordings might be directed, recorded music in Canada has been studied primarily in terms of its role as programming for this system" (Straw, The English Canadian recording industry, pp. 55–56).

18. For a survey of recent policies in film, publishing, and recorded music, see Berland, J., & Straw, W. (1994). Getting down to business: Cultural politics and policies. In B. Singer (Ed.), *Communication in Canadian society* (4th rev. ed.). Toronto: Copp Clark.

19. Laroche, K. (1988). *The sound recording development program: Making music to maintain hegemony.* Unpublished master's thesis, Carleton University. Wright, R. (1991). "Gimme shelter": Observations on cultural protectionism and the recording industry in Canada. *Cultural Studies, 5*(3), 306–316.

20. Mowitt, The sound of music, p. 178.

21. My approach to space and time is elaborated more fully in "Radio Space and Industrial Time" (Berland, J. [1994]. Radio space and industrial time: The case of music formats. In B. Diamond & R. Witmer [Eds.], *Canadian music: Issues of hegemony and identity.* Toronto: Canadian Scholars' Press. [Original work published 1993 in T. Bennett, S. Frith, L. Grossberg, J. Shepherd, & G. Turner (Eds.), *Rock and popular music: Politics, policies, and institutions.* London: Routledge.]) and in "Angels Dancing" (see note 8). It draws on Harold Innis's notion that all societies seek to reproduce and expand by organizing the dissemination of knowledge over time and/or space. Contemporary industrial societies privilege the mobility and speed of space-biased media and thus endanger the duration of oral histories and local cultures. The time–space paradigm combines media analysis, studies of the production of knowledge, and colonial history.

22. My use of this felicitous phrase—the canonization of the junior branch—derives from Tony Bennett's *Marxism and Form* (1980; London: Methuen).

23. Frith, *Music for pleasure,* p. 3.

24. Lehr, J. (1985). As Canadian as possible . . . under the circumstances: Regional myths, images of place and national identity in Canadian country music. *Border/lines, 2,* 16–19.

25. Kuhn, A. (1994). *Women's pictures: Feminism and cinema.* (2nd ed.). London: Routledge & Kegan Paul, p. 50.

26. Cf. Local Radio Workshop. (1983). *Nothing local about it: London's local radio.* London: Comedia. Berland, Radio space.

27. Of course "the local" can signify any number of alternative locations. In his taxonomy of "local" music practices, John Street identifies several discourses through which significance is attached to place: locality as industrial base, as social experience, as aesthetic perspective, as community, as scene, as political experience, etc. (Street, J. [1995]. [Dis]located? Rhetoric, politics, meaning, and the locality. In W. Straw, S. Johnson, R. Sullivan, & P. Friedlander [Eds.], *Popular music—Style and identity.* Montreal: Centre for Research on Canadian Cultural Industries and

Institutions, McGill University.). Sara Cohen adds that "locality could be a useful term for popular music studies if it is used to imply a particular methodological orientation, and a particular relationship between the spatial, the social, and the conceptual" (Cohen, S. [1995]. Localizing sound. In W. Straw, S. Johnson, R. Sullivan, & P. Friedlander [Eds.], *Popular music—Style and identity.* Montreal: Centre for Research on Canadian Cultural Industries and Institutions, McGill University, p. 61.). Clearly, different "locations" formulate diverse investments around the concept and the practice of the local. My account seeks to explain and analyze how radio became an important site for this investment in urban Canada.

28. Anderson, B. (1991). *Imagined communities: Reflections on the origin and spread of nationalism.* London: Verso. Cf. Toby Miller: "[The public presentation of identity] is far from a purely economic issue. The state's legitimacy is often drawn from its capacity to speak for its citizens, to be their vocalizing agent. This is achieved, depending on the type of society, at least in part through the doctrine of nations, the concept of a particular space defined by the state itself but informed affectively by a sense of cultural belonging" (*The well-tempered self [1993].* Baltimore: Johns Hopkins University Press, p. 24.).

29. Charland, M. (1986). Technological nationalism. *Canadian Journal of Political and Social Theory,* 10(1–2), 196–220.

30. The Canadian Broadcasting Corporation (CBC) has two national radio networks. The FM network features classical music; the AM network features a changing format of music programs and talk shows, dramas, and documentaries. In this discussion I focus on the latter, and necessarily bracket the privileging of classical music that occurred in the (post)colonial radiophonic enactment of "public interest." This was the subject of my PhD dissertation (Berland, J. [1986]. *Cultural re/percussions: The social production of music broadcasting in Canada.* York University, Toronto, Canada.).

31. Crisell, A. (1986). *Understanding radio.* London: Methuen, p. 17. Local Radio Workshop, Nothing local about it, p. 39.

32. I owe this formulation to Dale Bradley, who explores its implications for cyberspace in his unpublished PhD thesis, *Situating cyberspace* (1998). York University, Toronto, Canada.

33. Robbins, J. (1994). What can we learn when they sing, eh? Ethnomusicology in the American state of Canada. In B. Diamond & R. Witmer (Eds.), *Canadian music: Issues of hegemony and identity.* Toronto: Canadian Scholars' Press, p. 193.

34. Bradby, B. (1995). Lesbians and popular music: Does it matter who is singing? In W. Straw, S. Johnson, R. Sullivan, & P. Friedlander (Eds.), *Popular music—Style and identity.* Montreal: Centre for Research on Canadian Cultural Industries and Institutions, McGill University, p. 33.

35. Ibid., p. 34.

36. In a survey of (Anglophone) musicians conducted in Windsor, Ontario, a number of patterns emerged that may be characteristic of Canadian musicians. Asked about musical preferences and influences, only 12% made reference to Canadian nationality, while 18% named Canadian bands as models without mentioning their nationality. While there are musical features to such identification, its source is not primarily musical. Where such consciousness is expressed, it is likely (according to these sources) to have been affected by experience rather than by

music; by travels in Canada's North, by "wild, untouched nature," or by "northern people and culture."

37. Bradby, Lesbians and popular music, p. 35.

38. Crane, Mainstream music and the masses, p. 68.

39. I wonder if this could be conceived as a different version of the "bifocality" that Lipsitz and Cohen (Cohen, Localizing sound, p. 62) describe in immigrant cultures: a "common experience of being 'betwixt and between,'" but without having to leave the country.

40. Fenster, M. (1995). Two stories: Where exactly is the local? In W. Straw, S. Johnson, R. Sullivan, & P. Friedlander (Eds.), *Popular music—Style and identity*. Montreal: Centre for Research on Canadian Cultural Industries and Institutions, p. 86.

41. Dorland, M. (1987). A thoroughly hidden country: *Ressentiment* in Canadian culture. *Canadian Journal of Political and Social Theory*, 12(1–2), 130–164.

42. Barthes, R., & Havas, R. (1985). Listening. In R. Barthes, *The responsibility of forms: Critical essays on music, art, and representation*. New York: Hill and Wang, p. 260.

43. See, e.g., Eaman, R. (1994). *Channels of influence: CBC audience research and the Canadian public*. Toronto: University of Toronto Press.

44. Barthes & Havas, Listening.

45. Lefebvre, H. (1979). Space: Social product and use value. In J. W. Freiberg (Ed.), *Critical sociology*. New York: Irvington. See also Lefebvre, *The production of space*.

6

BORDERLINES
Bilingual Terrain in Scottish Song

STEVE SWEENEY-TURNER

> Amid decay lies the best soil of Renascence.
> —Patrick Geddes

A POLYGLOSSIC POSTMODERNITY

Scotland stands at the forefront of sociological concerns in the late twentieth century. Rather than being an awkward, ill-fitting case, it is at the centre of the discipline's postmodern dilemma.[1]

Scotland—like Switzerland—is (and always has been) a multi-lingual community—a "multi-ethnic" country, and the various strands of its popular tradition necessarily reflect this chequered linguistic past.[2]

Against any notion that Scottish culture is locked in some insular historical retardation outside the currents of contemporary politics, the sociologist David McCrone contends that the current "national question" places it firmly within the mainstream of postmodern concerns. Against any notion of a "national essence," the ethnographer Hamish Henderson contends that the linguistic and ethnic culture of Scotland is, and always has been, a multiplicity: multilingual, multiethnic.

In contemporary Scotland, we find three "indigenous" linguistic practices in parallel use: Scots, English, and Gàidhlig.[3] This polyglossic situation could in itself be enough to justify McCrone's reference to postmodernity, and could equally justify a lengthy sojourn with postcolonial theories of language. However, the question directly addressed below is how *just two* of these linguistic practices—Scots and English—react together within one of the most crucial cultural focal points within Scottish society.

The complex and resonant issues at stake here begin with the problematic of the ontological and political status of language. In locating ourselves within the margins of this border—the borderlines between Scots and English—it will be first a question of difference, but then, more critically, a question of certain differential strategies that can be used to cut across, through, and between the strict boundary lines required by ontological difference.

Following Henderson's cue, the site upon which these two linguistic territories will be interrogated is that of "popular tradition"—specifically, that of Scottish *song,* which has been a site of contestation throughout its entirety. In tracing across this cultural terrain (songs in Scots, songs in English, and songs that traverse or transgress the border between the two) the "production of place" within the space of music—the space of the language of song—will become a crucial problematic.

DECENTERING ONTOLOGIES OF LANGUAGE

> Let us be clear: there is no such thing as a Scottish language. It is true that in Scotland certain words and usages prevail that are not common to standard English, but this does not make it a language.[4]

> The unique characteristics of Scots ... its linguistic distinctiveness, its occupation of its own "dialect-island" bounded by the Border, its individual history, its own dialect variation ... —all of these are attributes of a language rather than a dialect. Manifestly Scots is to be seen as much more than simply another dialect of English.[5]

Here we have rival inscriptions of the borderlines between Scots and English: either Scots is a dialect of the English language; or Scots is a language separate from English, with its own internal dialects. Both views are motivated by opposing ideological forces, the former Unionist, the latter Nationalist. Yet both play out their battles within the same ontological space, within one and the same theoretical border. For each argument, there is no doubt whatsoever about the distinction between the categories of *language* and *dialect,* where languages are structures that encapsulate a series of lesser sublanguages, termed dialects. As a result, a *language* carries more ontological, political, and cultural significance than a *dialect.*

Within this ontology, the necessity for a nationalist agenda to prove the *linguistic,* rather than *dialectal,* status of Scots is clear—if Scots is a dialect of English, then Scotland is, by implication, a natural *subset* of the larger nation that would rule it by natural right. If, on the other hand, Scots is a language in its own right, then its attendant nation is accorded the natural right to self-determination.[6]

Politics, both cultural and constitutional, are played out within this ontological frame—a frame that is in turn framed by the institutional denial of official recognition to Scots at all levels, despite its previous historical claims to institutional hegemony.[7] At the institutional level, then, it becomes a question of strategy. As the French theorists Gilles Deleuze and Félix Guattari note:

> Even politically, especially politically, it is difficult to see how the upholders of a minor language can operate if not by giving it (if only by writing in it) a constancy and homogeneity making it a locally major language capable of forcing official recognition (hence the political role of writers who assert the rights of a minor language).[8]

But within Deleuze and Guattari's thought, there is a subtle swerve away from the ontological strictures that customarily circumscribe "the language question." Their two concepts here—"major" and "minor"—do not denote ontological categories as such, but instead "two possible treatments of the same language."[9] From this perspective, the argument is not whether Scots, for instance, actually *is,* in its ontological Being, a language or a dialect, but what kind of *operations* it can enter into in a given set of circumstances. From one direction, it is a question of *making* a "minor" language—a politically marginalized language—into a "major" language within a certain "local" frame. In this sense, ideologically motivated strategies can lead to a change in the institutional status of a linguistic practice; in other words, this status is not a fixed absolute, but is actively created by a political context. The institutional status of a linguistic practice is as variable as political structures themselves; there are no structural invariants.

From another direction, however, there is a certain interventional role that "minor" languages can play within the frame of "major" languages. For Deleuze and Guattari, this situation is "more compelling": "Take the way Gaelic and Irish English set English in variation. Or take the way Black English and any number of 'ghetto languages' set American English in variation, to the point that New York is virtually a city without a language."[10] Thus, for Deleuze and Guattari, it is not so much the case that "major" languages *successfully* govern "minor" ones, but that "minor" languages ceaselessly eat away at the margins of "major" languages, and therefore have the power to overwhelm them within a generalized multiplicity. Taking this idea further, Deleuze and Guattari argue that "the more a language has or acquires the characteristics of a major language, the more it is affected by continuous variations that transpose it into a 'minor' language."[11]

Taking a musical metaphor for their cue, Deleuze and Guattari contrast the organicist view of variation represented by the Schönbergian concept of *developing variation* with their own concept of *continuous variation,* a form of variation that is not teleological, not governed by an overall formal design, but that continues unabated despite all attempts to form it into a developed, static whole. *Continuous* variation is that which loosens and remobilizes the structural invariants required by *developing* variation. In the linguistic context, the attempt to establish a "major" language—a univocal, hegemonic structure—nevertheless leads to a situation where the "minor" languages it attempts to "speak" for begin to chip away at its uniform veneer. According to Deleuze and Guattari, it is always the case that marginalized languages (which are always multiple, as against the singularity attempted by and claimed for "major" languages) will rub up against the centralized language that claims to "speak" for them, and actively interfere with its structure, opening its singularity out once more into a field of multiplicities, or *minorities.*

Another kind of destructuralizing intervention is suggested by the writer W. N. Herbert, this one specifically within the context of the Scots–English axis:

> Scots is not a copy of English, matching the integrity of English orthography and dictionary definitions, it is an active criticism of such orthodoxies, a deconstruction by example . . . an attempt at the dehierarchisation of linguistic hegemony . . . . Scots is a language capable of doing something more than English; that criticises and, finally, extends English.[12]

Translating Herbert's argument into Deleuze and Guattari's terms, the "minority" of Scots actively intervenes in the "majoritarian" pretensions of English, and sends it spinning centripetally away from its centralizing tendency. According to Herbert, Scots is continually poised to effect a *deconstruction* of majoritarian linguistic orthodoxies. Yet, however far we are willing to accept this particular formulation of the question—however politically appealing it may appear to be—extreme caution should not be left aside. Not least since, if Scots does engage with English in a deconstructive, or even a crypto-deconstructive manner, then it is surely bound up in the problematic of remaining immanent to the text that it critiques.

As Derrida himself acknowledges: "It is a question of explicitly and systematically posing the problem of the status of a discourse which borrows from a heritage the resources necessary for the deconstruction of that heritage itself. A problem of *economy* and *strategy.*"[13]

More specific to our current endeavor is Hamish Henderson's work on the language of Scots ballads—work that is rarely read within a poststructuralist context, and yet which, as we will see, has certain resonances with both Deleuze and Guattari, and with Derrida. Henderson identifies a "formalized" Scots distinct from the vernacular, a "formal" Scots reserved for ballad and folk art in general. This form of Scots he terms *ballad-Scots,* and poses its problematics entirely within the immanence of its relationship to the "major" language of English:

> a curious "bilingualism in one language" has been a characteristic of Scots folk-song at least since the beginning of the seventeenth century ... a flexible formulaic language which grazes ballad-English along the whole of its length, and yet remains clearly identifiable as a distinct folk-literary lingo.... In the folk field.... Scots may be said to include English and go beyond it.[14]

In other words, ballad-Scots utilizes elements of English, effectively raiding the border between the two linguistic practices in order to expand its own structure—decentering itself while simultaneously exceeding the structure of English. In this, we can see Henderson's theory resonating along with Deleuze and Guattari's notion of the continuous variation that "minor" languages can subject their "major" neighbors to. Here, ballad-Scots cuts across the idea of absolute boundaries between linguistic singularities, and effects displacements along the lines of what postcolonial theories of language might refer to as an *interlanguage* or a *creole continuum.*[15]

In this, it is also very much "a problem of *economy* and *strategy*" of the kind posed by Derrida: if Scots, in its "critique" of the codes of "major" English, must remain to some extent *immanent to* the object of its "critique," then what effect does this immanence have upon its status as a discourse? Ultimately, in traversing the field of this question, it may turn out that the answer is not quite so politically appealing as writers such as Herbert suggest. In order to effect this traversal, it is time to engage with specifics.

THE TRANSGLOSSIC BALLAD

In order to examine these concepts, an analytical survey of textual practices within Scottish song is in order. Initially, we will follow Henderson's cue and consider the language of ballads in terms of its appropriation of English elements within the body of Scots.

The following is a transcription from a recording of Alison McMorland's version of "The Cruel Mither":

INTRO.	In Logan's Woods, aye an Logan's Braes A helped ma bonny lassie on wi her claes First her hose an then her shuin She gar me the slip when I was done
Stanza 1	She laid her back against a thorn There she has twa bonny bairns born *There she has twa bonny bairns born* *Doun by the greenwood sidey, O*
Stanza 2	She's put her ribbon frae aff her hair She chokit them till they grat sair *She chokit them till they grat sair* *Doun by the greenwood sidey, O*
Stanza 3	She's dug a hole baith lang an deep She's buriet them where nane cuid see *She's buriet them whaur nane cuid see* etc. . . .
Stanza 4	Right wanely has she gane hame That nane might meddle wi her fair fame. . .
Stanza 5	For days an weeks she wes pale an wan But she thocht, O, there's nane cuid tell . . .
Stanza 6	As she was sat at yon castle waa She saw twa bonny bairns playin at a baa . . .
Stanza 7	"O, bairns, bairns, if ye were mine A'd gie ye cou milk an reid wine . . . "
Stanza 8	"O, mither, mither, we wance were thine Ye didnae gie us cou milk an reid wine" *Ye didna gie us cou milk an reid wine* . . .
Stanza 9	"Ye put yer ribbon frae aff yer hair Ye chokit us till we grat sair . . . "
Stanza 10	"O, bairns, bairns, come tell me true Whit the future hauds fer you *Whit the future hauds for you* . . . "
Stanza 11	"O, mither, mither, we ken richt weel Tis we in heaven, in heaven must dwell An ye maun dread the fierce fires o hell *Doun by the greenwood sidey, O*."[16]

Throughout McMorland's version, linguistic codes are in continuous variation, transgressing the boundaries between Scots and English; her linguistic practice is, to coin a term, *transglossic*. The two main characteristics of this fringe of contact and displacement are (1) the interpolation of English words into the body of Scots, and (2) the juxtaposition of English and Scots forms of the same word. Of course, in order to establish the processes involved here, a certain questionably strict ontological division between Scots and English is required a priori, before we can begin to investigate the kind of mutual "grazing" of these practices that Henderson posits. Even more problematically, in order to effect an analysis within Henderson's terms, one almost inevitably has to rely (even if only in parentheses) on a concept of an ur-Scots in *opposition* to ur-English Received Pronunciation (R.P.; Queen's English). Not surprisingly, this leads to a highlighting of certain problematics in Henderson's thought—not least with regard to the question of which version of Scots one would base one's ur-language on, since Scots is a linguistic practice with no standard orthography and no R.P. dialect carrying more institutional power than any other. However, for the time being, let us suspend these questions (but only provisionally) and adopt a pseudo-Hendersonian mode of analysis in order to eventually arrive at a kind of interrogation of his concepts.

Analyzing McMorland's version of "The Cruel Mither" stanza by stanza, the following pattern emerges:

Introduction: juxtaposition of Scots personal pronoun "A" in line 2 with English form "I" in line 4. Equally, in line 4, substitution of English "was" for Scots "wes" (pron. "wiz"), and English "done" for expected rhyme on Scots "dune"/"duin."

Stanza 1: the least transgressive stanza, being well within the accepted common space between Scots and English. Aside from the refrain, only one word is specifically Scots here: "twa" (both "bonny" and "bairn" appear in N.English dialects).

Stanza 2: line 1, English "put" for Scots "pit," although its usage remains Scots, and in English proper would be "taken."

Stanza 3: as in stanza 1, we find both Scots and English forms of the same word—in this case, English "where" in line 2, which, on repetition in line 3, shifts to Scots "whaur."

Stanza 4: line 1, English "right" for Scots "richt." Line 2, English "might" for Scots "micht." Note also the substitution of English "*-ght*" for Scots "*-cht.*"

Stanza 5: line 2, reinstated Scots "*-cht*" in "thocht."

Stanza 6: line 1, English "was" for Scots "wes." Line 2, arguably, grammatical substitution of English "saw" for Scots "seen."

Stanza 7: line 1, English "if" for Scots "gin"/"gif."

Stanza 8: two different forms of the same Scots word: line 2, "didnae," changing on repetition to "didna" in line 3.

Stanza 9: line 1, "put," as in Stanza 3.
Stanza 10: line 2, Scots "fer," changing to English "for," line 3.
Stanza 11: line 2, English "must," changing to Scots "maun" in line 3.

Clearly, what we have here is a case of the "bilingualism within one language" that Henderson refers to as characteristic of ballad-Scots. What emerges here is a debatable territory between the linguistic regions of Scots and English, where the one appropriates certain forms from the other in order to achieve specific aesthetic affects. Indubitably, the greatest challenge to the stability of a particular language—whether it is viewed as "major" or "minor"—is presented by these strategies that organize the slippage from one linguistic practice into another.

Yet, while Henderson's "bilingualism within one language" is not in doubt here, the question of a political dimension to these practices has not yet been fully addressed. Does this transglossic practice really represent a kind of "deconstruction by example" of the "major" language of English? Can it be said that English is fully decentered here? How far does Scots approach English here in order to "set English in variation"? Surely the specific appropriation of English that sets up what Henderson calls the "formulaic" character of ballad-Scots rests on the assumption that English is a more formal and literary language than Scots, that is, that by accessing English, one accesses a "higher" linguistic register?

However, as Deleuze and Guattari state, as soon as a "minor" language is designated locally as a "major" language, it immediately becomes subject itself to the "continuous variations" that it used to inject into the body of its neighboring "major" languages. Perhaps what we have here is a formulation of an anglophilic dialect within Scots as a locally "major" language—a case of English as a now "minor" language that sends Scots itself into variation. Whatever the answer may be to this problem, or whether it can only be posed as an undecidable problematic, it is clear that the political ramifications are at best fractious for all sides of the debate around the "language question."

TOWARD A POLITICS

While Henderson focuses primarily on the ballad repertoire (a focus reflected in his term "ballad-Scots"), the practices that he draws attention to are prevalent within Scottish song in general.[17] Exactly the same kinds of substitutions are to be found, for example, in the popular bourgeois genre of "National Songs" from the 19th century in particular. It is here that the politics of linguistic practice within Scottish song becomes highly problematic, since with this genre, Victorian sentimentality and pseudo-nostalgia for the pastoral come to the fore, expressed specifically through the use of Scots lexis. In this, rather than acting as a "deconstruction by example," or even as a displasive force of variation, Scots comes to act as the perpetrator of its own minority, and dialectically upholds the majority of English. This is not so much a deconstruction of linguistic orthodoxies as a *reconstruction* of them.

Such a linguistic problematic can be seen from the following popular song, "The Auld House," by the prolific songwriter Lady Caroline Oliphant Nairne (1766–1845).[18] Artistically, with "The Auld House" (see Figure 6.1), we are indubitably a far cry from the classic ballads such as "The Cruel Mither," but at the same time it can be shown that—at the linguistic level—its politics revolve around similar axes.

Verse 1	The auld house, the auld house,
	What tho' the rooms were wee!
	Oh, kind hearts were dwelling there,
	An' bairnies fu' o' glee.
	The wild rose and the jessamine,
	Still hang upon the wa'.
	How many cherish'd memories
	Do they, sweet flow'rs, reca'!
Chorus	The auld laird, the auld laird,
	Sae canty, kind, and crouse;
	How many did he welcome to
	His ain wee dear auld house
	And the leddy too, sae genty,
	There shelter'd Scotland's heir,
	And clipt a lock wi' her ain hand,
	Frae his lang yellow hair.[19]

Within the terms of Henderson's "bilingualism within one language," note how the dynamics of the relationship between "major" English and "minor" Scots operate here: Scots is hardly used as a displasive force (even of resistance) against the majoritarian tendencies of English. What we have here is perhaps a slight but nevertheless far-reaching shift from the possibility of ballad-Scots as an anglophile dialect of Scots. Indeed, in Nairne's work, the overall feel of the language is quite English—Scots words crop up more as dialectal elements of English than as canonic terms in their own right. This occurs not least in the use of apostrophes to signify certain canonically Scots terms as truncations of their English counterparts, as in *fu'* (for "full") and *wa'* (for "wall")—a tendency shared by many "dialect" songwriters, Robert Burns included. This orthography of diminution is matched by the domestic image of "bairnies fu' o' glee" surrounding "the auld laird, sae canty, kind, and crouse" who lives with his aged "leddy" in

FIGURE 6.1. From "The Auld House," arranged by Adam Hamilton in his parlour song collection, *The Scottish Orpheus: A Collection of the Most Admired Songs of Scotland* (Edinburgh: Paterson, n.d.).

their "ain wee dear auld house" (see Figure 6.2). "Auld fowks an' bairnies"—the rural domestic scene is defined as a double past, with the narrator recalling her own childhood while at the same time identifying with the old folk of that childhood—two pasts that sentimentally elide to provide an organic continuity between the generations.

In "The Auld House," Nairne's concerns are very much within the frame of the genre that later became known as *kailyaird*—a genre within literature and song notorious for its trivialization of Scots. Kailyard operates through a representation of Scottish culture that is essentially conservative. The term itself signifies the traditional kitchen garden of the country croft (lit., "cabbage-yard"), and the term's aesthetic ramifications are drawn from this association. As a genre of song and literature, its predominant themes are (1) sentimentalization of rural life; (2) sentimentalisation of the lower classes (who are always happy with their simple lot); (3) celebration of the domestic scene (childhood, motherhood, old age); (4) valorization of the benevolence and rectitude of the upper classes; (5) praise for the righteousness of Presbyterian morality; (6) rejection of all forms of modernity; (7) condemnation of transgressions; and so forth. Linguistically,

The auld house! the auld house
What tho' the rooms were wee
Kind hearts were dwelling there,
Au' bairnies fu' o' glee.

THE AULD HOUSE O' GASK
The birth place of Lady Nairne.

The auld house, the auld house
Deserted tho' ye be,
There ne'er can be a new house
Will seem sae fair to me.

FIGURE 6.2. From "The Auld House," arranged by Adam Hamilton, *The Scottish Orpheus: A Collection of the Most Admired Songs of Scotland* (Edinburgh: Paterson, n.d.). In this collection Nairne's song appears first, preceded only by an engraving of "The Auld House o' Gask, The birth place of Lady Nairne," and the lines of the first stanza. This baronial mansion, however, is ill described by the lines "The auld house! the auld house / What tho' the rooms were wee."

kailyaird represents Scottish culture within a particularly British unionist, imperialist context: English is the language of the manor house, the church, and the school (the official, public, spiritual and educated life), while Scots is reserved for use by children, the aged, peasants, village idiots, and the like (innocence through ignorance—lack of sophistication in general).[20]

Nairne's "The Auld House" indubitably anticipates the concerns of kailyaird; indeed, her work overall can easily be read as one of the main determinants of its eventual development. According to Derek Scott, in his study of Victorian bourgeois song, Nairne's work is "an innocuous blend of romantic and sentimental Jacobitism."[21] However, the apparent innocuity of her work, when viewed from within the politics of language, is underscored by a serious irony. The irony, of course, is the disjunction between her overt nationalism[22] and her sentimentalization of Scots which constantly sways over the edge of trivialization, continually bordering on and anticipating kailyaird.[23]

No doubt class politics come into play here over and above national politics as such. By the 19th century, the Scottish gentry almost exclusively spoke English, and so Scots was, for them, at once the symbol of a lost historical moment and of a contemporary primitivism, symbol of a fallen Golden Age now preserved incompletely in the mouths of the lower classes. Again and again, the obituary of Scots was written in song collections garnered from "the folk" and edited by the middle and upper classes. Again and again, the question of preserving the once noble tongue was addressed at the moment of its apparently final spluttering. Again and again, the literary use of Scots signals a retreat from contemporaneity and a sentimental recourse to a lost state of grace: childhood, the Jacobite cause, the pastoralized–anglicized Gàidhealtachd, the heroic struggles of the past. Yet, again and again, despite the avowedly nationalist content of much of this work (from Ramsay through Burns to the lesser figures of Tannahill, Nairne, and beyond), the result was a gradual filtering out of Scots lexis and grammar, operating hand in hand with an increasing shift toward accepting anglocentric orthographic norms—a systematic process of anglicization in order to edit Scots song for a polite audience with its model of civilization as the capital city of the British Empire, and the nostalgic Scots diaspora of that empire as its market. Nairne and her contemporaries, in direct contrast to their ideological claims, represent both the continuation of a Scottish linguistic identity *and* its simultaneous erasure. Trivial their songs may be, but certainly not innocuous.

CONTEMPORARY STRATEGIES

These themes are carried through to the linguistic strategies of contemporary Scottish songwriting, whether in folk or rock genres. One of the most important songwriters who uses Scots today (mostly *outwith* folk genres) is Michael Marra, whose work emerges from the blues and soul traditions of Dundee. Marra's work raises further issues within the shifting perspective on language offered by Deleuze and Guattari's concepts of "major" and "minor" language, not least in terms of the question of further "minor" languages within Scots. Since the gradual decline of the "standard" Metropolitan Scots of the 16th century, one of the mainstays of the poetic and song traditions in Scots has been the use of local dialects. Marra's use of Scots tends to be within the Dundonian dialect, as, for instance, in the piece "O Penitence"[24] (which refers to the massacre at Dundee by the English Cromwellian army under General Monk in 1651):

Chorus	O Penitence O Penitence
	O harsh eternity
	Though Monk may hae the devils hands
	The deil himsel' he sprung fae me
Verse 1	When General Monk unpacked his trunk
	The devils a' gaed free
	And a hellish trail o' broken haids
	Was scattered ower Dundee[25]

Here, for example, we have the vernacular form "fae" in place of the more literary "frae," and also substitutions of Dundonian "haid" for standard "heid," and so on. This, added to Marra's characteristically gravelly delivery in a Dundonian accent, forms a specific regional linguistic identity within the overall body of Scots. Marra's own position on this issue is entirely couched within the question of regionalism. Of "O Penitence," he has said: "I never at any stage of the game thought of that as bein Scots—I only thought of it as bein Dundee, which A'm completely comfortable with. But in ither parts of Scotland, ye can't get away with it, ye know?"[26]

Marra's express concerns in this song are not so much with national linguistic issues as with the representation of a more local identity—even to the point of dislocation from other regional identities and sympathies within the nation.

On a more general level, Marra uses a "bilingual" juxtaposition in "O Penitence" in order to structurally illustrate an aspect of the narrative. A local story has it that a boy from Dundee gave Monk all the information he needed regarding defense positions, and the narrator of the song is in fact this boy's father. In this context, the bilingualism of the switch from English "devils-hands" in line 3 of the chorus referring to Monk, to the Scots "deil" in line 4 referring to the narrator's son, is significant. The actual *"deil himsel"*—the real Devil and not just his English "hands"—is approached in the narrator's own language, used effectively to set the

English phrase "devil's hands" in quotation marks, placing a distance between Scots and English precisely by utilizing both, while simultaneously denying the ability of English to bear full witness to the Scots narrator's experience. Indeed, Marra sees the whole field of usage within the fringe of contact between Scots and English as a daily problematic for Scots speakers:

> First thing ye've gottae do, if ye're gonnae wipe out any kin o power at all, then ye get rid of the language. And that, they've very successfully done. So we end up tryin 'ae claw it aw back, know? I don't like to do it as a gesture, at all, but when A spent time in London, A fund it a real strain, ye know, speakin Standard English.[27]

At this most political of junctures, a linguistic turn that we have already considered above reappears in a new form: the celebration of "localism," so crucial to Marra's work, is also one of the overriding features of kailyard approaches to language. To what extent does Marra avoid, lapse into, or engage with this problematic? In today's anglocentric pop industry, localism—often defined in national, rather than properly local, subnational terms—is actively discouraged. As Brian Hogg has noted, those like Marra who engage with these issues face serious career problems: "Marra's . . . desire to write and sing in a Scottish vernacular met resistance from London-based quarters. 'I wrote the *Gaels Blue* album to annoy my publisher,' Michael recounted in a BBC interview. 'He was horrified by it, which I began to enjoy.' "[28]

Marra's career has been strongly colored by his commitment to regionalism. After a period in London, he returned to Dundee to pursue a more solo career and he signed with the independent Edinburgh label Eclectic Records. This kind of decision to reject the centralization of the pop industry in London and return to Scotland has also been made by more internationally known bands like Hue and Cry and Deacon Blue. Their use of Scots is hardly prevalent, yet this has not ensured against the possibility of them—along with Marra—being accused of kailyard sentimentalities. According to Andrew O'Hagan:

> Pat Kane, the singer with Hue and Cry, bends over backwards trying to render the socio-linguistic contradictions of the here and now by lingering around the doorways of old tenements and yodelling fairly juiceless 3-minute pop songs, revelling in the ulterior glory of Glasgow's superior reality. "Ma hame toon" and "ma wee wean" run Kane's show: he's as sentimental as a lollipop. . . . Hue and Cry (who sing "Mother Glasgow" and "Rolling Home" with a straight face) and Deacon Blue (who sing "Raintown" with a shameless one), constitute the pop end of a new sweet urban Kailyard, the same belief in the virtues of normalcy and authentic,

harsh, real Northern life help them—like their rural counterparts—to be attracted to independence like moths to the burner.[29]

An accusation of adopting a kailyaird aesthetic cannot be taken lightly by such key figures of the Artists for Independence group as Pat Kane, Deacon Blue's Ricky Ross, and the less Scottish National Party–oriented Marra. Clearly, the ramifications of O'Hagan's accusations will have to be taken seriously (even if we can simply dismiss at the outset his journalese implication that Kane's work is written in Scots). O'Hagan's article attempts to effect a subtle reversal of the politics of kailyard. Rather than seeing it as being the product of an essentially Unionist, Imperialist "North Briton" identity, designed to pacify Scottish political aspirations, O'Hagan views it as the very crux of nationalist aesthetics.

However, the Michael Marra song that O'Hagan mentions Hue and Cry covering, "Mother Glasgow," is full of ironic manipulation of sentimental and unionist imagery, not to mention the ironic positioning of Glasgow's own creation myth, that of its 6th-century founder, Saint Mungo:

Verse 1	In the second city of the empire
	Mother Glasgow watches o'er her weans
	Trying hard to feed her little starlings
	Unconsciously she clips their little wings
Chorus	Mother Glasgow's succour is perpetual
	Nestling the Billy and the Tim
	I dreamt I took a dander with Saint Mungo
	To try to catch a fish that couldnae swim[30]

Here, Marra the writer and Kane the singer (both Catholics of Irish extraction) take an ironic sideswipe at the sectarian traditions of Green and Orange Glasgow. The use of the word "weans" could position us toward sentimentality in the kailyaird mode—not least since it is emphasized as a "dialect" word, being the only non-English word in the first verse. Yet the possibility of the term "weans" carrying any sentimental, nostalgic content is broken by the ironic contrasts between lexis and coding: in the chorus, these "weans" turn out to be the Orange and the Green, the Billy and the Tim of a vicious sectarianism succored by the Victorian imperialist principle of divide and rule. This is the legacy the empire leaves for the "weans" of its "second city." No peace here—the "Bitter Suite" of Hue and Cry's album title is pervasive.

Equally, the lame fish of the contemporary, polluted Clyde contrast with the magical fish of the St. Mungo myths.[31] Here, Glasgow has also fallen ecologically under imperial conditions. "Mother Glasgow" hardly represents the form of kailyaird aesthetic that O'Hagan charges it with, unless one ignores its ironic manipulation of the linguistic and aesthetic codes of kailyaird.

However, Marra's use of Scots is often also assembled as a humorous device, aimed at giving a certain amount of "local color." This device is common in kailyaird and in the more canonic works of Walter Scott, where "local dialect" is generally spoken by the comic pastoral chorus. Songs such as "Hermless" engage with precisely this kind of famously problematic usage, and yet nevertheless problematize it further by placing it within an overtly political context. As Marra writes of this song, it is a "suggestion for the National Anthem of Scotland, the others being too military for my liking"[32]:

Verse 1	Wi' my hand on my heart And my hert in my mouth Wi' erms that could reach ower the sea My feet micht be big but the insects are safe They'll never get stood on by me
Chorus 1	Hermless hermless there's never nae bather fae me I ging tae the libry, I tak oot a book And then I go hame for my tea
Verse 2	I save a' the coupons that come wi' the soup And when I have saved fifty three I send awa' fifty, pit three in the drar And something gets posted tae me
Chorus 2	Hermless hermless there's never nae bather fae me I dae whit I'm telt and I tidy my room And then I come doon for my tea[33]

In pieces such as this Marra engages with certain traditional problematics in Scottish culture and language and makes them spin on a different axis—rarely are his songs without irony. In "Hermless" we have the image of the comic Scots-speaking innocent who is so often found within kailyaird work—again, framed linguistically within the Dundonian locale ("bather," "ging," "drar," etc.). Equally kailyairdesque is Marra's attempt to arouse a sentimental sympathy in the audience for this character, who is, after all, honest, shy, big-footed, and ultimately "hermless." But this is also a personification of the nation, a nation that "daes whit it's telt," that "gies nae bather." Indeed, in the third chorus, it becomes apparent that "Naebody'd notice that I wasnae there / If I didnae come hame for my tea." The narrator in "Hermless," just as much as the kailyaird peasant, *kens his place.* If this song ever did achieve its alleged goal of becoming the National Anthem of Scotland (in place of Burns's "Scots Wha Hae," or even Henderson's "Freedom Come All Ye"), the effect of a whole nation simultaneously singing of its own utter insignificance on the face of the Earth would be striking indeed. As a candidate for the National Anthem of Scotland, we can read this song on the one hand as a celebration of nonthreatening behavior, but on the other, as an ironic indictment of Scottish political apathy.

The irony effected here comes from a subtle manipulation of kailyard characterization—much of which is delivered through the image of Scots as the language of the "inarticulate Scot," this time transplanted from the rural agrarian scene to the contemporary sphere of urban poverty—happy is our innocent with his impoverished, coupon-saving lot. Overall, it is an irony that effects a displacement at the heart of the kailyard aesthetic; rather than being a case of crypto-kailyairdism, Marra's work delivers a subtle critique of its codes.

THROW THE "R" AWAY?

Marra's song "Mother Glasgow" is one of the few in Hue and Cry's repertoire that carries any Scots lexis whatsoever. For their singer Pat Kane, the question of language within popular music and its intertext with politics opens out into a further problematic: "Every time I open my mouth to sing I'm American. This is not a matter of choice."[34]

Kane writes here not of a national linguistic contradiction,[35] but of a personal lack of choice such as any late-20th-century singer in Europe (and elsewhere) experiences. The homogeneity of the American version of popular culture is now so widespread that it has become a matter of personal experience that is not even questioned by the individual. To sing contemporary popular music is considered *naturally* to sing with an American accent, and with an American vernacular. To open one's mouth to sing and to therefore be American, to be singing in American English, is now an international condition.[36] Indeed, even in England itself, this condition is so strong within popular music that it took a movement as explosive as Punk to even begin to displace the linguistic hegemony of AmerEnglish, and it is easy to dispute the success of that attempt, despite Britpop's reinscription of that Punk strategy in the early to mid-1990s.

In Scotland, the issue is even more complex and even more finely balanced, with Scots battling against the dual claims of both AmerEnglish and Anglo-English. This is one reason why The Proclaimers, for example, both echo and extend the linguistic struggle begun within Punk. Within their avowedly Nationalist agenda, it is now necessary not only to reject AmerEnglish linguistic codes, but also to effect a double displacement by equally rejecting even those Anglo-English codes that Punk sought to reestablish. Pat Kane describes the problematic of the relationship to the new lingua franca in precisely this double context: "Does one simply accept that to love rock 'n' roll is to love America—or does one employ irony to enjoyably distance the music from the society, or even use its techniques to convey a critique of both American and British societies?"[37]

And within this dual displacement, it seems that, once more, it is a question of inhabiting the very structure(s) that one is attempting to shake: the immanence of ironic critique, with all of its crypto-deconstructive implications. In Hue and Cry's case, this can be expressed as a piece of consumer avant-gardism such as the sub–John Cage silent b-side to the single "Here Comes Everybody," titled "The Success of Monetarism," or as a simpler exercise in double coding, as in the title and lyrics of the single "Labour of Love":

> Chorus   Gonna withdraw ma labour of love
> Gonna strike for the right
> To get into your cold heart
> Ain't gonna work for you no more[38]

Kane describes this piece as "an anti-Thatcherite rant ... but it showed you could be political without being explicit."[39] However, the double coding here is achieved purely at the level of a generic juxtaposition: political innuendo is coded within a highly standardized love-song format. Linguistically, it conforms to Kane's idea of singing in the AmerEnglish lingua franca, but using its generic conventions against themselves.

However, this immanence to the object that one critiques is problematic in itself (as is well known within deconstruction)—especially if one retains a bit too much of the original structure, allowing it to cover over the traces of the parasitic devastation that one attempts to inject from within.

A further articulation of Kane's dictum which would appear to go further along his prescribed lines is the example offered by the already mentioned Proclaimers, who reintroduce a problematization of language as such into the body of pop conventions. As they sing in "Throw the 'R' Away":

> Verse 1   I've been so sad
> Since you said my accent was bad
> He's worn a frown
> This Caledonian clown
>
> Chorus 1   I'm just gonna have to hesitate
> To make sure my words
> On your Saxon ears don't grate
> But I wouldn't have another word to say

| | If I flattened all the vowels
And threw the "R" away |
|---|---|
| Verse 2 | Some days I stand
On your green and pleasant land
How dare I show face
When my diction is such a disgrace |
| Chorus 2 | You say that if I want to get ahead
The language I use should be left for dead
It doesn't please your ear
And though you tell it like a leg pull
I think you're still full of John Bull
You just refuse to hear[40] |

The reputation of The Proclaimers is centered on their highly specific Scottish identity, yet the above extract is plainly written in English. On the other hand, the text evidently deals with a language issue based on the difference between the "Caledonian clown" who sings these words and the "Saxon ears" of the addressee who has apparently objected to something in the former's linguistic practice. Thus, despite its delivery in English, the song negates the idea that the singer's language "should be left for dead." One assumes that this language is Scots, even if the linguistic turn of the song effects the very erasure that it laments. But the key point to this linguistic turn remains not one of language per se—or even of dialect—but of *accent*, a certain accent of *English* that could not operate if the singer "flattened all the vowels / And threw the 'R' away."[41] *Accent* becomes the main signifier of the difference between the two cultural identities of Scots and English. This difference is thus articulated not so much through language in the strong sense, but through the manipulation of one language by another by means of its timbral transformation according to external rules. In the same way that one can identify a French accent in English, so the normal codes of timbral and rhythmic articulation in Scots can impose themselves upon English and, as Deleuze and Guattari hold, "set it in variation"—even at this mere level of accent. Here, Scots acts as a parenthetical Deleuzian-Guattarian "minor" language that infects the very roots of English as a "major" language, turning it around on a new axis in the process.

Thus, the language that The Proclaimers use is a form of English that, in Henderson's terms, is "grazed" along its flank by the timbres, rhythms, and inflexions of Scots, only to become a subset of English (known to linguists as Standard Scottish English, the form of English now naturalized in Scotland as an indigenous language), such that it becomes a "minor" language form of the "major" English. Through the utilization of accentual articulation, English becomes decentered, its heterogeneity is increased—in other words, internal differences are generated within English, it becomes different from itself through this displasive multiplication. In this, it seems that the Proclaimers achieve the kind of immanent critique of pop Amer-English and Anglo-English that Pat Kane calls for—a critique that remains within its object while at the same time shaking its identity and structure.

CONCLUSION

> When Political combustion ceases to be the object of Princes & Patriots, it then, you know, becomes the lawful prey of Historians and Poets.[42]

To paraphrase Burns—who was, after all, more a songwriter than a poet—when a community loses even its right to political self-determination (let alone the democratic means with which to achieve it), culture often takes over where institutional politics leave off. This is a concept that resonates throughout contemporary Europe (and beyond). In the case of song, the struggle for cultural expression will almost inevitably be located at some level in the "language issue." The expression of a culture need not take the form of a political doctrine, espoused in a neutral language, but can easily, and perhaps more potently, be achieved by a neutral doctrine espoused in a politically charged language. The mere existence of any expression in an institutionally threatened or subordinated language—a Deleuzian–Guattarian "minor" language—can act as a strong affirmation of a culture's alterity to a political status quo.

Following Henderson, Deleuze–Guattari, and Kane, it is also possible to see various ways in which political confrontations can be played out in the spaces between closely related languages, and also in the spaces between various layers of the same language. At this level, the politics of subversion can shift into a kind of linguistic guerrilla warfare, sometimes paying more than just structural homage to Burns's concept of *political combustion*. It is all a question of context, and, in both the linguistic and the geographic sense, location.

How far current (and past) practices within Scottish song achieve this is questionable. As we have seen, the majority of Scots song that deals—overtly or covertly—with the "language issue" tends toward a situation that can be read as using English as an omnipotent counterpoint. If any real linguistic alterity is to be achieved (along the lines of that so easily achieved by Gàidhlig's greater distance from English), perhaps the crypto-deconstructive immanence to the object of critique needs to be deflected.

To call for this is indubitably to call for a revision of Scots well beyond the legacy of the 20th-century Scots Renascence—a revision that will take it forward into a new millennium, outside of ontological orthodoxies, but also outside of their immanent critique (a deconstructive problematic in itself with regard to the internality–externality axis). If this combustible field can be established, it will most definitely be the "lawful prey" of historians and poets—but also, and perhaps more influentially, songwriters. To effect a return to Patrick Geddes, perhaps it is the case that "Amid decay lies the best soil of Renascence"[43]—a cultural–political combustion in the presumed "Autumn" of our language? The question is: How do we negotiate this terrain to the fullest efficacy? ...

ACKNOWLEDGMENTS

This chapter, written in the dismal aftermath of the 1992 Tory general election victory (their fourth in a row) is dedicated to all of the singers and songwriters of Scotland who contributed to the sense of civic nationalism that ultimately led to the utter annihilation of all Scottish Tory MPs in the election on May 1, 1997, to the resultant installation of Tony Blair's New Labour administration in Westminster, and to the subsequent 75% backslide in favor of a Scottish parliament in the referendum of September 11. The final words of the last Scottish parliament on May 1, 1707, were, "Here's tae the end o ane auld sang." Two hundred and ninety years later (to the day), it seems we found our voices once more.

NOTES

1. McCrone, D. (1992). *Understanding Scotland: The sociology of a Stateless Nation*. London: Routledge, p. 1.
2. Henderson, H. (1992). *Alias MacAlias: Writing on songs, folk, and literature*. Edinburgh: Polygon, pp. 52, 78.
3. Which is most certainly not to deny the linguistic practices and contributions of the various "immigrant" populations in Scotland—in particular, the Italians, Asians, and Chinese.
4. Youngson, M. (1992, Autumn). A plea for respite from the "Aiblins" school. *Chapman, 69–70*, 91.
5. Aitken, A. J. (1987). A history of Scots. In *The concise Scots dictionary*. Aberdeen: Aberdeen University Press, p. xiii.
6. This particular formulation of the "language question" has been central to arguments over the Scottish identity throughout the last half-millennium, and is, no doubt, further complicated at its origin, since, until 1494, the term "Scottis" was reserved for the Gàidhlig spoken in the north and west, while what we now call "Scots" was at that time called—by its speakers—"Inglis," as opposed to the "Suddron" spoken in England. The nomenclative problematic is repeated today, with Scots also taking the names of "Lallans" and "Doric."
7. Of course, the "first" state language in Scotland was Gàidhlig, until the last Gàidhlig-speaking parliament was held shortly after the 14th-century Wars of

Independence. From that point on, Scots became the mainstay of state institutions, and officially remained so until the Treaty of Union with England in 1707. Latin, of course, had a certain function in the Middle Ages, but Scots seems to have taken precedence. Another difference from English linguistic history is that, since the Scots were in alliance with the Normans, rather than being a subject population of them, Norman French (while influential) never became a state language as such.

8. Deleuze, G., & Guattari, F. (1988). *A thousand plateaus: Capitalism and schizophrenia*. London: Athlone Press, p. 102. (Originally published in 1980 as *Mille plateaux: Capitalisme et schizoprénie*. Paris: Les Editions de Minuit.)

9. Ibid., p. 103. A similar attitude is struck by the Scots translator of Homer, William Neill, who writes in Scots:

> Gin I'm tellt that Scots is no a leid but a "mere dialect" I will mak repone that it's the yae "dialect" on the isle o Britain that hes a literarie tradeition raxin back ower mair nor sax hunner year. R. P. itsel is nocht but a dialect stellt up bi the establishment. A leid is a dialect wi its ain government, an thare's fouth o ensaumples o yon sempil meisure [1992]. *Tales Frae the Odyssey o Homer, owreset intil Scots*. Edinburgh: Saltire Society, p. 10)

10. Deleuze & Guatlari, *A thousand plateaus*, p. 102.
11. Ibid.
12. Herbert, W. N. (1992, Autumn). Carrying MacDiarmid on, *Chapman*, 69–70, p. 20.
13. Derrida, J. (1978) *Writing and difference*. London: Routledge & Kegan Paul, p. 282. (Originally published in 1967 as *L'écriture et la différence*. Paris: Les Editions de Minuit.)
14. Henderson, H., *Alias MacAlias*, p. 53.
15. Cf. Ashcroft, B., Griffiths, G., & Tiffin, H. (1989). *The empire writes back: Theory and practice in post-colonial literatures*. London: Routledge.
16. McMorland, A. (1977). *Belt wi' colours three*. London: Tangent. Given the close proximity of Scots and English, it is customary when writing on Scots in English not to fully translate passages, but to give them in the original Scots, with a footnoted glossary. GLOSSARY: *baith*-both; *brae*-hillside; *claes*-clothes; *cuid*-could; *frae*-from; *gane*-gone; *gar*-give/make/cause; *gie*-give; *grat*-cried; *hame*-home; *hauds*-holds; *ken*-know; *lang*-long; *maun*-must; *nane*-none; *richt*-right; *sair*-sorely; *shuin*-shoes; *thocht*-thought; *twa*-two; *weel*-well; *whit*-what.
17. Henderson also attempts to draw a strict line between his "ballad-Scots" and what he terms "punter-speak," the everyday usage of Scots. However, experience shows that most Scots speakers today continually slip in and out of English as much as Henderson's ballad singers. No doubt the explanation for this is simply the sheer weight of pressure that English brings to bear on Scots (and all other languages the world over), through the American media in particular.
18. Nairne is best known, of course, for sentimental Jacobite songs such as "Will Ye No Come Back Again," "Wha'll Be King but Charlie," "The Hundred Pipers," "The Land O' the Leal," and so on.
19. GLOSSARY: *ain*-own; *an'*-and; *auld*-old; *bairnies*-kiddies; *canty*-cheerful;

crouse-cheerful/proud; *frae*-from; *fu'*- full; *genty*-graceful; *laird*-lord; *lang*-long; *leddy*-lady; *mony*-many; *o'*-of; *reca'*-recall; *sae*-so; *wa'*-wall; *wee*-small; *wi'*-with. Also, note that despite the apparently anglicized orthography of "house," its "ou" vowel is pronounced according to standard Scots practice (like French) as "oo," as evidenced by its rhyme with "crouse" in the second line of the chorus. The importance of the distinction between Scots and English "ou" should be borne in mind while reading subsequent extracts (spellings such as "hoose" and "oot" are less classically derived, more vernacular practices).

20. However, in *Kailyard: A new assessment* (Edinburgh: Ramsay Head, 1981), Ian Campbell has written a challenging attempt to recover the ground of kailyaird for a less damning critique that problematizes our current relationship to it further. According to him, "The kailyarders invited pride in a Scottish Church, social fabric, educational system and historical sense which no Scot in the 1980s would wish to reject, grossly as it may be parodied. To reject the kailyard is to reject much that is central to any attempt to define 'Scottishness' " (p. 16).

21. Scott, D. (1989). *The singing bourgeois: Songs of the Victorian drawing room and parlour.* Milton Keynes, U.K.: Open University Press, p. 31

22. In "The Auld House," this is evidenced in the formulaically veiled reference in the chorus to the lock of Prince Charles Edward Stuart's hair preserved by the lady of the house, conjuring up the image of a bygone credibility for the Scottish gentry (Nairne was a baroness, mind), as well as associating the Scottish identity with the double bind of royalism and the lost Jacobite cause no longer recoverable in any contemporarily relevant political form—for the 19th-century Scots nobility, rebellion and political activism in general were safer and more romantic if kept well in the past.

23. Significantly, Derek Scott writes of another songwriter of this period, Lady Alicia Scott (often signed as "Lady John Scott"), that her use of language is "very much . . . English-with-a-Scottish-accent" rather than Scots as such (Scott, *The singing bourgeois,* p. 97).

24. Marra, M. (1991). *On stolen stationery.* Edinburgh: Eclectic Records. Copyright 1991 by Eclectic Records. Reprinted by permission.

25. GLOSSARY: hae-have; *deil*-devil; *fae*-from; *gaed*-went (*gae*-go).

26. Unpublished interview with the author, recorded at the Edinburgh Festival, August 1992.

27. Ibid.

28. Hogg, B. (1993). *The history of Scottish rock and pop: All that ever mattered.* London: Guinness, pp. 298-300.

29. O'Hagan, A. (1993). Homing: The anti-kailyard aesthetic of Bill Douglas. *Edinburgh Review, 89,* 81.

30. Transcribed from Hue and Cry (1989). *Bitter suite.* London: Circa Records. Copyright by Michael Marra. Reprinted by permission. GLOSSARY: *dander*-walk. Hue and Cry performed this piece, for example, at a pro-constitutional reform demonstration in Glasgow's George Square following the 1992 general election. The Tory party—the only party to deny the need for constitutional change—won the election overall in the United Kingdom, and so contin-

ued to rule in Scotland despite having a mere 11 seats out of 72. Their "mandate" to rule Scotland was a shaky 15% of the constituency vote (which was subsequently further depleted due to by-election defeats). In fact, even staffing the Scottish Office (SO) became a severe problem, with so few elected representatives to fill ministerial posts (the S.O. has more bureaucrats than the European Parliament), and so they increasingly resorted to giving senior portfolios to unelected Tory peers. Against the backdrop of these increasingly undemocratic conditions, the arrival of groups like Artists for Independence (whose signatories include major international figures such as Alasdair Gray) is hardly surprising. Equally unsurprising is the result of the subsequent 1997 General Election, with Scotland (and Wales, too) literally becoming a "Tory-free zone" in terms of parliamentary seats, and Blair's New Labour administration forefronting the promise of a devolved parliament in Edinburgh.

31. In Jocelinus's 12th-century hagiography, it is claimed that the saint recovered the queen of Strathclyde's lost wedding ring from a fish in the Clyde, thus acquitting her from the king's accusations of infidelity. Cf. (1989). *Two Celtic saints: The lives of Ninian and Kentigern*. Lampeter: Llanerch. N.B.: "Saint Mungo" is a more contemporary name for the original Saint Kentigern.

32. Marra, sleeve-notes to *On stolen stationery*, p. 3.

33. Marra, *On stolen stationery*. GLOSSARY: *ging*-dialect form of *gang*-go.

34. Kane, P. (1992). *Tinsel show: Pop, politics, Scotland*. Edinburgh: Polygon, p. 23.

35. That is, Kane is not arguing from the same position as Edwin Muir did, who, in discussing the basis of a national Scottish literature, claimed that both Scots and Gàidhlig were inadequate to the task, and that "Scotland can only create a national literature by writing in English" (Muir, E. [1982]. *Scott and Scotland: The predicament of the Scottish writer*. Edinburgh: Polygon, p. 111.).

36. Indeed, one might now argue that the "major" language that Scots must contend with is no longer British English, but this increasingly hegemonic status of the "major" language of American English, or, to coin a term, "Amer-English." For some, even British English has become a "minor" language in this context. For example, English newscasters no longer say "a week on Monday," but increasingly follow the American form "Monday week" (interestingly, a practice yet to be adopted by Scottish journalists). Further, while in an English Tesco's the other day, the author noticed the American form "specialties" being used to advertise fruit in place of the British form "specialities." It would seem that, in our postcolonial world, there is nowhere more postcolonial than the ex-imperial center. . . .

37. Kane, *Tinsel show*, p. 25.

38. Hue and Cry. (1987). *Labour of love*. London: Circa. Copyright 1987 by IMP. Reprinted by permission.

39. Quoted in Hogg, *The history of Scottish rock*, p. 298.

40. The Proclaimers. (1987). *This is the story*. London: Chrysalis. Copyright 1987 by Chrysalis Records. Reprinted by permission.

41. At this point, we also become embroiled in the dynamics of the notation of language, and its role in the distinction between Scots and English. For instance, although the Proclaimers write on the sleevenotes "I," they sing the Scots "A," and

equally they write English "was" while singing Scots "wes," "to" for their sung "tae," "my" for "ma," and so on.

42. Burns, R. (1985). Letter to Alexander Cunningham, March 11, 1791. In G. Ross Roy (Ed.), *The letters of Robert Burns*. Oxford: Clarendon Press, Vol. 2, p. 82.

43. Geddes, P. (1992). The sociology of Autumn. *Edinburgh Review, 88,* 39. (Originally published 1895.)

7

ENGLAND'S GLORY

Sensibilities of Place in English Music, 1900–1950

ROBERT STRADLING

> Now that other lads than I
> Strip to bathe on Severn shore,
> They, no help, for all they try,
> Tread the mill I trod before.
> —A. E. HOUSMAN

FROM BREDON HILL TO WENLOCK EDGE

It has become a scholarly platitude that the names marked on our maps often have a significance far beyond their geographical place and topographical characteristics. Such named locations possess a latent power that may far exceed that justified by any local material infrastructure, for example, its demographic or economic resources. This power may be characterized as a force of endowing human identification. It has been acquired historically, via a species of primitive accumulation unrealized by Marx, frequently through the applied intervention and investment of outside agencies inspired by wider and deeper motives. The power is released and articulated through cultural–linguistic discourses, and thus exerts an influence upon individuals and groups in society. Ultimately, therefore, this power is political.

The lands around the River Severn certainly provide an axial point of British geography. (See Figure 7.1.) The great tidal estuary penetrates deep into England, irrigating the very bowels of the nation, and contrariwise, via this channel the organic material of the community is excreted into the sea. The erosion by the estuary's swirling waters of the physical material of its mellow banks and meadows, themselves endlessly renewed by new strata of silt, is an organic symbiosis; it speaks of the land's elemental marriage with the sea, and of an even more primitive accumulation unconsidered by Marx.

In terms of representation, at least, no other region of the British Isles seems to have achieved quite the same relationship between sea, river, and land, or to have enjoyed an equal intensity of published reference to the

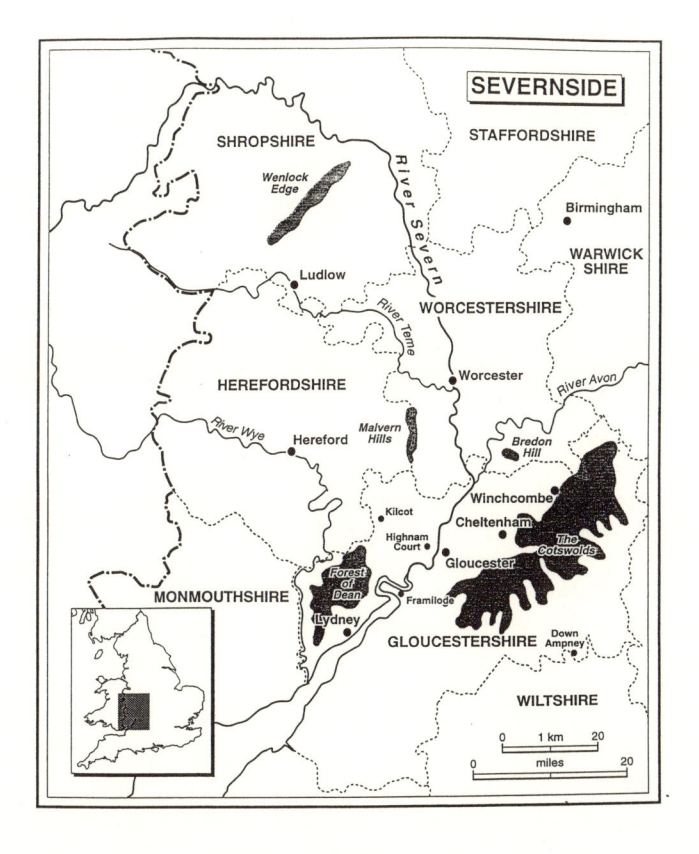

FIGURE 7.1. The River Severn and its environs.

culture, history, and destiny of our island race.[1] Or rather, our island races, because this area marks the border, the topographical and cultural frontier between Saxon and Celt. To the west, beyond the river, loom the mountains, the tribal homelands of culturally distinct Celts. The needs of defense lie not far beneath the surface of the collective consciousness. These resonances sing of danger, cooperative effort and self-sacrifice, mobilization and morale.

"Gloucester was, and is, a special city.... It is in every sense a crossroads: a place of arrival and departure, of mingling and sifting, blending and separating."[2] It was, accordingly, via a conjunction of factors, that the region of Severnside came to be selected as the most significant representational location of the phenomenon known as the "English Musical Renaissance." This dynamic movement in cultural politics aimed at nothing less than a national art music that could be both carefully defined and exclusively maintained. The movement had its headquarters in the academic centers established in late-19th-century London.[3] From these seminaries, a generation of missionaries went out, in the two decades before and after 1900, to proselytize, to convert, and in many cases to direct the musical masses in the provinces along lines set down by their London mentors. At the end of World War I, initial steps in government intervention in matters of music teaching and dissemination confirmed and strengthened the hegemonic tendencies established by the South Kensington academies and their allies in the critical press.

When the prime movers of the Renaissance began to construct a national framework for English art music in the 1860s, the cathedral cities of Severnside (Gloucester, Hereford, and Worcester) already boasted the longest unbroken performance heritage of art music in the country, by virtue of the Three Choirs Festival, which dated back to the early 18th century. For the Moses-like prophet of the English Musical Renaissance, Sir George Grove, this was an important tradition that demanded respect. As well as being a practicing engineer and the founder of modern English musicology, Grove was a committed Christian and a formidable biblical scholar—just the kind of universal man needed to initiate a renaissance movement. But those who took over from him in the 1890s were less appreciative of the Anglican musical tradition, and some even identified it as an enemy of progress. The National Church, for liberal humanists like Sir Hubert Parry, a Gloucester squire and Grove's successor as leader of the Musical Renaissance, had little to offer a national music. For him, composers had to look much deeper for inspiration, both inwardly into their own independent "souls" and outwardly, for the "true origins," or sources of English culture and civilization. They looked to the countryside, not to the city; to the farming seasons, not to the Christian calendar; to the village pub, not to the organ loft. They wished for secular modes of expression and aspiration, not religious ones, believing, as they mostly did, in the social triumph of science through evolutionary principles.

The importance of the Severnside area to the future of English music was not immediately obvious even to its ruling class. As far as Gloucestershire was concerned, another local squire—J. A. Gibbs—noted: "It cannot be said that Gloucester folk are endowed with a large amount of musical talent . . . but what they lack in quality they make up in quantity. . . . The village choirs do very well as long as their organist or vicar is not too ambitious in his choice of music."[4] This observation was made in 1898. Remarkably, within a few years, these same Cotswold clodhoppers were to become the ur-communities of a national music, and their hills, valleys, and streams the spiritual fountainhead of a whole civilization. Ultimately, they were transfigured, through the priestly offices of Ralph Vaughan Williams, into the Bunyanesque "Shepherds of the Delectable Mountains," denizens of England's musical Eden, above all a demonstrable source of "origins" of the kind that were so crucial to the late Victorian sensibility.

Yet it was not a composer who first fertilized this process, but instead a poet with little or no interest in music. A. E. Housman's *A Shropshire Lad*, set among the people and places of the Anglo-Welsh Marchlands, appeared around the same time as Gibbs's *A Cotswold Village*, quoted above. Enthusiasm for it gathered slowly, but by the early years of the new century a virtual craze for Housman's work was in evidence in intellectual circles, his verse being hailed as a modern version of Wordsworth's *Lyrical Ballads* and as holding a similar significance for English culture. Young poets made a beeline for the borderlands. These included writers like Robert Frost, from an American intellectual milieu in which the archtraditionalist Housman had suddenly become as influential as the archradical Walt Whitman was in England. When 1914 arrived, the English officer class packed a volume of Housman into its kitbag and took "the Shropshire lad" into the trenches.

During the period in question—surely the only one in which reading English poetry might remotely be said to have become a common pursuit—Housman, along with Kipling, attracted the largest audience. But, he never became a staple of the nation's classrooms or common rooms, and his unprecedented extracurricular popularity has long since vanished. To current sensibilities, by far the most important artistic symbol of the Severnside region is Edward Elgar. When he rehearsed an orchestra for his *First Symphony* (1908), Elgar was apt to suggest that the trio of the second movement should be played "like something you hear down by the river."[5] He was apparently recalling idyllic childhood days spent on the banks of the River Teme, a tributary of the Severn, which joins its great master a little south of Worcester. Elgar himself never set a line of Housman, despite the facts that the poet was his fellow countyman and that he had a strong interest in what was coming to be called "English Literature." He was his own man in every way, stubbornly resistant to the control of the Renaissance mandarins in South Kensington. At one point he even considered setting up a rival "Midlands School" of composers, masterminded from the chair of music established for him at the University of Birmingham. But in the last analysis, he was too dedicated to his own career to spare the time for such a project. Until 1914, at least, his childish games along the River Teme were the only sense in which he was ever a "team player."

The bed—it can hardly be called a valley—of the River Teme lies between Housman's two salient vantages of Bredon Hill and Wenlock Edge. The local "capital" of this region is the fortress town of Ludlow, once the center of royal administration in the area. During the Housman period, the collective attention of English composers was intensely focused here. Among many others, Arthur Somervell, E. J. Moeran, and the brilliant young hero George Butterworth contributed memorably to its promotion on the London artistic scene. As early as 1907 the teenaged Ivor Gurney began a series of Housman settings, later incorporated into cycles with evocative titles: "Ludlow and Teme" and "The Western Playland."[6] But the crucial conjuncture in the formulation of ideas and meanings was that Housman's popularity coincided with the publication of the new "scientific" folk-song research. Cecil Sharp, Vaughan Williams, and Butterworth were currently masterminding the decisive phase in the formulation of a national music, which was to be essentially a genre based on folk song, and folk dance and pastoral modes of expression.[7] Housman's evocative backdrop of village and farm; his diapason of work and play; his protagonists—simple but sturdy yeomen; his emotional range of stoic irony and bittersweet nostalgia—all these elements harmonized with the turn toward folk song. His lyrics became a meeting place for the Pastoral Music School, an agora where pupils engaged with the master in a Socratic dialogue about the essences of Englishness. At the same time, their expression of the tension between continuity and change, and of individual tragedy set in an timeless landscape, evoked the profoundest forebodings of a prewar epoch.

Sharp and his collaborators saw folk song as an indispensable source of patriotic, even of ethnic, feeling among the broad masses of English people. As the Boer War (1899–1902) ground on through initial setback into misleading triumph, and finally into bitter campaigns of attrition, Englishmen were being mobilized on a large scale for the first time in a century. On an immediate level of perception, at least, Housman's verse sings of belonging and peace. Yet the distant trumpets of war echo and reecho through the pages of *A Shropshire Lad,* whose personae often appear to be nostalgically looking back to their home across the seas from some foreign military posting. Butterworth isolated this feature in his celebrated orchestral tone poem, which (he explained to one critic) was "in the nature of a meditation of the exiled Shropshire lad."[8] Of course it is precisely the localized—and thus most intimately realized—essences of home and peace that are most worth fighting for: and the English husbandman (or "house-man") was to rise up in arms to defend his cottage and his village green in 1914. Housman's use of actual place-names allowed his readers to precisely locate their emotional reactions, encouraging a potent identification of place and feeling. Numberless letters home from the front in 1914–1918 were to echo the sentiments and cadences of Housman's verse in recalling particular places that represented an individual spiritual core.[9] Settings of Housman, possibly reaching four figures in total number in the years 1900 to 1950, became almost a passport for progress along what Vaughan Williams termed "the King's Highway," the officially prescribed route for national music.[10]

PLAY UP, AND PLAY THE TUNE

Housman explored other topics of crucial importance to national music, not all of them positive in their implications. His tragic muse set the life of the individual against the life of the community as a whole—if you like, protagonist against chorus. And despite the archaism of his lyrical style, Housman had not overlooked contemporary changes in the expressive character of the local community. He built into his verse references to cricket and football, team games that were spreading like wildfire to every part and every social class of the country. Apart from its broad cultural significance, the first era of nationally organized sport was also an insidious form of military mobilization. Housman's demotic use of "lads" to describe the members of sports teams (some of them, no doubt, later to be among the 30,000 British casualties in South Africa) also volubly conveys the importance of sport as a medium of male bonding, a factor crucial during the crisis of imperialism, and one that was to reach its greatest fulfillment in the trenches of World War I.

In Housman's "Reveille"—set to music by Ivor Gurney in 1908—the English yeoman is "called," almost as if to join the ranks of Kitchener's "Pals' Army" of 1914. The poem seems to exist in a cognate sphere to the celebrated poster "Your Country Needs You"—even if the country is Shropshire, rather than England.

>Up, lad, up, 'tis late for lying:
>Hear the drums of morning play;

> Hark, the empty highways crying
> "Who'll beyond the hills away?"
>
> Towns and countries woo together,
> Forelands beacon, belfries call;
> Never lad that trod on leather
> Lived to feast his heart with all.[11]

Another of Housman's attractions was that while his language was subtle, it was carefully modulated so as to enhance rather than to threaten the verisimilitude of rural simplicity. It provided an acceptable substitute for the original words of many folk songs, which were either in a dialect unintelligible to a metropolitan audience, or which upon "translation" revealed a shocking crudity of expression and an explicit sexuality—in some cases what would today (ironically enough) be called "industrial language." Using Housman's texts, the folk message could be carried without embarrassment into the recital room. However, there were other, contingent, embarrassments that proved more difficult to avoid. One of Housman's lyrics most frequently set to music was "Is My Team Ploughing?"—a title that carries various overtones. It refers to the team of horses that the speaker used to drive the plough, but also to his football (soccer) team, and to their collective endeavor in—as it were—another field. After his death, both team and teammates go on ploughing, the former in the fertile earth, the latter with the girl he left behind him.

When setting "Is My Team Ploughing?" in his song cycle "On Wenlock Edge," Vaughan Williams left out the two stanzas that referred to football.

> "Is football playing
>   Along the river shore,
> With lads to chase the leather,
>   Now I stand up no more?"
>
> Ay, the ball is flying,
>   The lads play heart and soul;
> The goal stands up, the keeper
>   Stands up to keep the goal.

The poet, who (not without justification) regarded football as part of the living tradition of English communities, protested strongly to his publishers against this act of bowdlerization. It remains an accident that has never been convincingly explained by Vaughan Williams' biographers.

What made football apparently as unmentionable as sex in the context of art song? Some critics corroborate a claim, made later by the composer, that the lines in question were rather bad poetry.[12] Vaughan Williams may have been confident in his literary judgment—though his much paraded lack of confidence in his own music makes this seem bizarre. Moreover, it was almost a cliché of musicology, certainly in Vaughan Williams day, that most of the great art songs had been set to indifferent poetry, to the extent that some writers argued almost a necessary correlation between bad poetry and good music.

But there is another reason that seems more convincing. The sports field was not one of the favored places of English music, the themes of its teams emphatically not to be played up on the *cor anglais*. Team sports were already apprehended as a populist alternative to art, an alternative potentially inimical to the spread of Arnoldian High Culture—which otherwise might have had a clearer missionary field in an increasingly post-Christian society. In other words, popular sport, increasingly commercially exploited and organized, represented a political threat to bourgeois social control. This thesis is valid not only in the limited sense that it set a term to the ambitions of "national music," but more generally; the rise of organized sport meant that the masses acquired a new public culture of their own—one soon to be amply supplemented by other new forms of "entertainment" in theater (the film) and music (jazz and jazz-derived dance music).[13] They poured into their arenas (in music, notably enough, often called "palaces") closing behind them the gates that shut out bourgeois culture. This, more than any other social phenomenon of the period, effectively confined art music to a socially sterile elite status as the music of the classes, not the masses; and thus crucially undermined the political-ethical project to create a populist, patriotic, art culture from the very start. It was a danger that composers other than Vaughan Williams sought to identify and condemn. Following a brief exile in England during the World War I, Frederick Delius noted that "nobody cares for art—especially the good things—sport tops everything"; Cyril Scott, questioned in postwar Germany about the lack of opera in England, was inclined to blame the national addiction to cricket and football.[14]

In the years after 1914, undoubtedly for the main reason that its nonmodernist aesthetic gave it the widest possible appeal, the pastoral style of Vaughan Williams and his associates became the dominant discourse of music in Britain, a kind of English, Morrisite version of the socialist realism soon to dominate musical life in the Soviet Union. It was rooted in an ambient physical reality which, through the rapid spread of public and private transport, was becoming steadily more familiar to the urban middle classes—to the extent that a meaningful encounter with it had become an essential part of belonging to that class, and for its millions of aspirant members literally a rite of passage. Location-specific music of hard geographical reference had—as it were—pride of place. In the 1920s it must have seemed that every site of outstanding natural beauty named on the

Ordnance Survey would sooner or later receive its musical apostrophe. Indeed, in 1929 Elgar actually jotted down the initial idea for the last of his "Pomp and Circumstance Marches" (No. 5) on the back of the Ordnance Survey One-Inch-to-a-Mile Map of the Gloucester–Cheltenham area (including Bredon Hill)! Notably enough, it was in these years, when the pastoralist trend reached its apogee, that Elgar produced the only work he ever endowed with a location-specific title, *The Severn Suite* (1927).[15]

Of course Elgar's was primarily a Worcestershire Severn, and—as an irate correspondent recently complained to BBC Radio 3—Bredon Hill is actually (if only marginally) in Worcestershire, not Gloucestershire. The occasion of broadcast reference to this complaint was a rare performance of Julius Harrison's rhapsody for violin and orchestra entitled "Bredon Hill." During World War I, Vaughan Williams had steeled his heart for grim work in an artillery regiment by summoning up the soft, inviolable tranquillity of the English countryside in the *Pastoral Symphony* and the violin rhapsody "The Lark Ascending." The importance of this idiom to a nation at war was illustrated again, in an even more critical moment, when Britain stood alone against the Nazi New Order in 1940–1941. The BBC commissioned Harrison's work in order to communicate to the listening world an aural picture of what Britons were fighting for. The chosen bard naturally turned to Housman. In a carefully scripted and rehearsed radio interview, the composer pointed out that "this part of Worcestershire speaks of England at its oldest. It is the heart of Mercia, the country of Piers Ploughman, and it is the spirit of Elgar's music too."[16] "Bredon Hill" was first transmitted to North America and soon afterward to Africa and the Pacific.[17] The exigencies of war had placed the Lark once again in the ascendant.

> Here of a Sunday morning
> My love and I would lie,
> And see the coloured counties
> And hear the larks so high
> About us in the sky.

LARKS IN THE CROW'S NEST

In fact, the lark ascended as far as the Crow's Nest. The Western Front of 1914–1918, where so many promising young composers died, was not England's only line of defense; arguably, it was not even the most important. The Royal Navy, the senior service (whose defeat, the public was often warned, could mean the war might be lost in one afternoon) was at once the guardian and the representation of British democracy. Accordingly, the seascape provided composers with a parallel dimension to landscape, a neatly complementary poetic-patriotic mode. The dryads of England's woods and fields shared the concert platform with the naiads of our maritime heritage. As in the case of terrestrial topography, the list of relevant works is long, providing a sequence as reassuring as the line of battleships in royal review at Spithead.[18] It is no accident that next to Housman, Kipling, Newbolt, and Masefield, all bards of the sea, were the contemporary poets most in demand with writers of art song. So important was the maritime environment that art music migrated to the seaside, in the south at Bournemouth under Dan Godfrey and in the north at New Brighton under Granville Bantock. Hundreds of city-based orchestral players spent the summer close-season with brass-and-wind bands playing "classical" medleys and arrangements on the sea—or, at any rate, on the pier. Even the young Gustav von Holst learned to pump his trombone almost literally on the ocean wave.[19]

In late 19th-century England, the sea came to assume a tribal-historical significance that was the equivalent of that of the forest in the Teutonic imagination. Since ancient Greece the warship has been a fertile metaphor for a national community. For generations of English public schoolboys reared on classical literature and history, Athens was not only the birthplace of democracy, but also the model of a successful *thalassocracy*, that is, a nation that bases its power upon the sea.[20] In 1904 Arthur Somervell had been the first composer to set a whole cycle of the *Shropshire Lad* poems to music. An inspector of music in schools, he later became a loyal disciple of Cecil Sharp and helped to supervise the introduction (or rather, the imposition) of folk song into the nation's classrooms.[21] Shortly before World War I, he completed his only symphony, giving it the title *Thalassa*, "The Sea." More explicitly chauvinistic examples of the maritime obsession were Stanford's "Songs of the Fleet," and Elgar's "Fringes of the Fleet," the former based on texts by the Bristol poet and "father of Eng. Lit.," Henry Newbolt, and the latter written to highlight "the Nelson touch" during World War I, by a composer whose significance to English music had been compared to that of Nelson in its naval heritage.[22] The atmosphere of the sea and ships lent itself ideally to choral (thus, communal and public) expression. In Boughton's Thomas Hardy opera *The Queen of Cornwall* (1924)—or rather, in the choreography of his partner, Christina Walshe—the chorus becomes the tumultuous sea, beating against the rocky coast. From Ethel Smyth's opera *The Wreckers* (1904) to Britten's *Peter Grimes* (1945), the elemental force of the sea is constantly resonated in the dynamic torrent of the community chorus. In the ongoing ritual of the Last Night of the Proms, the maritime aspect of our national identity seems set to retain its cultural prominence as we go toward the millennium. It is redolent in the name, and presiding image, of the composer of the celebrated "Fantasia on Sea Songs," written for the Trafalgar centenary in 1905, and culminating in "Rule Britannia": Sir Henry Wood, "Old Timbers," with his nautical beard and laurel wreath.

"National music" in the Sharp-Vaughan Williams sense, with increasing support from government and quasi-government sources, had a definitive role in the diffusion of this mythology. There can be little doubt that the aim was to establish throughout English musical life a sense of purposive and patriotic endeavor, a policy that related to and in some measure derived from the overall campaign for "national efficiency" espoused in the decade after the Boer War by many leading personalities across the political divide. In this respect, too, the national music movement, in its close definition of appropriate themes and styles, seems to recall musical life in the contemporary Soviet Union. Certainly they seem to reflect aspirations that are alien to conventional British perceptions of "the creative artist" and his proper milieu. From this mainstream, ostensibly liberal–individualist viewpoint, they are not only ideologically undesirable but also utterly impossible of practical achievement.

To whatever extent transgression of this principle is present on the British musical scene in this generation (an issue far too wide and complex to be followed up here) it does seem that in truly elemental ways the themes of the sea and democracy were already woven together in the mythical fabric of England. The sea was regarded as inculcating liberty as well as patriotism. Somervell's symphony, for example, was headed by the dedication: "Immortal Sea—a world whereon to triumph and be free." However, the freedom thus endowed is not subjective, but achieved only within the objectivized ambit of the ship and its crew. England expected that every man in the crew would do his duty—even if "he" were a single woman, like Grace Darling. A battleship provided the most magniloquent example of a "team" in action, a microcosm of all that was finest and most progressive in the nation. Before the age of propeller and steam, all the crew—as a phrase still in common usage reminds us—had pulled on the same rope. Indeed, film footage exists of George V, when Prince of Wales, helping the crew of his private yacht to hoist the sails. As they hauled the ropes or pushed the capstan, sailors (according to tradition) improvised the shanties that came to form a major element of the folk-song resource. The fact that so many folk songs were linked to the world of the Jolly Jack Tar added to their "democratic" attraction. Dozens of shanties discovered by Sharp and others at some evolutionary point had come amphibiously ashore, and, after passing through other phases of organic transformation, leached unobtrusively into the music of the National Pastoral School. Perhaps it is the faint trace of sodium chloride that leads many performers and listeners so "naturally" from the concert hall to the bar.[23]

In Vaughan Williams's *A Sea Symphony* (composed in the years 1904–1910), these fertilizing elements meet and mingle. The massed choirs sing an ecstatic paean to a vision of freedom and democracy. The choir, like a warship's crew, is a disciplined, highly trained, large-scale "team," drawn—in theory at any rate—from a wide social base. In this period both sides of the political divide struggled to maintain the traditions of choral music. For example, the socialist thinker Robert Blatchford, associate of Morris and Carpenter, had expatiated upon the potential importance of choral singing to the labor movement. This torch passed to Rutland Boughton, who in 1925—at the height of a fame as dazzling as it was ephemeral—was engaged by Herbert Morrison to lead the London Labour Choirs, conscripted from the slums of the capital. The initiative was later abandoned in the face of evidence that film shows and participation in football teams elicited far more interest (and thus subscriptions) from the workers. Escaping London workers and their football matches, the Labour prime minister Ramsay MacDonald visited the Cotswolds in 1929, and found there the heart of "the England of long past centuries."[24] Wealthy Londoners acted on the expert opinion of this Scots townsman, and began to colonize the Cotswolds. The communist Boughton, escaping the wealthy Londoners, went further and retired to a Gloucestershire smallholding at Kilcot, in the Forest of Dean, near the Welsh border, to resume work on his post-Wagnerian tetralogy about King Arthur.

The view of English opera—or, rather, of English music drama—maintained by Rutland Boughton was that it should be fundamentally choral in inspiration and style. "Write choral music," Parry had advised Vaughan Williams, "as befits an Englishman and a democrat."[25] Sir Hubert Parry himself was born at Highnam Court, located between the Forest of Dean and the Severn estuary shore. His secular oratorio *Scenes from Shelley's Prometheus Unbound,* which premiered in 1880, was selected by its early chroniclers as *the* foundation work of the English Musical Renaissance. In its review, the *Morning Post* felt it enlightening to add that it was composed by "one of Gloucester's children." A few years later, his *English Symphony* (No. 3) was greeted by a major critic as a masterpiece that obviously stemmed from the composer's Gloucestershire roots.[26] Parry's memorial in Gloucester cathedral was written by the contemporary poet laureate, Robert Bridges:

> From boyhood's eager play called by the English Muse
> Her fine scholar to be then her master composer.
> A Spirit elect whom no unworthy Thought might wrong
> Nor any fear touch thee, joyously o'er life's waves
> Navigating thy Soul into her holy Haven.[27]

It was Parry's duty to navigate not only his soul, but English music into a "holy Haven." In the 1890s, he became the leader of the Musical Renaissance in succession to Sir George Grove. Parry was a prolific writer as well as an energetic administrator, and acted as both teacher and personal exemplar to many other composers. More than any other patristic figure of the English Musical Renaissance, he set the agenda of its ethics and aesthetics, its topics and stylistics. He was a dedicated amateur sailor, photographed more than once (like George V) at the helm of his own yacht. He built a new home a few hundred yards from the slipway at Rustington in Sussex, and called it "Knight's Croft." It was here in 1916 that Parry composed his famous setting of Blake's "Jerusalem."[28] These epitomes of leadership and responsibility—captain, pilot, knight-errant, bard—evoke another fusion of ideas current among the burgeoning middle classes of the 1900s: the late Victorian obsession with neomedieval chivalry meshing with the naval-maritime fanaticism of the Edwardian age. It was evocative of this fusion that (also in 1916, the year the Battle of Jutland) Parry wrote a choral work called *The Chivalry of the Sea*. Years earlier, in his only opera, *Guinever*, the Knights of the Round Table were perhaps envisaged as a team of English composers set to deliver the people from the dragons of depression and the dungeons of darkness; luminaries to banish forever the city of dreadful night—the threat to civilization from the urban masses that he denounced in his inaugural speech to the Folk Music Society in 1899. When Parry died in 1918, the baton of leadership passed to his pupil and admirer, Vaughan Williams, who had for some time been recognized as his heir apparent.

GENIUS LOCI

Among the many hundreds of pieces written in the pastoral style of national music between the 1920s and the 1950s, it was "Gloster" that set the tone. So many composers were associated with the county that they constituted a loose (and unofficial) "school." In addition to Parry, Vaughan Williams was a native, as were Gustav Holst and the "specialist" Housman songwriter, C. W. Orr (both born in Cheltenham); while Herbert Howells, a great influence on the evolution of a definitive "pastoral" style, hailed from Lydney. Later, Gerald Finzi and Rutland Boughton developed strong links with the county.[29] In the first year of the new century, Holst composed a prototype work of the pastoralist idiom, the *Cotswold Symphony*. It reached fruition in 1922, when Vaughan Williams set his folk-opera *Hugh the Drover* in a Cotswold village, and Howells gave a string quartet the title "In Gloucestershire." The latter placed a massive coping stone on this cathedral with his large-scale choral work *Missa Sabrinensis*, completed in 1954. "Gloster" thus covered the whole spectrum of national music from the most representational to the most abstract genres.

But for many involved in its promotion or caught up by its emotion, the artist who epitomized the essence was the composer-poet Ivor Gurney, who from 1923 until his death in 1937 was consigned to a lunatic asylum. A well-connected group of advocates worked steadfastly to secure his recognition. By the 1980s they had succeeded in obtaining performances and recordings, eliciting favorable critical appraisals, and issuing biographies—though not, perhaps, in establishing Gurney upon the highest pinnacle of artistic greatness.[30] Yet, bizarre as it may seem to select such an "abnormal" personality as a key player in the "team," Gurney was evidently perceived as having an indispensable cultural centrality to the world of ideas discussed in this chapter. It was no accident that it was in a contribution to a volume issued in commemoration of Gurney that Vaughan Williams formulated his definition of "the King's Highway," and required adherence to it for his musical countrymen.[31]

Gurney was born in Gloucester city, and even in his teens, with the insight of the true artistic seer, he apostrophized the city's unique historical–geographical position in relation to its surrounding region.

> The surprising, enormous Severn Plain
> So wide, so fair
> Prom Crickley seen on Coopers, my dear lane
> That holds all lane-delightfulnesses there
> (O Maisiemore's darling way!)
> Framilode, Frampton, Dymock, Minsterworth
> You are the flower of villages in all earth.
> If one must die for England, Fate has given
> Generously indeed for we have known
> Before our time the air and skies of Heaven.[32]

An intensely pastoral patriotism, which as early as 1905 wished to write out the names in a verse of the places worth dying for, seems, in one sense, to supervene both Yeats and Brooke.[33] To be young in England, for a man who was destined to spend most of his life in hell, was very heaven; it was "Gloster" and Severnside, it was Housman, it was Vaughan Williams's music—the "Fantasia on a Theme by Thomas Tallis," which had a revelatory impact when heard in Gloucester cathedral in 1910. Within a few years *A Sea Symphony* had become a work of key significance for Gurney. As a child, he had messed about in his little boat on the lakes around Framilode, and a poetic imagination naturally allocated his homeland a leading role in the affair of the Invincible Armada:

> The spirit that sprang to height again
> When Philip would conquer the wide Main,
> And England, and her tigerish Queen.[34]

When the challenge duly came, Gurney joined the Gloucester Regiment—"The Glorious Glosters"—and was sent to France, shortly before the opening of the offensive on the Somme. A year later, he was wounded in action, and his first book of poems, *Severn and Somme,* appeared. In Gurney's letters from the trenches to Herbert Howells, the beauties of the Gloucestershire countryside are recalled and extolled lovingly, obsessively, and almost ad nausea. Howells is frequently exhorted to offer Gloster its due homage: "What about the *Forest of Dean* symphony?": "When are you going to write some Cotswold music?"[35] Gurney's origins were lower middle class and distinctly unprivileged. Perhaps, indeed, it was a bonus for the national music project that Gurney, who in terms of theme and style fitted the national music bill so perfectly, was well below hereditary mandarins like Parry and Vaughan Williams in the social scale, yet at the same time more completely powerless than any composer who had been definitively rejected by the London establishment. When setting "Is My Team Ploughing," Gurney—a keen footballer—had no trouble with the middle stanzas.[36]

"DO NOT FORGET ME QUITE, O SEVERN MEADOWS"

Even in the much wider context explored above, the city of Gloucester remains a rich and appropriate nodal point. As well as being a key rural–maritime annex, it also boasted an industrial dimension that was equally potent in terms of signification. Here—some readers may recall—the matches called "England's Glory" were manufactured by the firm of Samuel Moreland and Co., and retailed to the nation in little cardboard boxes. Such was the demand for the commodity it contained that at any given moment until the 1960s at least one example of this artifact could be found in the possession of any British male over the age of six. In an age when tobacco smoking was almost universal, after the original contents were exhausted, millions of boxes were passed on to small boys, who used them for storing collections of everything from spiders to sweets. The matchbox was decorated with a Union Jack and a superimposed picture of a prototype Dreadnought battleship—part of the navy that was "England's Glory." For the best part of a century, "England's Glory" advertisement posters could be seen in every Main Street and corner shop. Of course, the advertising emblemology of smoking was intimately bound up with its male-bonding aspects, that is to say, with teams and the team spirit: patriotism, sport, the sea, and the Senior Service.

In this way the daily lives of British citizens was accompanied by a familiar symbol of chauvinism and empire, nation and navy. England's forests, Housman's saplings plied double by the gale on Wenlock Edge, and plundered for centuries to provide the building materials of our wooden walls, our "hearts of oak," were now dedicated to another cause—but one that maintained the link (in two senses) with the Senior Service. Alongside

Moreland's factory site, English tree trunks were weathered in the complex of floats fed by the Severn, before being processed into millions of instantly expendable splinters. In 1914–1918, they went into watch stations with the sailors of the Home Seas Fleet, and into the trenches with the Shropshire lads and the Glorious Glosters. Moreover, many women also took up smoking during World War I, while (more prosaically) innumerable housewives used England's Glory matches to light the living room fire or the gas mantle. Quite literally, it was Gloucester's matches that kept the home fires burning.[37] Thus intellect, countryside, commerce, and the sea all came together at Gloucester. It was no accident that Vaughan Williams moved out of Wenlock Wood to write *A Sea Symphony* at a time when hopes for the survival of empire, nation, and culture were focused upon the Royal Navy, the land of Severnside, and English music.

The light and the warmth of "England's Glory" have proved ephemeral in every sense except—if one is susceptible to it (as many are, almost inescapably, through the genetic inheritance of class and culture)—the beauty of its landscapes and seascapes. Samuel Moreland's factory has long since been snuffed out, and even the firm's successors as proprietors of the Union Jack logo, Bryant and May, have gone up in smoke, a comparatively recent victim of the industrial holocaust of our times. But it is not only the material monuments, the factories and the dockyards, that have been dismantled. The aftermath of imperial disillusionment has led also to the massive deconstruction of our national mythology. Thus we are left with the contemplation of ironic and often bitter contradictions about the location-specific references of English culture and Culture. Just how authentic and elemental, for example, was that unique pride of place that inspired so much English art? The answer in many respects seems to be more accidental—even coincidental—than essential and generic. If the vicarage in which Vaughan Williams was born—and to which the young Gerald Finzi made a "pilgrimage" in 1921—had been situated a few hundred yards to the west, the apostle of national music would have been a son of Wiltshire, and perhaps the "Gloster" myth would have been stillborn. (In any case, he lived there only for his first two years, and later came to regard himself as a Londoner.) What is more (or perhaps, less) Vaughan Williams never succeeded in being "On Wenlock Edge." He was taken there by car in 1948, but the ridge "was hidden by a long bank of low cloud," and by this time the collector of authentic local experiences who had trudged half the country lanes of England was too frail to investigate on foot.[38] Likewise A. E. Housman never in his life climbed Bredon Hill to see the colored counties or to hear the larks. Despite all the touristic selling-points of Elgar Routes and Birthplace Cottages, inspirational villages, hills, and vales, the sense and sensibility of place was evidently not, after all, a necessary condition for the creation of English art.

Despite their profound sense of mission, nothing of what the apostles of national music did or failed to do made much difference to the vast majority of their contemporaries. One may consider, for example, the miserable workers in the sulphuric hell set alongside the Arcadian Severn, or of the pathetic tuberculosis-ridden match girls who trudged the smog-bound streets of London to promote the male bonding of empire. In another dimension of being, there was Mrs. Falge-Wahl, a Viennese refugee who came to live in Gloucester in the late 1930s. Not surprisingly, since she derived from the *beamtendel* bureaucratic class, she was a lifelong and intelligent follower of "classical music." Yet when she came to dictate her memoirs, after nearly 50 years' residence, apart from professing a love of the Three Choirs Festival, she was entirely unaware that her adoptive city and county claimed any special musical tradition:

> I used to laugh at how Gloucester people would take endless trouble to go to a concert in Cheltenham or Bath or Cardiff—Gloucester, no! . . . They say the amateur opera in Gloucester is quite good but I just can't stand it. . . . I just can't bear it in comparison to what I have heard in Vienna. . . . I remember *Der Rosenkevalier* with Richard Strauss conducting. . . . I mean it was so *fantastically* first-class.[39]

Perhaps the least "representative" of Gloucester's composer-sons should therefore be recognized as the most "representative"—I refer to Cornelius Cardew, the Maoist musical missionary and enemy of imperialism. Cardew was born and brought up in the village of Winchcombe—no more than a few miles from Bredon Hill—in 1936, became one of the most dedicated adversaries of the English musical establishment, and in 1981 met his death as a result of an accident that took place in mysterious circumstances in a London street. In 1974, Cardew asserted: "A book or a composition is not an end-product, not in itself a useful commodity. . . . The 'useful commodity' in the production of which [the artist] plays a role, is ideological influence. He is as incapable of producing this on his own as a blacksmith is of producing a Concorde."[40] This last sentence, a wonderfully English mixture of anachronism and modernism, innocence and experience, says it all.

NOTES

1. However, the dominance of the Severn counties was gradually replaced, during and after World War II, by the southeastern Downlands, above all, Sussex and Kent, a landscape—freer from industrial blots even than the southern midlands—that had always been a strong competitor; see Howkins, A. (1986). The discovery of rural England. In R. Colls & P. Dodd (Eds.), *Englishness: Politics and culture, 1880–1920*. London: Croom Helm, pp. 62–88.

2. Hurd, M. (1984). *The ordeal of Ivor Gurney.* Oxford: Oxford University Press, p. 18; this and subsequent quotations reprinted by permission of Oxford University Press.

3. For the institutional background and a representative foreground of these developments, see Stradling, R. A., & Hughes, M. (1993). *The English musical renaissance, 1860-1940: Construction and deconstruction.* London: Routledge. Here also (passim and bibliography) the reader will find more ample and detailed references to many sources drawn on for the present chapter.

4. Gibbs, E. J. (1983). *A Cotswold village, or country life and pursuits in Gloucestershire.* Hemel Hempstead, U.K.: Dog Ear Books, pp. 72-76. (Original work published 1898)

5. Quoted in Kennedy, M. (1970). *Elgar: Orchestral music.* London: BBC, p. 55.

6. Detailed treatment of Housman settings by English composers is given in Banfield, S. (1985). *Sensibility and English song: Critical studies of the early twentieth century* (2 vols.). Cambridge: Cambridge University Press, esp. Vol. 1, pp. 233-247.

7. See the excellent study by Boyes, G. (1993). *The imagined village: Culture, ideology and the English folk revival.* Manchester, U.K.: Manchester University Press.

8. Butterworth to Herbert Thompson, June 3, 1913, in Foreman, L. (1987). *From Parry to Britten: British music in letters, 1900-1945.* London: Batsford, p. 55.

9. See, e.g., Tapert, A. (Ed.). (1984). *Despatches from the heart: An anthology of letters from the front.* London: Hamish Hamilton.

10. See below, Note 30.

11. Housman quotations in this chapter are taken from Housman, A. E. (1994). *The works of A. E. Housman.* Ware, U.K.: Wordsworth Editions. Reprinted by permission.

12. Banfield, *Sensibility and English song,* Vol. 1, pp. 235-236.

13. LeMahieu, D. L. (1988). *A culture for democracy: Mass communication and the cultivated mind in Britain between the wars.* Oxford: Clarendon. According to a recent study, the sports craze of this period was also winning the battle for the allegiance of the middle classes; see Lowerson, J. (1993). *Sport and the English middle classes, 1870-1914.* Manchester, U.K.: Manchester University Press.

14. Delius to Philip Heseltine, March 15, 1916, British Library Additional Ms 52547, f.144. (Note: This item was not published in Carley, L. [1988]. *Delius: A life in letters 1909-34.* London: Scolar Press). Scott, C. (1969). *Bone of contention: Life story and confessions.* London: Scolar Press, p. 190 (see also p. 55). Some support for the hypothesis advanced in this paragraph can be found in Boyes, *Imagined village,* pp. 23-25 and passim.

15. For the "Pomp and Circumstance" story, see Moore, J. N. (1984). *Edward Elgar: A creative life.* Oxford: Oxford University Press, p. 785. In 1906, when the Elgars moved into their splendid new residence in Hampstead, they called it "Severn House."

16. The interview was "reconstructed" in the second of S. Johnson's BBC

Radio 3 talks on "British Music in the 1940s," March 7, 1995, from which the quotation in the text is taken.

17. Foreman, *From Parry to Britten*, pp. 240–241.

18. The titles of new English works performed at Promenade Concerts in the first half of the century show an overwhelming dominance of four themes: nature and the seasons, place and landscape, the sea and ships, and Shakespeare. Such works clearly belonged to a single complex of cultural–patriotic production. Since many of the last-named could be grouped with the first three under a generic "nature" classification, it is a complex that might be regarded as "organic"—were it not so much the product of careful political management. In each category the number of works achieving performance is only a small proportion of the number being written; moreover, in that period, "the Proms" was not the comprehensive music festival it later became, and did not embrace the fields of art song, opera, or choral work. See the program lists in Cox, D. (1980). *The Henry Wood proms.* London: BBC, p. 256ff.

19. Holst, I. (1969) *Gustav Holst: A biography* (2nd ed.). London: Oxford University Press, p. 15. Holst's *Cotswold Symphony* was first performed at one of Dan Godfrey's Bournemouth Winter Gardens concerts (*Gustav Holst*, p. 23).

20. This cultural *topos* is still retailed not only in the popular media but also in the teaching of ancient history. A revealing blend of these two elements was provided in an episode of ITV's celebrated detective series *Inspector Morse*, entitled "Greeks Bearing Gifts." It featured the obsession of an Oxford don with the contribution of the Athenian navy to the evolution of democratic norms. The galley reconstructed by English scholarship and rowed by English undergraduates is shown cutting through the Aegean to the music of Elgar's "Introduction and Allegro for Strings," more often associated with the Malvern Hills than the wine-dark sea. The claim in a lecture that "only the trireme saved Greek civilization and democracy for Europe" is greeted with justified indifference by his audience.

21. Somervell had originally been a strong opponent of Sharp, resenting his attempts to hijack the Folk Song Society, but later underwent a Pauline conversion to become one of his most fervent disciples; see Boyes, *Imagined village*, pp. 67, n. 121.

22. Hughes, D. (1989). The Duc d'Elgar: Making a composer gentleman. In C. Norris (Ed.), *Music and the politics of culture*. London: Lawrence & Wishart, p. 47.

23. On England's maritime "obsessions," see Behrman, C. F. (1977). *Victorian myths of the sea*. Athens, OH: Ohio University Press. On "national efficiency," see Newton, C. S. S. (in press). Joseph Chamberlain and the tariff reform movement. In C. S. S. Newton & R. A. Stradling (Eds.), *Conflict and co-existence: Cultures of nationalism and democracy in Europe since 1815*. However, the rise of Cecil Sharp to become unique mediator of the Folkish Muse was by no means a smooth process. On the contrary, it was marked by bitter struggles, first with C. V. Stanford and the "academic traditionalists" over folk song, and then with Mary Neal and her supporters over folk dance. However, as a recent analyst puts it, "Sharp won the battle. By 1914, a series of decisive events had left him sole leader of the only widely accepted form of the Folk Revival movement" (Boyes, *Imagined village*, p. 83).

24. Weiner, M. (1985). *English culture and the decline of the industrial spirit.* Harmondsworth, U.K.: Penguin, p. 121.

25. As related by Vaughan Williams in his "Musical Autobiography," printed in Foss, H. (1950). *Ralph Vaughan Williams: Study.* London: Harrap, p. 24.

26. Hughes, M. (1997). *The critical reception of English music, 1840–1914.* Ph.D. dissertation, University of Wales, in progress.

27. Quoted in Popkin, J. P. (1986). *Musical monuments.* London: Sauer, p. 71.

28. For biographical details about Parry, see Dibble, J. (1992). *C. Hubert H. Parry: His life and music.* Oxford: Oxford University Press.

29. See Norris, G. (1981). *A musical gazetteer of Great Britain and Ireland.* Newton Abbot, U.K.: David & Charles, pp. 331–338.

30. A list of this particular team is given in Trend, M. (1985). *The music makers: Heirs and rebels of the English musical renaissance from Edward Elgar to Benjamin Britten.* London: Weidenfeld & Nicolson, p. 196.

31. See Vaughan Williams, R. (1987). "Ivor Gurney (1890–1937)." In *National music and other essays* (2nd ed.). Oxford: Oxford University Press, pp. 256–257.

32. Quoted in Hurd, *Ivor Gurney,* p. 30.

33. It was a conceit echoed many years later by another poet, whose milieu was odd odes rather than Framilode, but who nonetheless subscribed influentially to the pastoral project. "There is a music about the names of the villages (of Norfolk) ... Brenzett, Lydd, Burmarsh and Dymchurch, Snargate and Snave, Brookland, Fairfield and Ivychurch" (Fletcher, C. [1985]. *A life in the country: Country pleasures and speculations.* London: Robson Books, p. 99).

34. Quoted in Hurd, *Ivor Gurney,* p. 29. Unfortunately, there seems little evidence to support Gurney's notion that Gloucester took an important part in the Armada campaign of 1588.

35. Thornton, K. K. R. (Ed.). (1934). *Ivor Gurney: War letters.* London: Hogarth Press, p. 46. Trend, *Music makers,* p. 202.

36. Thornton, *War letters,* p. 42. In training with the Glosters—as well as playing football—Gurney was able to do some useful folk-song research when he met "a great broadchested heavy chap who has been a morris dancer and whose father and grandfathers uncles and other relations know all the folk song imaginable" (*War Letters,* pp. 38, 44).

37. In passing it might be noted that the composer of the famous song referred to here, Ivor Novello, is claimed as Cardiff's most celebrated musical son, but he too was trained in Gloucester, under Herbert Brewer, the noted cathedral organist, and alongside Howells and Gurney (Hurd, *Ivor Gurney,* pp. 24–25).

38. Vaughan Williams, U. (1964). *R. V. W.: A biography of Ralph Vaughan Williams.* London: Oxford University Press, p. 286.

39. Murphy, C. (Ed.). (1986). *A stranger in Gloucester: Recollections of an Austrian in England.* London: Secker & Warburg, pp. 59, 65–66. Mrs. Falge-Wahl mentioned Parry's name to her interviewer, but only in connection with Highnam Court, which April Cantelo and Roger Smith were at that time (as it proved, abortively) attempting to turn into a music center for the region. She also expressed a liking for *The Dream of Gerontius.*

40. Cardew, C., et al. (1974). *Stockhausen serves imperialism and other*

articles. London: Latimer, p. 7. On the surface, Cardew seems to have been strangely impervious to the long shadow of Bredon Hill—or perhaps (alternatively) was always in rebellion against it. The history of the Scratch Orchestra, which Cardew founded, concludes thus: "SMASH THE DECAYING IDEOLOGICAL AND CULTURAL SUPERSTRUCTURE! SMASH THE BOURGEOIS CLASS AND ITS CORRUPT CAPITALIST SYSTEM! DOWN WITH IMPERIALISM!" (*Stockhausen*, p. 32).

8

SAMUEL COLERIDGE-TAYLOR'S GEOGRAPHY OF DISAPPOINTMENT

Hybridity, Identity, and Networks of Musical Meaning

GEORGE REVILL

At the turn of the century, Samuel Coleridge-Taylor was one of the most popular composers in Britain, and was championed by a number of influential people in the music world as the rising star of British music (Figure 8.1). Coleridge-Taylor was among the first generation of institutionally trained musicians in Britain. A vehement supporter of classical art music, he also had an almost unrivaled command of composition for a mass market. He saw himself as a composer in the Western romantic sense and as a champion of the idealistic current of European nationalist music. Of mixed African–British parentage, Coleridge-Taylor also needed to reconcile his British and African identities. The latter was most evident in his sympathy for the Pan-African movement and his cooperation with black musicians and social activists in the United States.

FIGURE 8.1. Samuel Coleridge-Taylor. Courtesy of Croyden Library.

This chapter examines the complex processes by which Coleridge-Taylor came to be represented as a black composer-genius. I will focus on the relationship between cultural and socio-technical hybridity. I will look at the ways in which his music became enrolled in both English and African-American discourses of cultural identity. In order to expore this cultural politics, I will adopt ideas from "actor–network theory" in the sociology of science and technology. It argues for an approach in which musical meaning is produced through a cultural geography consisting of heterogeneous networks of practices, institutions, and artifacts that together make music at once an imaginal and a material entity.

Coleridge-Taylor was born and brought up in suburban south London. His father, Daniel Taylor was a doctor born in Sierra Leone who first studied and then practiced in Britain. But he left his family and returned to Africa not long after Samuel was born. Samuel Coleridge-Taylor's youth was spent in poverty. He lived with his mother in rented rooms in Croydon. After displaying a precocious talent for music, he was "discovered" by a local "gentleman," Colonel Walters. Thanks to Walters's good offices, Samuel became a scholarship student at the Royal College of Music (RCM), where he began to study composition in 1892.[1] Under the tutorship of Charles Villiers Stanford, he became a star student, outshining the likes of his contemporaries Gustav Holst and Ralph Vaughan Williams. In 1898, while still a student, he witnessed the premier of "Hiawatha's Wedding Feast," the first part of his most famous work, the *Song of Hiawatha*. In his obituary tribute to Coleridge-Taylor, Sir Hubert Parry remembered this performance as "one of the most remarkable events in modern musical history."[2]

In 1895, Coleridge-Taylor began teaching at the grandly named Croydon Conservatoire of Music; suburban music teaching in south London was to be his main source of income for the rest of his life. Thus he joined the new generation of professionally trained musicians who existed wholly or substantially independent of church, state, or aristocratic patronage. Throughout his short life (he was only 36 when he died) Coleridge-Taylor had to balance his "serious" aspirations with the composition of "lighter" music intended for a mass audience and for domestic use. His large output of polite songs testifies to this need.[3]

In his argument concerning the heterogeneous constitution of black culture in Britian, Paul Gilroy follows the late-19th-century black writer and activist W. E. B. Dubois in identifying a quality of African identity that he calls "double consciousness,"[4] meaning an identity formed simultaneously from ethnic roots and Western modernity. As a romantic virtuoso composer in the Western mode whose work linked European, North American, and African traditions, and also as a follower of Dubois, Samuel Coleridge-Taylor certainly demonstrates this mix in the form of black Atlantic culture and British culture. Heterogeneous in terms of race and culture, Coleridge-Taylor also highlights a related form of hybridity, that of the simultaneously social and technical constitution of musical knowledges and practices. In his case, issues of race and identity were intimately bound up with his representation as a genius and with the specific interests of groups and individuals who sought to adopt his music for their own purposes. The connection between cultural and sociotechnical hybridity is made by JanMohamed in his essay on "border intellectuals."[5] Coleridge-Taylor could be thought of in this way. He certainly came to think of himself as an "intellectual" in the manner of Dubois. His "mixed" parentage and experience of life in imperial Britian and during visits to the United States suggest the "intimate experience of boundaries" necessary to such a subject position.

Coleridge-Taylor lived at a time of increasing isolation and separation for the black community in Britain. The significant communities of black people found in London in the early years of the 19th-century had substantially dispersed after the end of formal slavery.[6] Evolutionary theories of racial hierachy developed from the 1850s were widely accepted as a commonplace justification of Britain's formal empire.[7] Growing racial tensions within the United Kingdom were soon to be manifested in the race riots of 1919 and widespread discrimination against the communities of black seamen at port cities like Liverpool and Cardiff.[8] Nonetheless, black students from Africa and the Caribbean area were increasingly in evidence in London. These groups, blacks from the United States, and dark-skinned Indian students studying law and medicine formed elements of a nacent politically active black intelligentsia. This had early manifestations in the work of W. E. Blydon, who was resident in London at the turn of the century, and in the first Pan-African Conference organized in London in 1900.[9] But in the popular consciousness groups of African-American entertainers—singers, dancers, comedians, and minstrels who performed in U.K. music halls in the period 1890 to 1910 had a higher profile.[10] As a professional musician and supporter of Pan-Africanism, Coleridge-Taylor found himself located between these two groups: he was part intellectual, part entertainer. In order to explore this geography of identity, this chapter will begin by considering the problem of musical meaning and the relevance of actor–network theory to this question. It will then go on to examine aspects of Coleridge-Taylor's work using a conceptual schema adopted from actor–network theory.

MUSCIAL MEANING AND SOCIAL NETWORKS

Many authors agree that music does communicate, and that to a greater or lesser extent the meaning of such communication is shared with other listeners and performers. Yet the nature of music as some form of language remains an intractable problem.[11] Alan Durant argues: "for music there are no clear means of conducting meaning such as appear to exist for language."[12] Michael Chanan believes that "the effect is reinforced by the absence in music of the representational content by which other art-forms—the linguistic and pictoral—are more clearly related to the body social and historical."[13] Chanan argues that this is the difficulty semiologists refer to as the problem of a semiotic system without a semantic level, or content plane.[14] Chanan, and more recently Martin, have argued that rather than trying to understand musical meaning in terms of more or less fixed semiotic systems, we should look to the inherently social qualities of music as the key to understanding musical meaning.[15]

There is much common ground here with developments in the sociology of science and technology.[16] From the opposite end of the material–spiritual dichotomy, arguments for the value freedom of conventional scientific discourse echo those of conventional musicology: both preclude consideration of anything but the internal, formal properties of language and practice. Michael Callon's theoretical formulation is useful here as he tries to answer the questions: "How does science or technology interact with the social?" and "How do they shape one another?"[17] These questions echo those both Chanan and Martin address to the social construction of musical meaning.

Callon terms scientific texts, "technical artifacts" and calls the people who constitute scientific and technical activity "intermediaries." These link other human and nonhuman entities together into structures of social relationships he terms "techno–economic networks."[18] The social meaning of technical and scientific artifacts and practices are properties of the networks in which these entities are situated. The search for musical meaning, not in a one-dimensional content plane, but rather in some form of spatialized system of socioeconomic relationships (e.g., those suggested by Chanan's "chronotypes" and Martins's "interpretive communities") certainly exhibits similarities with Callon's formulation of "techno-economic networks." There are several aspects of Callon's work that are directly relevant to the study of Coleridge-Taylor and his music. I will now briefly examine each of these as starting points for an exploration of the relationships between the technics of musical production, musical meaning, its ideological valency, and the construction of identity for Samuel Coleridge-Taylor, the "Anglo-black" composer genius.

THE COMPOSER AS SOCIOTECHNICAL HYBRID

Callon argues that all human and nonhuman entities are potential actors, imbued with the capacity to make connections with others, thereby producing networks of social meaning from a heterogenous combination of human and nonhuman entities. Callon's description of the networking function of a conventional scientific text portrays this process: "A scientific text may be seen as an object which makes connections with other texts and literary inscriptions."[19] The choice of journal, of language and even title are the methods by which an article seeks to define and build an interested audience. The list of authors tells of collaboration, its citations rework the cited texts and insert them into new relationships, thereby identifying and linking new actors together.[20] Not only are conventional texts viewed in this way; the people and objects that make up techno-economic networks are all considered as textual intermediaries, active elements in the wider networks that function as signifying systems.

This approach is useful for the study of music because it enables the diverse elements of musical communication—from patterns of sound and embodied gestures, to technical skill in instrumental virtuosity or dance, to written scores, to theoretical treatises, to recordings of performances—to be considered together as mutually constitutive of musical meaning. Like Callon's scientific journal articles, musical works cast upon the world are network builders; they link back to previous works, and display evidence of artistic progression and creative individuality. They connect people with professional, economic, social, and aesthetic interests into networks of opinion and vested interest that constitute a composer's reputation. Just as intermediaries make connections between artifacts and people, it can easily be seen that intermediaries as entities themselves are not purely either social or technical but formed from networks of social and material practices and products.[21]

As Martin and Chanan have shown, music is also at once both a social and a technical activity. The creation of musical meaning through performance links together technologies of notation, instrument making, concert hall and venue architecture, the economics of promotion and marketing, training for musicians, sound engineers, advertising designers, the socialization of audiences and performers, and the mobilization of aesthetic codes and critical discourses.

The process by which Samuel Coleridge-Taylor came to occupy a position as a virtuoso composer/conductor highlights the simultaneously social and technical constitution of musical meaning. The construction of Coleridge-Taylor as this particular form of romantic genius was enabled by a network of sites and practices constituted from legal obligations, institutional and professional structures, economic opportunities, cultural preferences, and existing and developing musical practices. The absence of performing rights legislation in Britain ensured that composers did not receive royalties when their works were performed. In an age when the mechanical reproduction of music was primarily via the printed score, composers were placed in a highly dependent position vis-à-vis the publishers of sheet music. British publishers took the view that royalty payments would constitute a tax on the wider dissemination of compositions and would thus result in reduced sales of existing compositions and reduced demand for new works. This line of argument was used by music publishers to defend the existing policy on royalties ostensibly in the interests of the composer. In practice the only way for a composer to earn money from his existing work was to develop a reputation as the leading interpreter of his own music.[22] By this means a composer could earn income either by conducting or by playing his work on the concert platform. Though this situation was most extreme in Britain, Chanan shows this kind of system to be fundamental to the development of the romantic composer-interpreter within European art music as a whole.[23] After the staggering success of "Hiawatha's Wedding Feast," Novello, Britain's foremost music publisher, bought the rights to the second and third parts of the *Hiawatha* trilogy for £250 in 1899. Novello's also gave Coleridge-Taylor a five-year contract that guaranteed him a retainer of £100 per annum in return for the right to first refusal on his compositions.[24] These terms were not illiberal for the period, but they did little to release him from the need to augment his composition income by other means.

The precarious economic position of composers at this time was fundamental to this process. When Coleridge-Taylor took up his scholarship at the RCM in 1892 he was entering a profession that was already overcrowded. In Britain between 1870 and 1930 the number of musicians increased sevenfold from 7,000 to 50,000.[25] After the death of Prince Albert in 1861 there was little interest in music from those stratas of society that conventionally led patronage in the arts.[26] The lack of an indigenous tradition of opera, which was central to the livelihood of many European composers, and the small-scale nature of the established concert world resulted in a lack of permanent symphony orchestras and therefore a dearth of opportunity for orchestral players, conductors, and composers alike.[27] Under such circumstances it was virtually impossible for an aspiring writer of "serious" music to make a living from composition alone.

In spite of his obvious success with *Hiawatha* while still at the RCM and the publication of other works, Coleridge-Taylor was forced like many other British composers of his time—including senior figures like Edward Elgar, close contemporaries like Gustav Holst and friends like William Hurlstone—to join the vast ranks of private teachers, choir masters, and coaches to amateur groups. The burgeoning growth of amateur music making in industrial Britain supplied an endless succession of private pupils, choirs, and orchestras to be coached, not to mention a ready market for the composer.[28] After graduating from the RCM, Coleridge-Taylor continued to teach violin at the Croydon Conservatoire of Music while devoting the rest of his time to composition.

In some respects Coleridge-Taylor was fortunate to live in Croydon, a town in the rapidly suburbanizing area of Surrey well within London's sphere of influence. The town was close to the Crystal Palace which had perhaps the most advanced and extensive concert program in late-19th-century Britain.[29] Among the wealthy middle-class citizens of Croydon and neighboring areas were a constituency of amateur musicians with the leisure, financial resources, and sometimes the talent to take their hobby seriously. Coleridge-Taylor had staged his first concert in Croydon while still a first-year student at the RCM in 1893. Thus he began early to build a reputation in his hometown, a reputation soon to be reinforced by the success of his work at some of the primary venues for British music, including Henry Wood's Promenade Concerts at the Queens Hall (1898) and the Three Choirs Festival in Gloucester (1898).[30] When the amateur

Croydon Orchestral Society was formed in 1897, Coleridge-Taylor was the obvious choice for the position of director and conductor. Thus began an expanding range of coaching, adjudication, and conducting duties that came to dominate his working life. Increasingly, Coleridge Taylor was expected to fulfill the role of the virtuoso composer/conductor and conduct his own works at concerts throughout the United Kingdom. By the spring of 1900, for example, at the age of 25, he was occupied by a full program of engagements. On the April 31 he was in Bournemouth conducting his *Symphony in A Minor.* The next day he conducted "Hiawatha's Wedding Feast" and "The Death of Minnehaha." Two days later he was in Worcester conducting *Hiawatha.* On May 20 he was guest of honor at the esteemed Queens Hall in London to hear a complete performance of the *Hiawatha* trilogy. On May 24 he was back at the Queens Hall conducting his *Scenes from an Everyday Romance: A Suite for Orchestra in Four Movements.*[31]

The romantic conception of the virtuoso composer/conductor characteristic of the 19th-century fuses the social and technical around issues of interpretation. Compositional technique and command of musical language, an ability to exploit the strengths and explore the technical limits of instruments and performers are fundamental to the romantic conception of musical virtuosity. These characteristics relate directly to social attributes of interpretational skill and center on a perceived ability to communicate a particular personal experience, which in turn articulates broader social or "universal" human values. Samuel Coleridge-Taylor thought of himself as a composer in the romantic sense within the mainstream of European high art. He had a conventional European musical training and identified with a group of African-American thinkers led by W. E. B. Dubois. This group believed that people of African descent could build a civilization led by a black intelligentsia along parallel lines of development to those of elitist European culture.[32] The publication by Novello in 1891 of a choral anthem "In Thee O Lord" that Coleridge-Taylor composed at age 16, not to mention the successful performance of *Hiawatha,* are clear signs of early success. Thus he had good reasons for believing he could transcend the social restrictions on his "race" and demonstrate its technical capabilities by artistic virtuosity. Works such as the *Symphonic Variations on an African Air* and the *Twenty Four Negro Melodies* are deliberate attempts to apply European conventions to non-European subjects. He wished to do, he said, "what Brahms has done for the Hungarian folk-music, Dvořák for the Bohemian, and Grieg for the Norwegian."[33]

The transparent melodic sentimentality of Coleridge-Taylor's music could easily suggest superficial parallels with the emotionally charged work of European romantic composers. Elgar talked of him in relation to Tchaikovsky, while the African-Americans who invited him to the United States in 1904, 1906, and 1910 called him the "African Mahler."[34] Yet contemporary reports suggest he may have been ill-fitted for representation as the mercurial romantic virtuoso composer/conductor. Opinions about his conducting skills vary from assertions that he was, "a second-rate conductor even of his own works," to claims that he "conducted with his usual fiery energy ... always forceful and energetic."[35] In his early 20s he had been shy and retiring, choosing to watch the first performance of "Hiawatha's Wedding Feast" from behind the scenes. His biographers describe him as a creature of routine, with a passion for order, neatness, and tidiness amounting to obsession. At home with his wife and two children in a modest detached suburban villa with its "composing shed" at the bottom of the garden, he observed an unvarying routine. The product of "comfortable Croydon" in a number of ways, he was, apparently, "never known to complain."[36] This hardly suggests the romantic stereotype of material deprivation and emotional angst that constitute the wellspring of romantic genius.

However, at the same time he was also the product of a polite middle-class Orientalism that sought the savage in small harmless and easily manageable segments. Coleridge-Taylor was later to exploit this fashion for the exotic with numerous polite love songs and larger scale works like the cantatas *Kubla Khan* and *A Tale of Old Japan*. His music was frequently interpreted from a racial perspective. The idea of "barbarism" was a key concept articulating correspondences between racial identity and technical ability. It was central to the links forged between the figuration of the composer as a romantic genius and the interpretation of his music. It was not uncommon for his work to be described as "barbaric." Indeed, sometimes this adjective was mistakenly applied to music that was patently in a "classical" idiom, like the *Clarinet Quintet* reminiscent of Brahms.[37] Yet it is also clear that the notion of "barbarism" applied to Coleridge-Taylor was ultimately both ambiguous and double-sided. In addition to its African connotations, it was closely linked to a particularly European ideal of unrestrained emotion and to a romantic conception of musical virtuosity. This was closely connected with the late-19th-century European composers with whom his name was associated. This is evident from the report in the *Musical Times* of the first performance of the "Ballade in A Minor" at Gloucester in October 1898. The work, it was claimed, had its "barbaric moments, ... and is by no means unworthy of a youth who follows Tschaikowsky."[38] A review of his incidental music for the play *Herod* seems to have found the point of tension between these two versions of the "barbaric." His previous work, it was argued "would have seemed to make him the man most fitted to illustrate a semi-barbaric subject. But Mr. Taylor's barbarism is Western—*Herod* is Eastern."[39]

The material circumstances that constructed him as a virtuoso reinforced the racial stereotype that cast black people as perpetual child prodigies unable to develop their talent into maturity. After the instant success of music composed during his early years, critical acclaim for his later work was much less forthcoming. The need to earn a living as much as anything else ensured that Coleridge-Taylor became increasingly involved with teaching and conducting.[40] Though the *Hiawatha* trilogy continued to be very popular, Coleridge-Taylor received little financial advantage from its continued success.[41] However, his status as a popular celebrity continued to grow and by 1912 he was engaged in a very full program of engagements. On August 28, 1912, he collapsed at West Croydon station while on route for his teaching duties at the Crystal Palace Conservatoire. He died of pneumonia at home in bed on September 1, 1912. His obituary in the *Guardian* newspaper praised "his adaptability to European standards [which] must considering the racial admixture of his blood, be considered in itself a unique triumph." In doing this it reproduced the conventional wisdom about race and artistic virtuosity: "Once only had he spoken in an inspired way, when the enchantment of youth was upon him. He became, afterwards, no more than the successful practitioner."[42] As Berwick Sayers, his first biographer, put it: "Children of negro blood . . . usually showed a brilliant early promise which always suffered absolute arrest before they reached manhood.[43]

TRANSLATION, IDENTITY, AND THE POLITICS OF MUSICAL MEANING

The focus Callon places on what he terms the act of "translation" is also useful and relates the ways in which the establishment and functioning of sociotechnical networks generate their own systems of legitimation. This is something intrinsic and constitutive of the network rather than superstructural. Translation is a set of processes by which "definitions are inscribed in intermediaries." Meaning is given to particular animate and inanimate entities, placing them within the sphere of particular histories, practices, and ideologies, creating mutually supporting rhetorical structures. Through acts of translation and textualization, artifacts, practices, texts, specific individuals, and groups are embedded in the articulation of particular interests and goals. There is much in common here with the focus on "interpretive communities" stressed by Martin. Martin sees the establishment of norms, conventions, and reference groups, as well as the dynamics of their establishment through the expression of social, cultural, and economic power, as fundamental to our understanding of the production and practice of music. He argues that viewing artistic work as "collective action" enables us to understand how the works themselves are shaped by the opportunities, conventions, and constraints that present themselves in any given "art world" at any particular time.[44]

The complex division of labor involved in musical production is also critically important to the act of translation and the establishment of interpretive communities. Martin argues that a proliferating range of specialists—including critics, promoters, technicians, and teachers—and the growth of an increasingly segmented and differentiated audience promotes a variety of "perspectives, goals and interests." These will be dependent on "particular and disparate positions within the overall division of labour."[45] In this situation the shared cultural community is one in which different interest groups promote and defend their positions, and the ensuing discourse is constitutive of musical meaning.

The rise of nationalist schools of composition from the middle of the 19th century brings into focus the links between musical meaning, wider ideologies, and specific interest groups.[46] Coleridge-Taylor's music, particularly the enormously popular *Hiawatha* trilogy, was "enrolled" by a number of interest groups and "translated" into both African-American and English discourses of national identity.[47] In both cases his music and his position as a composer was advanced beyond that of his contemporaries. Central to each claim on Coleridge-Taylor's work was an image of the composer founded on a romantic conception of genius. As the embodiment of deep personal sensibilities that at the same time articulate wider social and human values, the romantic composer is both source and messenger. He/she is represented as a specific and particular voice who is independent of the strictures of everyday life, and therefore free to speak universal truths. At the same time, he/she must suffer the problems of wider society, and therefore, as the bearer of society's troubles, the romantic genius occupies a privileged position from which to represent those problems back onto society.

The composer as a sovereign universal voice is a powerful ideological force. To establish a particular voice as "universal" and then to claim that "universal" voice for a particular ideological position is clearly a strategy that universalizes the claims of that specific ideology. In spite of his fall from popularity since World War II, some recent scholarly interest has reproduced both the romantic ideas of genius and the ideological translatability of Coleridge-Taylor's music. For example, Tortolano's 1977 biography tries to reclaim him for the black consciousness movement.[48] But, in trying to stake out a place for Coleridge-Taylor as a genius, Tortolano uncritically reproduces many of the backhanded compliments made by white critics during Coleridge-Taylor's lifetime. These include praise for his sense of melodic invention and his liking for "color," both traced to his supposed lack of sophistication due to his racial origins. For another example, in what has been called a "misconceived" attempt to enforce an English reading of Coleridge-Taylor, Butterworth has attempted to prove "hidden" ties to the family of the great poet, Coleridge, confirming by hereditary association the composer's status as a romantic genius.[49]

Coleridge-Taylor studied composition at the RCM at the time when the music of the European nationalists was becoming influential in Britain. He was very interested in their work; the music of Dvořák in particular was fundamental to the development of his compositional style. During Coleridge-Taylor's student years certain senior figures in the English musical establishment were in the process of trying to reinvigorate British music, to create a "musical renaissance in England."[50] The very establishment of the Royal College of Music in 1871, in a country without distinguished conservatories dedicated to training professional musicians, was indicative of this project. This "rebirth" was necessary after the long "Dark Ages" of foreign domination ushered in by the death of Henry Purcell, the hegemony of Italian and Italianate opera, and the decline of the discredited and impoverished Royal Academy of Music. It was believed that only in the provincial choral tradition had the "true flame" of English music been kept alight.[51] Among those most actively involved in the renaissance movement was Coleridge-Taylor's teacher of composition at the RCM, Charles Villiers Stanford. Coleridge-Taylor was the first of a long line of composition pupils to be charged with the rebirth of English music. Stanford, Parry, and others looked back to a "Golden Age" of English music making in the 16th and 17th centuries. In a rather oddly shaped caricature that rewrote and oversimplified the social, cultural, and religious history of the period, they argued for an English music characterized by choral writing, honesty, and an understated directness of expression. The new English music would exhibit a degree of Protestant emotional restraint, while observing the good discipline of German theoretical practice. Further, and in contradiction of the preceding, they wished for a music liberated from the academicism, imitation, and the falsehood of fashion that had long stifled British music making.[52]

"Hiawatha's Wedding Feast" appeared to fit many of these criteria well. With the almost instant popularity of *Hiawatha* trilogy it is not surprising that August Jaeger, commissioning editor for Novello, the major publisher of choral music, believed he had found what both he and English music was looking for. On hearing the "Ballade in D Minor" at an RCM student concert, Jaeger told his wife: "I have long been looking for an English composer of real genius and believe I have found him."[53] Jaeger was one of the most influential figures in British music. Over the next few years his patronage gained for Coleridge-Taylor the support of Edward Elgar and a number of prestigious engagements and commissions. *Hiawatha* became a great financial success for Novello. Within four years of its premiere the work had enjoyed 200 performances and had become a major force in one of the most lucrative segments of the British market.[54]

In 1901, just one year after its first full performance at the Albert Hall, a performance of the *Hiawatha* trilogy was staged at the Metropolitan

Methodist Episcopal Church, in Washington, DC, by the newly formed Coleridge-Taylor Choral Society. The society's expressed purpose was to stage an all-black performance of the cantata. The audience for this performance totaled 1,500 mostly black people; at the earlier public rehearsal, nearly 3,000 people had been turned away.[55] In the decade up to 1910 Coleridge-Taylor's music and *The Song of Hiawatha* in particular became a rallying point for black consciousness groups and American black activists. One of these, Andrew Hilyer, wrote to Coleridge-Taylor from Washington: "In composing Hiawatha you have done the colored people of the U.S.A. a service which, I am sure, you never dreamed of when composing it. It acts as a source of inspiration for us, not only musically but in other lines of endeavor."[56]

It is clear from this that *The Song of Hiawatha* fits a particular ideological purpose. It is also probably true, as Hilyer observed, that Coleridge-Taylor's awareness of racial issues were not well developed at the time of the composition of the first part of the *Hiawatha* trilogy, "Hiawatha's Wedding Feast." His interest in issues of race, his connections with African-American groups in the United States, his reading of W. E. B. Dubois's book *The Souls of Black Folk,* and his attendance as delegate at the first Pan-African Conference in London in 1900 were largely forged through the network of people, texts, and institutions linked by *Hiawatha*.[57] Though his interest in issues of race and discrimination were genuine and heart-felt, they were also very much a product of the connections made by his music and the opportunities it offered to expand his professional horizons, providing him with further opportunities to travel and conduct. As Self has shown, Coleridge-Taylor's commitment to the cause of African-Americans did not remain unquestioned. In the period 1901–1905, he repeatedly tried to put off invitations to return to the United States, much to the irritation of his American patrons.[58]

The representation of Coleridge-Taylor's music as African could also be claimed for and inserted into a particular version of British identity that appears to have had Coleridge-Taylor's consent. He claimed that he has not suffered because of his race in Britain, and that he had only experienced racial discrimination in the United States. Though the circumstances of his life suggest otherwise, he projected all his fears about racial discrimination onto the United States and preferred to let his fame in the United States gain him respect at home, as a messenger of British civilization and humanitarian fairness.[59] At the time of his marriage, one newspaper, quoted by Self, unself-consciously appropriated the aspirations of African-Americans to the resolution of a specifically European conflict:

> It is an odd coincidence that while we are struggling in Africa the first coloured subject of the Queen who has acquired eminence as a composer

is the young Anglo-African, Mr. S. Coleridge-Taylor.... If the Boers would study music instead of the art of entrenchment how different things might be![60]

Here the Boers are represented as brutal and ignorant, while the cause of British imperialism is promoted as a benign quest for cross-cultural understanding.

Though important to the definition of Coleridge-Taylor as both "Anglo-African" and "Pan-African," there is nothing in *Hiawatha* that was readily identifiable as African or even Native American. The subject had previously been handled within the mainstream of European culture, for example, in a popular arrangement of the love song "On Away Awake Beloved" and in unfinished symphonic works by Antonin Dvořák and Frederick Delius.[61] However, *Hiawatha* clearly had an important symbolic meaning well beyond that which is immediately apparent in its story about a Native American chief and his people written by a middle-class white poet from New England. For African-Americans, the power of *Hiawatha* was its capacity to link together discourses of oppression, Christianity, African history, North American landscape, and social progress into a network of cultural resistance. Highly romantic and very distant from the actual experience of Native American societies at the hands of the whites, Longfellow's *Hiawatha* is written in a mock-realist pseudoanthropological style.[62] Coleridge-Taylor did not set the entire poem. Instead, he focused on the concluding sections beginning with the wedding of Hiawatha as a young adult and culminating in the arrival of the white man and Christianity. The most extensive and most deeply felt of the musical writing occurs in the concluding sections that deal with the acceptance of Christianity and the departure of Hiawatha advising his people to embrace the new faith. Recent authors have assumed that Coleridge-Taylor's treatment of this episode is steeped in irony, reflecting the betrayal and destruction of indigenous populations by Western civilization.[63] However, given the centrality of Christianity to the fight against discrimination in the United States and for self-determination in Africa, it is likely that the ideals of turn-of-the-century African-Americans were expressed quite directly in the music of the cantata.

For African-Americans during the 19th-century, the fight against discrimination involved constructing an image of Africa in Christian terms. In slave songs, for example, protest is couched in the figurative language of the Old Testament, a language that articulated their position within white society and offered hope of salvation. African-Americans represented themselves as the people of Israel in Babylonian or Egyptian bondage. Heaven, or Jerusalem, or Zion stood for Africa, a place of freedom and return after death.[64] As proof that Africans were able to produce an advanced culture, authors such as E. W. Blyden mixed biblical and classical sources, in order to argue that Africa was populated via Egypt by the sons of Noah and that therefore African "civilization" preexisted and nurtured that of modern Europe.[65] The cruelty of American whites toward blacks represented selfish materialism. Only black people with the resources of African civilization could redeem America and make it a truly Christian nation.[66] The biblical landscapes of wilderness and mountain related closely to concepts of personal revelation and salvation. For African-Americans fleeing slavery via the escape network known as the Underground Railroad, these took on new and very practical significance. "The Death of Minnehaha" tells of famine, death, and disease and centers on Hiawatha's journey through a forest wilderness. His return culminates in the acceptance of Christianity and the salvation of his people from the prospect of dispersal. In this regard these sections closely follow African-American representations of their own experience in the landscape and society of North America.[67] The Coleridge-Taylor Society's performances of *Hiawatha* were unprecedented. For the first time in the United States groups of black musicians gathered to perform European art music in public concert performance. They sang of the redemption of a dispersed people reunited and restored to strength. Using language wrapped in the metaphorical landscape of the new continent, they appropriated from the white middle class a vision and a means of expression. By bringing music written for the English choral tradition into the American Baptist Church they created a specifically African-American ideal for the land of opportunity.

"ACTORS," "NETWORKS," AND MUSICAL MOBILITY

The idea that all intermediaries whether human or nonhuman have agency is perhaps one of the most controversial aspects of Callon's formulation.[68] How, one may ask, can an insensate artifact have any form of volition or self-determination? Arguably, Callon describes a set of potentialities that reside in the nature of the object rather than any form of self-reflexive action. One might describe this as a tendency toward multivalency that allows the artifact or class of artifacts to resist or escape definition within any particular network. In terms of musical meaning, it is perhaps the quality of music, what Said calls "transgression," that relates to this most closely. He sees this as something "completely literal and secular at the same time: that faculty music has to travel, cross over, drift from place to place in a society, even though many institutions and orthodoxies have sought to confine it."[69] Many phenomenological studies recognize an intrusiveness and invasiveness of the aural, and music's ability to "touch" the individual. Said acknowledges the relevance of this romantic conception of music, which he calls "music's unique magic," and lays the foundation for turning it toward a social theory of musical production. When Said speaks of the literalness of transgression in music he seeks to stress music's physical quality of inhabiting many times and places. But it does not follow from this idea that the consequences are limited to either a utopean idealism or to mere presence. Rather, he points toward music's adaptability for a variety of purposes, its ability to cross social boundaries, and the malleability and reversability of its symbolic codes. This has a whole range of hegemonic and counterhegemonic implications that foreground both the limits and potentialities of different forms of sound in different places and the exercise of social power that legitimates or denies such transgressions.

The apparent ability of music to escape or defy the meanings assigned to it is reflected in the multiplicity of readings possible from Coleridge-Taylor's music. His music is heard as African, though references to African music, in terms of rhythm, melody, or instrumentation, are almost nonexistent.[70] His music is heard as English, but it contains no folk songs and no references to the music of the 16th and 17th centuries, which many argued was critical to construction of a "truly" English music. His harmonic and melodic language derives largely from Slav and Bohemian sources.[71] Coleridge-Taylor was promoted as a classicist, though he made no major statements in symphonic form; indeed, his primary success came in popular genres. Though his early music was abstract and "serious" his later compositions were not marked by increasing abstraction. The case was just the opposite: his music became "lighter" and was characterized by his diversion into composition for the theater. In the end, his music, when taken as a whole, is very difficult to classify. It is perhaps not surprising that historians have been unable to accommodate him within the story of English music. Not until Michael Trend's book of 1985 did Coleridge-Taylor receive any recognition for his role in the late-19th-century English Musical Renaissance.[72] The apparent multiplicity of readings possible even with his songs, not to mention a choral work like *The Song of Hiawatha* with its verbal description and literary associations, suggests the importance of extramusical meaning. Coleridge-Taylor's music appears to be defined entirely through a cultural geography of extramusical associations. A set of translations connects his music into networks formed from economic imperatives, critical discourses, political projects, and academic exercises that are both historically and geographically specific.

The mobility of Coleridge-Taylor's music is made apparent in efforts made by various groups and individuals to capture his music for a range of discourses serving their own interests. This chapter, no less than other interpretations, enrolles his music into a particular academic discourse with its own agenda. Constantly, critical evaluation of his music engages in a process of categorization and classification that reads the work for certain types of meaning directed toward particular ends. These trajectories themselves are not simple and unidirectional; instead, they are formed from complex networks bound together by the sociotechnical practices of making music. His music furthered the progress of the English Musical Renaissance no less than the profitability of the publisher Novello, the careers of a new generation of senior figures in English music and musicology, and the local celebrity of Coleridge-Taylor's friends and promoters back in Croydon. It advanced the cause of African-Americans, the political aspiration of a group of black community leaders, Coleridge-Taylor's own artistic aspirations, and perhaps also the social and cultural status of the wealthy Americans who invited him to the United States. In each instance musical meaning is intimately bound up with attempts to define the composer, to delineate the nature of his talent, and to figure the technical in the name of the social.

The very language of professional music with its developing institutions of criticism and analysis worked first to mark Coleridge-Taylor as "the coming man" and then to write him out of the history of English music. Ironically, the development of these practices in Britain centered on Coleridge-Taylor's home territory, those places that nurtured his talent, the R.C.M. and the Crystal Palace.[73] Here music's transgressive capabilities threaten well-entrenched notions of social and personal identity and connect these to the classification of music. Coleridge-Taylor was not unaware of this fusion of technical capacity and social identity: indeed, he consistently made this link with the assertion that he was an *English* composer with a *British* education. Sir Hubert Parry's recollections of the first performance of "Hiawatha's Wedding Feast" at the R.C.M. clearly relate musical and racial purity:

> By the time it [*Hiawatha*] came into existence the narration type of musical cantata was getting discredited. But Coleridge-Taylor was peculiarly fitted by racial combination to produce an exception to the conventional tendency. The primitive nature delighted in stories. He himself said that he was mainly attracted to Longfellow's poem by the funny names in it. At any rate it was simple, unanalytic, straightforward pleasure which appealed to him. He did not thirst for intellectual analysis. ... Like his half-brothers of primitive race he loved plenty of sound, plenty of colour, simple and definite rhythms, and, above all things plenty of tune.[74]

Parry's words carefully mark out a space for Coleridge-Taylor's music well outside the Royal College. By describing his music as having "plenty of colour, simple and definite rhythms ... like his half-brothers of primitive race," Parry links it to the commercial music making of the music hall and to black minstrelsy. Depicting Coleridge-Taylor as the dapper suburban gent, whose sphere of influence is that of female domestic leisure time, and as a writer of "tuneful" music that provides "unanalytic straightforward pleasure," is to represent his music as little more than a pleasant diversion. Represented in this way as undemanding, it was also unproductive in the sense that it did not contribute to the intellectual development of music. Coleridge-Taylor's music is dismissed as the product of a juvenile, unsophisticated mind. His ability to handle "feminine cadences" is attributed to a particular empathy unavailable to the sophisticated, white, Anglo-Saxon male.[75] Thus arguments couched in terms of race, class, and gender excludes Coleridge-Taylor's music from the "official" canon of English music. Instead, it is dismissed as a hybrid music produced by a hybrid identity.

The polyvalency of his music created a geography of opportunity that took Coleridge-Taylor and his music well beyond the bounds of his home base in Croydon. In this sense Coleridge-Taylor's music did not suffer from the lack of exposure and the incompetent performances that dogged the careers of many British composers. In one sense the very values of Croydon, represented in the polite conformity of much of his music, gave it a broad appeal based on a suburban rather a than cosmopolitan universality. However, though rooted in Croydon economically as well as aesthetically, it had long been Coleridge-Taylor's aim to transcend his localism. In this way the apparent ambiguity of his music, its reluctance to have order imposed upon it by critics and enthusiasts alike, reflects his own desire to escape the prescribed paths that others had charted for him. Self has traced Coleridge-Taylor's attempts to make his work known in Europe. Given his affection for certain European composers and his desire to escape the drudgery of teaching, coaching, and adjudicating, his motivations were probably economic as much as artistic. Possibly following advice from August Jaeger, as early as 1899 Coleridge-Taylor was trying to learn German, planning to give up his teaching, and preparing to visit Jaeger's hometown of Dusseldorf.[76] As early as 1900 Coleridge-Taylor's growing independence was beginning to lose him the support of his erstwhile champions. In correspondence, both Edward Elgar and August Jaeger began to comment on what they perceived as his "upishness": "Really nothing succeeds like success. Produce one work that will become *really* POPULAR and you get commissions chucked at you!"[77] Coleridge-Taylor's desire to escape is reflected in the substantial length of time he spent trying to compose the opera *Thelma* during 1907–1908. The postponement of other remunerative engagements and commissions in order to devote time to the project indicates a concern for his work well beyond the purely mercenary. Given the remote possibility of having the opera successfully staged in Britain, the project has been interpreted by Self as Coleridge-Taylor's principal attempt to gain acceptance in Europe.

Given the multiplicity of networks, the sets of interests and expectations embedded within and connected by his music, it was almost inevitable that these networks of opportunity with their mutually conflicting and contradictory trajectories would add up to a geography of disappointment. Coleridge-Taylor's opportunism and his mobility enabled him to make the most of these networks, while at the same time locking him into a semiotic web of interpretation that made him a hostage to fortune. His early death at age 36 meant that Coleridge-Taylor did not live long enough to begin to fulfill the plans he set for himself as he tried to move from being a suburban to a cosmopolitan composer. By this age neither Edward Elgar nor Ralph Vaughan Williams had made any significant impact on the musical world, and had certainly not written the definitive works that had been demanded from Samuel Coleridge-Taylor since the age of 20. In one sense his death confirmed racial stereotypes and the assertion that he would never be a "great composer." Yet in another sense, it enabled his rehabilitation and reinsertion into the myth of romantic genius. In the years immediately after his death, the financial insecurity of his widowed wife and two children was used by the musical establishment as a means of mobilizing support for a successful campaign to gain performing rights legislation in Britain. Coleridge-Taylor was represented as an innocent victim of the music business, a man who had suffered for his art to the point of working himself to death. This is a curious turn for a composer who had been criticized for pandering to popular taste by writing reams of mundane commercial music for profit. Thus condemned as a populist, Coleridge-Taylor's geography of disappointment was revalorized to underpin the subsequent economic security of British composers and the continuation of a "classical" music to which he was deemed irrelevant.

NOTES

1. There are four book-length biographies of Samuel Coleridge-Taylor: See Berwick Sayers, W. C. (1927). *Samuel Coleridge-Taylor—Musician*. London: Augener. The author knew Coleridge-Taylor, but his book is highly influenced by then-current theories of race. Tortolano, W. (1977). *Samuel Coleridge-Taylor: Anglo-black composer, 1875–1912*. Metuchen, N.J.: Scarecrow Press. This book was written as an attempt to reclaim Coleridge-Taylor for African-Americans. Coleridge-Taylor, A. (1979). *The heritage of Samuel Coleridge-Taylor*. London: Dennis Dobson. This book is written from the perspective of his daughter. The most recent biography is Self, G. (1995). *The Hiawatha man: The life and work of Samuel Coleridge-Taylor*. Aldershot, U.K. Scholar Press. This book includes much new material in addition to a thorough appraisal of existing sources, an up-to-date bibliography, and a discography. Because Self's book has replaced the others as the

primary biographical source, references in this chapter will be primarily to this text. The most substantial archive of material relating to Coleridge-Taylor is in the local studies section of Croydon Library.

2. *Musical Times,* October 1912. Quoted in Scholes, P. (1946). *The mirror of music.* New York: Books for the Libraries Press, Vol. 1, p. 129.

3. Self (*Life and work,* Appendix A) lists 132 published songs including, e.g., "Five southern love songs" (1896); "The soul's expression," (1900); "Five fairy ballads" (1909); "Songs of sun and shade" (1911).

4. Gilroy, P. (1993). *The black Atlantic: Modernity and double consciousness.* London, Verso.

5. JanMohamed, A. (1992). Worldliness-without-world, homelessness-as-home: Toward a definition of the specular border intellectual. In M. Sprinker (Ed.), *Edward Said: A critical reader.* Oxford: Basil Blackwell. Reprinted in Munns, J. & Rajan, G. (Eds.). (1995). *A cultural studies reader: History, theory, and practice.* London: Longman. Suggesting the connections between cultural and sociotechnical hybridity, JanMohamed argues that in many ways the specular border intellectual is homologous with Donna Haraway's definition of the "cyborg" (p. 459).

6. Walvin, J. (1973). *Black and white: The Negro and English society, 1555–1945.* London: Allen Lane, pp. 189–199; Shyllon, F. (1992). The black presence and experience in Britain: An analytical overview. In J. S. Gundara & I. Duffield (Eds.), *Essays on the history of blacks in Britain.* Aldershot, U.K.: Avebury, pp. 208–209.

7. Bolt, C. (1971). *Victorian attitudes to race.* London: Routledge & Kegan Paul, pp. 210–214. See also Lorimer, D. A. *Colour, class, and the Victorians: English attitudes to the Negro in the mid-nineteenth-century.* Leicester, U.K.: Leicester University Press, pp. 21–44.

8. Fryer, P. (1984). *Staying power: The history of black people in Britain.* London: Pluto Press, pp. 298–316; Walvin, *Black and white,* pp. 206–207. These authors show how racial hatred often consolidated around the issue of mixed marriages, which had become increasingly prevalent in the United Kingdom because resident black men greatly outnumbered black women.

9. Shyllon, *Black presence,* pp. 210–211; Walvin, *Black and white,* pp. 196–197; Fryer, *Staying power,* pp. 272–277.

10. Fryer, *Staying power,* pp. 442–443; Alexander, Z. (1987). Black entertainers. In J. Beckett & D. Cherry (Eds.), *The Edwardian era.* London: Phaidon, pp. 44–46. For an overall assessment of the role of black musicians in the United Kingdom, see Oliver, P. (Ed.). (1990). *Black music in Britain: Essays on the Afro-Asian contribution to popular music.* Milton Keynes, U.K.: Open University Press. Of special relevance is Green, J. Afro-Amercian symphony: Popular black concert hall performers, 1900–40, pp. 34–44.

11. An interesting discussion of this in an historical context is Miller, S. (1993). Towards a hermeneutics of music. In S. Miller (Ed.), *The last post: Music after modernism.* Manchester, U.K.: Manchester University Press, pp. 5–27.

12. Durant, A. (1984). *Conditions of music.* London: Macmillan, p. 7.

13. Chanan, M. (1994). *Musica practica: The social practice of Western music from Gregorian chant to postmodernism.* London: Verso, p. 38.

14. Ibid., p. 38.

15. Chanan, *Musica practica*; Martin, P. (1995). *Sounds and society: Themes in the sociology of music.* Manchester, U.K.: Manchester University Press.

16. See, e.g., Law, J. (Ed.). (1986). *Power, action, and belief: A new sociology of knowledge?* London: Routledge & Kegan Paul; Law, J. (Ed.). (1991). *A sociology of monsters: Essays on power, technology, and domination.* London, Routledge; and Latour, B. (1991). *We have never been modern.* London: Harvester Wheatsheaf. An example of the use of actor–network theory in the study of music is Hennion, A. (1987). An intermediary between production and consumption: The production of popular music. *Science, Technology, and Human Values, 14,* 400–424.

17. Callon, M. (1991). Techno-economic networks and irreversibility. In J. Law (Ed.), *Sociology of monsters,* p. 134. See also Callon, M. (1986). Some elements of a sociology of translation: Domestication of the scallops and the fishermen of St. Brieux Bay. In J. Law (Ed.), *Power, action, and belief,* pp. 196–229.

18. Callon, Some elements, p. 134.

19. Ibid., p. 135.

20. Ibid., p. 136.

21. Ibid., p. 139.

22. Ehrlich, C. (1989). *Harmonious alliance: A history of the Performing Rights Society.* Oxford: Oxford University Press, pp. 1–21. Also see Ehrlich, C. (1985). *The music profession in Britain since the eighteenth century: A social history.* Oxford: Clarendon Press, pp. 102–103; and Chanan, *Musica practica,* pp. 150–156.

23. Chanan (*Musica practica*) claims that "the first generation of modern conductors were primarily composers going about their business" (pp. 158–159). He also shows how the first composers to exploit this possibility were the composer/soloists of the 1840s such as Paganini and Liszt. He also shows how the developing complexity of the romantic-era symphony orchestra was intimately tied to the developing cult of virtuosity in the conductor and the increasing centrality of the composer as interpreter. Wagner, for example, while earning considerable sums from copyright, "made it practically impossible for his works to be staged without him" (p. 149). See also Dahlhaus, C. (1989). *Nineteenth-century music.* Berkeley and Los Angeles: University of California Press, esp. Virtuosity and interpretation, pp. 134–142.

24. Self, *Life and work,* p. 99.

25. Ehrlich, *The music profession,* p. 51.

26. Ibid., p. 73.

27. As Ehrlich (*The music profession*) says: "The London season was short, irregular and dominated by arbitrary fashion, while provincial events were confined, at best, to scratch performances by impoverished touring companies.... No orchestra offered full-time employment, and even the best musicians spent much of their time sight-reading, and playing far below their capabilities" (p. 74).

28. Trend, M. (1985). *The music makers: Heirs and rebels of the English musical renaissance, Edward Elgar to Benjamin Britten.* London: Weidenfeld & Nicolson, p. 48. See also Mackerness, E. D. (1964). *A social history of English music.* London: Routledge & Kegan Paul; and Ehrlich, *The music profession.*

29. See Musgrave, M. (1995). *The musical life of the Crystal Palace.* Cambridge: Cambridge University Press.

30. The "Four Characteristic Walzes" for Henry Wood's Promenade Concerts at the Queens Hall (1898) and the "Ballade in A Minor" at the Three Choirs Festival in Gloucester (1898).

31. Self, *Life and work,* pp. 111–112.

32. see Geiss, I. (1974). *The Pan-African movement.* London: Methuen, 1974; Padmore, G. (1956). *Pan-Africanism or communism? The coming struggle for America.* London: Dennis Dobson; and Ranger, T. O. (Ed.). (1966). *Emerging themes of African history.* London: Heinemann. See the reassessment of Dubois by Gilroy, P. (1993). "Cheer the weary traveller": W. E. B. Dubois, Germany, and the politics of (dis)placement. In P. Gilroy *The black Atlantic,* pp. 111–145. Dubois was leader of the Niagara Movement of militant black intellectuals. After studying at Fiske University, he entered Harvard, and then won a special grant to study abroad, which he used to spend two years in Berlin (Geiss, Pan-African movement, p. 212). Gilroy (*Black Atlantic,* pp. 134–135) demonstrates the influence of Hegel on Dubois and also that of Bismark. See also Revill, G. (1995). Hiawatha and Pan-Africanism: Samuel Coleridge-Taylor (1875–1912). *Ecumene,* 2(3), 254–257.

33. Tortolano, *Samuel Coleridge-Taylor,* p. 146.

34. Self, *Life and work,* p. 217.

35. Ibid., pp. 83–84.

36. Ibid., p. 110.

37. Ibid., p. 47; first performance July 10, 1895.

38. Ibid., p. 66.

39. Ibid., p. 116. Self reports this review from the *Musical Times.*

40. "By 1910 Coleridge-Taylor could be thought of alongside the first rank of conductors: Mr. Coleridge-Taylor himself comes to the Town Hall to conduct the Birmingham Symphony Orchestra and to praise it, after the manner of Richter and Safonoff and Sir Charles Stanford and other distinguished conductors" (Self, quoted in *Life and work,* p. 208).

41. "A statement produced after his death showed that between 1905 and his death, an average annual royalty accruing to him (on sales of sheet music where the work had not been sold outright) of just £119 p.a." (Self, *Life and work,* p. 265).

42. Ibid., p. 262.

43. Berwick Sayers, *Samuel Coleridge-Taylor,* p. 15.

44. Martin, *Sounds and society,* p. 174.

45. Ibid., pp. 174–175.

46. On nationalism in European music during the 19th century, see, Dahlhaus, *Nineteenth-century music,* pp. 35–41, 217–226, and 302–311. See also Dahlhaus, C. (1980). *Between romanticism and modernism: Four studies in the music of the later nineteenth-century.* Berkeley and Los Angeles: University of California Press; Dahlhaus, C. (1985). *Realism in nineteenth-century music.* Cambridge: Cambridge University Press; Longyear, R. M. (1973). *Nineteenth-century romanticism in music.* Englewood Cliffs, N.J.: Prentice-Hall; and Mellors, W. (1988). *Man and his music, Part 4: Romanticism and the twentieth century.* London: Barrie & Jenkins.

47. For a discussion of the relationship between European and African nationalism in Coleridge-Taylor's music, see Revill, *Hiawatha and Pan-Africanism,* pp. 254–259.

48. Tortolano, *Samuel Coleridge-Taylor.*

49. See Stradling, R. & Hughes, M. (1993). *The English musical renaissance, 1860–1940: Construction and deconstruction.* London: Routledge, p. 208. Also see Butterworth, S. (1989). Coleridge-Taylor: New facts for old fiction. *Musical Times, 130,* 202.

50. See Stradling & Hughes, *English musical renaissance,* pp. 34–35. Also see Howes, F. (1966). *The English musical renaissance.* London: Secker & Warburg; and Trend, *The music makers.*

51. Stradling & Hughes, *English musical renaissance,* p. 36

52. Ibid., pp. 36–37.

53. Self, *Life and work,* p. 61.

54. Stradling & Hughes, *English musical renaissance,* p. 208.

55. Tortolano, *Samuel Coleridge-Taylor,* p. 32.

56. Quoted in Trend, *Music makers,* p. 58. In addition to the Washington performances, there were performances by the Boston Cecilia Society between 1900 and 1902, and by the Orpheus Oratorio Society in Easton, Pennsylvania (Young, P. M. [1975, August]. Samuel Coleridge-Taylor, 1875–1912. *Musical Times,* p. 704.

57. In 1896 the American black poet Paul Lawrence Dunbar visited London. Dunbar's father had been a slave in Kentucky and died when his son was 12. In London, Dunbar and Coleridge-Taylor joined together to give several concerts at the Salle Erard in Great Marlborough Street and in Coleridge-Taylor's home of Croydon. Among the compositions he supplied for these concerts were a set of "Hiawathan Sketches" for violin and piano and settings of three of Dunbar's poems. According to his daughter, this collaboration was a key moment in introducing him to the black civil rights movement in the United States (Coleridge-Taylor, *Heritage,* p. 27).

58. Self, *Life and work,* pp. 143–153.

59. There is considerable anecdotal evidence to suggest that Coleridge-Taylor did experience racial prejudice in Britain. For example, he was called "Blackie" in the street, and once at the Royal College of Music he was dismissed as "nothing but a damned nigger"; see Berwick-Sayers, *Samuel Coleridge-Taylor,* p. 97, and Coleridge-Taylor, *Heritage,* pp. 42–44. Butterworth (Coleridge-Taylor, p. 202) suggests that Colonel Walters secured a place for him at the RCM primarily because his business friends in the City would not take a black person as a clerk. For further examples, see Self, *Life and work,* pp. 143–158. An interesting study of the "coloured" violinist and composer Joseph Emidy, who worked as a teacher and performer in Cornwall in the first half of the 19th century, suggests that he experienced little racial prejudice; see McGrady, R. (1991). *Music and musicians in early nineteenth century Cornwall.* Exeter, U.K.: University of Exeter.

60. Reported in Self, *Life and work,* p. 100.

61. Scott, D. (1989). *The singing bourgeois: Songs of the Victorian drawing room and parlour.* Milton Keynes, U.K.: Open University Press, pp. 149–150. Clapham, J. (1966). *Antonín Dvořák: Musician and craftsman.* London: Faber & Faber. See also Self, *Life and work,* pp. 70–79.

62. Not only does the poem mix together elements from different American nationalities, those used did not have any form of written language. The poem was loosely based on Longfellow's own association with the Algonquins and his reading

of Henry Rowe Schoolcraft, an American ethnologist and explorer. See Wagenknecht, E. (1966). *Henry Wadsworth Longfellow: Portrait of an American humanist*. Oxford: Oxford University Press, p. 108, 130; Ziff, L. (1982). *Literary democracy: The declaration of Independence in American poetry*. Harmondsworth, Middlesex, U.K.: Penguin, p. 56; Lee, A. R. (Ed.). (1985). *Nineteenth-century American poetry*. London: Vision Press, p. 149; McWilliams, J. P. (1989). *The American epic: Transforming a genre, 1770–1860*. Cambridge: Cambridge University Press, p. 117; and Fielder, L. A. (1968). *The return of the vanishing American*. London: Jonathan Cape, p. 117

63. See Alwyn, K. (1991). *Coleridge-Taylor: Hiawatha*. London: Argo, p. 10; Stradling & Hughes, *English musical renaissance*, p. 29; Tortolano, *Samuel Coleridge-Taylor*, p. 67; and Self, *Life and work*, p. 103. Fielder (*The return*, pp. 77–78) makes this point in the context of Longfellow's poem.

64. Geiss, *Pan-African movement*, pp. 42, 28. On the Pan-African movement, see also Padmore, *Pan-Africanism or communism?*, and Ranger (Ed.), *Emerging themes of African history*.

65. Geiss, *Pan-African movement*, pp. 97–102.

66. Carroll, P. N., & Noble, D. W. (1977). *The free and the unfree: A new history of the United States*. Harmondsworth, Middlesex, U.K.: Penguin, p. 256.

67. See Dixon, M. (Ed.). (1987). *Ride out the wilderness: Geography and identity in Afro-American literature*. Urbana and Chicago: University of Illinois Press.

68. For a discussion of this point within the geography literature, see Matless, D. (1996). New material? Work in cultural and social geography, 1995. *Progress in Human Geography, 20*(3), 379–391; also see Harvey, D. (1995). A geographer's guide to dialectical thinking. In A. Cliff et al. (Eds.), *Defining geography: Essays for Peter Haggart*. Oxford: Blackwell; Haraway, D., & Harvey, D. (1996). Nature, politics, and possibilities. *Environment and Planning D: Society and Space, 13,* 507–528; and Philo, C. (1995). Animals, geography, and the city: Notes on inclusionary and exclusions. *Environment and Planning D: Society and Space, 13,* 655–681. While discussing very different subject matter, Philo arrives at a similar conclusion to the one suggested here.

69. Said, *Musical elaborations*, p. xv.

70. Revill, *Hiawatha and Pan-Africanism*, p. 256. Kwabena Nketia, J. H. (1982). *The music of Africa*. London: Victor Gollancz; Manuel, P. (1988). *Popular musics of the non-Western world: An introductory survey*. Oxford: Oxford University Press, pp. 82–93; Roach, H. *Black American music: Past and present*. Boston: Crescendo.

71. Clapham, J. (1966). Antonin Dvořák: Musician and craftsman. London: Faber & Faber, pp. 30–31, 39, 45; Revill, *Hiawatha and Pan-Africanism*, pp. 256–257, 265.

72. Trend, *Music makers.*; Stradling comments on the fact that Coleridge-Taylor is not even mentioned by Howes in his *The English Musical Renaissance*, the standard work on the subject.

73. The definitive *Grove's dictionary of music and musicians* originated in the concert notes produced when Sir George Grove was secretary of the Crystal Palace Company (Musgrave, *Musical life*, pp. 113–116).

74. *Musical Times,* October 1912; see also Scholes, *Mirror,* pp. 129–130.

75. Parry says: "The pure occidental composer would have gone wrong trying to do something subtle and uncanny to show the fineness of his insight. . . . But Coleridge-Taylor had no such temptations" (quoted in Scholes, *Mirror,* p. 130). See also Berwick-Sayers, *Samuel Coleridge-Taylor,* p. 57, and H. Ancliffe, quoted in Tortolano, *Samuel Coleridge-Taylor,* p. 129. Tortolano does not criticize these statements, but instead uses them as evidence to establish Coleridge-Taylor's genius (p. 39). For discussion of the gendering of "classical" music, see, e.g., Citroen, M. J. (1993). *Gender and the musical canon.* Cambridge: Cambridge University Press. Leppert, R. (1991). *Music and image.* Cambridge: Cambridge University. Is a very useful account of the gendering of musical practices as "productive" and "unproductive." See also Shepherd, J. (1987). Music and male hegemony. In R. Leppert & S. McClary (Eds.), *Music and society: The politics of composition, performance, and reception.* Cambridge: Cambridge University Press, pp. 151–172; and Scott, D. (1993). Sexuality and musical style from Monteverdi to Mae West. In Miller (Ed.), *The last post,* pp. 132–149.

76. Self, *Life and work,* p. 86. He believes that the more serious abstract tone set, for example, in the "Ballade in A Minor" reflects a deliberate attempt to write music that would suit German tastes.

77. Self, *Life and work,* p. 115.

9

GLOBAL UNDERGROUNDS

The Cultural Politics of Sound and Light in Los Angeles, 1965–1975

SIMON RYCROFT

This chapter explores the constitution of musical meanings in 1960s Los Angeles and suggests that such meanings frequently transcend lyrical content, socioeconomic constraint, or stylistic influences. Conscious manipulation of the contexts of performance augments, subverts, or refigures the messages contained within musical texts, providing situated meanings. Throughout the 1960s and early 1970s, Western countercultures experimented in audiovisual technologies and alternative forms of mediated expression in an attempt to transcend theoretically received notions of technocratic and mechanistic modern social order.[1] These experiments were grounded in an appreciation for contemporary social, cultural, and media theory, and aimed to transmit a radical consciousness based upon a holistic vision of a global community. The multimedia environments such activities spawned, usually in clubs and occasional festivals, fused the aural with the visual in innovative ways, mixing musical sounds and poetry with lighting effects, film, television, and video. Within these environments, it was hoped that each audience member would become involved in the construction of the performance's meaning and form part of a radical global consciousness.

Such experiments constitute some of the basic tactics of 1960s underground revolt.

Definitions of what might comprise a counterculture generally limit themselves to material and structural relations as overriding explanatory mechanisms, subordinating any artistic or expressive dimensions of definition in to the socioeconomic base.[2] These definitions are prescriptive; they rarely consider the intellectual or aesthetic aspects of counterculture, interpreting instead from encoded modes of dress and behavior; as a direct result of this method, they reinforce the stereotypical *image* of the "hippie" as a member of a doped-out hedonistic tribe. The limits of any revolt in which they might be engaged are thus prescribed. In short, it is naïve to presume that the counterculture of the 1960s formed in a discursive vacuum. At the moment that critics such as Raymond Williams, E. P. Thompson, and Richard Hoggart began asserting the role of culture in the makeup of political consciousness and social reproduction, actors in the counterculture were simultaneously recognizing the same perspectives in the formulation of their own cultural politics. For me, it is perhaps this emphasis on the self-conscious appropriation and application of "social" theory—utilized in a variety of tactics from the written word to musical expression—that best defines the counterculture. To distance this account from previous definitions, therefore, it is more apt to employ the term "underground."

Notions of underground dissent not only recall a continuous heritage of intellectual revolt, from, say, the French bohemians of the 1830s and the Russian nihilists of the 1860s,[3] but also accurately reflect the aesthetics and poetics of countercultural expression in the 1960s. Writers and editors in the underground press, for example, exploited the romanticism of this heritage, counterpointing the "overground" establishment to the "underground" vanguard, and countercultural performance played on underground motifs in music, lightshows, and film.[4] By extending the limits of received notions regarding countercultural revolt and by considering certain intellectual and discursive influences, therefore, it is possible to envisage an oppositional force that augmented certain traditions. And while the globalized or internationalized politics of underground revolt are frequently asserted by theorists as well as practitioners, many of these influences are rooted in particular locations or situations. In short, by engaging with the discourse of the underground in its myriad textual forms, a more nuanced reading lays bare the complexities of the geographies of underground dissent.[5]

In 1960s Los Angeles (L.A.), for instance, different musical practices played out within the space of the city. Each practice represented a peculiar understanding of cultural politics relating to differing notions of "environment" and "geography." A broad tension is apparent between a universalist underground philosophy based upon media and drug experimentation and a localized, socialistic, radical agenda based upon communal values and civil rights. The former practice was characterized by the "globalized" genre of psychedelic (or acid) rock which absorbed influences from beyond the city. The latter practice had its roots in the 1940s' Beat movement, found a coherent identity in the city following the Watts rebellion, and was much more geographically and culturally localized. The geography of both is apparent in the morphology of countercultural L.A. and forms the logic of this chapter's structure: each had a different but related geography. Media experimentation found a place within most scenes within the city but tended to be resisted in the highly defined and demarcated zones of communal socialism such as Venice West. Frequently, however, this geography is a negotiation of the two strands. Because they share similar traditions in terms of postwar intellectual protest and experimentation with the form and content of aural and visual expression, they are difficult to distinguish. Broadly, however, multimedia musical practices stressed the role of (countercultural) technological developments in expanding consciousness in a global embrace, while localized "radical" musical practices, conversely, attempted to make false consciousness apparent, particularly that false consciousness identified in multimedia experimentation itself. This same conflict occurred throughout the Western underground movement and was represented in a series of opposing publications and protest styles, but in Los Angeles it is striking thanks to its spatialization. This chapter thus proceeds from a general analysis of situated media experimentation politics and aesthetics, to the specific cases of situated protest in Venice West and the Sunset Strip, and then to the less definite geographies of the global underground in L.A. in the form of the "Human Be-In" and multimedia.

SITUATED ENVIRONMENTS

The geographies of the 1960s underground are characterized by a series of synchronicities; developments in the aesthetics of countercultural revolt appear almost simultaneously in underground communities across the globe. This synchronicity was facilitated by the development of a global network of communications in the form of the Underground Press Syndicate and the mobility of key personnel and groups in the movement. But in each center of countercultural dissent, the character of that dissent played a series of variations on a theme. Perhaps the most familiar "scene" is that of San Francisco. But, while central to the development and day-to-day currency of the worldwide underground movement, the allure of San Francisco's scene tends to obscure other scenes on the West Coast.

Acid rock—the founding aesthetic of San Francisco's late 1960s music scene—emerges as a self-consciously universal, tribalist genre, attempting to make subconscious connections with the primeval and create a radical global consciousness. Most accounts of psychedelia play on this theme, identifying common phrases in words and music, constructing it as a global phenomena. Sheila Whiteley's account suggests precisely this, stating that the stylistic complexity of a range of performers—such as Cream, Hendrix, Donovan, Jeffersen Airplane, the Beatles, and the Doors—captured and defined the cultural characteristics of the counterculture: musical elements of "surprise, contradiction and uncertainty suggested alternative meanings which supported the hippies' emphasis on timeless mysticism."[6] Whiteley "proves" her case by musicological analysis, noting common musical sequences across the board. It seems from this that there was no geography of countercultural music. But her account ignores the contexts of performance and the situatedness of music itself. To be sure, those common elements were present, but so were a whole series of situated traditions that negotiated those universal characteristics. It follows that a more nuanced reading of situated undergrounds is required.

The ecologies of situated undergrounds were products of local traditions and discourses of dissent and representation. Los Angeles's underground was influenced by a particular discourse of the city itself, one that eschewed traditional narratives of urban form and formulated tactics of dissent in their light.[7] Music and performance played a significant role in the formation of this dissent in L.A., but messages were consciously augmented and altered via other means of expression and further complicated by events in the city. It is impossible to delineate the aesthetics of this revolt, therefore, without recourse to other media genres and to historicize and spatialize their occurrence. A series of sites and events demonstrate the peculiar geography of music in L.A. in the 1960s. There are, in short, a number of defining moments and situations in which music played a key role in refiguring the spaces and environments of countercultural dissent. First, however, it is important to delineate the peculiar character of the L.A. underground scene.

Much of this chapter draws upon the content of the underground press in L.A. between 1964 and 1975, and maps sites, texts, and contexts of countercultural musical performance in the city. The nature of these sites, while conceptually attuned, varied according to the nature of the local underground community. Different musical aesthetics and functions arose throughout the city, for example, on Venice Beach, in the clubs of the Sunset Strip, and in the Human Be-In festivals held at Griffith Park. Each reflected the situated cultural politics of their organizers and localized communities. This is not to infer in this instance that musical style was determined by urban ecology, but to emphasize that the geographies of music are influenced and defined by a series of discourses surrounding politics, social order, and culture. These structuring frames negotiate to produce sometimes subtle, sometimes explicit localized musical genres. To access this complex, therefore, the important sites and events of 1960s L.A. are considered with a specific emphasis upon the ways in which seemingly globalized countercultural genres (such as acid or psychedelic or folk rock) become situated and localized, influenced by the character of situated cultural politics. But L.A. musical aesthetics also defined a southern Californian style, characterized by a commitment to a conventional socialist communitarian agenda. Some attention, therefore, needs to be given to the broader discursive terrain of L.A. itself.

CULTURAL POLITICS AND URBAN ECOLOGY

In *The Sounds of the City* Charlie Gillett found that most L.A. music of the mid-1960s was labeled "folk rock" and "pop" but some music was less easy to categorize, especially that of Frank Zappa, Captain Beefeart, and Dr. John.[8] Consequently their evasion of Artists and Recording categorization meant relatively few records were sold. But in general, the "sound of Los Angeles," from the Doors[9] to the Mothers of Invention, was a variation on a theme of classic rhythm and blues with a particularly strong black (southern) influence. Acid rock or psychedelic rock, while influential in the city, was not the all-encompassing 1960s sound characteristic of many other scenes, especially further north in San Francisco. Indeed, in most senses San Francisco and Los Angeles represent two sides of the West Coast renaissance of the 1950s and 1960s, with the former building cultural politics upon a more entrenched and widespread tradition of Beat revolt characterized by a stronger emphasis on experimentation in modes of consciousness and expression,[10] and with the latter more influenced by situated events and discourses surrounding civil rights and urban territoriality.

To explore these differences some recourse to the influential narrative of urban ecology in L.A. is apposite. Los Angeles and southern California generally has always been constructed as somehow "Other": "mysterious, seductive, unsettling and enigmatic."[11] Accounts of L.A.'s morphology frequently explain the shape of the urban zone in terms of the automobile. But increasingly in the early 1960s critics jettisoned reductive explanations based upon the automobile, modernity, and Keynesian economics, and became more flexible considering, for example, the automobile as *reflected* in urban form but not necessarily determining it. The car, which remained a cultural icon central to the "L.A. look" and to the "L.A. lifestyle,"[12] was seen to contribute to "a highly decentred urban morphology,"[13] and formed a large part of the established (eastern) critique of L.A. as "a non-traditional city without ordered urban structure,"[14] while other explanatory narratives, or "L.A. stories," layered the narrative.[15]

Barry Miles from London's *International Times*[16] in a 1969 feature reemphasized the importance of the automobile as a structuring myth in the city's material and cultural–political spheres. L.A.'s lifestyle, he felt, thought of space in terms of routes, "organic movements on a central city archetype," which had a tendency to sort underground communities into discrete territories.[17] The music of the city, one expression of countercultural identity, was also profoundly affected by an automotive narrative, with its sound almost "derived from the sound of the automobile"[18] and characterized by variations around a standard rhythm and blues backbeat that literally drove the music.

Urban theorists pointed toward the state of flux that seemed to denote the city's identity, an identity that only in Disneyland seemed to re-create the Mandarin vision of an East Coast town.[19] Architecture critic Reynar Banham perhaps best captured this fluidity in his conception of the city's "Four Ecologies," an organic notion that described the functioning of L.A. in terms of the interaction of four diverse urban ecologies. In suggesting that all four betrayed "mechanisms natural and human that have made these ecologies support a way of life,"[20] Banham therefore connects differing social and cultural practices with distinct urban districts, a local discourse which was adopted by the underground and by urban theorists today. Contemporary scholars of the "L.A. school" view a similar diversity, and Soja in particular highlights a single important event in the genesis of urban–industrial restructuring, a moment from which traditional narratives of urban ecology no longer seemed to apply to the city: the Watts uprising of August 1965. Similarly, a study of the L.A. underground bears out this proposition. The riots became a defining moment in the cultural politics of underground dissent in the city.

The Watts riots articulated a series of local discourses of racism, economics, politics, infighting between the Downtown elite and their Westside challengers, and the ideological realignment of a number of L.A.'s civil rights groups.[21] Occurring at a time when the city's underground community was relatively young and surrounding issues of territoriality, the riots necessarily had a profound effect on the semiotics of dissent in L.A. Despite their Westside bases of operation remaining geographically distant from South Central, the underground was influenced by an emergent "Watts aesthetic," the events having "galvanised artists and writers on the first broad scale since the Hollywood witchhunt."[22] Although this commitment was augmented by a similar questioning of white morality concerning United States involvement in Vietnam,[23] the L.A. underground was characterized by a more traditional Old Leftist libertarian discourse which, likewise, took the Watts uprising as a galvanizing moment.

L.A.'s most prominent underground patriarch in the 1960, Art Kunkin, editor and founder of the *Los Angeles Free Press* (the city's first and largest underground paper began its run in the summer of 1964), was influenced by the "Watts aesthetic." For Kunkin, freedom of artistic expression was the hallmark of a healthy liberal community and civic consciousness: "Our [the *Free Press*'s] fundamental and overall concern is with the creation of those conditions where each one of us can really live a deeply personal life as we see fit, with due regard for our fellow human beings."[24] The *Free Press*'s support for the 1966 Artist's Tower of Protest in favor of peace on the troubled Sunset Strip bears this out. The Protest Tower was constructed from a series of painted panels by various artists, and exhibited for a week with concurrent impromptu performances from local folksingers and actors, and mediated by Situationist guards, challenging passersby to express their feelings on its message.[25] Central to exhibitions in one media therefore were the messages contained in another, each contributing to negotiated and *democratic communal* messages as a direct result of the breakdown of communication witnessed in the riots.[26] In the L.A. underground more so than in other scenes, art, therefore, was a legitimate mode of voicing dissent.

Watts, while a territory that played a minor role in the production and consumption of underground culture in the city, therefore had a disproportionate influence upon the aesthetics of revolt. The riots coincided with the establishment of the *Free Press,* a number of socialist and artists cooperatives and communes in the city, and a range of civil rights organizations. These groups found cohesion through their attachment mainly to the events in the district, for their members rarely resided in Watts. But this involvement helped formulate the "Watts aesthetic" that defined the grounds of revolt throughout the 1960s and 1970s.[27] The "Watts aesthetic" as it emerged throughout the 1960s coupled traditional civil rights concerns with radical artistic expression in a variety of media, the defining characteristic of the L.A. underground.

Throughout its run, and particularly during Kunkin's editorship, the *Free Press* deliberately involved itself in Los Angeles's underground community, sponsoring events, parties, and some of the first "Acid Tests" in the city.[28] From the outset, most of the festivals had some sort of backing from the paper, including the first "Love-In" in Griffith Park, in conjunction with another in San Francisco, and a series of free concerts held mainly on the Westside, the first of which was the Great Underground Arts Masked Ball and Orgy (GUAMBO). GUAMBO was an indoor event originally scheduled to take place on the corner of Fairfax and Beverley at the Aeronautical Institute. Confusion over the meaning of Kunkin's appeal for people to bring "junk" (interpreted as drugs) in order to make a junk sculpture caused the institute to cancel 24 hours before the event. Consequently the concert, featuring the Mothers of Invention in their first-ever performance, was held in a hotel downtown on Western Boulevard. Afterward the *Free Press* generally held open-air concerts with no admission charges. Kunkin used his connections in the cultural community to hold concerts and happenings throughout the city, but especially on Venice Beach where a concentration of sympathetic community leaders, some of whom were already involved with the paper, were willing to cooperate. Indeed, the Westside of the city, including Venice and the Sunset Strip, became the geographical focus for most underground activity.[29]

L.A.'s underground operated amid a discourse of the city's ecology (literally, its way of life) and formulated tactics in its light. Reading through the city's underground press of the 1960s and 1970s, it is apparent that the articulated target of their revolt was the nature of the urban form itself. Underground groups worked locally and citywide to resist, for instance, the demolition of particular buildings and the redrawing of a district's political boundaries, emphasizing continuity and tradition amid chaos. And the sounds of L.A. music were similarly structured, rarely experimenting beyond a more standard manipulation of words, music, and the context of performance that characterized the underground in other places, and being slow to take up developments in the manipulation of medium and message.

MEDIUM, MESSAGE, AND MANIPULATION

The 1960s underground deployed new techniques from contemporary theories on the media, technocracy, and the written word. The mid-1960s witnessed an explosion in communication forms. Acid-influenced multimedia events and sound and light shows of the late 1950s and early 1960s, such as the "happenings" at the Albert Hall in London, Andy Warhol's experiments in New York City, and the Fillmore Ballroom in San Francisco, grew out of a fusion of formerly distinct media types and contributed to revolutions in all forms of media. Sights and sounds were experimented with and blended in new ways to provide "total media" happenings or "environments."[30]

Light became a significant new art medium, one that could break the bounds of elite cultural expression. Lightshows were complemented by electronic sounds. New electronic groups played on stage in front of "head-lights," multicolored psychedelic light shows regarded as integral to the music itself. Acid rock, a new genre of rock music, emerged from these experiments, owing something to hallucinogens but just as much to multimedia aesthetics themselves. Celebrated by many in the underground press, experiments with feedback, primitive video technology, and putative synthesizers were considered primeval sounds, natural sounds of the electronic age: "both fact and metaphor, conjuring up aural images of the current that drives our daily living."[31]

Technology enabled a spiritual leap backward, breaching the barriers between art and everyday life,[32] a fusion of art and science, the sensory and the intellectual in "a cosmic cauldron of psychedelic experience." Participation in such psychedelic environments imparted enlightened awareness: "We projected our eyes around the moon and realized for the first time that we are just elements of an atom in the vastness of the cosmos ... artists, and scientists, creating synthetic lightshows, are the first manifestation of this awareness."[33] Such rhetoric highlights the contradictory understanding of technology and technological vistas as both liberating and restricting. And it also suggests the centrality of a countercultural understanding of technology to the emergence of contemporary environmental consciousness[34]: the function of the psychedelic artist limned the function of the ecologist in a performance situation, revealing the "relationships between the organism [participant] and its environment."[35]

As simulacrums of the cosmos, these new environments owed much to putative media theory, particularly that of Marshall McLuhan. He was adopted by the counterculture as one of a number of contemporary theorists and patriarchs, including Herbert Marcuse, R. D. Laing, Theodore Roszak, and Buckminster Fuller. But the "telegraphic immediacy" and opacity of McLuhan, perhaps, had the most significant impact—the epistemological contradictions between each theorist were of little concern to the first television generation.[36] McLuhan's jettisoning of media content as a major constituent of transmitted messages in his *Understanding Media*[37] and other works opened media analysis to broader socioeconomic and cultural environments. Changes in the social order were explained by the decline in the dominance of linear print media and the rise of nonlinear computer and electronic communications. While redirecting social science, McLuhan's insistence that technologies were central to the alteration of life and consciousness became central, if implicit, to the intellectual revolt of the 1960s.[38]

For McLuhan, in the preelectronic mechanical age all forms of media were extensions of our physical bodies in space. In the technological age, with the advent of electronic mediums, however, we "extended our central nervous system itself in a global embrace abolishing both space and time as far as our planet is concerned."[39] And the message of any medium was therefore the change in scale, pace, or pattern introduced into human affairs. So the message of, say, television was not broadcast schedules, but the effect of television upon culture: the way it changed people and social relations.[40] The potential for these new technologies as liberating devices were clear, but so too were their dangers as devices of "violent" control of consciousness.[41]

But the attractiveness of McLuhan's rendering of media and consciousness to the underground was founded upon the notion of participation and interaction in the formulation of media messages. The Mechanical Age broke the social networks of traditional oral societies (those with a high level of interaction and participation) by the introduction of "hot" or dense linear mediums such as mass-produced printing. The Technological Age had introduced "cooler" interactive mediums (T.V., movies, telephones, etc.). Within the new mediums lay the potential to replicate a primitive tribal social order:

> A tribal and feudal hierarchy of traditional kind collapses quickly when it meets any hot medium of the mechanical, uniform and repetitive kind. ... Similarly, a very much greater speed-up, such as occurs with electricity, may serve to restore a tribal pattern of intense involvement such as took place with the introduction of radio in Europe, and is now tending to happen as a result of T.V. in America. Specialist technologies detribalize. The non-specialist technology retribalizes.[42]

"Put more simply, the Orientalization of the West, the insight brought by media, is that people want roles, not goals, style not objectives."[43] And the universality of McLuhan's media–society dialectic necessarily implied some form of transcendent commonalty, or the "Global Village." Electronic media caused an implosion effect, localizing, despacing, and retribalizing, creating a neoprimordial world in which participation and interaction are maximized. Media technologies, as extensions of humanity, were naturalized; nature and the cosmos were reasserted into culture.[44] Eventually, the climax of the Technological Age would be the "technological simulation of consciousness, when the creative process of knowing will be collectively and corporately extended to the whole of human society,"[45] or the development of a single common transcendent consciousness. And for McLuhan, the advertising industry was the vanguard in the retribalization process: "Bless Madison Ave for restoring the magical art of the caveman to suburbia."[46]

McLuhan courted the attention of the counterculture. His books were advertised widely in the underground press, and his magazine, *Aspen,* was intended expressly for them: "Our medium will massage you about the tribal man."[47] Indeed, the underground press saw the widespread knowledge of the new media theory as a defining quality of the new revolutionary movement, a movement whose "members seem to have an instinctive understanding of McLuhan-style media theory: they know how to use the media to strongest advantage."[48] Within the movement much was made of these new technologies of liberation, particularly in the United States. Underground papers began advertising and reviewing developments in video and audio technologies. Readers were encouraged to set up media collectives, to subvert the dominance of straight media, to "seize the media and save the world."[49] In New York City the collective Global Village and in San Francisco Video Free America experimented with nonlinear forms of expression and collective media messages. Electronic media became, in the late 1960s, the latest sacrament of the counterculture, one whose theory showed the interconnectedness of all things: "The mystics and visionaries all saw this clearly but the rest of us need video (and acid) to make it evident."[50]

Clearly, these are transcendental notions suggesting a uniform cultural politics and musical aesthetics, but as the remainder of this chapter demonstrates, local traditions in, among other things, the politics of dissent, shape the geographies of music and performance. There were conflicts and contradictions within the L.A. scene itself between different styles and genres of music and musical performance. Most significantly, each of these styles rests upon different perceptions of "environment" in a McLuhanesque sense and conflicting geographical imaginations that in turn formed the foundation of very different cultural politics in various enclaves of the city.

VENICE WEST: BONGOS AND BEARDS

The Venice West district, on the coast north of Marina Del Rey and south of Santa Monica, presents a legacy of subversive groups whose history can be read in the architecture and geography of the region. From its conception as a vast leisure resort mirroring the "real" Venice, to its current image as the center for Angelenos wishing to live alternative lifestyles (a legacy from the 1950s and 1960s), Venice West presents itself as catering to the more artistically and socially aware of L.A.'s citizens.[51] The district was founded in 1905 as the embodiment of the dream of Abbott Kinney, a property developer who wished to reproduce his romantic vision of the real Venice. To this end he imported gondolas for the sea water canals that were spanned by authentic bridges and lined with colonnaded facades. Kinney's intention was to create a fantasy city that would serve as a retreat for the business community of L.A. and bring a West Coast culturally progressivist style of end-of-the-pier entertainment to Angelenos in the form of an auditorium that hosted his Chatauqua, or assembly of culture. This fantastic dream would, however, eventually come to be maintained by the kind of community that Kinney certainly did not have in mind.

Lawrence Lipton, a detective fiction writer who wrote with his wife under her pseudonym Craig Rice, moved to Venice from Santa Monica with more serious literary ambitions after their divorce in 1948. Lipton's intention was to live cheaply and write his poetry while living off the earnings of the best-selling series of Rice books. During the 1950s, Lipton gathered about him a number of local poets and artists, and became the figurehead of a cultural community in Venice, which he eventually labeled the "Holy Barbarians."[52] Lipton viewed the artists' disposition as that of a shaman, calling for a "the restoration of the ritual life and of the many gods that had once presided over it."[53] The artists and performers he attracted, many of them Korean War veterans, bore out his philosophy in their lifestyles and made up Venice's disaffiliated Beatnik community. Even though the core group of cultural producers never grew to beyond 30 in number, this elite began colonizing the run-down buildings in Venice, converting them into coffeehouses and jazz–poetry dens and attracting daily and seasonal visitors. The ocean front walk became the focus of their activities, including John Haag's Venice West Cafe, the Gas House, and the exclusive artists' colony on an upper floor of the Grand Hotel which supported the most disaffiliate of Lipton's disciples.

Lipton outlined his philosophy of their way of life as "The New Poverty," which "is the disaffiliate's answer to the New Prosperity."[54] A philosophy of art became inseparable from a philosophy of life: "If disaffiliation really made the artist free, it could also turn him into the prototype of a new kind of free human being."[55] The Holy Barbarians were compared to the first Christians, developing their own rituals and sacraments unadorned with civilized trappings. Rituals and myths were seen to give cohesiveness to a community whose ultimate objective was to find new ways of knowing: "wholeness, personal salvation, in a word, holiness, and the artist has always been in search of it. . . . What then is this self that the Holy Barbarian is constantly exploring? It is a search for the 'Original Face' [after Alan Watts]. His basic, original nature."[56] In a McLuhanesque sense, the reading of poetry in the district, particularly when accompanied by free-form jazz, was interpreted by Lipton as part of a revival in certain lost elements of oral or tribal culture, "sparked by the electronics revolution in communication, by the phonograph, radio, tape recorder, and the audio-visual media of motion pictures and television."[57]

Lipton's community of disaffiliates managed to amass significant physical assets in the Venice district: venues for poetry and jazz, coffeehouses, bars, and hotels—many of which occupied Kinney's old infrastructure. These monuments became imbued with new countercultural meaning and the original vision of Venice West was redefined in their own image. Throughout the 1960s and 1970s, the protection of Venice from developers and real estate agents was articulated around these monuments through music and carnival. Venice became a contested territory, an identifiable enclave that served as the site for a series of attacks on, and expressions of, countercultural lifestyle throughout the period. It became the focus of attention not only for the young, but for the Los Angeles Police Department (LAPD) and city hall. Disputes usually surrounded the coffeehouses and other poetry-reading and music venues because most provided entertainment without the required police permit. The first arrest was that of the Venice West Cafe owner, John Haag, on September 19, 1964. Haag interpreted his detention as politically motivated, claiming that it followed his sponsorship of a demonstration against police malpractice in the city through an ad hoc committee that he chaired. Police had been present at performances in the cafe for the previous six years, only choosing to enforce the law when provoked by Haag's activities: "Wherever there is anything different from the commonplace, you can expect the Los Angeles Police Department to interfere. Wherever there is criticism of the police you can expect the LAPD to retaliate."[58] In Venice, Haag felt that by enforcing quirky citywide ordinances, the police were waging a campaign against bohemians and other minority groups, "acting more like an army of occupation than like the guardians of law and order they pretended to be."[59]

Later in the same year, the city attorney was instructed to draft a new anti-drumming ordinance. As with the entertainment permit, the city council member for Venice, Karl Rundberg, with his self-confessed hatred of bohemian lifestyles, was pivotal in the attempt to curb their activities, claiming that he was being pressed to act by the Venice community. Significantly, the proposed ordinance covered musical instruments synonymous with the culture of alternative living in the district: guitars and wind instruments. Councilman Rundberg complained that beatniks "sleep all day. They start out in their beards about 10 pm and get all ginned up on beer and raise hell all night long. . . . I want to get rid of these beatniks who beat on garbage cans."[60]

Developers were increasingly interested in the region, attracted by cheap property prices, and police harassment was interpreted as part of the same conspiracy. Lipton was called before a consortium of "realestateniks," and chastised for labeling Venice the "Slum by the Sea" in *The Holy Barbarians*. For Lipton, the "slum" was a place of refuge for artists disaffiliates, where it was possible to live in voluntary poverty. Plans to hold the Los Angeles World Fair in Venice also worried him. It would solve in one "fell swoop the problems of profitable property neglect, cockroaches, dry–wet rot and slum lords, along with such menaces as writers, poets, painters, bookstores, bongo drums, folk guitars, jazz, beards, sandals and all forms of dissent and non-conformism."[61] But the artists, he was confident, who were experienced in living at a subsistence level under tyranny would "continue to make their contribution to the West Coast Renaissance of the arts."[62]

But these incursions appeared to strike at the heart of all that the

Venice counterculture was attempting to achieve. The enforcement of particular laws was clearly targeted at certain facets of the lifestyle and philosophy that had evolved within the district: narcotics, music, poetry, and street entertainment. The systematic enforcement of ordinances concerning the reading of poetry and the holding of dances that had first to be vetted by the Los Angeles Board of Recreation and Parks was seen not only as an attack on countercultural lifestyles and the kind of spontaneity they depended on, but also as part of a broader objective to redevelop Old Venice.

During the late 1960s, in Venice West, Lipton's tradition of beatnik experimentation with aural and poetic expression evolved. A series of cooperatives and communes that began experimentation in more contemporary technologies resided in the district. A new consciousness required a new language, and the cooperative "Single Wing Turquoise Bird" sought, with light and sound, to define "the first words of an entirely different vocabulary, a tribal language which expressed not ideas but states of consciousness—not of individuals but of groups."[63] Given the equipment— three overhead projectors, two movie projectors, and a series of strobe and spot lights—this seemed overambitious, and Single Wing Turquoise Bird were undercapitalized, frequently played down the importance of the bands they provided the lightshows for and consequently were short-lived. The relative failure of this venture says much about the character of music and performance in Venice and in L.A. generally. While prepared to indulge in multimedia experimentation, Venice was certainly not in the vanguard; the weight of artistic tradition in the district and the battle for independence affected its development.

But, as this brief review of events in the Venice district shows, music and performance in conjunction with other activities played a crucial role in formulating the politics of dissent and protest and in constructing a community identity. While posited on a transcendent and universal philosophy of expression, these genres found particular significance in Venice West. The mix of situated events, especially various political and territorial disputes, and the peculiar tactics of the local underground formed the context of musical performance and shaped its meaning. And while not averse to more progressive musical experimentation, Venice remained tied to largely traditional musical styles of revolt, reminiscent of the early Campaign for Nuclear Disarmament (CND) protests in Britain. Local musical practices and social practices (or cultural politics) are thus inseparable, as I have implied, and the nature of L.A.'s fragmented ecology seems to emphasize this trait. So, while Venice West may have relied upon less "evolved" forms of musical protest, the Sunset Strip hosted more familiar countercultural performances.

THE FUNSET STRIP

> They came to me and asked me to head up that committee to save the Sunset Strip for the hippies. They were running up and down yelling "This is Our Strip!" But I mean, Sunset Strip belongs to Gloria Swanson or the Indians if it belongs to anyone and what's all the noise about one little piece of land anyway? It's not really that important.[64]

Although an important territory for battles between the underground and establishment, the Sunset Strip in the Hollywood district was hyped beyond any real propensity to erupt in a similar manner to Watts, perhaps also reflecting the weight of the Strip's meaning to the entertainment industry worldwide. Unlike Venice, there was no important dissentient history to latch onto and exploit, nor was there a sizeable indigenous radical population. Rather, the Sunset Strip served as a shopping mall for L.A.'s countercultural dabblers, full-timers, or just interested onlookers. The major countercultural factions residing on the Strip were the Diggers and the Provos, an international Situationist-influenced group; the latter stoked the more violent confrontations in the district.

If there were a district in L.A. that emulated the cultural politics of dissent characterized by the Haight-Ashbury district in San Francisco between 1967 and 1968, it would be the Sunset Strip. The community of Diggers in both places at this time were in the ascendant. In San Francisco they reaffirmed Haight territoriality with a series of "happenings" in the district, many organized by the Digger community and those who ran outlets in the local hippie economy. What distinguished the Diggers, "an amorphous, shifting and sometimes contentious amalgam of ex-political radicals, psychedelic mystics, Ghandians and Brechtian avant-garde thespians,"[65] from other community members was their commitment to direct action, spectacle, and the redefinition of political expression. Wherever they appeared in urban underground communities, the Diggers' efforts were focused on the creation of an alternative community. By distributing free food, free accommodation, and free clothing, and through ceremony and festival, they declared the changing nature of a territory. In Haight, they successfully established a "sense of community for hippies."[66] San Francisco Diggers attempted to formulate an anarchistic "antistructure" philosophy, warning against "structure freaks." Leaders were neither good or bad, but leading per se was bad. Amalgamating McLuhan's concept of medium as message, the message of leadership was "Vietnam. Concentration camps. The Great Society. Riots on Haight Street."[67]

In 1967, Los Angeles boasted some 30 headshops (places to buy drug and related paraphernalia) and a series of underground music clubs, a large cluster of which were centered on the Sunset Strip and served a nomadic population. Beginning in June 1967, the Diggers held "Feed-Ins" in parking lots on the Strip as part of an initiative to create an alternative economy that would include workshops producing hippie goods.[68] The Strip also had a "hip minister" at the West Hollywood Presbyterian Church, the "Missionary to the Sunset Strip," whose calling was to guide the "return to naturalism and an attempt to escape the vast urbanization of man into his cement cities."[69]

As the radical community's Central Business District, the Sunset Strip appeared to serve a surrogate Watts role, where ideas and their expression formed in the crucible of the riots were played out within the conflicts and "happenings" on the Strip between 1967 and 1968. Its proximity to South Central and the recent escalation in clashes between the underground and the authorities on the Strip meant that events logically suited to a reaffirmation of Watts's identity were sited within the Sunset Strip district. Events/happenings like the Artists' Peace Tower, prompted by Watts and the "Watts aesthetic," and expressing a commitment to a more general radical L.A. aesthetic, that would promote civic (underground) pride, took place in this district on La Cinega and Sunset Boulevard, for example.[70] More suitably, the Strip played host to some of the countercultures' more traditional happenings, including in September 1967 the first in a series of sporadic processions, involving an old Twin Coach, on which the city's new underground bands were showcased.[71]

MULTIMEDIA

Influenced primarily by the writings of McLuhan and occasionally by those of Buckminster Fuller, the L.A. *Free Press*'s multimedia correspondent, Gene Youngblood, followed the lightshow and acid rock scene in the city and throughout the country. Curiously, it was precisely the sense of tradition and citizenship characterized by the Venice community and the broader L.A. underground that the message of multimedia electronic environments blurred, evoking more primeval associations and a radical communitarian politics based less on socialism and more on tribalism:

> Someday, New York will be preserved under a mile-high plastic dome and exhibited like a museum piece. That dome will be manufactured in Southern California.... On the West Coast—where tradition has died, where change is the only constant, where technologist visionaries are constructing a super world, where television extends our senses into space, where the ears of science listen to pulsar messages from the cosmos—here on the West Coast, a new consciousness is being born ... more occult than psychedelic, mystic rather than Maoist.[72]

There was a general view that L.A. could not match up to multimedia events held elsewhere in the global underground. This dearth was frequently expressed, as above, in terms of the city's peculiar urban ecology and the ephemeral nature of its existence. On a visit to San Francisco to review the underground film community, the *Free Press* correspondent Richard Whitehall bemoaned the L.A. scene in this light: "After the urban sprawl of Los Angeles, the Bay area was a great place to be, ... it isn't just that San Francisco is a city and not just a succession of tract-housing developments in search of a city." And, evoking the lack of tradition and tangible history to draw on in L.A., he noted that in San Francisco, "There is still a sense of the past reaching into the present. . . . There is an intellectual stimulation comparable only to Paris in the communication and interaction between painters, sculptors, poets and film makers, so the distinctions blur, and each one seems involved in the totality of the artistic life around him."[73]

And the fragmented nature of L.A.'s underground was implicated in a similar lack of coherence in the music of dissent; the different genres in general only reflected the self-interests of individual communities. Why, it was asked, were performances on the Strip not mirrored elsewhere in the city, providing much-needed cohesiveness to L.A.'s radical liberal community? "What if some black kids in L.A.'s ghetto and some white young hairs from Fairfax and the Strip and Laural Canyon and parts of the Far East etc., started to plan some Gatherings of ALL the tribes in ALL the parks?"[74]

According to Gene Youngblood, the clubs in Los Angeles were behind their counterparts in San Francisco or New York and even they did not fully appreciate the potential, scope, or mind-altering possibilities of a multimedia environments in the strictly McLuhanesque sense: "Of course every corner bar [in The Strip] from the Whiskey to the Magic Mushroom now has its sheet and light piddle, but they don't count as 'total environment.' "[75] Gene Youngblood pointed to the Doors and the Mothers of Invention as among those who had fully understood "environmental theater" (after Artaud) and begun to deploy it.[76]

It was the Sunset Strip that witnessed most of the city's explorations in sound and light. The Magic Mushroom rather than the Whiskey A-Go-Go hosted most of the city's "electronic" groups of which there were, perhaps surprisingly, many: Kaleidoscope, Electronic Zit, the Amplified Trinity, and the Stuffed Ereworm.[77] Musical expression within the L.A. underground therefore took on a character that matched the peculiar ecology of the city and its dissentient communities. The Mothers of Invention were considered the most prominent of the city's groups, although they chose New York for many of their shows. Returning to perform sporadically in the city, the Mothers provided a critique of L.A.'s musically unprogressive rebellion in fliers and ads for their 1967 Wilshire gig: "In order to insure that our concert will have no commercial potential and so as not to disrupt that framework of the existing social–cultural structure an evening with The Mothers will have no dancing no liquor no light show no age limit . . . just 2 hours of unadulterated musak." But the Mothers set played on the theater of cruelty and the absurd, wholly in tune with much of L.A's underground rebellion: "We'll mention the police and Gov't a lot and we can all nod our heads together while we cop out. . . . We've been rehearsing new numbers like 'BROWN SHOES DON'T MAKE IT' 'I'M LOSING MY STATUS AT THE HIGH SCHOOL' and a new Funset Strip version of 'WHO ARE THE BRAIN POLICE?' that is guaranteed to titillate your liberal backgrounds."

HUMAN BE-INS

For L.A., festivals were more commonplace than multimedia experimentation, but their structure frequently differed from the original models born in San Francisco. The era of the mass festival, the Happening, or the Be-In was short-lived, and particularly so in L.A., where they came and went between 1965 and 1969. Be-Ins or Love-Ins frequently took place simultaneously in cities on the West Coast and occasionally elsewhere. The San Francisco Be-Ins sprung organically from Haight-Ashbury. For Jay Stevens, in his account of LSD and the American dream, it was the strategic geographical position of San Francisco, the "Queen city of California," that gave the Love-In special meaning there, making it, in the second half of the 20th century, the "Paris of discontent."[78] There was also the heritage of the Beat movement to draw upon in the city; indeed, the Beat poet Allen Ginsberg played a pivotal role in the organization of the first Be-Ins.[79] In its context, the Be-In amplified the impact of Haight, pointing up the disintegrating social fabric of San Francisco and America. San Francisco was the main media port of call, after Saigon. Even Gray-Line buses made a point of altering their routes so that passengers could see the hippies of Haight.[80]

As many as 25,000 people attended the first Be-In or "Pow-Wow" at Golden Gate Park in January 1967. San Francisco's underground press presented the Be-In as a celebration of the tradition of North American Indians, gathering on the plains, praying to the spirits that the "great muds would flow down and cover the 'white epidemic.' "[81] Similarly, this generation "considered by many to be the reincarnation of the American Indian, has been born out of the ashes of World War Two, rising like a Phoenix, in celebration of the slightly psychedelic zeitgeist of this brand-new Aquarian Age." Be-Ins expressed the greening of a new generation, seeking the "return of this once voluptuous country."[82] On stage, Allen Ginsberg and Gary Snyder chanted mantras and even the Hells Angels, hired as "security" guards, were reborn in the atmosphere of peace and love, becoming noble warriors, a cross between the "collectiveness of the Centurion Guard, and the individuality of the Samurai."[83]

The first Human Be-In in San Francisco also affected the course and patterns of underground dissent in the city. Significantly, the event represented a departure from conventional political expression. Berkeley radicals and the Students for a Democratic Society (SDS), previously the dominant group, were dwarfed by the ascendancy of Haight, and their calls for a political rally were ignored. The hippie lobby pushed for a musical festival punctuated by readings and talks from poets and prophets. When the radicals approached the microphone toward the end of the day, the crowds dispersed. For Rorabaugh, this experience resulted in a new understanding between the two groups: "The radicals learned that rock music and LSD were more popular than the New Left.... Both groups were rebelling against social norms ... so [a] shared joint went a long way toward a hippie-radical fusion."[84]

During 1967, there was a season of Be-Ins and festivals coinciding with the summer in which Los Angeles saw its largest influx of countercultural revellers to date. The first event was held on Saturday, January 14, in Griffith Park, in conjunction with the first in Golden Gate Park, San Francisco, and organized jointly by the *San Francisco Oracle* and the *Los Angeles Free Press* underground papers. Meeting in a house in the Hollywood hills, the two groups devised the Be-In as a promotion of a "Tribal System," for which they detected a "mass yearning" among the young.[85] This first Human Be-In in the city was alternatively promoted as a "Pow-Wow"—a gathering of the Braves—in the hope that it would encourage a "genuinely democratic social movement outside the major political parties."[86] Such a new social movement would recognize seers, visionaries, and gurus as their appointed leaders, following the doctrine of Timothy Leary, also present at the planning meeting. It was an attempt to "get Western man out of the cities and back to tribes and villages."[87] Significantly, Leary spoke at the San Francisco Be-In but not at the L.A. ones.

The Griffith Park Be-Ins were the first time that L.A.'s public parks were used for such an event, although they were already established traditions in New York and San Francisco. But they also encapsulated a curious and short-lived development in the cultural politics of underground dissent in the city. Even the language of their "invitations" jarred with the more staid socialist character of the local counterculture: revellers were encouraged to bring "the color gold, incense, flowers and pictures of your favorite guru."[88] Entertainment was "impromptu" and eclectic, mixing folk, jazz, poetry, and acid rock. Later in the day of the first Be-In, festivities moved to the Hullabaloo club on the Sunset Strip where a much larger crowed gathered and were entertained by the day's performers in more conventional surroundings. While 600 attended the first Be-In, crowds at the second were much greater and the music festival was proclaimed by some as a new development for the city, a turning point in the local politics of dissent from the city's characteristic form of theater of cruelty to the theater of love: "Hey Antoinin Artaud, you poor old dead junkie, faggot funny farm commuter genius. It's really a drag that you weren't around in freaky L.A. this past weekend"; the "new" hippies had become a community.[89]

The police were expecting trouble at this event since it came on the back of disturbances in the nearby Sunset Strip. There was, however, very little trouble. For the organizers in L.A., the only blot on an otherwise peaceful day was the presence of the local Provo group, who, indulging in a little self-promotion, and to make an absurdity of the proceedings, carried placards reading "PROVO PRESENTS HUMAN BE-IN."[90]

Throughout 1967, events on the Sunset Strip[91] impinged upon a series of Be-Ins in Griffith Park, gradually politicizing them as police infiltration and the violence increased. The second Be-In held in March 1967, was seen as the most successful, when "THE NEW HIPPIES OF LOS ANGELES BECAME A COMMUNITY FOR THE FIRST TIME."[92] They year 1967 saw not only more violence but also a particularly high in-migration to the city, with the arrival of some 100,000 would-be hippies "full of adventure but empty of purse."[93] Latter, an uneasy alliance between the city's Hells Angels and the countercultural community was forged, causing problems with the police and resulting in a near riot at the July Be-In when "police cleared the Love-In and busted more than 40 people ... and incurred the further enmity of a mostly pacifist hip community which is getting increasingly bitter about blue-coat harassment."[94] Eventually, the violence heralded the end of the Love-In era in L.A. Some 11 months after they first appeared, a commentator reported the "social dream which the 'Be-In' originally represented has degenerated into the fierce reality of muggings, rapes, arrests and shootings."[95] Even the global, tribal, and unifying phenomena of the Be-Ins as they were grafted onto the city seemed affected by the different character of L.A.'s underground community.

After the 1967–1968 seasons, occasional Be-Ins or festivals occurred in other parts of the city. The character of these later events was similarly forged by the peculiar circumstances within the territory where they took place. In April 1969 Venice Beach hosted its first free concert, attempting to build upon the success of Be-Ins in the previous two years. In the mythology of L.A., the "Beach" was considered an ideal ecology of life for such revelry.[96] Symbolically situated on "America's edge," the festival was once again portrayed as an event that could unite a disparate underground. Unfortunately, the territory was not free of city ordinances, and despite the transcendental music, other sacraments were strictly outlawed in the beach, including alcohol. A bottling incident caused the LAPD, with whom the show's sponsors the L.A. *Free Press* had cooperated in the planning, to crack down on the crowds, declaring the gathering an unlawful assembly and causing a minor riot.[97] Unknown to the organizers, prior to the festival, the LAPD had applied for and obtained an emergency ordinance banning electronically amplified music from the city's beaches. Compounded by a series of other skirmishes and disputes occurring already in Venice, the home of many of L.A's underground intelligentsia, the "LAPD riots" were presented as a flash point of conflict between the establishment and the underground: "You [the establishment] have closed or severely restricted various establishments which offered the brand of entertainment or music we enjoy and appreciate. . . . You are and have been and we are becoming."[98]

SOUND, LIGHT, AND THE GLOBAL UNDERGROUND

A series of musical genres jostled for place and function in the geographies of underground L.A. Clearly, these styles were not grafted onto, or unmediated by, the discursive environment of the city and the more localized character of underground revolts. Musical meanings are thus constituted by situations, a complex of grounded influences: political, economic, cultural, media, and style. The music of dissent, in general, is defined by localized ecology and politics. And while these situated cultural politics and related musical expressions clearly had a geography in terms of aerial differentiation, a much more complex and subtle geography of music is apparent. Each enclave described here, as I have implied, held related but different notions of environment and "environmental consciousness." And these notions reflected the scope and operation of located and seemingly contradictory geographical imaginations.

In Venice, the weight of local traditions of difference (in design, performance, and expression) and territorial pressures from the LAPD, the government, and real estate developers served to found a cultural politics of music in the 1960s that took as its referent much more localized discourses. These were related to a situated tradition of beatnik revolt characterized by a notion of a globalized communal politics through experimentation with the mix of various modes of expression (impromptu performances, jazz, poetry, etc.). This cultural politics engendered an environmental consciousness that helped redefine the meanings of the district and its peculiar infrastructure itself, and had a significant influence throughout L.A.; but it was reluctant to take influences from beyond the district. Conversely, the human Be-Ins held at Griffith park were transposed from earlier and similar events in San Francisco to which music, especially acid and folk rock, became central in forming the politics of dissent. These events certainly did tap into a transcendental notion of dissent based upon a McLuhanesque construction of global media environments, but their character in L.A. was molded by a pervasive geographical imagination, influenced in part by events in and characteristics of the Venice district, in which many underground patriarchs resided, and by their significance as sites of conflict between local underground factions, but also by a broader citywide commitment to a more conventional communitarian politics in the wake of the Watts uprising. Similarly, in the Sunset Strip, more "transcendental forces" were operating in the form of the Diggers and Provo, and the district's international media and film image enabled it to become the only significant enclave experimenting in medium and message in L.A. But musical expression in the Strip relied as much upon the L.A. underground concerns of art dissent and democracy, following the earlier riots in the proximate Watts district and skirmishes in the Strip itself, as they did upon advances in the technologies of light and sound. Again, then, events in South Central provided ideological impetus to the cultural politics of dissent in the 1960s and 1970s across the city, delimiting the scope of a radical geographical imagination.

The styles and genres of 1960s music, while philosophically grounded in notions of a global underground community, found meaning within L.A.'s territories of underground dissent. As this chapter demonstrates, a series of countercultural enclaves witnessed very different developments in musical performance, but the cultural politics of each was conceptually related through a discourse of media theory, the collapsing of space and time, and the notional development of a single transcendent consciousness. This seems true for San Francisco, for New York, for London and for other centers of dissent in the 1960s. The aural, the visual, and the textual were fused in ways peculiar to the environments and territories of dissent. The geographies of music thus arise from complex dialogues between discursive environments and palpable environments, between situated dominant and subversive geographical imaginations.

ACKNOWLEDGMENTS

The research for this chapter was funded by the Economic and Social Research Council. Much of the material presented arises from a broader study of the 1960s underground press. Where various histories, events, and situations are presented, they have been drawn from accounts in numerous countercultural periodicals. I am grateful to Steve Daniels, Peter Jackson, and Douglas Tallack for their commentary on earlier drafts. I am also indebted to the editors of this volume for their valuable comments on earlier drafts.

NOTES

1. These issues were covered particularly well in two books published in the late 1960s which, judging by accounts in the underground press, were very influential: Reich, C. A. (1971). *The greening of America*. Middlesex, U.K.: Penguin Books (Original work published 1970); and Roszak, T. (1971). *The making of a counter culture: Reflections on the technocratic society and its youthful opposition*. London: Faber and Faber. (Original work published 1968)

2. Consider, e.g., the explanations of rebellion and self-conscious differentiation contained in Clarke, J., Hall, S., Jefferson, T., & Roberts, B. (1975). Subcultures, cultures, and class. In S. Hall, & T. Jefferson (Eds.), *Resistance through rituals: Youth subcultures in post-war Britain*. London: Hutchinson, with the C.C.C.S., University of Birmingham, pp. 9–79, and in Willis, P. E. (1978). *Profane culture*. London: Routledge & Kegan Paul.

3. For this history, see Esler, A. (1971). *Bombs, beards, and barricades: 150 years of youth in revolt*. New York: Stein and Day.

4. For a fuller account of this facet of 1960s underground rebellion, see Rycroft, S. (1993). *Mapping the underground: British and American counter-cultures, 1950–1975*. Unpublished Ph.D. thesis, University of Nottingham, pp. 16–74.

5. This approach is elaborated in Daniels, S. (1993). *Fields of vision: Landscape imagery and national identity in England and the United States*. Cambridge, U.K.: Polity Press.

6. Whiteley, S. (1992). *The space between the notes: Rock and the counter-culture*. New York and London: Routledge, pp. 2–3. It must be noted, however, that as an exercise in the theory of music, the geographies and environments of musical expression were not the focus of Whiteley's account.

7. Consider, e.g., Banham, R. (1971). *Los Angeles: The architecture of four ecologies*. Norwich, U.K.: Fletcher & Son; Davis, M. (1990). *City of quartz: Excavating the future in Los Angeles*. New York: Verso. Rycroft, *Mapping the underground*; and Soja, E. W. (1989). *Postmodern geographies: The reassertion of space in critical social theory*. London: Verso.

8. Gillett, C. (1983). *The sound of the city: The rise of rock and roll* (rev. American ed.). New York: Pantheon Books, pp. 347–349.

9. The Doors are frequently presented as a typical acid rock or psychedelic Band (see Whiteley, *The space between*). Here, however, considering the peculiar circumstances of 1960s Los Angeles, it is less easy to categorize them (or indeed any other band so labeled) in such universal terms.

10. Rycroft, S. (1996). Changing lanes: Textuality on and off the road. *Transactions of the Institute of British Geographers, 21*, 412–419.

11. Palmer, W. J. (1984). Book review: Los Angeles in fiction. *Modern Fiction Studies, 24*(5), 757.

12. Banham, *Los Angeles*; Davis, *City of quartz*.

13. Soja, *Postmodern geographies*, p. 195.

14. See Krim, A. (1992). Los Angeles and the anti-tradition of the suburban city. *Journal of Historical Geography, 18*(1), 132.

15. Consider, e.g., another perspective on the globalization of Los Angeles in

Rieff, D. (1993). *Los Angeles: Capital of the third world.* London: Phoenix Paperbacks/Orion Books.

16. *International Times* was the first in a series of British underground publications that were produced in London. The fact that Los Angeles and other sites of countercultural rebellion were represented in the pages of a paper consumed by a mainly London readership is interesting in itself. The presentation of other scenes, or other ecologies, is a testament to the existence of a self-consciously global underground that was constituted by a series of localized characteristics (see Rycroft, *Mapping the underground*).

17. Miles, B. (1969, March 14). Internal combustion city has no legs, no weather. *International Times*, p. 3.

18. Ibid.

19. Banham, *Los Angeles*, pp. 128–129.

20. Ibid., p. 235.

21. On the evolving politics of the civil rights movement in the United States see Fraser, R. (1988). *1968: A student generation in revolt.* London: Chatto & Windus; and Harman, C. (1988). *The fire last time: 1968 and after.* London: Bookmarks. On the conduct and events of the Watts rebellion, see Sears, D. O., & McConahay, J. B. (1973). *The politics of violence: The new urban blacks and the Watts riot.* Los Angeles: Houghton Mifflin. On the disputes between the Westside and Downtown business districts that form one context of the uprisings, see Davis, *City of quartz*.

22. Davis, *City of quartz*, p. 67.

23. Cleaver, E. (1982). Domestic law and international order. In G. Howard (Ed.), *The sixties: The art, attitudes, politics, and media of our most explosive decade.* New York: Washington Square Press, pp. 125–132.

24. Kunkin, A. (1965, July 23). One year of the *Free Press. Los Angeles Free Press*, p. 3.

25. Wilcock, J. (1966, March 4). Internationally important art exhibit played down by L.A's press, radio, T.V. *Los Angeles Free Press*, pp. 1–2.

26. The *Free Press* ran the headline "The Negroes Have Voted" following the Watts uprising. It was the disenfranchisement of South Central's black community, that was of most concern here. And in a period that saw the redefinition of political expression to which issues of the cultural politics of medium and message were central, it was logical that the underground's explanation of the riots should be couched in terms of a breakdown in communication. What was needed, it was felt, were new forms of expression uninhibited by old categories of art and of society.

27. Kunkin, A. (1992, May). personal communication, interview; reproduced in Rycroft, *Mapping the underground*, pp. 359–372.

28. These tests were carried out initially in a South Central Unitarian church and are recounted in Wolfe, T. (1968). *The electric kool-aid acid test*, New York: Bantam Books. They were not, however, particularly successful, largely due to the clientele and the curious moral leadership local underground groups such as the Black Panthers provided to the young.

29. Kunkin, personal communication, 1992.

30. The use of the term "environment" is significant. Different factions within the underground constructed correspondingly different "microcosmic environ-

ments," most of which are described in the underground press. For some of the "theories" surrounding these countercultural practices, see Nuttall, J. (1968). *Bomb culture*. London: MacGibbon & Kee; Neville, R. (1970). *Play power*. London: Jonathan Cape; and Stevens, J. (1988). *Storming heaven: LSD and the American dream*. New York: Harper & Row.

31. Youngblood, G. (1968, May 10). Environment as light/scale as content/Lear Jet as music/rock as theater/electricity as god. *Los Angeles Free Press*, pp. 34–35.

32. In this sense, the underground continued a tradition of 20th-century revolt (including surrealism and dadaism) that sought to redefine the contours of art and the everyday; see Bonnett, A. (1990). Art, ideology, and everyday space: Subversive tendencies from Dada to postmodernism. *Environment and Planning D: Society and Space, 10,* 69–86.

33. Youngblood, G. (1969, January 10). Intermedia. *Los Angeles Free Press*, p. 14.

34. Consider Cosgrove, D. (1994). Contested global visions: One world, whole-earth. *Annals of the Association of American Geographers, 84,* 270–294.

35. Youngblood, G. (1969, June 13). Intermedia: The artist as ecologist. *Los Angeles Free Press*, pp. 34–47.

36. Ferguson, M. (1991). Marshall McLuhan revisited: 1960s zeitgeist victim or pioneer postmodernist? *Media, Culture, and Society, 13,* 71–90.

37. McLuhan, H. M. (1964). *Understanding media: The extensions of man*. London: Routledge & Kegan Paul.

38. Wolfe, T. (1969). Suppose he is what he sounds like, the most important thinker since Newton, Darwin, Freud, Einstein, and Pavlov—What if he is right? In G. E. Stearn (Ed.), *McLuhan: Hot & cool*. New York: Signet Books, pp. 67–75.

39. McLuhan, *Understanding media*, p. 3.

40. Feigen, G. M. (1989). The McLuhan Festival: On the Road to San Francisco. In G. Sanderson & F. Macdonald (Eds.), *Marshall McLuhan: The man and his message*. Golden, Colo.: Fulcrum, pp. 65–69.

41. McLuhan, H. M. (1989). Violence of the media. In G. Sanderson & F. Macdonald (Eds), *Marshall McLuhan: The man and his message*. Golden, Colo.: Fulcrum, pp. 91–98; Widmer, K. (1973). Sensibility under technocracy: Reflections on the culture of processed communications. In B. N. Schwartz (Ed.), *Human connection and the new media*. Englewood Cliffs, N.J.: Spectrum Books, Prentice-Hall, pp. 28–41.

42. McLuhan, *Understanding media*, p. 24.

43. Ponte, L. (1972, May 4). Kandy kolored massage. *International Times*, p. 35.

44. This was expressed most characteristically in graphic and textual form in McLuhan, H. M. (1970). *Counterblast*. London: Harley Parker, Rapp & Whiting.

45. McLuhan, *Understanding media*, pp. 3–4.

46. McLuhan, *Counterblast*, p. 131.

47. Advertisement. (1967, July). Marshall McLuhan was here. He left a message for you. *Ramparts*, p. 27.

48. Stansill, P., & Mairowitz, D. Z. (1971). *BAMN: Outlaw manifestoes and ephemera, 1965–70*. London: Penguin, p. 80.

49. Menkin, L. (1971, August 6). How to fuck the networks: Space time continuum memo #2. *Los Angeles Free Press*, p. 46.

50. Benhari. (1971, September 15). TV or not TV. *San Francisco Good Times*, p. 10.

51. Venice's beatnik history is well documented in Maynard, J. A. (1991). *Venice West: The Beat generation in southern California*. New Brunswick, N.J.: Rutgers University Press. For details of the forms of Beat expression in the district, see Rycroft, *Changing lanes*.

52. Lipton's portrait of the scene is presented in Lipton, L. (1959). *The holy barbarians*. New York: New York: Julian Messner.

53. Maynard, *Venice West*, p. 41.

54. Lipton, *The holy barbarians*, p. 150.

55. Maynard, *Venice West*, p. 51.

56. Lipton, *The Holy Barbarians*, pp. 168–170.

57. Ibid., p. 221.

58. Venice poetry den raided. (1964, September 24). *Los Angeles Free Press*, p. 2.

59. Ibid., p. 1.

60. Cummings, R. (1964, December 3). Ban on bongos, guitars at beaches and parks proposed by city council. *Los Angeles Free Press*, p. 1.

61. Lipton, L. (1964, September 24). The wasp. *Los Angeles Free Press*, p. 2.

62. Ibid., p. 2.

63. Youngblood, G. (1968, November 22). Single wing turquoise bird. *Los Angeles Free Press*, p. 31.

64. Spector, P. (1967, May 19). *Open City*, p. 5.

65. Davis, F. (1967, December). Focus on the flower children: Why all of us may be hippies someday. *Transaction: Culture and Modern Society Special Edition*, p. 10.

66. See Rorabaugh, W. J. (1989). *Berkeley at war: The 1960s*. Oxford: Oxford University Press, p. 144.

67. C.C. (1967). Sheep? Baa. *Communications Company* (San Francisco). In J. Hopkins (Ed.), *The hippie papers: Notes from the underground press*. New York: Signet Books, p. 17.

68. Pine, R. (1967). The Diggers Create a Society. *Communications Company* (San Francisco). In J. Hopkins (Ed.), *The hippie papers: Notes from the underground press*. New York: Signet Books, p. 26.

69. Bryan, J. (1967, August 24). The hippy minister. *Open City*, p. 25.

70. Wilcock, J. (1966). Internationally important art exhibit played down, pp. 1–5.

71. Taylor, G. (1967, September 21). Wailing on Sunset Strip. *Open City*, p. 4.

72. Youngblood, G. (1968, October 11). Acid mantra: Part two. *Los Angeles Free Press*, p. 31.

73. Whitehall, R. (1967). Underground films grow in importance. *Los Angeles Free Press*, p. 16.

74. Margolis, W. J. (1967, March 10). A plot to underthrow the overground. *Los Angeles Free Press*, p. 10.

75. Youngblood, Environment as light, p. 34.

76. Youngblood, Acid mantra: Part two, p. 18.
77. Garcia, B. (1967, September 21). About the kaleidoscope. *Open City,* p. 5.
78. Stevens, *Storming heaven,* p. x.
79. Draper, R. (1990). *The Rolling Stone story.* Edinburgh, U.K.: Mainstream, pp. 53–56.
80. Rorabaugh, *Berkeley at war,* p. 144.
81. Levine, S. (1967, January). A gathering of the tribes—A baptism: Notes from the San Andreas Fault. *San Francisco Oracle,* p. 12.
82. Ibid.
83. Ibid., p. 13.
84. Rorabaugh, *Berkeley at war,* p. 141.
85. Johnson, O. (1967, January 20). Pow-Wow. *Los Angeles Free Press,* p. 3. While its was the underground press editors who were the main organizers, Chet Helms of the Family Dog was also present at the San Francisco meeting (Kunkin, personal communication).
86. Ibid., p. 3.
87. Ibid., p. 8.
88. Hopkins, J. (1967, January 20). A gathering of the tribes for a human be-in. *Los Angeles Free Press,* p. 1.
89. Freedland, N. (1967, March 3). Be-In Opens a Loving Weekend. *Los Angeles Free Press,* p. 4.
90. Hopkins, A Gathering of the tribes, p. 3.
91. The Strip witnessed some minor skirmishes in the late 1960s arising mainly from LAPD enforcement of vagrancy and narcotics laws and culminating in 1967 in a minor riot, labeled by the underground the "Pandora's Box" uprising. The local Provo group and some Diggers were also involved in stoking the fires.
92. Freedland, Be-In opens a loving weekend, p. 4.
93. Bryan, The hippy minister, p. 20.
94. Bryan, J. (1967, May 5). Open city. *Open City,* p. 7.
95. Gold, R. (1967, November 17). End of love-in era in L.A. *Open City,* p. 3.
96. see Banham, *Los Angeles..*
97. Hastings, C. R. (1969, April 25). Venice free show smashed by LAPD. *Los Angeles Free Press,* pp. 1–4.
98. Burgess, J. G. (1969, April 25). Notice to the dead and dying: You are standing on a generation. *Los Angeles Free Press,* p. 41.

10

FROM "DUST STORM DISASTER" TO "PASTURES OF PLENTY"

Woody Guthrie and Landscapes of the American Depression

JOHN R. GOLD

> When the sun comes shining, and I was strolling
> And the wheat fields waving and dust clouds rolling;
> As the fog was lifting a voice was chanting:
> This land was made for you and me.[1]

These lines from Woody Guthrie's "This Land is Your Land" are a familiar part of a song now widely regarded as the unofficial U.S. national anthem. Yet when originally written in February 1940, they told a different story. The song was then entitled "God Blessed America" in conscious parody of Irving Berlin's hit "God Bless America."[2] Rather than a straightforward celebration of things American, Guthrie's version was a bittersweet reflection on the state of the nation. Its verses offset the splendors of the landscape with references to class, poverty, unemployment, and inequality. The mention of "dust clouds" alluded to the storms that had recently ravaged the drought-stricken states of the southern Great Plains, stripping off the desiccated topsoil and bringing desolation to large tracts of farmland. In a few words, Guthrie elegantly juxtaposed the frontier dream of abundance with a new imagery of scarcity and despair.[3]

This example indicates something of the power of his musicianship, but it also hints at the underlying complexity of the man himself. Guthrie was a singer/songwriter whose works powerfully portrayed the social and environmental conditions of the Great Depression. His group of 20 songs collectively known as the "Dust Bowl Ballads,"[4] together with the film and novel of *The Grapes of Wrath*[5] and the work of the Farm Security Administration's photographers,[6] were instrumental in alerting the nation to the hardships faced by the common people.

Guthrie's personal views and political attitudes, however, remained inherently complex. In the case of "This Land Is Your Land," for example, the original manuscript shows it to have been a six-verse song with a compassionate, strongly socialist message. Yet despite its composer's continuing reputation as a figure on the American left, he developed a four-verse rendition (verses 1–3 and 5) that stripped the song of an important part of its message. The so-called radical verses (4 and 6), with their references to the inequity of private property and unemployment lines, were deliberately omitted.[7] The popularity of the song in the postwar, and especially the post-McCarthy, period was thereby assured at the expense of some of its meaning. Seen against this background, any analysis of Guthrie's music needs to be carefully rooted in the social and cultural context of the times in which it was composed and performed.

This chapter focuses on the representation of the drought lands and the subsequent fate of their inhabitants as they appeared in Guthrie's "Dust Bowl Ballads" composed between 1936 and 1941. Unlike other studies[8] that have focused primarily on the ethnomusicological, biographical, or topographic aspects of these songs, the aim here is to situate the allusions to landscape found in Guthrie's lyrics within the wider context of American popular culture. Guthrie's references to landscape are interpreted not just as the backdrop to the social history of the Dust Bowl but also as support for environmental interpretations that endowed land and climate with the "kind of creative unpredictability conventionally reserved for human actors."[9] Above all, his lyrics are shown to have reflected and assimilated a set of themes that were of broader significance in the development of the American West[10]: namely, the Dust Bowl itself as prophetic fulfillment of biblically based millenarianism; the highway (the migrants' escape route to the states of the Far West) as a test of resolve and endurance; and the lure of the Far West, especially California, as the "Promised Land."

The ensuing chapter contains six sections. The first briefly describes the social and environmental conditions prevailing in the Great Plains during the Dust Bowl years. The second part supplies biographical and musicological context to Woody Guthrie's early career, ending with background material about the "Dust Bowl Ballads" and the influences that helped to shape their content. The three subsequent sections examine the powerful landscape imagery that these songs contain, the roots of that imagery, the traditions that Guthrie embraced, and the symbolism he employed. The concluding section reflects on Guthrie's achievements in telling the social history of large migrant groups in terms of the environmental history of the areas in which they lived.

THE DUST BOWL

Present-day conceptions of natural disaster do not always accord with those that held sway in the United States in the past. Soil erosion is a case in point. Until around 1930, for example, the American farmer commonly regarded it as a "spasmodic phenomenon" largely confined to lands subject to washing. Many believed that moderate blowing was beneficial because it mixed the soil and thereby helped to maintain its fertility.[11] The scale of the drought and dust storms of the 1930s, however, left no room for such interpretations. The events associated with the Dust Bowl forcibly brought home the fact that land was finite and that action needed to be taken if the future of rural society was to be safeguarded.[12]

The term "Dust Bowl" has a specific and identifiable origin. On April 14, 1935, Robert Geiger, an Associated Press staff reporter working for the *Washington Evening News,* was in Guymon in the Oklahoma Panhandle to write a series of articles on the drought and dust storms. After witnessing the damage inflicted by the most severe storm yet experienced, when dust blackened the daytime sky and visibility was reduced to zero, he coined the term "Dust Bowl" for the afflicted area.[13]

It immediately caught on. Due to where he was writing, the term became associated with Oklahoma, but it could equally be applied to the surrounding states. During the early 1930s the whole Great Plains, a remarkably uniform area of 550,000 square miles extending from Canada southward to Mexico, suffered drought and dust storms. The greatest impact, however, was experienced in a 150,000-square-mile region in the south including western Kansas, eastern Colorado, northern New Mexico, and the Texas and Oklahoma Panhandles (Figure 10.1).

At the outset, it should be noted that drought and dust storms were not new to the region. They had been recorded in Kansas, for example, throughout the 19th century and high rates of population turnover as a consequence of soil erosion were not unusual.[14] The significance of recurrent drought, however, became more acute when successive waves of agricultural innovation allowed greater exploitation of marginal land.

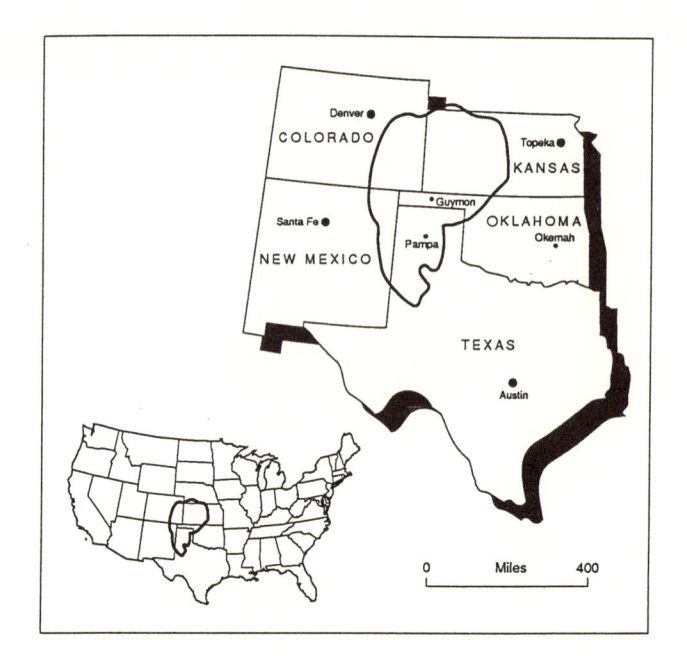

FIGURE 10.1. The Dust Bowl. The bounded area shows the region suffering the most severe dust storms, 1935–1940.

The Great Plains were an area of natural grassland, originally covered with a thick matting of galleta, grama, wire, and buffalo grasses. Underneath the turf layer was a rich, powdery soil.[15] The coming of the steel plough in the 1880s and of tractors, gang ploughs, and headers in the period before World War I provided opportunities for the expansion of wheat farming in place of ranching. It also presaged one of the most rapid environmental transformations seen in the Western world. The railroad companies, their agents, and the land companies were quick to seize the chance to engage in boosterism designed to encourage migrants to settle. Between 1870 and 1910, the Great Plains experienced the fastest demographic increase in the United States as people were attracted to newly created farms. Seventeen million acres were added to the area under wheat cultivation between 1909 and 1924.[16] One might assume that agricultural depression, falling wheat prices,[17] and the occurrence of dry years in the early 1920s would have changed matters, but the opposite was in fact the case. Farmers expanded their acreage further to offset their declining incomes. This occurred particularly in the southern Great Plains. Between 1925 and 1931 wheat acreage increased 200% with many counties experiencing expansion ranging between 400 and 1,000%.[18]

The policy of expansion briefly achieved its aims, but fell into disrepute in the early 1930s when the rains repeatedly failed to materialize. Wheat itself offered good protection against wind erosion when the ground was covered, but successive droughts in the early growing seasons meant that the crops were decimated and the light powdery soil was exposed to the steady westerly winds. By 1933, severe dust storms had started. Their impact was exacerbated by the abandonment of failed farms, where now nothing was planted to tie down the soil.[19] Complex patterns of erosion and deposition developed. Some areas saw their topsoil completely removed down to the hardpan. Others experienced local deposition, with drifts reaching the eaves of deserted buildings and piling up along fencerows and ditches. At times dramatic "black blizzards"—walls of dust reaching up to 8,000 feet in the air—would sweep across the Plains transporting material much further. Dust was commonly carried as far as New York, Philadelphia, and New England, or even deposited on ships far out at sea.[20]

The social responses to these testing environmental conditions were complex and varied. There was already a high propensity to migrate, given the small size of the farms, the frequency of drought and other hazards (e.g., prairie fire, hail, floods, cold, heat, blizzards, and plagues of grasshoppers), and the cyclical vagaries of the international agricultural trade system.[21] There were some 10,000 abandoned farmhouses on the Great Plains, with 9 million acres of farmland quickly reverting to nature.[22] The highest incidence was seen in the southern states. In Colorado, for example, a survey of seven drought-afflicted counties showed 2,878 farmhouses still occupied and 2,811 abandoned. Oklahoma witnessed similar movement. Settled during recurrent booms in oil as well as land, the population was considered "under the influence of the moving itch."[23]

Yet the experience of Oklahoma also demonstrated the care that must be taken before drawing connections between the dust storms and the mass migration of displaced agricultural families. A significant proportion of migrants were not farmers, but mechanics, storekeepers, and others whose livelihood crumbled when depopulation drastically reduced local spending power. Many moved only a short distance to the nearest town or the next county. Even those migrants who crossed state lines were not necessarily going far. Almost half of the 500,000 people who left Oklahoma in the 1930s, for example, went to a contiguous state such as Texas.[24]

Wherever the destination, it is also worth emphasizing that comparatively few migrants actually came from the Dust Bowl. The Oklahoma Panhandle was sparsely populated.[25] Surveys indicated that although 25% of the migrants entering California in the 1930s were from Oklahoma, only 2-3% of the state's out-migrants came from the westernmost districts where the dust blizzards blew.[26] Instead the overwhelming mass were poor white sharecroppers and tenant farmers from the cotton lands in the south and east of the state. They were displaced by a cyclical downswing in the cotton economy that hit bottom in 1935. Paradoxically, too, their position was further weakened by the impact of federal government measures intended to support farmers. The Roosevelt administration did not include sharecroppers and tenant farmers in agricultural recovery programs designed to help farmers who owned land. Many were forced to leave their holdings, they were "tractored out by mechanization, displaced by land owners (farmers, not bankers) . . . not 'dusted out' as many believed."[27]

Across the South most sharecroppers and tenants were black. Displaced blacks migrated north. In Oklahoma and Texas, however, they were white. Displaced whites migrated west, and they received the bulk of the nation's attention. They were also, as we shall see later, the people with whom Woody Guthrie associated when he reached California.

WOODY GUTHRIE AS FOLK MUSICIAN

Woodrow Wilson ("Woody") Guthrie's musical career was brief. Struck down by the hereditary disease Huntington's chorea in 1952 at the age of 39, his working career lasted just 17 years. Despite this, Guthrie's productivity was prodigious: he wrote more than 1,000 songs, several books, and a quantity of short folksy writings, and he collaborated on several films.[28]

Analyses of Guthrie's career have followed the passing fashions of historical writings, focusing on specific phases of his work and avoiding complexity.[29] Early writers tended to treat him as a self-taught rustic folk musician, who gave a voice to his people.[30] Later studies, recognizing his socialist leanings, regarded him as a heroic defender of the exploited—a "guerilla minstrel" who was a precursor of the "protest movement" in 1960s folk music.[31] Later still he was viewed as a "prophet singer" who, like Walt Whitman, preached the restoration of community and democratic fairness.[32] In reality, all such views supply only partial understanding of Guthrie's work. More balanced interpretations recognize the fluidity of the folk traditions that his music absorbed and his constant willingness to change his music to suit the audiences for whom he was playing.

Guthrie was born in the small town of Okemah in the Oklahoma cotton belt in 1912. Living in a town only founded in 1902,[33] Guthrie grew up in a frontier zone with ethnically diverse people and rich musical traditions. The music played at family and community gatherings, for example, included traditional fiddle tunes, ballads, Tennessee church songs, and hillbilly music. Guthrie later supplemented these with other styles he heard on the radio in the 1920s or collected while wandering around the rural South in his youth.[34] These included nascent country music (especially the music of the Carter Family and Jimmie Rodgers), blues, hoedown, gospel—indeed just about anything apart from the jazz emanating from New Orleans.

From the beginning Guthrie, like other musicians around him, freely absorbed these various styles and influences without any particular concern for authorship. This attitude continued throughout his career. Guthrie's early songs were set to existing tunes. Klein,[35] for instance, argued that Guthrie assiduously aped Maybelle Carter's guitar style and later "lifted several dozen Carter Family melodies for his own purposes." These included the tune for "This Land Is Your Land." This was taken from the Carter Family's "Little Darling, Pal of Mine," which the Carters in turn had taken from an old Baptist hymn, "Oh My Loving Brother." Guthrie was forever rewriting his songs or performing them in different ways—altering the words, changing the order of the verses, and modifying the tempo. Very few, not even those that were essentially narratives, ever reached final and definitive versions.

They could also be tailor-made for different audiences. I alluded earlier to the way in which the meaning of "This Land Is Your Land" was changed by the omission of the so-called radical verses. The same trend can also be witnessed in his treatment of the Dust Bowl Ballads. As originally written, the chorus of "Dusty Old Dust (So Long It's Been Good to Know Yuh)" ended with the lines: "This dusty old dust is a-getting my home / And I've got to be drifting along." A subsequent "popular" version altered this to: "What a long time since I've been home / And I've got to be drifting along." The meaning was completely changed by the alteration. The time- and place-specific words of the original version were replaced by the comforting and timeless sentiments of the popular version. In the process, Guthrie fashioned a contemporary American equivalent of "Auld Lang Syne" at the expense of the song's critical edge.

He absorbed other influences during his career. In 1929 he moved to Pampa, an agricultural town in the Texas Panhandle then experiencing an oil boom. It was from here, rather than Oklahoma, that he gained his firsthand experience of the dust storms. Later he moved to California (1937) and finally to New York (1940). As he traveled, he came into contact with three marginal groups whose causes Guthrie embraced in his music. The first were the "orphans of the storm," who made their way west after losing their homes in Kansas, Arkansas, Texas, and Oklahoma. The second consisted of hoboes, mostly single men thumbing lifts and riding railway boxcars in search of work. The third group comprised members of the radical Left, with whom Guthrie associated when he moved to California. Guthrie was not naturally a member of any of these groups but he assimilated himself to each of them during the period in which he wrote the "Dust Bowl Ballads." They supplied him with ideas and inspiration. He in turn championed their needs and was probably their most articulate spokesman.

Yet while drawing attention to the range of influences he absorbed, it must be stressed that Guthrie was a relatively conservative composer in terms of the form of his music. Unlike the free experimentation of his literary efforts,[36] Guthrie deliberately composed within the southern folk music traditions with which he was most comfortable. As Reuss[37] points out, they were "by far the strongest reservoir of form and content his talents could draw upon." Moreover, Guthrie had strong feelings about authenticity in folk music form. He would later quarrel with close associates in left-wing musical circles when he felt they were straying too far from prescribed folk models or drifting into pretentiousness or pseudofolksy affectation.[38]

The "Dust Bowl Ballads," therefore, fit firmly in the traditional rhythmic and melodic pattern of southwestern U.S. folk ballads. Their innovative quality and power derives from their lyrical content. Collectively, they present the travails of the Dust Bowl migrants stylized into a modern biblical tale, with debts both to the Old Testament (especially the Book of Exodus) and the New Testament's Book of Revelation. As such, the story was set against three distinct landscapes. The first was the Dust Bowl itself, with the everyday agricultural landscape turned to barren aridity by the unremitting droughts. The second was the landscape of the highway, experienced as families overloaded their possessions onto battered cars and headed west in search of hope and a better life. The third was the vision and subsequent reality of the "Promised Land." Each merits further discussion.

"DUST STORM DISASTER"

From his home in Pampa, Woody Guthrie responded to precisely the same storm that had led Robert Geiger to coin the term "Dust Bowl." His song "Dust Storm Disaster" began:

> On the fourteenth day of April
> Of nineteen thirty-five,
> There struck the worst of dust storms
> That ever filled the sky.
>
> You could see that dust storm coming
> The cloud looked death-like black
> And through our mighty nation
> It left a dreadful track....

> It fell across our city
> Like a curtain of black rolled down
> We thought it was our judgement
> We thought it was our doom.[39]

The references to death, doom, and judgment are significant. The clearest precedent in the popular imagination for the drought and dust storms was biblical. Across the drought lands, the churches filled with anxious congregations as a fundamentalist religious revival took place. Its tone embraced a millennialist strain long present in American popular culture that could always be pressed into service to meet the needs of particular historical circumstances. "Millennialism" could come in many different forms,[40] but in this instance it promoted an eschatological outlook that may be termed "premillennial dispensationalism." Here "individuals saw omens of disaster as increasing trials that would precede the imminent return of Christ in judgment and salvation."[41]

The extent to which Guthrie shared such beliefs is open to considerable dispute,[42] but this imagery was a readily accessible means of characterizing events of dimensions beyond immediate understanding. The dark dust clouds were like the Grim Reaper; the Final Judgment was at hand. The contrast was made starker by viewing the past in an idyllic manner. Although living conditions in this frontier region had always been hard and uncertain, what had gone before now seemed an era of peace and plenty. The song "Oklahoma Hills," written with his cousin Jack, painted a picture of an Edenic landscape of recent memory. It celebrated the endless spaces and primeval freedoms of the frontier, of being able to ride for miles "where the oak and black-jack trees / kiss the playful prairie breeze." The family farm, even if of recent creation, also seemed a haven of peace and tranquillity. In "Talking Dust Bowl" (also known as "Talking Dust Blues"), Guthrie sang:

> Back in nineteen twenty-seven
> I had a little farm and I called that heaven.
> The price was up and the rain came down
> And I hauled my crops all in to town.
> I got the money, bought clothes and groceries,
> Fed the kids and raised a family.[43]

Into this blissful state came the dust that destroyed the bases of life and, like the Last Judgment, was impossible to escape. It got everywhere: it was on the fields, on the roads, in people's clothes, and in the air they breathed. There was even a local respiratory condition known as "dust pneumonia" associated with the storms.[44] In "Dust Pneumonia Blues,"

Guthrie sang that when you got the "dust pneumony," "you ain't got long, not long," although ironically observing in a later verse that his "gal" was so shocked when it rained that she had fainted and had to have "a bucket o'dirt" thrown in her face to revive her.

The dust could be resisted defiantly for a time. In "Dust Can't Kill Me," Guthrie invoked the popular notions of the frontier spirit.[45] In its verses, he triumphantly proclaimed that although the dust storms could destroy all his possessions, "it didn't get me, girl / It can't stop me." Similarly, there were songs praising those who were willing to act against predatory financial institutions when they sought to evict families from their homes.[46] Songs such as "Pretty Boy Floyd" and the Steinbeck-inspired "Tom Joad" commended Robin Hood–like outlaws who defended the people against grasping corporate capital. In "Pretty Boy Floyd," for example, the actions of the real-life Oklahoman outlaw were praised, with lines about families being handsomely rewarded for hospitality—even to the point of having their farms saved by an outlaw willing to pay their mortgage.

Yet defiance and the sporadic interventions by outlaws had their limits. The agricultural community could only stand losing just so many crops before facing ruin. "Dust Storm Disaster" spoke of the view from the people's "oil-boom shacks" of fields coated with a "rippling ocean of dust the wind had blown." Moreover, their enemy was an insidious force that searched out any weakness and whistled through the cracks to invade even the sanctity of the home. In the long term, only flight offered salvation. The last verse of the song states what seemed the inevitable:

> We loaded our jalopies
> And piled our families in
> We rattled down that highway
> To never come back again.[47]

"I AIN'T GOT NO HOME"

The highway and its landscapes supply the second major set of images to be considered here. Movement, the car, and the highway itself have exerted a fascination for Americans and permeates U.S. literature and popular culture.[48] Going down the highway, the notion of the traveling man, and the spirit of moving west had a long-established place in the American consciousness. A generation before Jack Kerouac, Woody Guthrie was drifting around, thumbing rides and riding the rails. He understood the attractions of moving for its own sake, of traveling light in expectation of new experiences and excitements. Nevertheless, he readily appreciated that the river of migrants pouring west along Routes 10, 90, and 66 (the Will Rogers Highway) shared little of this enthusiasm. For them, this was the "Hungry Gut Highway."[49] It was traversed by people who might never previously have traveled more than 20 miles from their homes, yet were now heading 2,000 miles west in old and hopelessly inadequate cars. Their desperate anxieties were only too apparent.

One of the best known of the "Dust Bowl Ballads," "I Ain't Got No Home," highlights the social and psychological problems involved. Loss of home and the inability simply to move on to new lands, as in the classic days of the frontier, led to large groups of migrant workers roaming around, searching for work. Their plight, the symbolic loss of their "place" in the world, and, implicitly, their loss of their sense of self was highlighted in the first verse:

> I ain't got no home,
> I'm just a-ramblin' 'round,
> A hard wanderin' workin' man,
> I go from town to town.
> The police make it hard wherever I may go,
> And I ain't got no home in this world anymore.[50]

These people were effectively the "Dust Bowl Refugees," a name that clung to them when they moved on to California and elsewhere in search of casual work. Their insecurity was admirably encapsulated in the song "Dust Bowl Refugee." The southwesterners made their way from the Dust Bowl to the Peach Bowl, but they were welcome only when seasonal fruit picking was available. At other times, they were forced to be "ramblers" who travel "with the seasons." The "never-ending highway" was perforce home for such people.

The continual references to home are important. The refugees from the once-productive drought lands were forced to wander in the wilderness. Yet this is not something that would necessarily last forever. Returning to the biblical theme, Guthrie suggests that the forced period of wandering was effectively a trial that the people must endure before entering the "Promised Land." The highway was not just the thread that tied origin to destination, it was also a test. The lyrics of "Dust Bowl Refugee" mentions two specific landscapes with scriptural resonances—the arid desert and the high mountain—through which the refugees had to pass. Like their biblical antecedents, the migrants could only enter the Promised Land if they successfully withstood the trials that these landscapes imposed.

Some would not make it. In the ballad "Tom Joad," Grandpa Joad dies and is buried by the side of the road, while Grandma is buried "on the California side." For the remaining members of the family looking to the west from the mountain side, they saw what looked like the Promised Land, a bright green valley with a river running through. In this manner, the vision of the "Promised Land" replete with the River Jordan was assimilated into the story. Whether or not this landscape of hope was also a landscape of illusion would not be learned until after arrival.

"PASTURES OF PLENTY"

Every hell has a heaven against which it is compared. For these American migrants, the principal image of terrestrial paradise was, as it had been for previous generations, a mythologized California. More than any other state of the Union, California exercised a beguiling attraction for the migrant that made it "almost impossible to separate the place on the map from the legends that have kept it alive in the imagination."[51] It was the land of the booster—a "golden state," a land of economic opportunity where droughts were unknown and "where the water tastes like wine."[52]

Guthrie himself, as noted above, moved to California in 1937 and worked and reworked most of the "Dust Bowl Ballads" while he was living there. From mixing with the migrants and personal observation, he harbored no illusions about the state and knew that for each person that immediately found employment many others failed to do so. The illusory nature of California's promise for the migrant was also belied by squalid labor camps, with insanitary wooden shacks, built on unwanted fragments of land in the river bottoms, on hill sides, and even on the edges of parking lots.

Despite this, Guthrie's songs portray the desperate hopes and aspirations of those for whom clinging to the myth of California as paradise was so important. In the song "Pastures of Plenty," Woody indicated that it was a paradise to which they will have only brief admittance, a green land, with a fine climate and abundant crops, in which they were only welcome as a temporary labor force at harvest time:

> I worked in your orchards
> Of peaches and prunes,
> Slept on the ground,
> In the light of your moon,
> On the edge of your city,
> You've seen us and then,
> We come with the dust
> And we go with the wind.
>
> California and Arizona,
> I make all your crops,

> And it's north up to Oregon
> To gather your hops,
> Dig the beets from your ground,
> Cut the grapes from your vines,
> To set on your table
> Your light sparkling wine.[53]

In addition, despite being themselves recent settlers, the existing Californian population was nervous about the impact of the "Okie" influx on its social fabric and unwilling to commit funds for resettlement programs. Paradise was thus infested by deputy sheriffs. A view was conveyed of migrants who were continually harassed and forced to move on. "Vigilante Man" referred to the shooting of Preacher Casy, a character from Steinbeck's *The Grapes of Wrath*, before issuing a more general condemnation of the tactics of the law enforcement officers who herded the people around like "wild cattle." In the song "Do Re Mi," Guthrie pointed to the actions of the deputies at the county line, refusing admittance to those who lacked the money (the "do re mi") to support themselves.

When this version of events is set alongside the historical evidence, qualifications are immediately necessary. Half the southwesterners moving to California settled in Los Angeles, San Francisco's Bay Area, or San Diego. They may have been initially destitute, but many had skills. As the economy picked up after the Great Depression, especially as the defense industries boomed with the advent of World War II, the migrants settled into regular jobs and created lasting communities. New Deal measures back in the South worked to staunch the flow of migrants. Settlement even occurred quickly in the agricultural San Joaquin Valley, the scene of considerable hostility in the late 1930s.[54] Cultural assimilation proved to be no long-term problem in the way that Steinbeck had predicted.[55] Certainly the crisis had abated by the time that the "Dust Bowl Ballads" appeared.

CONCLUSION

This last point is important. Guthrie may well have composed the "Dust Bowl Ballads" within traditional folk-song form, but they related to a community that had already lost the temporary definition of its migrant status. There is no evidence that any of the "Dust Bowl Ballads" even entered the musical traditions of the "Okies" while they were a distinctive group in the Far West. As Reuss[56] comments:

> The Dust Bowl community disappeared into the American mainstream after World War II, but even before it did, none of Woody's song

compositions showed any signs of entering that group's oral tradition. There are no Guthrie creations, for instance, in the extensive Todd and Sonkin collection of Okie Ballads recorded in California in 1939–1941, just after Woody's period of maximum exposure among migrants in the state through radio and personal appearances. If any of his songs stood a chance of being absorbed into the Okie folksong repertory, they should have turned up at that time. None did.

By the same token, neither the "Dust Bowl Ballads" nor any of Guthrie's other music relating to the southwestern United States had any significant impact on the traditional folk music of that region.

In part, that outcome was influenced by Guthrie's own activities after he left California for New York. This period saw him forsake his former confidants, the migrants and the hoboes, in favor of the radical Left. At this stage, Guthrie began grafting a more theoretical base onto the folk-song form that he had utilized previously without any sociopolitical rationale. He drew increasingly on the mass media rather than on traditional narratives for themes in his work. Songs of the 1945–1950 period were still composed in folk style, but their themes moved further and further from his old folk cultures.[57] The "Dust Bowl Ballads" were assimilated into a canon that emphasized popular struggle and worker protest rather than the specific events connected with the 1930s dust storms.

In due course the vitality of the labor-radical songwriting circles drifted away, but Guthrie's music retained its appeal. It benefited from the rise of the short-lived folk protest movement in the 1960s[58] and, more importantly, from the political ambiguity that allowed his songs to be drawn into the sentimental mainstream of American music. His best known tunes retained wide public recognition, with his role as a keen observer of the problems of rural America in the 1930s being belatedly recognized in April 1966 when Secretary of the Interior Stewart Udall honored Guthrie with a Conservation Service Award for his efforts to awaken the American people to "their heritage and the land."[59]

Viewed from a gap of more than 50 years, as has been emphasized above, it is apparent that Woody Guthrie was selectively relating the saga of the Dust Bowl. The people with whom he associated after moving to California were "Okies" either living in the Los Angeles area and homesick for rural Oklahoma or still actively searching for agricultural work. They tended to view their difficulties in biblical terms rather than in Marxist terms of abstract market forces. They were also more inclined to blame nature than socioeconomic forces for their loss of home and subsequent migration, even though, as noted above, most were not from the Dust Bowl at all but people evicted from the cotton areas. However much they personally related their circumstances to the events of the Dust

Bowl, they remain unreliable witnesses of the history of the drought lands.

Yet to question the reliability of the source of the imagery does nothing to reduce its power when viewed as part of popular culture. In common with other migrant peoples faced with new and unwelcoming environments, the Dust Bowl refugees constructed stories that expressed their plight, and tried to make sense of complex realities to explain how they came to be there and what, if anything, the future might hold for them. Guthrie's songs dramatically recounted those stories. They depicted a people driven from their lands by natural disaster and forced to venture into the unknown in search of a better future. Within the fabric of these songs were woven together three key strands of landscape imagery: the dystopian landscapes of the all-enveloping, all-powerful dust storms; the testing mountain and desert landscapes of the road; and the utopian landscapes of the West. Whatever embellishments and interpretations were added to the story, the "Dust Bowl Ballads" imaginatively related the social history of the migrants to the environmental history of the areas in which they lived. In doing so, Woody Guthrie provided a marginal and dispossessed group with an articulate champion and drew attention to a national scandal. As such, his music remains one of the most potent evocations of place and social hardship to be found in 20th-century folk music.

ACKNOWLEDGMENTS

I would like to express my thanks to Joseph Hickerson and his staff at the Archive of Folk Culture, Library of Congress, Washington, DC, for their wholehearted assistance while I was preparing this chapter. It should be noted that the lyrics from Woody Guthrie's songs quoted in this chapter are used with permission of TRO Essex Music Inc., of New York and London. Specific copyright attributions can be found in the footnotes.

NOTES

1. "This Land Is Your Land." Words and music by Woody Guthrie. Copyright TRO. Copyright 1956 (Renewed), 1958 (Renewed), 1970 Ludlow Music, Inc., New York, N.Y. Used by permission.

2. The original manuscript bears the title "God Blessed America," which was also the chorus, but the composer later scrubbed out that title and replaced it with the more familiar "This Land Was Made for You and Me." For a description of the writing of "God Blessed America" and a transcript of the original words, see Klein, J. (1980). *Woody Guthrie: A life*. New York: Knopf, pp. 140–141. For a facsimile of the original manuscript, see ibid., p. 447. See also Pascal, R. (1990).

Walt Whitman and Woody Guthrie: American prophet-singers and their people. *Journal of American Studies, 24* (particularly p. 44).

3. This develops a point made by Cronon, W. (1994). Landscapes of abundance and scarcity. In C. A. Milner II, C. A. O'Connor, & M. A. Sandweiss (Eds.), *The Oxford history of the American West*. New York: Oxford University Press, p. 623.

4. There is no fixed list of these songs, as a large number of Guthrie's songs relate to Dust Bowl themes. For the purposes of this chapter, the "Dust Bowl Ballads" are taken to include all tracks on the collection of that name (C-1040) issued by Rounder Records of 1 Camp Street, Cambridge, Mass. 02140 in 1988. (They were originally produced for RCA Records by Frank Driggs.) The 15 tracks on that collection were "The Great Dust Storm (Dust Storm Disaster)," "I Ain't Got No Home," "Talking Dust Bowl Blues," "Vigilante Man," "Dust Can't Kill Me," "Dust Pneumonia Blues," "Pretty Boy Floyd," "Going (Blowin') Down This Road (I Ain't Going to Be Treated This Way)," "Tom Joad, Parts 1 and 2," "Dust Bowl Refugee," "Do Re Mi," "Dust Bowl Blues," and "Dusty Old Dust (So Long It's Been Good to Know Yuh)." Five additional songs dealing with similar or related themes may also be added to that list: "Hard Travelling," "Will(y) Rogers Highway," "Rambling Round," "Pastures of Plenty," and "Oklahoma Hills." For an accurate impression of Guthrie's musical style and views at the end of the 1930s, there are few better guides than *Woody Guthrie: The Library of Congress Recordings* (Rounder Records C-1041, parts 1 and 2). These recordings feature Guthrie playing a selection of his songs and engaging in brief conversations with Alan Lomax, then the director of the library's Archive of Folk Song.

5. Steinbeck, J. (1939). *The grapes of wrath*. New York: Viking Press. The resulting film of the same name was made by Twentieth Century Fox in 1940 and directed by John Ford.

6. A good overview is found in Hurley, F. J. (1993). The Farm Security Administration file: In and out of focus. *History of Photography, 17*, 244–252. See also Lange, D., & Taylor, P. S. (1969). *An American exodus: A record of human erosion*. New Haven, Conn.: Yale University Press for Oakland Museum. (Original work published 1939). Meltzer, M. (1978). *Dorothea Lange: A photographer's life*. New York: Farrar, Strauss and Giroux. Ohrn, K. B. (1980). *Dorothea Lange and the documentary tradition*. Baton Rouge: Louisiana State University Press. Sandweiss, M. A. (1988). The way to realism, 1930–1940. In J. Enyeart (Ed.), *Decade by decade: Twentieth-century American photography from the Collection of the Center for Creative Photography (CCP)*, pp. 35–47. Boston: Little, Brown, for the CCP, University of Arizona.

7. Klein, *Woody Guthrie*, pp. 140–141.

8. E.g., Lomax, A. (Ed.). (1967). *Hard-hitting songs for hard-hit people: Notes on the songs of Woody Guthrie*. New York: Oak Publications; Dillsaver, J. D. (1975). Woody Guthrie's Depression: A study of situation. Unpublished Ph.D. dissertation, University of Columbia at Missouri; Lookingbill, B. (1994). Dusty apocalypse and socialist salvation: A study of Woody Guthrie's Dust Bowl imagery. *Chronicles of Oklahoma, 72*, 396–413. The only contribution that has previously dealt with landscapes per se is Curtis, J. R. (1975). Woody Guthrie and the Dust Bowl. In G. O. Carney (Ed.), *The sounds of people and places*. Washington, D.C.:

University Press of America, 197–210. Curtis, however, does not provide any sustained link between portrayals of landscape and wider cultural traditions.

9. Schama, S. (1995). *Landscape and memory.* London: HarperCollins, p. 13. Among a large literature that takes this point further in the North American context, see Worster, D. (1985). *Rivers of empire: Water, aridity, and the growth of the American West.* New York: Pantheon Books; Brown, J. D., Anderson, N. K., Cronon, W., Dippie, B. W., Sandweiss, M. A., Schoelwer, S. P., & Lamar, H. R. (1992). *Discovered lands, invented pasts: Transforming visions of the American West.* New Haven, Conn.: Yale University Press; and Cronon, W. J., Miles, G., & Gitlin, J. (Eds.). (1992). *Under an open sky: Rethinking America's western past.* New York: Norton. For more debate on environmental history itself, see the special section (1990). on "Environmental History." *Journal of American History,* 76, 1087–1147.

10. Although a problematic term, the "West" is taken in its historic context as the lands lying to the west of the Mississippi. The states of California, Oregon, and Washington can be considered as the "Far West."

11. Hurt, R. D. (1979). Agricultural technology in the Dust Bowl, 1932–1940. In B. W. Blouet & F. C. Luebke (Eds.), *The Great Plains: Environment and culture.* Lincoln: University of Nebraska Press, p. 139.

12. There is no room here to deal with the development of the American soil conservation movement which stemmed directly from reaction to the Dust Bowl. For more information, see Browning, G. M., Cohee, M. H., Fuqua, N. J., Hill, R. G., & Pritchard, H. W. (1984). Out of the Dust Bowl. *Journal of Soil and Water Conservation,* 39, 6–17.

13. Logsdon, G. (1991). Woody Guthrie and his Oklahoma hills. *Journal of the Mid-America Folklore Society and the Kansas Folklore Society,* 19, 64.

14. See, e.g., Malin, J. C. (1946). Dust storms, 1: 1850–1860; 2: 1861–1880; 3: 1881–1900. *Kansas Historical Quarterly,* 14, 129–144, 265–296, 391–413. Further discussion may be found in Bogue, A. G. (1991). James C. Malin: A voice from the Grassland. In R. W. Etulain (Ed.), *Writing Western history: Essays on major Western historians.* Albuquerque: University of New Mexico Press, pp. 215–243.

15. Lauber, P. (1958). *Dust Bowl: The story of man on the Great Plains.* New York: Coward-McCann, p. 41.

16. Hurt, *Agricultural technology,* p. 139.

17. The wheat price declined from $1.16 per bushel in 1926 to $0.68 in 1930. See Lookingbill, B. (1994). "A God-forsaken place": Folk eschatology and the Dust Bowl. *Great Plains Quarterly,* 14, 275.

18. Ibid.; also Lauber, *Dust Bowl,,* p. 41.

19. Lauber, *Dust Bowl,,* p. 20.

20. Worster, D. (1979). *Dust Bowl: The Southern Plains in the 1930s.* New York: Oxford University Press, pp. 10–25; also Cronon, *Landscapes of abundance,,* p. 623.

21. Stein, W. J. (1973). *California and the Dust Bowl migration.* Westport, Conn.: Greenwood Press, p. 4.

22. Logsdon, *Woody Guthrie,* p. 20; Worster, *Dust Bowl,* p. 49.

23. Duncan, O. D. (1939). *The significance of the migrations of Oklahoma*

farm populations. Stillwater: University of Oklahoma Press, p. 1, quoted in Stein, *California*, p. 9.

24. Worster, *Dust Bowl*, p. 49.

25. There was also considerable adaptability among a population who primarily owned their farms. See, e.g., Miner, C. (1993). Here today, here tomorrow: G-K farms in the Dust Bowl years, Thomas County, Kansas. *Kansas History, 16*, 148–165. For a discussion of a literary response, see Quantic, D. D. (1991). Frederick Manfred's *The Golden Bowl*: Myth and reality in the Dust Bowl. *Western American Literature, 25*, 297–309.

26. Worster, *Dust Bowl*, p. 61.

27. Logsdon, *Woody Guthrie*, pp. 64–65.

28. The best full-length biography on Guthrie is undoubtedly Klein, *Woody Guthrie*. A variety of personal reminiscences from contemporaries are also useful: see, e.g., Yurchenco, H. (1960). *A mighty hard road: The Woody Guthrie story*. New York: McGraw Hill; and Robbin, E. (1979). *Woody Guthrie and me: An intimate reminiscence*. Berkeley, CA: Lancaster Miller. With respect to Guthrie's own writings, see Guthrie, W. (1943). *Bound for glory*. New York: Dutton; and Guthrie, W. (1965). *Born to win* (R. Shelton, Ed.). London: Macmillan.

29. Lookingbill, Dusty apocalypse, p. 397.

30. E.g., Terkel, S. (1961, December). Woody Guthrie: The last of the great balladeers. *Climax*, (December) 45–69; Turner, F. (1977). Just what the hell has gone wrong here anyhow?: Woody Guthrie and the American dream. *American Heritage, 28*(6), 34–43.

31. Denisoff, R. S. (1971). *Great day coming: Folk music and the American left*. Urbana: University of Illinois Press; Reuss, R. A. (1975). American folksongs and left-wing politics. *Journal of the Folklore Institute, 12*(2–3), 89–111; Fiori, U. (1978). *Joe Hill, Woody Guthrie, Bob Dylan: Storia della canzore popolaire in USA*. Milan: Mazzotta; Hampton, W. (1986). *Guerrilla minstrels: John Lennon, Joe Hill, Woody Guthrie*. Knoxville: University of Tennessee Press.

32. Pascal, *Walt Whitman and Woody Guthrie*.

33. In passing, it is worth noting that Oklahoma itself had only gained statehood in 1907.

34. On radio, see, e.g., the discussion in Gazert, C. (1992). 'Tis sweet to be remembered: Independent radio performance pioneer Bradley Kincaid. *Journal of American Culture, 15*(3), 17–25. It must be pointed out, however, that Guthrie's role as a collector should not be overestimated. He was far more interested in finding useful material or musical styles for his own use than with any desire to collect music for its own sake.

35. Klein, *Woody Guthrie*, p. 57.

36. For example, while in California, Guthrie self-consciously experimented with writing in regional dialect in his "Woody Sez" column for the left-wing periodical *People's World*.

37. Reuss, R. A. (1970). Woody Guthrie and his folk tradition. *Journal of American Folklore, 83*, 273–303.

38. Ibid.

39. "Dust Storm Disaster." Words and Music by Woody Guthrie. Copyright

TRO. Copyright 1960 (Renewed), 1963 (Renewed). Ludlow Music, Inc., New York, N.Y. Used by permission.

40. See, e.g., Ketterer, D. (1974). *New worlds for old: The apocalyptic imagination, science fiction and American literature*. Bloomington: Indiana University Press; and Moorhead, J. H. (1984). Between progress and apocalypse: A reassessment of millennialism in American religious thought. *Journal of American History*, 71, 524–542.

41. Lookingbill, "A God-forsaken place," p. 273. This author contrasted premillennial dispensationalism with the inherently more joyful postmillennial version in which such events would be seen as the precursors of a progressive evolution into the Kingdom.

42. Lookingbill, Dusty apocalypse, provides interesting but contentious arguments on this point.

43. "Talking Dust Bowl." Words and Music by Woody Guthrie. Copyright TRO. Copyright 1960 (Renewed), 1963 (Renewed) Ludlow Music, Inc., New York, N.Y. Used by permission.

44. The four small hospitals in Meade County, Kansas, found that 52% of their admissions in April 1935 were acute respiratory cases (Worster, *Dust Bowl*, p. 20).

45. Lowenthal, D. (1982). The pioneer landscape: An American dream. *Great Plains Quarterly*, 2, 10.

46. Guthrie's lyrics, however, express no particular ideological standpoint on the matter. See Menig, H. (1975). Woody Guthrie: The Oklahoma years, 1912–1929. *Chronicles of Oklahoma*, 53, 262–263.

47. "Talking Dust Bowl." Words and Music by Woody Guthrie. Copyright TRO. Copyright 1960 (Renewed), 1963 (Renewed) Ludlow Music, Inc., New York, N.Y. Used by permission.

48. Zelinsky, W. (1973). *The cultural geography of the United States*. Englewood Cliffs, N.J.: Prentice Hall; Dettelbach, C. G. (1976). *In the driver's seat: The automobile in American literature and popular culture*. Westport, Conn.: Greenwood. For a comment on the ambiguities of mobility in the American consciousness, see Cresswell, T. (1993). Mobility as resistance: A geographical reading of Kerouac's On the Road. *Transactions of the Institute of British Geographers*, 18, 249–262.

49. Called this in Guthrie's song "Willy Rogers Highway."

50. "I Ain't Got No Home." Words and Music by Woody Guthrie. Copyright TRO. Copyright 1960 (Renewed), 1963 (Renewed) Ludlow Music, Inc., New York, N.Y. Used by permission.

51. Houston, J. D. (1989). From El Dorado to the Pacific Rim: The place called California. *California History*, 68, 173.

52. From verse 2 of Guthrie's "Going Down the Road (I Ain't Going to Be Treated This Way)."

53. "Pastures of Plenty." Words and Music by Woody Guthrie. Copyright TRO. Copyright 1960 (Renewed), 1963 (Renewed) Ludlow Music, Inc., New York, N.Y. Used by permission.

54. See Stein, *California*; and Gregory, J. N. (1989). "Dust Bowl legacies: The Okie impact on California, 1939–1989. *California History*, 68, 74–85.

55. Gregory, *Dust Bowl legacies*, p. 74.

56. Reuss, Woody Guthrie and his folk tradition, p. 297.

57. Some of the better known songs are "The 1913 Massacre," "Song of the Deportees," "Belle Starr" and "The Dying Miner." See Reuss, Woody Guthrie and his folk tradition, p. 302.

58. Bob Dylan's "Song to Woody" (1962). is perhaps the most tangible indication of this interest.

59. Semple, R. B., Jr. (1966, April 17). US Award given to Woody Guthrie. *New York Times*, p. 47, quoted in Reuss, Woody Guthrie and his folk tradition, p. 298.

11

SOUNDING OUT THE CITY

Music and the Sensuous Production of Place

SARA COHEN

    This chapter explores the role of music in the production of place. It does so through biographical information concerning 88-year-old Jack Levy drawn from a case study he participated in on popular music and Liverpool's Jewish "community."[1] The chapter points to connections between some of the musical styles and places that have been important to Jack, focusing in particular on the relationship between music and the neighborhoods and city in which Jack has lived.

    The first part of the chapter discusses music and place in terms of everyday social relations and interactions, looking at some of the ways in which place could be said to be socially, culturally and materially "produced" through musical practice. The second part emphasizes the fact that this "production" is always a contested and ideological process. The third part considers the dynamic interrelationship between music and place, suggesting that music plays a very particular and sensual role in the production of place, in part through its peculiar embodiment of movement and collectivity.

    I first met Jack in 1992. His wife had died two years earlier, after which he had become bored, depressed, and ill. He found walking difficult; his trips outside his apartment were less frequent than he would wish. He occasionally visited a nearby home for the Jewish elderly, and when he could manage it he walked to the synagogue round the corner. Each week he attended social activities held either at the Jewish community center a couple of miles away or at the apartment complex where he lived, which had been built and was serviced for the Jewish elderly by the Liverpool Jewish Housing Trust. Through such activities Jack keeps in contact with people he has grown up with, but frequently tires of. A friend, Les, used to visit Jack everyday, and a volunteer sometimes stopped by to help him with the shopping, but last year Les moved abroad and the volunteer can no longer spare the time to visit. Jack regularly telephones his sister who lives in a home for the elderly in Southport. Jack has no children; his only daughter died in the early 1970s.

Since our initial meeting I have visited Jack at his home on a regular basis. His front room is dingy and cramped. The walls are a dark yellow and the patterned carpet has faded. There is a table, a television that is rarely turned on, an armchair, and a pale brown sofa. A dark patch at one end of the sofa marks the spot worn by the familiar pressure of Jack's head. Beside the sofa is a wooden chair upon which sits a small radio and a telephone. The sideboard is crammed with old photographs. To help pass the time, Jack listens to music on the radio, particularly dance band music. In 1992 he also began to write what he refers to as "stories." He would choose a particular subject familiar to him—a Liverpool Jewish family, street, event, or activity—and write a paragraph or several pages on what he remembered about it. He used some of his life savings to publish his reminiscences in two small booklets.[2]

Talking to Jack is often a frustrating experience. He frequently contradicts himself, he can appear surprisingly naive, and he could not be described as terribly articulate or perceptive. His memory, however, is phenomenal. He can envision a particular Liverpool street in the 1920s and list by number all the houses or businesses along its length, describing the Jewish people who lived or worked in them and tracing their family histories. In addition, Jack has a tremendous sense of humor and he adores music. Like others he finds it hard to describe music, often relying upon commonplace statements and clichés to explain the way it can make him feel, but he talks of music and dance with a passion and intensity that colors and animates his face and gestures. While recalling for me some of the people and events he has known, he has introduced me to a world of music through which places are produced and reproduced.

LIVING AND DEFINING PLACE
Relations of Kinship and Community

Jack was born in London's East End in 1906. His parents were part of a wave of Jewish immigrants who came to Britain from Eastern Europe in the late 19th century, many of them fleeing the ravages of the Crimean War. The port of Liverpool acted as a staging post for hundreds of thousands of Jews who passed through it on their way westward. Some, however, remained in Liverpool. When Jack moved there with his family at the age of eight, the city's Jewish population had increased to around 11,000, and has created what is generally referred to as a Jewish "quarter" around a street called Brownlow Hill, a name that retains symbolic significance for many Liverpool Jews. Jack's family finally settled in that street after occupying a series of dilapidated apartments in neighboring streets. His sisters ran a milliner's shop on the street.

Jack left school at 14, after which he held 37 different jobs including selling trinkets and other items door-to-door mostly in Jewish neighborhoods, collecting money for Jewish charities, selling advertisements for the local Jewish newspaper, and working on commission for other Jewish organizations. Over the years Jack was also hired by various Jewish tailors whenever work was available. Jack's employment experiences were typical of those of many Jewish immigrants. Throughout the 19th century Liverpool suffered chronic unemployment. Unlike other big industrial towns, such as Manchester, it had little manufacturing industry, and as a port it attracted large numbers of unskilled laborers. Fluctuations in trade made for an unstable labor market, a situation exacerbated by the flood of Irish, Jewish, and other immigrants to the city during the latter half of the 19th century. Most of the Jewish immigrants lived in poverty. About 40% were unskilled, and many of these took to some form of peddling (selling drapery, crockery, furniture, tobacco, stationary, pirated sheet music, etc.). But there also existed within the Brownlow Hill neighborhood a small-scale industrial economy of Jewish tailoring and cabinet-making workshops, many of which were situated in people's homes. (Jack's mother worked as a buttonholer, his father was a tailor, his father-in-law was a cabinet-maker.) There were also quite a few Jewish shops in Brownlow Hill: bakers, butchers, booksellers, and so on. In contrast to Manchester and Leeds, commerce predominated among Liverpool's new immigrant Jews, perhaps largely because of the city's lack of manufacturing industry.

The first generation of immigrants, including Jack's parents, aunts, and uncles, spoke Yiddish and they tended to work, socialize, and worship only with fellow Yiddish-speaking Jews. They established tightly knit social networks based on relations of kinship and fellowship with others from the same country of origin. Together these groups constituted quite an isolated population. As a young boy Jack also associated only with fellow Jews. Later, he and his Jewish peers had Gentile friends but they never visited their houses or entertained the idea of marrying a Gentile. In 1939 Jack, like his sister, entered into an arranged marriage.

The impoverished situation of the new immigrants, and that of Liverpool's laboring classes generally, contrasted greatly with the wealth of the city's elite which included a small established Jewish population. By the beginning of the 19th century there already lived in Liverpool about 1,000 Jews, including a middle class of merchants, bankers, and shopkeepers (largely of German and Dutch origin) that was well integrated into the upper echelons of Liverpool society but, as a minority, was concerned to be seen as well behaved and to fit in with wider society. This highly anglicized Jewish elite lived a few miles outside of the "Jewish quarter" in the large mansions situated around two of Liverpool's finest parks. They had little in common culturally or economically with the new immigrants. In 1906 a lawyer and renowned member of this elite, Bertram B. Benas, gave a presidential address to the Liverpool Jewish Literary Society in which he said:

> A self-imposed ghetto is for the first time in process of formation in our city. Entire streets are being wholly occupied by Russo-Polish immigrants in the Brownlow Hill district. . . . The non-Jewish residents are removing to the more distant outskirts. . . .

> To see them at prayer is quite a revelation to modern Liverpool Jewry. Their services are full of emphatic, vivid, even uncouth devotion. To listen to their ready and soulful responses, to see the weird swinging of their bodies during their orisons, to hear the loud and earnest sounds of their great Amen, their hearty unison in songs of praise, wanting perhaps in musical culture, yet giving food for inspiration.

Class and other distinctions among Liverpool Jews were reinforced in the popular press. A series of articles entitled "The Liverpool Jew" appeared in the *Liverpool Review* in 1899. The articles were full of anti-Semitic references to Jewish character and culture. Four classes ("specimens") of Liverpool Jew were portrayed, from the uppermost "English Jew," down to the "newly-imported Foreign Jew" based in the "little colony," as the Brownlow Hill neighborhood was referred to, a term that, like "ghetto" or "quarter," implies a position of powerlessness and incarceration. Second-generation immigrants comprised the second class of Liverpool Jew, which was typified as frequenting music and dance halls, "exhibiting his 'light fantastic toe' at cheap cinderellas and dances," while the fourth class, the English Jew, was portrayed as much more "cultured"—artistic, literary, and "Musical—to an acute degree"—found at almost every concert devoted to the classical productions of the world's great composers. Such stereotypes illustrate the way in which music (in this case through writing and verbal discourse) is used to define and distinguish people and places according to class and ethnicity. As Stokes has emphasized,[3] this underlines the importance of turning from "defining the essential and 'authentic' traces of identity 'in' music ... to the question of how music is used by social actors in specific local situations to erect boundaries, to maintain distinctions between us and them."

Musical Performance, Exchange, and Interaction

The consumption and production of music also draws people together and symbolizes their sense of collectivity and place. For the immigrant Jews of Brownlow Hill, music (religious, folk, popular, and classical) played an important role in everyday life and the rituals, routines, and discourses that comprised it. Music was in fact the focus of many social gatherings, helping to establish and strengthen the immigrants' relations with each other or their relationship with God, and music also framed particular events such as wedding ceremonies and religious festivals, setting them apart from other daily activities, heightening their symbolic significance.[4]

Most of the immigrant Jews were indeed very religious, and religious music and practice undoubtedly helped maintain their individual and collective identity in a context of considerable uncertainty and unfamiliarity. The immigrants set up Chevra, societies through which those who had originated in a particular Eastern European town or district met together to worship and socialize, often in someone's house. Gradually they set up their own synagogues which contrasted greatly with the opulence and grandeur of those frequented by the Jewish elite. (They also set up their own welfare organizations, assisted by the Jewish elite for whom charitable activity played an important role, as it has done in many Euro-American Jewish circles, acting as a source of collective cohesion and prestige.)

Within Judaism, particularly its Eastern European traditions, vocal music is believed to provide the closest communication with God, with the Hasidic song or wordless chant possessing "more power than any other prayer; representing pure religious ecstasy"[5]; and embodying the notion that while the life of a text is limited, the melody lives on forever. The chanting is traditionally done by and for men (chazans). Hasidic song has left a strong imprint on Eastern European Jewish music as a whole. Today, synagogue attendance has declined among Liverpool Jews, but the symbolic meanings and ritual imagery of the synagogue are deeply internalized. Jack's stories often incorporate religious references, and synagogue music has great emotional significance for him. "It shows you your place," he explains, "[It is] traditional. They daren't alter it. That music goes on and on and on. Fathers play to sons, and sons play to sons. Always the same. It never alters . . . that music is there forever." He thus depicts the music as a timeless (and gendered) tradition representing security and stability.

When Jack was young his parents listened on the family gramophone to recordings of the great chazans imported by a nearby record retailer from a Jewish wholesaler in London. They also listened to recordings of Yiddish folk music. One of Jack's strongest memories of music as a young child is of his mother and aunts sitting together, singing Yiddish songs and weeping to the mournful sounds that reminded them of Poland, their homeland ("der heim"). Such songs typically depict aspects of daily life and work, or tell tales about separation and parting, or focus on the worlds of children and women. Jack said of the women, "They loved to weep, that was their pleasure." Many people maintain a link with their past through attachment to specific places, and music is often used to remember such places. The Yiddish music provoked and structured particular emotions in Jack's female relatives, emotions through which they expressed their feelings about their country of origin and the relations and practices they had left behind. The music brought them together and symbolized their collective identity. Listening to that music today, Jack is reminded of those women and the female domestic space or home that they represented.

Referring to the recordings that his relatives listened to, Jack said, "And somehow those records came around. And one person got hold of one, and it was passed all round. . . . And bit by bit we used to have records." This description conforms with Jack's depiction of Liverpool Jews as living "in one circle," a spatial metaphor for neighborhood that incorporates Jewish records and songs as part of the circle, and part of the process of defining it. Likewise, there existed for a short period a Liverpool Yiddish book publisher, Ghetto Press, and a regional Yiddish newspaper that Jack also described as being passed around the neighborhood from house to house.

But what Jack talks about most in relation to the past is film and dance music, which he describes as "the whole life and soul of [his] generation." As a young man he attended the cinema on a weekly basis and the films and music he saw and heard there inspired him. He has sung, for example, the songs of Al Jolson's for me, demonstrating through his voice and the movement of his arms the emotional intensity that they evoke. Jolson too was the son of Jewish immigrants struggling to find their place in a new country, and Gabler[6] has written that he was "caught between the old life and the new . . . of both and of neither." Jolson's on-screen performances often articulated this experience, which is perhaps one reason why his music appealed so strongly to Jack.[7]

Since he left school in 1920, dancing and dance halls have been Jack's major obsession. "Dancing," he told me, "was my life." At one time he went out dancing six nights a week at Jewish functions, at the tailor's club, and at various dance halls in the city. During his early 20s he started running dances himself and acted as Master of ceremonies (MC) in local dance halls. Jack's reminiscences indicate the attraction that dance-hall culture had for him, the sense of excitement and occasion, as well as the anticipation and preparation, that a dance provoked, and the escape that it offered from the worries and routines of everyday life. He describes in vivid detail the women he danced with, their beauty and glamour, and the fashionable dress of them and the men.[8] Sitting on his sofa, he sways his torso and arms, closing his eyes in an expression of blissful engrossment, attempting to convey to me the physical attraction of the dance and the heightened sensuality and pleasure it evoked, displaying a sense of pride in the talents he had as a dancer and the proficiency and skill with which he mastered the various dance steps.

For Jack's bar mitzvah his parents bought him a piano. Although none of his family could play it, there was always someone in the neighborhood who could. Jack remembers social gatherings in his house when people would stand around the piano and sing popular songs of the day (e.g., "Rambling Rose"). Others in the neighborhood played instruments on a semiprofessional basis. During the 1920s and 1930s there were quite a few Jewish dance bands based in the Brownlow Hill neighborhood. Jack was close friends with these musicians, and he refers to them with affection and pride as "local musicians," "local" here meaning not just musicians from the Brownlow Hill neighborhood, but that neighborhood's Jewish musicians (i.e., he is claiming them as the community's own). Similarly, Jack sometimes talks of "Liverpool," or "this town" when he is referring only to its Jewish community. "Local" is, of course, a discursive shifter or variable determined by factors such as ethnicity and class.

Jack yearned to perform in a dance band himself. Later, during the 1940s, he took the plunge and spent all his savings on a saxophone. He joined a band but eventually decided that he wasn't a very good musician. Like many of his peers, he also dreamed of being a professional dancer, but again decided that he wasn't good enough, saying, "The only place to be a professional was London, and all my family was in Liverpool. I wouldn't leave them for the world to go to London." However, the beginnings of the modern British entertainment industry coincided with Jewish immigration from Eastern Europe and that industry did attract may enterprising immigrants. Access was relatively easy compared with entry into other industries due to lower financial barriers and less discrimination. Entertainment was an area not yet dominated by Gentile talent and capital, partly because it was considered risky and disreputable. Consequently, Jews entered the industry at every level. Close inspection of reports and publications on Liverpool's theaters and cinemas, for example, and of local Jewish archives, reveals passing references to Jewish performers, entertainment agents, and owners, managers, and promoters of clubs and cinemas. (This situation was mirrored in other British cities, particularly London, Manchester, and Birmingham and it was magnified in America). On the music retail side, there have been several Jewish-owned music instrument and record shops in Liverpool (hence the Jewishness of the entertainment infrastructure surrounding the Beatles, including clubs, agents, managers, retailers, and solicitors).

Music and the Social, Cultural, and Economic Production of Place

This account of the social and cultural life of the immigrant Jews of Brownlow Hill has been brief, fragmented, and rather superficial. However, it has promoted a view of music and place not as fixed and bounded texts or things, but as social practice involving relations between people, musical sounds, images and artifacts, and the material environment. It has also highlighted the importance of place in defining Jewish ethnicity,[9] and indicated some of the ways in which music is involved in the social, cultural, economic, and sensual production of place.

Jack is very proud of Liverpool and its history. Explaining why he feels so strongly about the city he said, "I live here. My home's here. My mother and father, my daughter, they're buried here. So where they're buried is my home." Places thus reify or symbolize social relationships, and kinship relations are obviously of particular emotional significance.[10] Although Jack has few living relatives in Liverpool, he is bound to the city through relations with dead kin and relations of affinity with fellow Jews. Music is one means through which such relations of kinship and community are established, maintained, and transformed.

A particular Liverpool neighborhood like Brownlow Hill has been shown to be lived and shaped through music. Musical events, whether involving small family gatherings or grander community rituals, festivals, and celebrations, and musical practices such as the exchange of musical artifacts, illustrate music's role in the social production of that neighborhood. Via performance or through the peddling of sheet music, music was also a means of generating individual income and developing that neighborhood economically and materially. Music was also used to represent the neighborhood, whether through well-known local musicians who came to symbolize it and acted as its ambassadors; or through the use of particular musical genres and styles that evoked a collective past and tradition; or through the musical stereotypes in the local press that used music to present alternative images of the neighborhood.

But music is not just represented and interpreted: it is also heard, felt, and experienced. For Jack it is sound as well as sight and smell that conjures up images, emotions, and memories of Brownlow Hill and its atmosphere. His attempts to demonstrate the physical pleasures of music and the way in which it resonates within the body, stimulating movement and emotion, emphasize the intensity of experience evoked by music and its effectiveness in producing a sense of identity and belonging.

The musical practices and interactions of the immigrant Jews helped to define and shape the particular geographical and material space within the city that they inhabited. At the same time, they invested that space with meaning and a sense of place, thus distinguishing it from other places within the city. Hence neighborhoods, cities, and other places are socially and materially produced as practical settings or contexts for social activity, but through such activity places are also produced as concepts or symbols. To describe places as being "produced" is to emphasize the processes that shape their material, social, and symbolic forms. Music is part of such processes. Music reflects aspects of the place in which it is created (hence "different cities make different noises"),[11] but music also helps to produce place. Hence Appadurai[12] has described locality as both figure and ground.

Comparative material on Liverpool's Irish and black populations emphasizes music's role in the production of place, the spatial politics of everyday life, and the expression of ethnic identity. One musician, for example, describes how in the 1930s a black neighbor would play his records loudly and open all the windows so that the sound would travel and publically proclaim his status as the owner of a gramophone. Meanwhile, a color bar operated in many of the city's clubs and dance halls, which led to a situation in which black musicians performed in "white" spaces, but the leisure activities of black people were restricted to one particular area of the city. Elsewhere in the city marching concertina bands have acted as a focus and trigger for Irish sectarian conflict, representing an appropriation or invasion of public space and a marker of territory.[13]

In defining a sense of "this place," music also marks relations of kinship, alliance, and affinity with places elsewhere. Yiddish music, for example, was commonly used by the immigrant Jews to maintain relations with Eastern Europe, and from the 1920s onward various Hebrew songs were used to forge relations with another home or promised land and to express Jewish nationalism.[14] Zionism and other political movements have used music to reify particular places in the pursuit of common goals so that those places come to embody the future and alternative ways of living. Many songs of Eretz Israel represent a synthesis of elements from Eastern

European and Middle Eastern folksong. They are usually about the land and those who work on it, and many have an assertive, patriotic ring, thus contrasting with the Yiddish songs that conjure up images of everyday life in homelands like Poland. Jack finds it hard to relate to the songs of Eretz Israel, partly, perhaps, because unlike his contemporaries who have established connections with other places (especially London and Israel) through their middle class children and grandchildren, Jack has few such connections. The songs are in a language he can't understand, and he sees them as belonging to another generation. "I don't want to know," he says, "they're not in my era. Once we became a land of our own, a State, the whole thing changed. The youngsters took over ... and it was different then." Thus Jack sometimes expresses a sense of alienation from his contemporaries and from the younger middle class Jewish establishment in Liverpool, yet says at the same time "I knew their parents," again expressing a sense of community and belonging through kinship ties.

Relations between Liverpool Jews and Jews in Israel, America, or elsewhere are reinforced via visiting musicians and through other musical exchanges. Jack's reminiscences frequently allude to Liverpool Jews who are now, in his words, "scattered all over the world." Like other Jews of his generation, he discusses the music of Jewish immigrants from Eastern Europe, such as Al Jolson, Irving Berlin, and Sophie Tucker (all based in America), in a manner that suggests a sense of affinity with those sharing similar heritages and experiences. In addition, however, Jack frequently cites Irish songs and songs of black slaves in America, acknowledging through them a sense of unity with other immigrant or oppressed peoples. He said of the latter: "They all had their songs ... they've got their roots here, their roots there ... Nobody wants them. They're a misfit. They get out, but where can you go? They've got no home."

The images and information that Jack has acquired about such people have been largely obtained through popular song and film. He talks with affection about the "black mammy women" from the American South, describing the little spectacles they wore and their warm-heartedness. He also quotes at length from the song "Danny Boy," linking the lyrics to Irish experiences of oppression, and linking that form of oppression to Jewish experience and history, thus suggesting the marking of "families of resemblance" through music.[15]

This highlights the way in which music enables Jack to travel in an imaginary sense to different times and places. Illustrating how music inspires his fantasy, transporting him from one place and immersing him somewhere else, Jack described his Monday afternoons at a Liverpool ballroom during the 1920s. Monday, he explained, was traditionally washing day. The women used to take off their aprons after a hard morning's work, do their hair, put on their finery, and take the bus to the city center, arriving at the ballroom for the 2:30 P.M. start. Jack once danced there to a tune entitled "In a Garden in Italy," and he enthused about how the music made him picture that garden, and how wonderful that experience was. Jack said of music: "It doesn't matter if it's dance music or what, it's there in my radio, and you're in another world. It takes you to a new world." He cited songs with American places-names in their title such as "Back Home in Tennessee," "Chicago," "Memphis Blues," "California Here I Come." He depicted the scene at the Swanny River: "All the women with their wide dresses. The men with their bowler hats. . . . So there you are, that's the Swanny. I don't even know where it is. I don't even know if there is a Swanny River. . . . I used to lie awake at night going through all the districts of the tunes. . . . Marvellous. . . . You'd go off to sleep thinking of them."

Jack began his dancing life in the dance halls based in the Brownlow Hill neighborhood, but as he gradually became more involved with dancing he frequented halls beyond that neighborhood, thus extending his music "pathways"[16] and broadening his knowledge and experience of the city. As a profession, music also offered other Liverpool Jews a "way out" of the neighborhood or city they lived in and the possibility of creating a new place. Gabler,[17] in his portrayal of the Eastern European Jewish immigrants who founded and built Hollywood, argued that the desire of these immigrants to assimilate and achieve status and power led them to a "ferocious, even pathological embrace of America." Through film these Jews created an idealized image of the America that they aspired to. "Prevented from entering the real corridors of power, they created a new country, an empire of their own, and colonized the American imagination to such an extent that the country came largely to be defined by the movies." The same was achieved through song by George Gershwin, Irving Berlin, Jerome Kern, and other Jewish composers. The experience of migration can thus exaggerate attachments to romanticized homelands, but also lead migrants to stridently assert an adoptive belonging.[18]

In the biography of Vesta Tilley, a well-known music hall performer and wife of Walter de Frece, a Liverpool Jew and theatrical entrepreneur involved with the music hall business, Maitland[19] suggests certain parallels with the experience of the Hollywood Jews. Walter spearheaded the move to make the music hall more respectable and enhance its appeal to the middle classes. He himself had political and social aspirations that eventually led him and Vesta Tilley to drop their associations with the music hall. Eventually he was awarded a knighthood, and in 1924 he became a member of Parliament and a deputy lieutenant. This suggests that the music hall both helped and hindered Walter's efforts to achieve upward mobility and embody respectable Englishness, and it highlights the ideological significance of music in the production of place.

So far I have discussed music's influence on social relations and activities in particular places, on people's aesthetic experiences of place, and on the economic and material development of place. I have suggested ways in which music is used to represent or symbolize a place, distinguishing it from, or linking it to, other places, and associating it with particular images and meanings. Now I would like to explore the ideological nature of this process.

REPRESENTING AND TRANSFORMING PLACE
Music, Ideology, and Social Mobility

Jews like Jack gradually assimilated with wider Liverpool culture not just through interaction with Gentiles at dance halls and elsewhere, but through pressures brought to bear upon them by the Jewish establishment. While Jack's mother and aunts wept to Yiddish music at home, Jack and his peers were singing "Land of Hope and Glory" at school, undergoing a social and educational program instigated by the Jewish elite. The program was designed to anglicize the immigrants, by ridding them of their Yiddish language and culture; to control their leisure, by directing it away from disreputable activities (e.g., gambling and frequently dance halls); and to depoliticize them, by exorcising the socialist, anarchist, and trade union activity that some of them promoted. The elite were motivated by a variety of reasons. They feared, for example, that the foreign ways of the newcomers would threaten their own acquired respectability and standing and promote hostility to the Jewish population as a whole. Alternatively, popular culture has commonly acted as a focus for moral panic and social control, particularly in connection with working-class or immigrant youth. The concern of the Jewish Liverpool elite with anglicization, and with fitting Jewish tradition into the wider culture, can be detected early on in the rapid changes they introduced in their synagogues. A choir was introduced in one Liverpool synagogue at the beginning of the 1840s, for example, and an organ in another during the 1870s. These and other changes have continually reflected and provoked divisions among British Jews regarding processes of assimilation and distinctiveness.

The social and educational program aimed at the new immigrants was instituted via a framework of Jewish societies and clubs, many of which were based upon models in the wider English society. They included a Jewish Working Men's Club that ran classes in English, and a branch of the Jewish Lads' Brigade—a national Jewish cadet force based on the Church Lads' Brigade, whose letter-headed paper states that its object "is to train its members in loyalty, humour, discipline and self respect that they shall become worthy and useful citizens and be a credit to their country and their community." The Brigade was backed by a number of social clubs, including the Jewish Lad's Club, the Jewish Boy Scouts, and the Jewish Girls' Clubs. The process of anglicization was continued in the Hebrew school founded in 1840. Pupils were encouraged to change their names, mark British celebrations, and enter choral competitions and similar events.

These societies and clubs represented leisure and entertainment, but they were also highly politicized, combining both power and pleasure. Music was used to mold particular identities and allegiances, whether it be the military brass band music of the Jewish Lads' Brigade, the choral and orchestral societies of the Jewish Working Men's Club, or songs and anthems that acted as symbols of Englishness and expressions of national loyalty and unity. The program indicates pressures of assimilation, but also the simultaneous concern with maintaining distinctiveness as Jews. Jewish societies, clubs, and dances were regarded as safe contexts in which Jewish people could meet and form suitable friendships with people of their own kind. The program was extremely successful. Within a single generation, Yiddish had practically disappeared from the cultural scene.

Yet the production of national or other place-bound identities is always a contested process, and not all the Jewish immigrants were totally influenced by the social and educational program instigated by the Jewish elite. Many kept to their own more informal leisure activities based around their homes. Some, like Jack, attended organized walks, played football, and participated in other activities organized by Jewish societies, but also went to "outside" functions held at local dance halls frequented by Gentiles and forbidden to many Jewish young people. Meanwhile the Jewish elite patronized different clubs and venues and Jack never mixed with them. They also had their own social and cultural institutions—for example, literary societies—and gradually began to encourage the more up-and-coming of the new immigrants to join their activities until members of this nouveau riche started setting up their own similar organizations. Most such societies organized regular dances, concerts, and gramophone recitals in addition to dramatic, sporting, and fundraising activities, and debates and lectures. According to their minute books, many talks focused on politics and high culture.[20] Debates addressed issues such as the division between established and immigrant Jews, and the generation gap between immigrants and their "English children." These societies gradually died out in the face of growing competition from the newly flourishing entertainment industries.

Music, Stability, Security

Like many other immigrant Jewish populations, Liverpool's immigrant Jews experienced rapid social and economic advancement. Within two generations a significant transformation of the class position of the immigrants had occurred. This was due to a mixture of social, cultural, and economic factors, including the fact that the city's high rate of unemployment discouraged further Jewish immigration. Most of the pedlars progressed as entrepreneurs. They came into contact with Gentiles because they moved around a lot, and they did better economically than the masses of skilled cabinet makers and tailors who worked long hours in small shops for a fixed wage. However, the latter's occupational structure also eventually shifted, toward clothing, drapery, and furniture businesses, and toward the professions which many were encouraged into as a means of improving themselves and their families.

Biographical information on some of the Jewish individuals and families involved with the Liverpool entertainment industries illustrates the way in which they were able to quickly establish themselves in those industries, but also indicates the cultural transformation that enhanced status and respectability might demand. Mal Levy, for example, had a recording contract in the 1960s and toured the country as a performer until he succumbed to parental pressure and returned to Liverpool to join the family tailoring business. "I think it was 'Don't put your son on the stage,'" says Mal, "You know, the old-fashioned Jewish outlook—it's not a good job, it's not a decent job.... They looked down on music in those days." Such attitudes help explain why Liverpool Jews have tended to work in the business- and management-ends of music rather than in the performance end, and why rock and pop music have received such little attention from the city's Jewish institutions.

Brian Epstein came from a respected Liverpool family that ran a lucrative furniture business. Epstein opened a record retail branch within this business before taking up management of the Beatles and setting up his own music management company. According to Coleman,[21] Epstein's father, along with other relatives, wasn't too thrilled about Brian's association with the Beatles ("those yobbos"), and persuaded him to take on his brother Clive as joint director.[22] Although Brian Epstein's success eventually earned him respect from Liverpool's Jewish community, his obituary in the *Jewish Chronicle* stated: "The sad thing is that Brian was never completeley au courant with the music that he was so much involved in.... His strength of character came from the solidarity of his upbringing and the integrity of his background. It was this strength that he relied on when his artistic judgement failed."[23] During Epstein's funeral in Liverpool, the officiating rabbi ignored his achievements and fame and described him as "a symbol of the malaise of the 60s generation."[24] News of Epstein's death in the *Liverpool Jewish Gazette* was limited to a few short lines in the obituary notices at the back. It began, "Brian Epstein, manger of the Beatles ... " and went straight on to mention his donations to Jewish charities.

While the first part of this chapter pointed to music as a fundamental part of everyday life, and to its role in the production of identity, belonging, and place, the second part has emphasized the ideological dimension to this process. Particular musical styles and activities come to symbolize particular values, and they can be used as a tool to transform notions of place and identity in order to maintain or challenge a particular hierarchical social order. Music is thus bound up with the struggle for power, prestige, and place. It reflects but also influences the social relations, practices, and material environments through which it is made.

Place, Image, Status

As the immigrants made their way up the economic and social scale, they gradually moved out of the Brownlow Hill neighborhood. During the 1930s that neighborhood underwent massive slum clearance which hastened the Jewish exodus. By the late 1930s only a small minority of Liverpool's Jews remained in the Brownlow Hill area. The Jews moved along Smithdown Road to settle in the more affluent neighboring suburbs of Allerton, Woolton, and Childwall where the overwhelming majority of Liverpool Jews are now based. As one informant put it, "It is easier to be Jewish when you live with other Jews." During Jack's lifetime a great transformation in Liverpool's Jewish population has thus taken place. It has involved a shift from notions of Russian or Polish Jews to Anglo Jews; from notions of a Jewish "quarter" or "ghetto" to a Jewish "area" or "district"; and from a social split between the elite, more established Jews and the immigrant Jews, to a single unified middle-class Jewish community based in that area or district. Notions of being inside, outside, or "on the fringes" of the community have strengthened as socioeconomic homogeneity among the Jewish population intensified, increasing pressures for conformity.

Many young Liverpool Jews describe the community as "incestuous" and "traditional." The head of music at the Jewish school told me that Jewish religious "rules" make it impossible for many of the Jewish children to join in some musical events and activities, and that even if they aren't religious they have to be seen to be. "That's why it's such a close-knit community," she said, "because they make their fun together." When Liverpool's economic situation worsened after the 1960s, young Jews, along with those from other social groups, began to leave the city in search of economic and social opportunities elsewhere. This, along with emigration to Israel, a significant drop in the birthrate, and the high rate of intermarriage, led to a significant decline in the Jewish population. At present there are around 4,000 Jews in Liverpool. The Jewish authorities recently launched a "Come Back to Liverpool" campaign and video to encourage younger people to stay in, or return to, the city. The video emphasizes the uniqueness of the Jewish community and the area in which it is located. The smallness and safeness of the community is also emphasized, pointing out that it is easier to be someone in such a context, rather than be a small fish in a big pool somewhere else. The video features leisure amenities that project an image linked to classical music, emphasizing, for example, longstanding Jewish associations with the Royal Liverpool Philharmonic Orchestra. Hence place, "community," and "Jewishness" have become more commonly defined through so-called high culture.

EMBODYING PLACE

Travel and Migration

The story of Jewish migration is a familiar one that features strongly in Jewish collective memory. Judaism has been likened by one Liverpool Jew to a "mental map by which we find each other as Jews in every part of the globe."[25] Jack's mental maps of the world, of Britain, of Liverpool, are partly based upon collective knowledge and experience of the geographical global movements of Jewish people, particularly the movement of Jews from Eastern Europe to particular British and American cities, and the movement of Liverpool Jews from the city center to the suburbs.

In contexts of change and mobility the production of place is often intensified. Stokes,[26] writing about Turkish and Irish migrants, points out that place, for many migrant communities, is something constructed through music with an intensity not found elsewhere in their social lives.'[27] Concerning today's global mobility, Stokes wrote that "the discourses in which place is constructed and celebrated in relation to music have never before had to permit such flexibility and ingenuity." Musical sounds and structures reflect but also provoke and shape such movement.[28] Hebrew songs, for example, helped inspire the Zionist movement, while Irish traditional music has developed through continual movement between Ireland (the "home country") and the more distant countries adopted by Irish emigrants. Irish music influenced and blended with different musical styles in America, for example, and some of the resulting hybrid styles and sounds were then reimported to Ireland and treated as authentic, traditional expressions of Irishness.

Many musical compositions address the experience of migration or travel more directly through lyrics or through the culturally specific semiotic coding of musical sounds and structures. American country and blues musicians, for example, frequently write about the experience of being on the road,[29] and Jack sings songs about leaving and returning written by Irish and other migrants. Such songs are prevalent in ports like Liverpool with their mobile and displaced populations, for whom concepts of "home" and "homeland" can evoke strong emotions—although relations with, and notions of, homeland depend on the particular circumstances of those involved, for example whether they emigrated individually or, like the Jews, in family groups. Today in Liverpool, songs from *Fiddler on the Roof* are often played at social gatherings of elderly Jews like Jack, songs that remind them of their collective origins and experiences of homelessness and emigration.

Place is also produced through the shorter journeys, routes, and activities of everyday life. All Jack's stories are about the city and people and places within it. Sitting in his front room he has taken me on a tour of parts of the city, house by house, dance hall by dance hall, street by street,[30] pointing out relevant events, individuals, family and other relationships as we pass by, and transforming my own view of the city. Jack's phenomenal memory of, and emotional investment in, these buildings, locations, and social networks may be partly due to the daily door-to-door journeys he conducted around the city by foot as a traveling salesman.[31] His leisure activities as a dancer, which took him on a nightly basis to various parts of the city, have added to his perspective on the city and its spatial geography. "I've been round this town for the last 70 years," says Jack, "and I know it backwards. I know everybody, and almost everybody knows me, except the growing generation. . . . "

In this sense places can be seen to be literally embodied. Through their bodies and bodily movements (whether through long-distance travel, walking, conversation, etc.) people experience their environment physically. Depending upon the circumstances surrounding them, some movements, such as long-distance journeys, can be quite stressful. Other more repetitive movements, such as the day-to-day journeys involved with work, or the sensual and expressive movements of dance, can be particularly memorable or intense. All can have a deep impact upon individual and collective memory and experiences of place, and upon emotions and identities associated with place.

Bodies, Sounds, Sentiments

Music can evoke or represent this physical production of place quite well. There is no space here to explore evidence for this in detail, but personal observations supported by the work of several critical musicologists indicate, without essentializing music, the particular way in which music produces place.

First, music is in a sense embodied. Musical performances also represent repetitive physical movements, whether through the fingering of instrumentalists, or the gestures of dancers. Music can move bodies in a way that distinguishes it from everyday speech and action and from the visual arts. Although music is part of everyday life, it can also be perceived as something special, something different from everyday experience.[32]

Hence many people in Liverpool and elsewhere have prioritized music, making enormous financial sacrifices so that their children might learn how to read and play it, and even write it.

In addition, we listen to music and hear the presence and movements of the performing musicians. Hence Tagg describes music as an "extremely particular form of interhuman communication"[33] involving "a concerted simultaneity of nonverbal sound events or movements ... [that makes music] particularly suited to expressing collective messages of affective and corporeal identity of individuals in relation to themselves, each other, and their social, as well as physical, surroundings."[34] Music also creates its own time, space, and motion, taking people out of "ordinary time."[35] Blacking[36] points out that, "we often experience greater intensity of living when our normal time values are upset ... music may help to generate such experiences." Furthermore, as sound, music fills and structures space within us and around us, inside and outside. Hence, much like our concept of place, music can appear to envelop us, but it can also appear to express our innermost feelings/being. Travel writers or journalists often single music out as representing the essence, soul, or spirit of a place, perhaps because music appears to be "more natural" than visual imagery since its social constructedness/semiotics is less familiar.

The images and experiences engendered by music are, of course, dependent upon the particular circumstances in which the music is performed and heard, and upon the type of musical style and activity involved. But through its embodiment of movement and collectivity, and through the peculiar ambiguity of its symbolic forms,[37] music can appear to act upon and convey emotion in a unique way. It represents an alternative discourse to everyday speech and language, although both are of course ideologically informed and culturally constructed. Hence male, working-class, rock musicians in Liverpool use music to express ideas and sentiment in a manner that may be discouraged in most public settings, or that aren't so easily expressed through other means.[38] Their music is very personal, although it is at the same time created for public performance. This can make music a particularly precious resource in the production of place and local subjectivity. As popular culture, music can be a particularly powerful and accessible resource. For the general listener just one simple musical phrase can simultaneously represent a private world of memory and desire and a collective mood or a soundtrack to particular public events. (Hence the contrasting use of music in BBC Radio 4's "Desert Island Discs" and BBC1's "The Golden Years.")

For Jack, sitting alone and listening to music on the radio, or simply talking about music, can evoke some of his most intense feelings and experiences. His musical tastes and experiences are individual, reflecting his personal biography. At the same time, however, his reminiscences have been shown to be shaped by the social relations, networks, and collectivities that he has been a part of. All this indicates music's effectiveness in stimulating a sense of identity, in preserving and transmitting cultural memory, and in establishing the sensuous production of place. Individuals can use music as a cultural "map of meaning," drawing upon it to locate "themselves in different imaginary geographies at one and the same time,"[39] and to articulate both individual and collective identities.

CONCLUSION

This chapter has been rather wide ranging, encompassing both real and imaginary places, and places of different scales, types, and times. However, I have explored the relationship between music and place through a specific biography bound up with specific social relations and situations, rather than through more abstract discussion. I have presented place as concept and as social and material reality, representing social and symbolic interrelations between people and their physical environment.

Music reflects social, economic, political, and material aspects of the particular place in which it is created. Changes in place thus influence changes in musical sounds and styles (hence the gradual anglicization of Eastern European synagogue music brought to Liverpool). My discussion has highlighted ways in which music not only reflects but also produces place. I have illustrated ways, for example, in which music acts as a focus or frame for social gatherings, special occasions, and celebrations; provokes physical movement or dance; and involves everyday social interactions such as the exchange of records and other musical artifacts, as well as business and industrial activity. Such musical practices have been shown to establish, maintain, and transform social relations, and to define and shape material and geographical settings for social action.

At the same time music has been shown to be bound up with the symbolic production of place. Music can, for example, be intentionally used to categorize or to represent place. Obviously, lyrics can refer directly to specific places, but musical sounds and structures too can represent place, either through the use of culturally familiar symbols (e.g., accordians to represent France), or in more particular ways, as illustrated by the musical stereotyping of Brownlow Hill (the "little colony") in the Liverpool press. Such collective musical symbols associate places with particular images, emotions, and meanings, and they provoke or shape social action. Hence anthems and Zionist songs inspire nationalist sentiments and movements, while other musical styles are linked in similar ways with issues of class and hierarchy.

Music is not only bound up with the production of place through collective interpretation. Music is also interpreted in idiosyncratic ways by individual listeners. Songs, sounds, and musical phrases evoke personal memories and feelings associated with particular places—as indicated by Jack's account of Yiddish and dance hall songs. I have shown that places like Liverpool, Poland, and parts of America have emotional and symbolic significance for Jack because of the relations of kinship, affinity, and alliance that they embody. Such relations are maintained, strengthened, and transformed through musical practices and interactions. This includes listening to and producing music, the verbal discourse and physical movements surrounding such practices, and the ideology informing them.

Music thus plays a unique and often hidden or taken-for-granted role in the production of place. Through its peculiar nature it foregrounds the dynamic, sensual aspects of this process, emphasizing, for example, the creation and performance of place through human bodies in action and motion. Stokes[40] has gone so far as to suggest that "the musical event, from collective dances to the act of putting a cassette or CD into a machine, evokes and organizes collective memories and present experiences of place with an intensity, power and simplicity unmatched by any other social activity." The production of place through music is always a political and contested process. As I hope I have shown, music is implicated in the politics of place, the struggle for identity and belonging, and power and prestige.

ACKNOWLEDGMENTS

This article originally appeared in *Transactions of the Institute of British Geographers*, 1995, 20, 434–446. Copyright 1995 by *Transactions of the Institute of British Geographers*. Reprinted by permission.

NOTES

1. I would like to thank the Leverhulme Trust for funding the research project that enabled the study to be carried out.

2. Levy, J. (1993). *Yiddisher scousers*. Liverpool: Author. Levy (1994). Memories are made of these: More stories by Jack Levy. *Yiddisher scousers*, No. 11. Liverpool: Author.

3. Stokes, M. (Ed.). (1994). Place, exchange and meaning: Black Sea musicians in the West of Ireland. *Ethnicity, identity: The musical construction of place*. Oxford: Berg, p. 6.

4. Finnegan, R. (1989). *The hidden musicians: Music-making in an English town*. Cambridge: Cambridge University Press.

5. Werner, E. (1990). Jewish music: Liturgical Ashkenazic tradition. In S.

Sadie (Ed.), *The new Grove dictionary of music and musicians* (Vol. 9). London: Macmillan, p. 629.

6. Gabler, N. (1989). *An empire of their own: How the Jews invented Hollywood.* London: W. H. Allen.

7. This common experience of being caught between different places, or of "bifocality," has of course been widely studied. Much has been written, for example, on the dual allegiance experienced by Anglo-American Jews, with a Jewish nationality existing alongside a British or American one (e.g., see Goldstein, S., & Goldscheider, C. [1985]. *Jewish Americans: Three generations in a Jewish community.* Lanham, Md.: University Press of America.).

8. Fashion played an important role in the lives of Jews like Jack, perhaps because of their domination of the local tailoring industry. An emphasis upon being fashionably dressed might also have given them a sense of status and prestige. Gabler (*An empire of their own*), writing on the immigrant Jews of Hollywood, frequently refers to their smart and fashionable attire, as do the satirical articles on "the Liverpool Jews" published in *Liverpool Review* (1899).

9. See Hall for a reconceptualization of ethnicity as a politics of location (Hall, S. [1995]. New cultures for old. In D. Massey & P. Jess [Eds.], *A place in the world.* Milton Keynes, U.K.: Open University Press).

10. See Werlen's writing on Pareto (Werlen, B. [1993]. *Society, action, and space: An alternative human geography.* London: Routledge, p. 180).

11. Street, J. (1993). (Dis)located? rhetoric, politics, meaning and the locality. In W. Straw et al. (Eds.), *Popular music: Style and identity.* Montreal: Centre for Research on Canadian Cultural Industries and Institutions.

12. Appadurai, A. (1993). *The production of locality.* Unpublished paper delivered at the decennial conference of the Association of Social Anthropologists, Oxford University.

13. McManus, K. (1994). *Ceilies, jigs, and ballads: Irish music in Liverpool.* Liverpool: Institute of Popular Music, p. 5.

14. Zionism was brought to Liverpool by immigrant Jews early in the century when anti-Semitism was rife throughout Europe. The movement was opposed by the Jewish elite who saw it as a threat to their acquired respectability, status, and Englishness.

15. Lipsitz, G. (1989). *Time passages: Collective memory and American popular culture.* Minneapolis: University of Minnesota Press, p. 136.

16. Finnegan, *The hidden musicians.*

17. Gabler, *An empire of their own.*

18. Lowenthal, D. (1985). *The past is a foreign country.* New York: Cambridge University Press, p. 42.

19. Maitland, S. (1986). *Vesta Tilley.* London: Virago.

20. One, e.g., was on Mendelssohn as an example of a fine Jewish composer.

21. Coleman, R. (1989). *Brian Epstein: The man who made the Beatles.* Harmondsworth, U.K.: Viking, p. 83.

22. Ibid., pp. 102–103.

23. Ibid., p. 415.

24. Ibid., p. 410.

25. Kokosolakis, N. (1982). *Ethnic identity and religion: Tradition and change in Liverpool Jewry.* Washington, D.C.: University Press of America, p. 199.

26. Stokes, Place, exchange, and meaning, p. 114.

27. See also Clifford, J. (1992). Travelling cultures. In L. Grossberg, C. Nelson, & P. A. Treichler (Eds.), *Cultural studies* (pp. 96–112). New York: Routledge.

28. Stokes, Place, exchange, and meaning, p. 114.

29. Metaphors of roads, trains, and the like have infused much of Euro-American popular culture, which may also be attributed to fantasies of escape and celebrations of distance or modernity.

30. He is particularly proud of the fact that he can list every dance hall that ever existed in the city.

31. Lynch and other human geographers have studied people's mental maps of their immediate locality in relation to their habitual movements through that locality (see Lynch, K. [1960]. *The image of the city.* Cambridge: Massachussetts Institute of Technology Press.).

32. Finnegan, *The hidden musicians,* pp. 336–337.

33. Tagg, P. (1981). On the specificity of musical communication: Guidelines for non-musicologists. In *Stencilled papers from Gothenburg University Musicology Department. 8115.* Gothenburg: Gothenburg University Press, p. 1.

34. Tagg, P. (1994). *Introductory notes to music semiotics.* Unpublished paper, p. 18.

35. See Tagg on musical time (Tagg, P. [1979]. Kojak—50 seconds of television music: Toward an analysis of affect in popular music. In *Studies from Gothenburg University, Department of Musicology* [Vol. 2]. Gothenburg: Gothenburg University Press.).

36. Blacking, J. (1976). *How musical is man?* London: Faber, p. 51.

37. See Tagg, On the specificity of musical communication, on the nonreferentiality of music.

38. See Cohen, S. (1991). *Rock culture in Liverpool.* Oxford: Oxford University Press.

39. As Hall, New cultures for old, has written of "diaspora."

40. Stokes, M. (1994). Introduction. In M. Stokes (Ed.), *Ethnicity, identity: The musical construction of place.* Oxford: Berg, p. 3.

12

DESIRE, POWER, AND THE SONORIC LANDSCAPE

Early Modernism and the Politics of Musical Privacy

RICHARD LEPPERT

Whereas western music history is written on the complex grid of relations between the public and the private, Western musicology remains focused on public musical life, as filtered through the institutions of state, church, concert hall, opera theater, and the semipublic court. The history of private musical life remains largely unwritten.[1] I want to speculate and to theorize about the social and cultural "problem" of the public and private spheres in relation to each other. My purpose is to suggest some implications of the tension between the public and the private in music as a product of discursive practice intimately tied to sociocultural relations, constructions of the human subject, and human subjectivity. Hence, I shall suggest something about the alliances between human desire, on the one hand, and the manipulation of power, on the other, as these entities are played out on the field of activities I shall call "sonoric landscapes" over stakes that are in every sense always already political.

The phrase "sonoric landscapes" embeds the following observations and assumptions, some obvious, other perhaps not: (1) sounds surround us, helping to construct us as human subjects and to locate us in particular social and cultural environments; (2) sounds produced or manipulated by humans result from conscious acts, and hence carry a semantic and discursive charge; (3) all sounds—even those not produced by humans but "merely" heard by them—can be read or interpreted; and (4), drawn from the preceding three givens, sounds are a means by which people account for their versions of reality—as it was, is, and/or might be. That is, people do not employ sounds arbitrarily, haphazardly, or unintentionally—though the "intentionally" haphazard may itself constitute an important sort of sonoric discourse.

A number of musicologists have begun the awesome and long overdue task of reconsidering how music "means" and how its meanings help produce both society and culture. A few musicologists have attempted—often in the face of considerable opposition—to reopen issues of musical semantics that were dropped from musical discussion thanks to a deadly combination of 19th-century hard-line aesthetics and 20th-century humanistic pseudoscience borrowed from the social sciences, which in turn borrowed, in lamentably nonscientific fashion, from the "hard" sciences. One notable result of this combination is what now constitutes mainline music theory: nothing if not rigorous, profoundly similar to literary New Criticism, where the only questions asked—indeed, the only questions that can be asked, given the "methodology"—involve the notes in relation to the notes. And whereas literary New Criticism has been on life-support in English Departments for well over a decade, slowly fading with faculty retirements, the analogue in musicology and music theory is anything but threatened. It continues to overshadow and marginalize all other research.

In the past decade a few scholars have examined music as a discursive practice.[2] This is not the place to survey their work, but I do want to draw attention to the opening chapter of Lawrence Kramer's *Music as Cultural Practice, 1800–1900*, "Tropes and Windows: An Outline of Musical Hermeneutics."[3] Here Kramer lays out his case for musical criticism organized largely according to poststructuralist, especially deconstructive, cultural theory. The strength of his proposal lies precisely in his insistence that the hermeneutics he undertakes is located in the musical text. His criticism combines social groundedness, historicity, and the generic specificity of musical discourse—all elements of poststructural practice and all argued for nearly 30 years ago by Theodor W. Adorno, whose work indeed articulated several facets of poststructuralism, at least in generative form, via a systematic examination of music.[4] Kramer and, among others, Susan McClary and Rose Subotnik, organize research on *particular* musical texts. This is altogether necessary. My purpose is to offer an "even more than this" to these scholars' conceptions about the discursive practices of music.

The part of music-as-discourse and musical hermeneutics I address is differentially embedded or encoded in any particular musical text at the same time that it both *exceeds* the text and exists *prior* to it, either as an unrealized but notated composition or as a performance. This "it" has at least two antecedents, or referents: the first is a spoken and unspoken, conscious and unconscious relation of people in a given social unit to music in general and to different sorts of music in particular, and the second is the relation of music, in its phenomenological ubiquity, to everything nonsonoric. In other words, prior to *and* simultaneous with any given musical text and/or its performance are the relations of music to lived experience. This notion "lived experience" identifies the second antecedent for my "it": the human body—not just the ears but also the eyes and the effect of seeing and hearing on emotion, physicality, and consciousness (in his introductory chapter, in passing, Kramer identifies music's connection to the body).

My point is this: musical discourse necessarily both precedes and exceeds the semantic quotient of any particular musical text. Musical discourse operates, in other words, even in silence, a fact brilliantly articulated years ago by John Cage, who made specific use of human sight as the problematizing agent of "musical" silence—you had to "be" there and to "see" the silence to know that what was happening was nonmusically musical. If musical discourse functions even in silence, can the meaning of this "silent precedent" be demonstrated? How?

In a tentative, exploratory way, and by moving into a relatively distant preelectronic, prephotographic past, I hope to get at these issues via a few paintings, whose *topoi* do not, however, privilege music as primary subject matter. I have intentionally picked examples where music is compositionally somewhat ancillary yet where its visual representation is nonetheless semantically crucial to a proper understanding of the image. I argue for an understanding of music's discursive power as a sight and for music's ubiquitous presence—paradoxically always prior to and simultaneous with any particular musical event—in people's readings of reality.

THE SONORIC LANDSCAPE, REPRESENTATION, AND EMBODIMENT

The seriousness and intensity of debate over sonoric meaning is notable in the histories of musical codification, virtually all of which focus on the different social and cultural consequences of authorized and unauthorized sounds. Indeed, so significant is the need to exert control over sonority, I would suggest, that the history of the West itself could profitably be rewritten as an account of sonoric difference: from Plato to the Parents' Music Resource Center, I doubt there is a generation that has escaped the deeply self-conscious concern for ordering the world sonorically.[5]

The landscape, as opposed to the earth as a physical entity, is a perception, a specific and ultimately confined view of a portion of the land that seems "worth" viewing because it is somehow noteworthy. Thus landscape is the different within the same; it is what draws attention to itself. What we define, and separate out, as a landscape appears in our consciousness as something at once "itself" and as a representation of itself. That is, when a portion of land is raised in our consciousness to the status of land*scape,* the physical entity is reconstituted in our minds as something in excess of the factual. This excess is experienced as a representation—and as such is discursive. By the phrase "sonoric landscape" I wish to evoke the ubiquity of sonority—a sweep of sound as broad as the land itself. But I also wish to evoke the particularity of *musical* sonority in the larger agglomeration of sounds and the particularities of different musical sonorities.

Sonoric landscapes are both heard and seen. They exist because of human experience and human consciousness. Music (the part of the larger sonoric landscape that interests me) connects to the *visible* human body not only as the receiver of sound, but also as its agent or producer. The human embodiment of music is central to any understanding of music's sociocultural agency. The semantic content of music—its discursive "argument"—is never solely about its sound and the act of hearing. It is instead about the complex relations between sound and hearing as these are registered and as they mediate the entire experience of being. That experience is physical; intellectual, in the broad meaning of the word; and spiritual, though hardly restricted to the religious or the mystical. But it is especially to be understood as the result of mediations between the ear and the eye. The sonoric landscape is peopled and hence interactive. It is external to the human subject yet internalized by its sight and sound.

The terms *power* and *desire* in my chapter title foreclose the discursive particularities that can be explored in a chapter-length essay. I did not choose this pair arbitrarily. After all, to argue that musical discourse possesses agency is to raise questions about power. Yet I do not mean any and all power, but power operating at the level of social and cultural organization—power, that is, in its most obvious connection to the political, narrowly defined. Since music, especially art music, so often these days seems removed from power (this is one of aestheticism's more peculiar "accomplishments," though resulting from an utterly false consciousness if ever there was one), then arguably I should try to relocate it precisely in this more "difficult" space. The category "desire" provides me with an entry into the *embodied* relations between the private and the public, which, through music, act to shape individual human subjects as well as classes of subjects.

SOUND AND SOCIAL ORDER

In 1607 the Antwerp painter Abel Grimmer produced a small panel representing spring, one of the four seasons (Figure 12.1). The image represents a feudal hierarchy and the beneficent prosperity it presumably provided. The subject is poignant given the historical circumstances, namely, the end of a period of bloody conflict between the Spanish Netherlands and its overseers in Spain.[6] Embedded in European representations of the seasons—popular from the Middle Ages onward—are ideals of recurrence, predictability, and the banishment of chaos, as well as antagonisms and anxieties about nature and culture and the roles they assigned to people. Spring located the dialectical relation between nature and culture in human desire and sexuality, and in expressions of hope for new life and general social fecundity. What especially interests me is the role that certain kinds of music play in the representation.

FIGURE 12.1. Abel Grimmer, *Spring* (1607), oil on wood panel, 33 × 47 cm. Antwerp, Koninklijk Museum voor Schone Kunsten. Photo copyright IRPA-KIK, Brussels.

The painting frames a society that is coherent, ordered, hierarchical, static, and peaceful. Hierarchy is evident in the differences between persons, notably between the landed nobility and the peasants who work the land. Stasis, represented perhaps less obviously, is the quality most directly tied to peacefulness. This is not "Spring 1607"; it is "Every Spring" or, more accurately, the visualization of a desire for, and possibly a confidence in, perpetual recurrence.

The cycle of time encoded by definition into representations of the seasons is as integral to agricultural societies as images encapsulating the loss of a day-to-day relation to nature—the calendar imagery of endangered species, the Public Television specials on the destruction of the Amazon rain forest, and so forth—are to our own society. To perceive the cycles of time does not eliminate anxiety over the powers that operate in a seasonal spiral. The cycle of all life is biologically established, but any particular life, however its experiences may be constrained by the individual's position in the social hierarchy, is nonetheless lived actively, dynamically, and consciously. Before taking up these issues in detail, I need to describe the picture.

In Grimmer's *Spring* the château of a feudal lord looms in the background, emphasizing his formal garden, probably an herb garden, with all that suggests about medicine and healing. The area under cultivation is laid out geometrically but lacks the statuary or fountains appropriate to a purely decorative garden. Workers prepare the beds, turning soil, raking the earth, seeding, planting slips, spreading fertilizer, and watering. Just outside the garden enclosure two men prune a tree, while two women shear sheep. They are all either servants or serfs. Those for whom they labor disport themselves on the grass (Figure 12.2) in a bower, where musicians play while the listeners drink or embrace, as well as above the bower, beneath a topiary shrub, where several more people, sketchily painted, enjoy social intercourse. Some of them appear to be making music, though it is hard to be certain of this. Nearby a couple by themselves embrace in a small boat on the river, within earshot of the music making. On the horizon, behind a forest, rooftops and a tower stand in for a town or city. In sum, the image's primary details are those of landscape architecture (the beds), intense horticulture (topiary), and architecture proper (not only buildings but also such details as the fencing), though the whole is not rationalized to the degree found in later bourgeois art.[7]

The painting's composition is simultaneously medieval and early modern, its form confronting the changing social constructions in the region during the early 17th century. Its modernity locates itself in the strong, off-center diagonals of the garden bed that direct our eyes toward the aristocrats under the bower. Its medieval character, a conflicted one, locates itself in the activities of the foreground, where our eyes cannot rest on any

FIGURE 12.2. Abel Grimmer, *Spring* (detail). Photo copyright IRPA-KIK, Brussels.

one figure but instead wander from person to person, vignette to vignette. A medieval harmony asserts itself in the full social hierarchy represented; I have said as much already. But the stasis necessary for this hierarchy is flawed.

The first flaw, an especially dangerous one, is evident even before we sort out the picture's narrative. It locates itself in the painting's compositional vanishing point, though it is not so neatly established as it will be in later art. Is it the castle tower, the town tower, or the meeting of land and sky between the two? The vanishing point is nothing if not a conception of *dynamic,* not static, space. The far horizon establishes difference; it is neither town, nor castle, nor cultivated land, and its ownership is ambiguous. Yet the horizon is made visually relevant once it is incorporated into the composition by means of the vanishing point. Its status rises; the faraway means something to the near-at-hand. Its emptiness, which draws us, is powerful. Like something repressed, it returns; indeed it intrudes. Without the vanishing point, what matters is the world "as shown." Once our eyes are drawn to the distant by means of the vanishing point, the world "as shown" is at once "enriched"—literally and metaphorically deepened—and made more terrestrial, less philosophical. But it is also made relative, part of something else, hence inadequate and unfinished. The guarantee of stasis is undercut. The horizon is a threat whose semantic power acts within the dimension of time, guaranteeing change; it makes space a problematic category, a discursive terrain. Land is no longer a static, unproblematic category for representation; it is instead a depth, a space, a distance: a more-than-this. Land ownership becomes visually fetishized once the land one possesses (here the space close up) is differentiated from what one does not possess (distant, unconvincingly "claimed" space). Thus this painting incorporates and problematizes the perception of space and time central to the formation of the modern world. To perceive these elements as dynamic was at once to challenge feudalism and to mark the prerequisites for capitalism.

I ask indulgence for an apparent detour, for this history is fundamental to my discussion of music. The connection I seek to establish is this: music, like no other medium of discursive practice, acts simultaneously in space and in time. Although theater does too, it does so differently, because its predominant "text" is words, whereas music's "text" is sonorities as such—even when words are present (worded music). Music is simultaneously more and less than the concrete: it is abstract, yet it is inevitably made and experienced as embodied. Music, unlike theater, has a mystical substance; as an "embodied abstraction" it simultaneously is and is not. It fills space but cannot be measured; and it disappears as absolutely as a shadow once light fades.

Music bears relation to the shadow: it is the *is not* of that which is; it is the account of the real that itself is both real and not real. In no other human practice does agency depend so specifically on being and not being; in this respect music relates to spirituality. This much is true of music throughout human history. What is different and additional at the moment of *Spring,* 1607, is that now and for the first time representationally, hence experientially, the dimensions of time and space in which music operates were severely problematized in Western European experience. The comparatively static and cyclical feudal world, which had been slowly dying for more than a century, was being subsumed under the dynamism of mercantilism and soon-to-be capitalism. Space and time were becoming the dimensions through which human dynamism and agency were understood to operate most fruitfully, in the process giving rise to modern conceptions of the human individual and the activities of individualism. Cycle was about to disappear in favor of vector. Music's history could be read as the prophet. But the feudal and protocapitalist sides of this history would necessarily read the prophecy differently, each according to its own interests. The ideal audience for this image would find its visual pleasure in a reading premised on feudal continuance, even though the representation itself could not but acknowledge feudalism's decline.

In the center foreground of *Spring* a man bends to his shovel. He and a companion at the extreme left, also holding a shovel, occupy more picture space than other figures and far more than any of the nobility. Our interest in them develops not from any individuality, for they have none, but from their roles as workers and their proximity to our own space. Their faces are not shown; what matters is their strength, marshaled to a task. If we shift our focus to the other workers, men and women alike, we see that they too are mostly faceless and that those whose faces are represented betray not individuality so much as the hardness of their labors (the woman at the extreme left foreground), their contentment (the woman at farthest right poking seeds into the ground), and even a kind of lumpish stupidity (the men raking and casting seeds). I say "lumpish" advisedly, for the painter consistently represents the workers as low to the ground, their bodies, shaped like swelled turnips, differentiating them from the two women of superior class looking on at the right side of the garden and giving instructions. The workers' bodies also contrast with those of their social superiors under the bower, notably the male lutenist stretched out comfortably on the ground and his servant who pours wine: long-legged, far from the ground, so to speak.

Yet the nobility themselves are little more than dashes of color; they too are essentially "faceless," so small that we can do little more than distinguish them by their social type. But we see enough, because difference is the key, and difference is unquestionably and unambiguously established. Faces or portraits are not at issue. The scene is a bit of Flanders—as though Flanders were the whole world, excepting again the difficulty with the vanishing point. That represented world—I am not arguing about the "real" world of Flanders, only the pictorial one—is typecast, and only the roles matter, not who fills them. So long as the roles hold, everything else matters less and can be made to fit the general scheme. The aristocracy's certainty of position and authority is visually enhanced by its retreat into the background to pursue its pleasures. In later bourgeois images the self-image is foregrounded, openly asserted, and such retreats seldom occur; even in Grimmer's painting, however, prebourgeois anxiety about social position may be evident in both the revelers' proximity to their fortress and the river-as-moat that separates them from their workforce.[8]

CONTEMPLATION AND THE BODY

The image is structured by three related differences: work from leisure, peasant from aristocrat, and *silence from music*. I am not arguing that the painting's foreground—the nonmusical portion—strikes us as "literally" silent, for the memory traces it activates in viewers do include sound. Sheep, for example, commonly bleat when being sheared, not liking to be held for shearing and often being nicked. And workers are hardly silent during their labors. Gardeners may hum to themselves, making their own music while engaged in light labor like scattering seeds, if not during more taxing jobs like spading earth. But for the most part the sounds their labors suggest are not musical. More to the point, the painter offers us no encouragement to "see" the laborers singing, whereas he requires us to acknowledge the music of the nobility.

Thus the painting represents two landscapes and two soundscapes. In the foreground is a formal garden, of the sort that would reach its apogee and richest discursive manifestation at Versailles roughly two centuries later. In the background, at the vanishing point to the right of the château, is a forest in an apparently primeval state. The forest is a privileged space, both legally and symbolically. (Poaching game carried severe penalties in forested lands held as private hunting preserves, where the authorized killing of game served not only to supply the princely table with exotic meats but also to signal the princely power of life and death within the domain.) The soundscapes register themselves by simultaneous presence and absence: music fills the air under the bower, opposing the putative silence of the foreground. Expressed via Saussurian semiotics, the *is* (music) defines itself by means of the *is not* (silence, or nonmusic) and vice versa. As such, music—a particular kind of music—represents itself as the sonoric simulacrum of one sort of life, private life, with *private* conflated with privilege and prestige. Private music, ironically represented "in public" so that privacy as such can be visually valorized, is the sonoric overlay that gives meaning to the entire scene, both for the revelers and for the laborers who may overhear sounds that define what they themselves are not.

The immediate function of the music under the bower is love. Those for whom that music is played are the couple with their backs to us between the men playing viol and lute, the couple in the boat, and the couple standing and embracing in dark recess. But overriding the music's amatory function is its role as an agent of social order, manifested in the contemplation of the couple listening between the two instrumentalists. That is, music's pleasure is "purposeful" and not merely something in the air, like the chirpings of birds. It invites conscious audition, of sufficient seriousness that the one couple turn their backs to us to hear. What they listen to and for—by definition—is a sonoric discourse, probably one that interpolates them less in the present, which after all is momentarily uncontested to the extent that it simply *is*, than in the future, which more than ever before is up for grabs, not only because feudalism is dying but also specifically because Flanders was experiencing upheavals at the moment of the painting's production.

The incorporation into the image of "art music" and its audition as the central "event" among the nobility establishes an opposition between contemplation (thought) and physical labor (in essence, nonthought). Such music is self-conscious, intentional, inherently and necessarily "rational." It is not spontaneous but planned, so as to sanction and articulate sonorically a meaning regarding the physical events transpiring not only under the bower but also in the painting's foreground. To the extent that this music is listened to, it is a passive engagement; but because passivity functions here as a sign of social division, it is a means of valorizing social difference. Not accidentally, it recapitulates the ancient Boethian precedence of the critic/auditor over the producer.

It is well known that opera houses, until well into the 19th century, were as much the locus for conversation and other activities as for listening and that audiences commonly quieted down en masse only to hear their favorite musical bits. It is also established that the gradual silencing of talk and the increasing expectation that audiences attend to musical performance in both opera theater and concert hall developed with the middle class's enshrinement of symphonic instrumental music. Attentiveness to music—what Adorno termed "contemplation"—may of course be explained as a laudable enhancement of high art, but it is neither that simple nor so entirely benign.

The problematics of contemplation, a "mental" activity, emerge the moment mind intersects with body. The etiquette of "contemplation" is, before anything else, a controlling of the body in time, a working against the body, whether self-imposed or imposed by others (like parents who discipline their squirming children). And it is an etiquette that turns music from an inherently participatory activity into a passive one in which the listener maintains physical stasis by exerting the cultural force of will against the body's desires. The auditor may move toes in time to the beat but he may not hum, stomp his feet, sway his torso, or bob his head: bodily reaction to music in the concert hall must be neither audible nor visible. To give oneself over to any of these reactions invites rebuke.[9]

I will not sort out here the full complexities and ramifications of this etiquette, but will instead identify just one facet that applies most directly to my concerns, namely, that the etiquette invokes, mirrors, and replicates macrocosmic mechanisms for establishing social order. The etiquette of physical passivity, simultaneously socially imposed and self-imposed, reflects the achievement of social hegemony in part through cultural practice. "Consent" is manufactured, gradually learned and internalized, rather than imposed by raw force, as Antonio Gramsci pointed out many years ago.[10] Further, a socially required passivity of reception becomes a simulacrum of the socially correct meaning of the performance itself. Both the sonorities heard and the act of performance itself are disciplines.[11] The music being contemplated draws attention to itself, raises the stakes of its presence, specifically as an "activity" whose valorization is organized by rendering the body static. Music in this guise acts as a sonoric surveillance on the body, holding it captive to contemplation with the social proscription of physical reaction.[12] Not incidentally, whether the auditor actually contemplates any music is perfectly irrelevant to the demand.

MUSIC AND DIFFERENCE

In *Spring* music possesses and creates prestige by imposing its presence in relation to lived, *linear* time, this despite the typically cyclical experience of time in agricultural societies. I want to connect this matter first to erotics, then to music. One common feudal articulation of linear time occurs in the mythology of courtly love. Though the "literary practice" of courtly love predates by several centuries the period of my concern, the courtship central to it occupies the group under the bower. Courtly love, as idealized and theorized by Andreas Capellanus in the 12th century,[13] valorized relationships whose intensity depended on the indefinite postponement of the physical. The lover's platonic suffering could be enjoyed for many years; indeed, the longer the wait, the sweeter the agony. Any reader of *The Romance of the Rose,* the best known verse account of chivalric love, is aware that delay—prolonged through tens of thousands of lines—articulated desire and was itself an object of desire worthy of intense contemplation. Delay and desire are premised on a grid of time. And that grid, on which one plays out one's life by willfully waiting, charts an excessive control over time, one that enables the lover to wait in a world where the ability to wait establishes status.

In the painting time is valorized in an equation, whose product is prestige, that depends on our witnessing simultaneous but opposing events confirming that while some must work, others must not, and also that if one kind of work is physical, the other is overtly and actively mental: contemplative listening. Contemplative listening is not philosophically removed from the world, as later aesthetic theory would have it; it is instead the sign of one's control and domination of the world. Music, as a phenomenon that acts through time, when heard contemplatively stops all other activities. As such, it *is* an exercise of power, a political act. It is worth noting that "contemplative" sensual desire, that odd privilege of "doing without," is explicitly opposed to the sensual archaeology of the lower social strata, as characterized in endless numbers of contemporaneous representations, where the order of the day is rampant physical groping in an uncertain, unstable time frame. For the peasantry, the sensual is formulated temporally as instantaneous, the mythology of chivalric love disappearing in the lunge of bodies striving to copulate.[14] Nonetheless, as regards the private music making represented in *Spring,* an irony has to be faced. To account for the political capital of privacy, the sonoric–visual signs of that privacy, music making and lovemaking together, have to be made visually public, have to be voyeuristically displayed. In this sense representation, whether visual or sonoric, is the simulacrum not of strength but of weakness, an acknowledgment that culture is process and that all process incorporates the promise of change.

Music is a possession to be paraded before Grimmer's laborers, and before viewers outside the picture frame, as the sight and sound of difference. But since music itself is "simply air," what it encodes of power is the power over time. For some, the world can be made to stop while the air is filled with music's emptiness. Music's power, according to this formulation, *is* its emptiness, which constitutes itself ironically as a sign of fullness and excess. It can be no wonder that with the advent of the bourgeois world, but with notable recourse to Plato, so much anxiety was manifested about music as a waste of time. That the emergent bourgeoisie were so consistently reproachful about musicians in their ranks, especially male musicians, is hardly surprising given both the class's hatred for the perquisites and discursive practices of the nobility and its ironic fetishization of time as money. Nor can it be surprising that the bourgeoisie themselves quickly figured out how music—to be sure, music of their "own sort"—could be engaged sonorically to represent their interests.

Representations of the seasons are visual idealizations of feudal ideology, feudal hierarchy, and feudal consciousness. They are mental projections, visually articulated, about a future that continues and perfectly realizes the present. They are less the world as it truly is than the world as it is desired, but with desire seamlessly constructed out of present circumstances. Not incidentally, therein lies the inherent anxiety of representation: "A visual image, so long as it is not being used as a mask or disguise, is always a comment on an *absence.* The depiction comments on the absence of what is being depicted. Visual images, based on appearances, always speak of *dis*appearance."[15] As for music, the representation does not, strictly speaking, address the reality of performance practices. But that is not to suggest that musical images like Grimmer's bear no relation to musical life. Grimmer's musicians and their audience must relate closely to the functions of music in the society represented; if not, their presence would be nonsensical: discursive practice disallows "empty decoration."

Grimmer, in deciding to organize his image around the full social spectrum, had to face the issue of what he would have the nobility *do.* Apart from warring and hunting, the nobility ordinarily conveyed their rank by an absence of physical activity. But in an image whose subject—spring—requires an orderly presentation of peace (no warring) and growth or new life (no hunting), the nobility nonetheless need to be shown *using* the time they supposedly controlled, over which no power is so absolute as that of appearing to do nothing while others do for you. Music is the ideal activity to make that point clear. One can make music oneself with a minimum of physicality, like the lounging lutenist, or one can pay someone else, like the violist, to make it in one's presence; the result is something at once beautiful *and* produced. It is something cultural, not natural; the manifestation of another level of power, it is nevertheless *nothing*. The power of music making is not only the power to control time through the expenditure of leisure; it is also the license to waste time. Music is visually extravagant. (The possibility that music, as a productless entity, was trivial has troubled philosophers, moralists, and politicians throughout Western history, though these concerns only reached their zenith in post-Renaissance Europe.[16])

Music's pleasures and relevance have virtually never been denied. Indeed, music's most virulent enemies have often condemned music, or at least some music, precisely for the pleasures it provides and the effects of its audition on the social fabric. Even when judged a trivial pursuit, in other words, music retains its relevance, a negative one. Throughout history music has existed in conflict with what, sonorically, it is its purpose to define. Music is condemned, if not interdicted, as much as it is praised and supported. It is necessary to realize that debates about music are not about nothing. The disputes in any age between ancients and moderns concern the sonoric portion of the social order and the identity of the human subject, especially the sensual human subject, therein. That is why Grimmer, ultimately responsible to the interests of his patrons—who might sit under a bower but would not wield shovels—represented the only music possible, just as music itself is very nearly the only "activity" ideologically and politically available to project ideological "correctness."

There is a complementary way of expressing this point. *Spring* is a narrative that strives visually for closure, doubly postulated as a successful ending, a nonchallenge, and an account sealed off from the outside. Any narrative not only produces a world but also, by that very act, necessarily excludes some of the world. The activities of including and excluding are never innocent, accidental, or semantically void. They betray an interest—stakes. Moreover, the concern with closure in representation incorporates a gendered response to storytelling, a characteristic of male psychosexual efforts to gain and maintain control.[17]

In hierarchical societies there cannot be one undifferentiated body of music. The musics that exist must be classified, and their differences must be articulated *in words*. Unclassified sound, soundscape without the registration of difference, is the sonoric allowance of either democracy or anarchy. Valorization must occur; sound as a dimension of human activity and human agency cannot be left out of the sociocultural equation. The Platonic metaphor conflating musical harmony and world harmony was not accidental, as Plato himself makes clear in his diatribe on listening—however abstract his conception and however nonscientific his "astronomy." Musical classification for Plato is essential because sonoric control is one guarantee of the utopia he envisions.

ENVELOPMENT

In human sensing, whereas sight distances, hearing envelops.[18] Envelopment counted for everything in feudal society's understanding of itself, even in its late stages of decay. Envelopment meant mutuality. At the social apex it incorporated noblesse oblige; indeed, the war between Spain and the Spanish Netherlands, in truce at the moment of Grimmer's painting, was in part waged over the deterioration of that fundamental principle. Society was neither held together by raw coercive power nor even conceived in terms of it.

A painting that represents the hierarchy of the social totality, like Grimmer's, thus incorporates a problem. To the extent that sight distances us from the world, providing a primary means by which we measure and classify, the medium of painting becomes socially and politically problematic to the self-representation of feudal society. This is so because the world the painting represents is made silent. As such, the image stands off, separates itself from us like something to be studied. It is a medium easily given over to the clinical.

Sound, by its enveloping character, brings us closer to everything alive. Hearing musical sound, with or without words, makes us especially aware of proximity and thus of connectedness. Parents sing lullabies to their infants, and their infants respond: this is music at its most enveloping, for it connects the baby's consciousness to the parent's body via the parent's warm, moist breath, the sonoric articulation of life itself. Music fills breath with substance, fleshes it out, so to speak, and doubly touches the body of its infant auditor, whose ears hear and whose skin feels the breathy imprint. The reassurance is formed by a bond at once utterly abstract and profoundly embodied.

Sight can accomplish none of this, though not for want of trying: "Sight as a drive attaches itself to pleasure-giving, or anxiety-alleviation. Objects become symptoms, referring back to the psyche, as it robs them of their true nature as material things and gives them a new meaning and significance."[19] But sight nonetheless holds us at arm's length—even when we embrace our lovers. Sight distracts lovers in embrace; eyes close to erase sight's distancing; we close our eyes, and the eye-produced classifications shouting out our separateness disappear. We become one. Sight reminds us of difference but also of the promise of loss. Feudal society's structural connectedness—its metaphoric familial linkage—is severely strained in this painting's raw articulation of extreme social difference. This tension must be overcome.

Of all human activities only music can reproduce the breath of connectedness in painting, because the visual trace of its activity insists on its operation. Music is there only because it must be; it cannot be done without. And it exists in thousands of paintings because its function is central to lived experience. Music is the "argument" that the spring idealized in Grimmer's painting is still possible.[20]

OWNERSHIP, FAMILY, AND THE PROMISE OF DOMESTIC PRIVACY

A half century after Grimmer's *Spring,* two Flemish painters, Guilliam van Schoor and (perhaps) Gillis van Tilborgh, collaborated on a representation of the Nassau mansion in Brussels (Figure 12.3). The canvas, over 6 feet wide, commanding by itself, depicts a commanding architectural and quasi-agricultural enclosure in which open land is as abundant as it is scarce

FIGURE 12.3. Guilliam van Schoor and Gillis van Tilborgh (?), *Nassau Mansion at Brussels* (1658), oil on canvas, 123.5 × 206 cm. Brussels, Musées Royaux des Beaux-Arts de Belgique. Photo copyright IRPA-KIK, Brussels.

in the city that abuts the estate on the right. In this representation the prestige of the Nassau family depends on the vastness of the open space they control in a larger, crowded, geography. The power fueling prestige is horticulture, both the garden plantings and the lack of plantings. There is space within the enclosure for a nonfunctional formal garden—the sections closest to the château—whose geometries delineate nothing so much as the imposition of mathematical, hence intentional, order on nature. In the middle distance are an herb and perhaps a kitchen garden, where individual plants are accorded fallow space. The lower right quadrant of the enclosure closest to the viewer is entirely fallow, a radical spatial excess in an urban setting. There are only two or three workers but more than a dozen aristocratic observers. The activities of the aristocrats, to the extent they can be discerned, are contemplative, leisured, and, with reference to the five figures in the right foreground, familial and musical.

The man and woman at the extreme right are posed as icons of *mesure*, metaphoric agents and living microcosms of everything else visible in the enclosure. In one sense the guitarist provides the imaginative sonoric completion of what is visible, eliciting in the viewer's memory sounds that trace the universalizing, politically totalizing tendency asserted alike by the order of the ornamental garden design, the physically imposing dwelling that towers over the rest of the visible city, and indeed the land itself.

Lest we react to the musical event as a pictorially "innocent" *tranche de vie,* the painter reminds us that it counts for more. Perched atop the guitar's neck is an exotic bird, apparently a parrot, a perfect visual substitute, because of its exotic coloration (not because of its own "voice") for the music we cannot hear. Visually excessive, the bird is precisely on that account both functional and essential in a discourse about, and an argument for, a particular way of life. (Such pets, together with various small primates, were a common badge of prestige among the upper classes in the Low Countries.) On the surface, it might seem that the painters could have filled that corner of the picture's space with anything or anyone, or perhaps with nothing. To have chosen a musical vignette, and to have added to it the detail of a bird, one whose color draws our eyes to the guitarist, was a rhetorical act.[21]

This rhetorical gesture would seem useless if we did not understand the significant role of sonority in social organization, one that I can articulate in two ways. First, the guitarist's placement near the wall at her back helps define her act as private. The wall forms the boundary between the private and the public, privilege and the lack of privilege. The painters show the distinction by means of a raised perspective, a quasi–bird's-eye view, that allows us to see over the wall to the other side. The space within the garden wall, and the activities occurring there, gain meaning as the viewer sees differences outside the enclosure. Second, the horticultural emptiness of the front-most garden plot, although it encodes prodigality, is nonetheless pictorially "dangerous," taken by itself, to the extent that it might be read as lack; in an image where cultivation is the visible analogue to power, noncultivation is ambiguous. This ambiguity is stabilized by twin components: family (the couple with the child) and music (the guitarist and her male companion). Together these two groups form a human and sonoric "garden" where art rather than vegetables is cultivated and where the fallow earth serves as a visual frame.

The painting contains few distractions; it fetishizes not people but a building. Its compositional lines invariably pull us viewers toward the mansion, whose inhabitants at the front picture plane seem to wait almost helplessly for our glance to leave them so as to focus on the mortar and brick icon of their identity. The walls of their garden are merely extensions of the architecture, in that they guarantee a privacy almost as complete as that afforded by the walls of the château. This is not a trivial matter, and it has consequences for the history of music. In the half century that passed between Grimmer's *Spring* and this picture's execution, the role of music had changed. Music's social circumstance now approaches the bourgeois ideal of a private sphere totally separate from the public. The music of the nobles in *Spring*, performed in a quasi-agricultural setting, where a river physically separates it from the laboring peasants, nonetheless carries to their ears. By contrast, the urbanites on the other side of the wall in the later painting could hear little of the guitar. The wall limits both sound and sight.

Earlier, in 16th-century Flanders, townsfolk commonly heard the public music of the town pipers performing in municipal towers, their playing a sonoric promise of social order and shared municipal vitality. It was shawm and sackbut music, meant to be heard—indeed, a music not to be denied. What goes on, musically or otherwise, behind the walls of the Nassau mansion, however, depends on access; to see and hear one must first be admitted. That difference—between private and public—becomes a driving force in the history of modern society; it also becomes a fundamental distinction in the history of music. The enclosed garden of the Nassau mansion is the prototype of the concert hall, which delineates a physical space for a certain kind of music, whose sonorities are the acoustic signs of a certain privileged group of people.

NOISE

David Teniers the Younger repeatedly painted the lower and upper classes together in scenes that commonly incorporate musical activity (Figure 12.4).[22] His *Landscape with Shepherds, Swineherds, a Harvest, and a*

Genteel Couple at Music exudes fecundity, its soil supporting an ample harvest gathered by peasants and its grasses the fatness of sheep and pigs and the swelling of cows' udders. It is a specific landscape in that the distant city towers resemble those of Mechlin and Antwerp. There is labor in the background, business in the center foreground, and intimations of love among the couples on the left and right. Abundance is shared; there are tables at either extreme from which sustenance is enjoyed. Human subjects of different classes are separated spatially, with the hierarchy established by a sweeping movement of the eyes from left to right, the aristocratic couple and their servant occupying, in effect, half the pictured landscape, the crowd of peasants the remainder.

The two other fundamental distinctions that mark difference and prestige involve the implied aurality of the image. On the right half is the noise of activities both necessary and mundane: the squeals of pigs being captured and the discourse of money or business. On the left, in sharp contrast, a contemplative and cultured "discourse" ensues between the socially elevated couple: she reads, he plays the violin. The vignette creates the impression of serenity, but the man and his violin also replicate the

FIGURE 12.4. David Teniers the Younger, *Landscape with Shepherds, Swineherds, a Harvest, and a Genteel Couple at Music* (1677), oil on canvas, 180 × 270 cm. Cologne, Wallraf-Richartz-Museum. Photo: Rheinisches Bildarchiv, Cologne.

effect of Orpheus charming the animals; this was a pictorial subject much in evidence in 17th-century Flanders, against which Teniers's painting necessarily resonates (Figure 12.5) and to which I will return. Even though the man's noble status required that he remain aloof from peasant tasks such as animal husbandry, that social "rule" is momentarily violated for a higher purpose, though the violation is not likely to be noticed. What I mean is that the man's violin playing pulls the sheep, lambs, and even cows to his side, as though he were their attendant.

This "violation" or license nonetheless serves a purpose. Orpheus charming the animals, after all, is a subject organized to represent a man who commands all nature as the measure of all things. The Orpheus story locates virtually magical powers in a single individual; it aestheticizes his power into music and poetry; and it promises an Edenic order as the result of that power. Where Orpheus plays, the world is at peace (thus the appeal of the story during this period of Flemish history). The political dimension of the subject, obvious and incontestable, is that a particular music—Apollonian, or art, music—commands the world, and at the same time confirms the propriety of the man's position. Music closes a sonoric circle around the man, marking and authorizing his identity and providing the source of his power. The potential stakes of music's ability to sanction one's identity, it seems to me, were what Beethoven registered in removing the original title page of the *Eroica* carrying his dedication to Napoleon.

Teniers's landscape is a soundscape as well as a blatant, even heavy-handed, visualization of smugly managed power. His aristocrat may appear

FIGURE 12.5. Roelant Savery, *Orpheus Charming the Animals* (1617?), oil on wood panel, 62 × 131.5 cm. The Hague, Mauritshuis Museum. Photo copyright IRPA-KIK, Brussels.

a bit too much a farmer and not enough a cousin of Orpheus for our taste, but that ultimately matters little when even the tree under which he sits bends to envelop him in a compositional acknowledgment of who he is and what he can do—incidentally in perfect union with the original story where even the trees and rocks were moved by the sounds of Orpheus's lyre.

The violin in the 17th century was a popular instrument among the lower classes, who used it principally to accompany dance.[23] It is an instrument thus commonly associated with intense physicality and frenetic movement. Yet there is no invitation to the dance here; indeed, no movement whatever is suggested save that of the bow across the strings. Therein lies the point: music itself is tamed (and an actual "taming" occurred during this century in northern Europe as the violin was slowly adopted by the upper classes for art music). The noble couple, stationary, are bearers of status. They remind us of an essential distinction in music between the physicality of the popular (noise, nonart) and the comparative passivity of the aristocratic (art).

Teniers accords his aristocratic sitters status by emphasizing the striking incongruity of his compositional arrangement. In effect, he poses the couple and their servant as if they were in private chambers, complete with basic furniture and accessories: table, tablecloth, wine glasses, and serving tray. He translates an interior enclosure into the outdoors, with the protective shade of the tree under which the couple sits as architecture: chamber music in a chambered landscape. The charge of prestige the image carries is constructed in visual and aural terms that are the opposite of those that make prestige possible. That is, prestige here accrues from physical inaction, or as close to that as possible, although in reality it depends on physical actions, typically, to be sure, those of dependable others under one's charge. Leisure as culture, in other words, is the mask for the action against nature by which culture is achieved. In the nature–culture equation, disharmony is the constant, but its presence must be neither seen nor heard.

SURVEILLANCE AND JUDGMENT

An alternate means by which artists of the period incorporated sonority's trace into paintings was to look to the other end of the social spectrum and represent the music of the lower classes. Two examples will suffice, the first, by Theodoor van Thulden, probably representing a wedding feast (Figure 12.6), the second, one of a seemingly endless number of so-called kermis scenes or peasant celebrations painted by Teniers the Younger (Figure 12.7).[24] Both depict the two extremes of the social hierarchy within a single pictorial frame.

Wedding Feast (Figure 12.6) is composed like a stage set. The bridal couple sit at a table beneath a temporary canopy hung from an outside wall. The building itself, hyperpicturesque, is also like a theater flat with one outside wall removed so we can look in on events. The crowd scenes are distributed throughout the canvas as vignettes; many concern lovemaking and peasant drunkenness. An entrance onto this "stage," already overburdened with actors, is in progress; at the lower left, an aristocratic couple have emerged from their coach (compositionally framed by the poles supporting a lean-to shed). Their costumes are very different from those of the peasants, and that difference is heightened by a noteworthy detail: the woman in the foreground, wearing the painting's most elaborate costume, is masked. She is hardly rendered incognito to her audience by this gesture. The painting's inhabitants would know exactly who she was, for it was the role of the feudal aristocracy to honor peasants by appearing at major rituals like weddings. The mask does not disguise; it establishes identity, difference, and distinction. It marks presence and the simulacrum of absence.

An additional compositional detail makes clear the separateness of social spheres. Near the standing aristocratic couple is another pair of the

FIGURE 12.6. Theodoor van Thulden, *Wedding Feast*, oil on canvas. Brussels, Musées Royaux des Beaux-Arts de Belgique. Photo copyright IRPA-KIK, Brussels.

same class. They are seated and also elevated physically; compositionally, they rise above the peasant couple near the painting's center who head a dance line. The aristocrats are observers, not participants, an audience for a play-within-a-play that we also witness. We as viewers—and originally this "we" must have constituted people similar in social rank to the feudal lords—are twice removed from the events that occupy the bulk of the picture's space. The only justification for painting the small rise of land on which to seat the nobility is visually to increase the distance between social ranks otherwise made evident by costume. But there is more, and here I will state my point.

The scene's action is governed by music, specifically by a man at the right who stands on a barrel and plays the bagpipe. As the Flemish instrument most characteristic of peasant life, it figured in countless 16th- and 17th-century paintings. It provided, in life, the sonoric accompaniment to village fairs, weddings, and the like. (As to weddings, a popular proverb made clear the visual similarity of the instrument to the male genitalia—windpipe and windsack together—and, indeed, some peasant wedding subjects of the period refer to male sexuality.) The bagpiper is a kind of Pied Piper: he calls the tune. How his audience of peasants visually reacts to the sound is crucial. In painting the only way to establish that reaction is through the body.

As one might expect, the music sets people dancing. But the point is how they dance, and how their physical movements are embodied differently from those of the aristocrats who view them. It is crucial that van Thulden connects the viewer visually to the two couples on whom the matter turns; hence he not only places the standing lord and his wife near the couple at the head of the dance line, but he also has them look at one another. Moreover, the peasant couple "perform" for their masters. The peasant man doffs his hat, the characteristic gesture of deference. And, most important, he lifts his leg high in the exaggerated dance step of the *Hoppaldei*.[25] This gesture is almost certainly the most eye-catching, prominent detail in the painting. It is a movement of intense physicality, visually contrasted with the extreme reserve of the noble couple.

The painting's naturalism is severely curtailed. Everything is too posed; the buildings are too stagey; the break between foreground and background is too clear. But ideologically it is entirely correct. It is a representation not of an event as such but of a social ideal where there is no uncertainty and nothing is challenged. The lives of the peasantry are inevitably public. Their space can be entered and surveilled. It is clear that the nobility's entrance is unexpected, for nearly all the peasantry nearby engage in activities—drunkenness and groping lovemaking—ordinarily inappropriate to the decorum and deference superior rank demands.

This is Bakhtin's carnival.[26] That is, the wedding celebration is a bracketed event, where the momentary suspension of normal activities is structured into a long season of a religious and political Lent.[27] There is an unmistakable sign reminding us of this fact. In the lower foreground, directly in front of the peasant whose dancing leg is suspended so high, lies an upturned rake. It visually connects to the barn at the back of the scene filled with gathered hay. These two details frame the celebration and provide its "excuse": the peasant "time-out" occurs after work is finished. The rake and the hay in the barn, in their relation to human events, problematize the dimension of time. Equally important and closely related, these details establish the character actors as "good" peasants.[28]

Sonorically associated with intense physical labor, hence encoding silence, the rake and the hay are visual antidotes to the bagpiper and the dancers. The bagpipe is a profoundly sonoric instrument whose ability to pierce silence is nearly unparalleled. The only exclusively aristocratic instruments that could match it were trumpets and kettledrums, employed as the celebratory and signaling instruments of the exclusively aristocratic cavalry. (The right to play trumpets and kettledrums was tightly, even violently, controlled, and extreme pageantry accompanied the performance, with sight and sound merging in the representation of the sign.[29] Apart from kettledrums and trumpets, the only "loud" instruments of the period were the shawms and sackbuts played by those in the employ of Flemish towns, musically representing the interests of the urban trade centers in a social space between the nobility and the peasantry.) The "private" instruments of the nobility were of the *bas,* or soft, variety. All this being true, the peasant bagpipe is a sonoric simulacrum of and for difference. It is not accidental that the painterly conventions of the period (late 16th century to nearly the end of the 17th) manifest concern over peasant activities in representations of peasants' musical practices.

In van Thulden's painting, just as in Teniers's (Figure 12.7), the immanent threat peasants posed to aristocrats is in part diminished by a heavy dose of the picturesque. But that cannot silence the sonority of the bagpipe, because the bagpipe's sound was ubiquitous in Flemish life. It penetrated vast space, especially by comparison with that of the bowed strings and soft winds (e.g., recorders) favored by the aristocracy. Sonorically, it represented the social majority whose lives it helped define and order at events like fairs, tavern gatherings, and weddings. Its insistence was public, just as the "soft" music of the upper social orders was largely private. The opposition between outside (public) and inside (private) is crucial, even at this early stage of modernism. It looks forward to the troubled fetishization of privacy that serves as a defining characteristic of the bourgeoise in the 19th century.

Tenier's version of this subject (Figure 12.7), although similar to van Thulden's, divides more neatly into two halves. On the right are the bagpiper,

FIGURE 12.7. David Teniers the Younger, *Kermis*, oil on canvas 157 × 221 cm. Brussels, Musées Royaux des Beaux-Arts de Belgique. Photo copyright IRPA-KIK, Brussels.

a high-stepping dancing couple, and their peasant auditors. At the left the local lord and his spouse enter, having arrived in their coach. Directly above the coach stands their château, informing us whence they came. It is closed off, with only its towers and battlements visible through the trees; it is identifiable on account of its defensive function. Everything on the left side of the picture is serene, reserved, private, and *silent*. What lies within its precincts can only be imagined. It is for neither seeing nor hearing.[30]

NATURE AND WORD

Among the more curious pictorial subjects popular in 17th-century Flanders were so-called bird concerts (Figure 12.8). These are the most imaginary of natural and sonoric landscapes; they gather birds, both local and exotic, from climates hot and cool, dry and moist. Bird concerts are analogous to contemporaneous still-life paintings of flowers that incorporate the ordinary with the unusual, the governing factor being visual splendor (flowers are placed together that bloom at different times of the year, an arrange-

FIGURE 12.8. Jan van Kessel the Elder, *Bird Concert*, oil on canvas, 53 × 72 cm. Private collection. Photo copyright IRPA-KIK, Brussels.

ment achievable, if at all, only through forcing in hothouses). In this aviary, whose inhabitants come from the Old World and the New, predator birds commingle with their putative prey in an Eden without humans—but not without the trace of humans.

The ordinarily violent intra- and interspecies relations are held in a suspension that allows the Australian ostrich to be sighted with the New World parrot and the ostrich and parrot with the European swan. That suspension is music—not the natural "music" of the birds, for their sounds are not in fact musical—but the music of men, inscribed on the choirbook propped on the ground around which the birds gather like a *schola cantorum*. What can this mean if not the control of nature by the Word, wherein text is accorded privileged status over the things of this earth? Yet the Word is more than text; it is texted music.

This subject demarcates the visual beginnings of aesthetics, wherein music as a practice and music as a metaphor for society meet in a self-conscious and problematic relation. Music in this instance is problematized in a "society" of birds not only as a sonoric, texted suspension in which geographical impossibilities and violent instincts are held (and held in check) but also as a practice that draws attention to itself something separate and momentary. The music governing the birds' song is a music of unison (that much is clear, though not much else, in the notation). The birds are "asked" to sing what humans have given them. We classify them; they are ours. Their very naturalness is an affront to our status, and as such it is subsumed in the Word. This is a dialectic of enlightenment wherein nature, simultaneously the enemy, the tool, and the resource "given" us to exploit, comes to us only at the cost of splitting the body, our "nature," from the mind.[31]

It is also the dialectic into which music is culturally located as music, and not as mere sound or noise. Music is not "in the air" like the natural sounds of birds or, for that matter, the sounds of people generally[32]; it is instrumentalized, understood as a behavior to be defined, characterized, rationalized, made purposeful and useful. The music of the bird concert, that is, does not define the birds; instead, it violates them by misrepresenting their nature. The pleasure of their "music" is not theirs, but ours. Their pleasure is no longer innocent in its purposelessness. It is coerced. It is no longer Orpheus who charms the animals but man's rule that classifies them. I would go so far as to suggest that the musical text at the base of the tree, on the banks of a river, is more than a little akin to the passenger list for the Old Testament Ark; it is hardly accidental that most of the birds are shown in pairs. Music is charged with providing the aestheticized cover for what is metaphorically the determinate text for survival.

So in the end this is pretty serious business: Platonic metaphors of music of the spheres, expressed in explicitly terrestrial terms, to be sure, nonetheless define the terms for life itself. That music organizes the terms provides ample evidence for what is otherwise disguised in the visual splendor of the painting's rich colors. Aesthetics is never passive and music is never drained of meaning. In aesthetics and music alike purposelessness is only a mask or a sweetener for something deemed more important, namely, the shape of society and the human subjects within it. Pleasure is never without consequences: it is a component of history and comes with a price to be paid.

ACKNOWLEDGMENTS

This chapter originally appeared in *The Sight of Sound: Music, Representation, and the History of the Body*. Berkeley and Los Angeles: University of California Press, 1993. Copyright 1993 by The Regents of the University of California. Reprinted by permission.

NOTES

1. The work of Walter Salmen is perhaps the most distinguished effort to date to address this imbalance. See, e.g., Salmen, W. (1969). *Haus- und Kammermusik: Privates Musizieren im gesellschaftlichen Wandel zwischen 1600 und 1900.* (Musikgeschichte in Bildern, Vol. 4/3). Leipzig: Deutscher Verlag für Musik; and the recent festschrift dedicated to Salmen: Fink, M., Gstrein, R., & Mössmer, G. (Eds.). (1991). *Musica privata: Die Rolle der musik im privaten leben.* Innsbruck: Helbling.

2. A brief account of some of this work is available in Leppert, R. & McClary, S. (Eds.). (1987). Introduction. In *Music and society: The politics of composition, performance, and reception* (pp. xi–xix). Cambridge: Cambridge University Press. Among the studies published most recently, see esp. Kramer, L. (1990). *Music as cultural practice, 1800–1900.* Berkeley and Los Angeles: University of California Press; McClary, S. (1991). *Feminine endings: Music, gender, and sexuality.* Minneapolis: University of Minnesota Press; and Subotnik, R. R. (1991). *Developing variations: Style and ideology in Western music.* Minneapolis: University of Minnesota Press.

3. Kramer, *Music as cultural practice,* pp. 1–20.

4. See, e.g., Adorno, T. W. (1976). *Introduction to the sociology of music* (E. B. Ashton, Trans.). New York: Continuum. On Adorno and deconstruction, see Jay, M. (1984). *Adorno.* Cambridge: Harvard University Press, pp. 21–22; and Jameson, F. (1990). *Late Marxism: Adorno, or, the persistence of the dialectic.* London: Verso, pp. 9–10 and p. 254, n. 10. Jay properly cautions against an unproblematic acceptance of Adorno as a proto-poststructuralist.

5. The best attempt to date—by no means wholly successful—to develop a theory for this history is Attali, J. (1985). *Noise: The political economy of music* (Brian Massumi, Trans.). Minneapolis: University of Minnesota Press.

6. See Leppert, R. (1993). *The sight of sound: Music, representation, and the history of the body.* Berkeley and Los Angeles: University of California Press, pp. 246–247 n. 21.

7. See the different, though partly complementary, accounts of what I would call rationalized landscape painting by Bermingham, A. (1986). *Landscape and ideology: The English rustic tradition, 1780–1860.* Berkeley and Los Angeles: University of California Press; and by Barrell, J. (1980). *The dark side of the landscape: The rural poor in English painting, 1730–1840.* Cambridge: Cambridge University Press.

8. In the painting a small river separates foreground from background; it marks the division between the two types of human subject represented. But the stream's presence is obscured or disguised at the crucial point where the two groups of people come into closest proximity. Here the division seems momentarily to disappear, as if the river itself disappeared, as if the two groups engaged in free intercourse after all. But this is merely an illusion of oneness. Indeed, the river disappears as a barrier only to have its function taken up by a hedge, and the hedge opens up, like a gate, to lead to the river bank: access is controlled. To cross the barrier one needs a boat, and the only boat in the picture is occupied by aristocratic

lovers, who look, not toward the workers, but toward the chateau, the architectural confirmation of their identity and the guarantee that they will retain their status.

9. Cf. Mulvey, L. (1989). *Visual and other pleasures*. Bloomington: Indiana University Press: "The mind/body opposition is characteristic of other oppositions of dominance (black/white, colonised/conqueror, peasant/noble, bourgeoisie/worker) and in each case the oppressed are linked to nature (the body) and the dominant to culture (and the mind)" (p. 167).

10. Gramsci, A. (1988). *An Antonio Gramci reader: Selected writings, 1916–1935* (D. Forgacs, Ed.). New York: Schocken Books, pp. 306–307. In a later passage (p. 356), Gramsci acknowledges music in his list of "sources of linguistic conformism" through which the socially dominant articulate their interests and inculcate them in the population at large. He is primarily concerned here with the linguistic means of mass-producing consent: the educational system, newspapers, theater, film, radio, and so forth. Music enters in a discussion of relations between "the more educated and less educated strata of the population" via the following lengthy parenthetical insight:

> A question which is perhaps not given all the attention it deserves is that of the "words" in verse learnt by heart in the form of songs, snatches of operas, etc. It should be noted that the people do not bother really to memorize these words, which are often strange, antiquated and baroque, but reduce them to kinds of nursery rhymes that are only helpful for remembering the tune.

Gramsci does not consider how the music itself performs the role of agent via its own sonorities beyond the semantic quotient of the word text the music accompanies, which is the argument I am advancing, though he implies as much when he points out music's power to overwhelm words.

11. I am borrowing here from Foucault, M. (1979). *Discipline and punish: The birth of the prison* (A. Sheridan, Trans.). New York: Vintage Books.

12. See further Small, C. (1977). The perfect cadence and the concert hall. In *Music, society, education* (pp. 7–33). New York: Schirmer.

13. Capellanus, A. (1969). *The art of courtly love* (J.J. Parray, Trans.). New York: Norton.

14. Among the best painted examples are works by David Teniers the Younger, on which see Leppert, R. (1978). David Teniers the Younger and the image of music. *Jaarboek, Koninklijk Museum voor Schone Kunsten*. Antwerp, pp. 63–155 and passim.

15. Berger, J. (1985). Painting and time. In L. Spencer (Ed.), *The sense of sight* (p. 207). New York: Pantheon Books.

16. I have written extensively about this phenomenon in Leppert, R. (1989). *Music and image: Domesticity, ideology, and socio-cultural formation in eighteenth-century England*. Cambridge: Cambridge University Press.

17. See Mulvey, Film, feminism, and the avant-garde, in *Visual and other pleasures*, pp. 111–126.

18. See on this point Lowe, D. M. (1982). *The history of bourgeois perception*. Chicago: University of Chicago Press; and Shepherd, J. (1987). Music and male hegemony. In R. Leppert & S. McClary (Eds.), *Music and society: The politics*

of composition, performance, and reception (pp. 152–158). Cambridge: Cambridge University Press. (Reprinted in Shepherd, J. [1991]. *Music as social text*. Cambridge: Polity Press, pp. 152–173)

19. Mulvey, *Visual and other pleasures,* p. 135.

20. Whether the argument was unvaryingly "accepted" by viewers is hardly the issue. The narrative must be "read," and the reader-viewer in the act of reading can never be fully controlled. The discursive activity of the painting is a plat or map, and a plot—in the double sense of a narrative or story and a scheme. The representation, like any other, makes an argument the viewer may or may not accept, though not freely, for the reading-viewing is invariably constructed in part by the society and culture of which the image is a projection. The ideal viewer, in other words, has partly internalized the image prior to its being painted.

21. I have not located any emblematic connection between the guitar and the parrot, though the striking combination hints at one.

22. See Leppert, Teniers; a discussion of this painting occurs on pp. 143–144.

23. According to the Dutch poet Jan van der Veen, "De Vedel of Fiool die wert God betert, meer/Gebruyckt tot ydelheyt, als tot Godts lof en eer" (The fiddle or violin is, alas, used more in the service of vanity than in the praise and glory of God). See Bergström, I. (1956). *Dutch still-life painting in the seventeenth century.* (C. Hedström & G. Taylor, Trans.). New York: T. Voseloff, p. 156; and Leppert, R. (1977). *The theme of music in Flemish paintings of the seventeenth century* (Vol. 1). Munich and Salzburg: Musikverlag Emil Katzbichler, p. 77.

24. See further Leppert, R. (1978). *Arcadia at Versailles: Noble amateur musicians and their musettes and hurdy-gurdies at the French Court (c. 1660–1789); A visual study.* Amsterdam: Swets, pp. 29–31. For another example by Teniers similar in composition and subject see Leppert, Teniers, Figure 54, pp. 133–134.

25. See Sachs, C. (1937). *World history of the dance* (B. Schönberg, Trans.). New York: Norton, p. 280.

26. Bakhtin, M. (1984). *Rabelais and his world* (H. Iswolsky, Trans.). Bloomington: Indiana University Press. For a history of the difficulty of maintaining political control over carnival, see Le Roy Ladurie, E. (1979). *Carnival in Romans* (M. Feeney, Trans.). New York: Braziller. Carnival purposely structures the transgression of the law of the dominant; it acts as a safety valve for pressures building from below. But the entire point of carnival is ultimately to contain, to channel, to control by other means. Mockery was not only tolerated but expected and encouraged. It was comic; its purpose was to take charge of the serious: body over mind, peasant over aristocrat, the immoral over the moral, nature over culture, low art over high art. And carnival is contradictory in that the spontaneity is in effect organized; so long as organizing principles hold, it remains a mask that fails to transform the face of surveillance underneath.

27. See the discussion of this phenomenon in Attali, *Noise,* pp. 21–24; the sonoric difference between carnival and Lent is the organizing principle of this book.

28. The concern with the "good" peasant has a long history in Western art, extending into the early romantic period, with its nostalgia for a disappearing agricultural economy. See Barrell, *Dark side of the landscape*.

29. See Leppert, *Theme of music* (Vol. 1), pp. 201–223.

30. Teniers's own interests and self-location in this history are evident in his representing in the background the chateau, known as De Drij Toren, that he himself rented and eventually bought; it marks his lifelong quest to be granted a title. See Bocquet, L. (1924). *David Teniers*. Paris: Editions Nilsson, pp. 41–46, 62–75, and passim.

31. See the moving, insightful account in Horkheimer, M. & Adorno, T. W. (1972). Man and animal. In Cumming, J. (Trans.), *Dialectic of enlightenment* (pp. 245–255). New York: Continuum. See also the excellent account by Johnson, M. (1987). *The body in the mind: The bodily basis of meaning, imagination, and reason*. Chicago: University of Chicago Press.

32. The best visual account of the ubiquity of musical sonority in European history, a history very imperfectly known, is by Salmen, W. (1976). *Musikleben im 16. Jarhundert* (Musikgeschichte in Bildern, Vol. 3/9). Leipzig: Deutscher Verlag für Musik.

Index

Abhinaya, 65
Acid rock
  concerts/festivals, 228–229
  emergence of, 224–225, 226
  multimedia events, 229–232
Addis, Thomas, 66–67, 68
African-American music. *See* Black music culture
Audiences
  cultural/geographical expansion of, 132–133
  fragmentation of, 16–17
"The Auld House" (Nairne), 159–162
Automobiles, in Los Angeles lifestyle, 226–227

B

Bandmasters, professional military, 124
Barbarism, 205
Batānā, 75
Bilingualism, within one language, 158, 159
Bird Concert (van Kessel), 315–317
Black music culture
  Coleridge-Taylor and, 199–200, 210–211
  commercialization and, 33, 100*n*
  "gangsta rap," 19
  Liverpool Jews and, 277
  northern soul and, 90–94
Booth, William, 123
Bootlegging, 90, 100*n*
Boral, Lal Chand, 64
Brass band movement, 117, 118
Brass bands
  categorizations, 118–119
  contests/prizes for, 120–123
  establishing, 113–116
  images of, 106–108
  in late 20th century, 104–105
  leisure time and, 112–113
  mainstream music and, 125
  middle/upper classes and, 111–112
  moral concerns and, 112–113
  musical identities of, 116–118
  names of, 106
  before 19th century, 108–109
  in Northern Britain, 123–124
  repertoires, 116–117
  social functions of, 117–119
  in Southern England, 124
  sponsorship of, 106, 113
  stereotype of, 125
  uniformity/nationalism of, 122
  women in, 123, 127*n*
  working-class and, 105, 106, 107, 125
Brass instruments
  hire-purchase schemes, 110, 111
  in 19th century, 108–109
  invention of valves and, 109–110
  self-teaching primers and, 110
  standard pitch for, 122, 127*n*
Britain. *See also* English art music
  cathedral cities of Severnside, 178, 179
  geography of, 177–178
  Gloucester, 178, 179
  London, as "cultural capital," 88
  music industry in, 40
  Northern, brass bands in, 123–124
  northern soul. *See* Northern soul
  royalty payments and, 202
  spending on recorded music, 41–42
  Victorian, musical life in, 104–106, 112. *See also* Brass bands
  working-class, identification with America, 91
"The Brit Awards," 40
British pop invasion, 39, 47
Bund, 85, 95, 98*n*
Business cycles, 37–39

C

California
  Los Angeles. *See* Los Angeles
  paradise theme, Guthrie and, 260–261
  San Francisco, 224–225, 226, 236
Canada
  listening to music in, 134–135
  local music in, 136
  music industry in, 135–137
  place identity absence in music, 138–139
  radio programming in, 16, 136–137, 139, 140
  recorded music expenditures in, 135–136

Index

Capitalism, music development and, 33–34
Cardew, Cornelius, 192
CD format, 34, 35, 38, 45
Clairino technique, 109
Classical music, 5, 6, 8–9. *See also* English art music
Coleridge-Taylor, Samuel, 197–198
  barbarism and, 205
  black music culture and, 199–200
  "feminine cadences" and, 214
  interest groups and, 207
  mobility of music, 212–213
  musical acceptance in Europe, 214
  musical meaning and, 200–201, 211–213
  networks, 214–215
  obituary, 205
  polyvalency of music, 214
  racial discrimination and, 209–210
  as romantic genius, 207–208
  as sociotechnical hybrid, 201–206
  student years, 198–199, 208
Commissioning agents, 12
Commodification
  of embodied performance, 35–36
  of Indian music/musicians, 58
  of music, 33–35
  musical knowledge and, 7
  new music development and, 46, 49
  Northern soul and, 89–90
  product consolidation and, 43–44
  product differentiation and, 35
Communication, musical, 200, 201–202, 286
Composers. *See also specific musical composers*
  categorization of, 9
  English, 180
  as sovereign universal voice, 207
Concerts, Los Angeles music scene and, 228–229, 239–242
Concert-tourism, 40
Consumption, music
  motives for, 39
  production and, 12, 14, 33
  shifting geography of, 46–47
  Western, 17–18
Copyright legislation, 11
Corporate restructuring, 46
Counterculture, 223
"Cover version," 36
Criticism, musical, 292–293
Croydon Orchestral Society, 203–204
"The Cruel Mither" (McMorland), 156–158
Culture
  globalization of, 35
  music and, 3–4
  values, commodifying/universalizing of, 12

D

Dance forms, Indian, 65–66
Double consciousness, 199
Durgā, 72
"Dust Bowl Ballads" (Guthrie), 249–251, 255, 256–263
Dust Bowl region, 251–254

E

Economics, of music, 9–10, 33–39
Electronic media
  listening/reception and, 131–134
  space and, 129–131
  transcendent consciousness and, 231–232
Elgar, Edward, 179–180, 184
England. *See* Britain; English art music; Liverpool, England
"England's Glory" advertisements, 190–191
English art music, 178–181
  English Musical Renaissance and, 178, 187, 213
  Gloucester or "Gloster" and, 188–190
  nationalism in, 181–182, 184
  operas, 187
  rebirth of, 208
  sea themes and, 185–187
  sports themes and, 182, 183
  during World War I, 184–188
Entrepreneurs, 12, 37, 113
Environment, of music, 21–25
Epstein, Brian, 282
"Etane Yauban Daman Na Kariye," 76–77
European music. *See also specific types of European music*
  American influence on, 38–39
Experience, musical, 131, 286

F

Festivals, Los Angeles music scene and, 228–229, 239–242
Folk music, 33, 254–256
Free Press, 228–229, 237, 238, 242
Frost, Robert, 179

G

Gaisberg, Fred, 59, 60–62, 74
Gauharjan, 58, 62–63, 64, 75, 77
Gender ambivalence, 7–8
Globalization, of music industry, 41–42, 49
Government, commercial radio in Canada and, 137
Gramophone industry
  early, in India, 57–66
  marketing, in India, 66–74
Great Plains, Dust Bowl region of, 251–254
Grove, Sir George, 178
GTL (Gramophone and Typewriter Ltd.), 59, 66–71
Gurney, Ivor, 188–190
Guthrie, Woody
  California paradise theme, 260–261
  "Dust Bowl Ballads," 249–251, 255, 256–263
  as folk musician, 254–256
  highway themes, 258–260
  personal views/political attitudes, 250

H

Hawd, John Watson, 59–60
Hiawatha (Longfellow), 210
"Hiawatha's Wedding Feast"
  (Coleridge-Taylor), 202–203, 208–209, 213
Hindu goddesses, 70–72
"His Master's Voice" dog, 69, 70, 79, 80
Horns, brass, 108–109
Housman, A. E., 179–180, 181–183

I

Impresarios, 12
India. *See also* Indian music/musicians
  dance forms in, 65–66
  early gramophone industry in, 57–66
  gramophone marketing in, 66–74
  Hindu goddesses, 70–72
  musical entertainment in, 64–65
Indian music/musicians, 79
  adaptations in recorded performances, 78
  commodification of, 58
  early recordings of, 74–78
  "Etane Yauban Daman Na Kariye," 76–77
  first recordings of, 59, 61
  flexibility of, 78
  forms of, 74–78
  Gauharjan, 58, 62–63, 75
  low-status of, 63–64
  men, 64
  performances of, 75–78
  with rāgmālā, 72–73
  recruitment of, 60, 65
  social level of, 65
  Western misconceptions of, 61
  women, 63–64
"Industrial language," 182
Infotainment, global, 44–45
Intellectual property, 34
Interpretation, musical, 32
Interpretative communities, 92, 207
"Is My Team Ploughing?" (Housman), 182

J

Jackson, Enderby, 124
Jaeger, August, 208
Jews, Liverpool
  kinship/community relations, 271–273
  migration/travel and, 284–285
  music, stability/security and, 281–283
  musical performance/exchange and interaction, 273–276
  social culture, 276–280
  social/educational programs, 280–281
  status and, 283–284
Joint ventures, 42

K

Kailyaird, 161–162
Kathak, 65–66

Kermis (Teniers), 314–315
Khan, Faiyaz, 64
Khyāl, 75–76
Kunkin, Art, 228–229

L

Landscape with Shepherds, Swineherds, a Harvest, and a Genteel Couple at Music (Teniers), 308–311
"The Lark Ascending," 184
Legal regulations/aspects, of music industry, 11, 34
Lesbian identification, in popular music, 141–142
Levine, Ian, 87
Levy, Jack, 269–272, 274–279
Lightshows, psychedelic, 229–230
Lipton, Lawrence, 232–233, 234, 235
Listening
  animation of sense of location and, 134
  in Canada, 134–135
  commercial processes in, 133
  habits, reshaping of, 133–134
  space and, 6, 129–131
Liverpool, England
  British pop invasion and, 38–39
  Jewish community. *See* Jews, Liverpool
  "Merseybeat" phenomenon, 48
Local music
  at beginning of 21st century, 48–49
  commercial Canadian radio programming and, 139, 140–141
  contemporary Scottish songwriting and, 163–167
  defined, 47–48
  scale, social nature and musical content of, 47–48
London Punk, 19–20
Longfellow, W. (*Hiawatha*), 210
Los Angeles
  concerts/festivals, 228–229, 239–242
  cultural politics in, 226–229
  electronic media and, 231–232
  global underground community and, 242–243
  human be-ins, 239–242
  multimedia events, 229–232
  multimedia events/experimentation, 222, 224, 229–232, 237–239
  Sunset Strip, 236–237
  underground movement in 1960's, 223–226
  urban ecology in, 226–229
  Venice West district, 232–235, 241
  Watts riots and, 227, 228

M

McLuhan, Marshall, 230–231
McMorland, Alison, 156
Marketing, of music, 33, 34, 35

Markets
  Pacific Asia, 42
  sound-carrier, forecasts for, 42
  Western, 43
Marra, Michael, 163–167
The Mothers of Invention, 238–239
Multimedia events, 237–239
Music. *See also specific aspects of*
  as art form, 8
  as communication, 200
  definition of, 286
  development, music industry and, 32
  diversity, 46, 47
  genre development, 46
  meanings of, 206–207, 292
  production, shifting geography of, 33, 46–47
  universal standards, 6–7
Music companies/corporations
  Big Five, 40
  big/major, 36–37
  changing geography of, 38–39
  GTL, 59, 66–71
  internationalization of, 44–46
  small/independent, 37
  vertical integration, 38
Music education, budgetary cuts in, 4
Music industry. *See also* Music companies/corporations
  boundaries of, 10
  in Canada, 135–137
  capitalistic view of, 33–39
  contemporary, 9–14
  corporate networks in, 11–12, 13
  corporate strategies, 41–43
  employment, 40–41
  in future, 44–45
  global expansion, 12, 48–49
  income, 34, 40
  international development, 43–44, 45–47
  legal regulations, 11, 34
  music development and, 32
  profits, 34
  restructuring, 11, 37–39
  structure, 37

N

Nairne, Lady Caroline Oliphant, 159
Nassau Mansion at Brussels (van Schoor and van Tilborgh), 306–308
Naturalization process, 6
Noise, 2–3
Northern soul, 83–85
  black America soul and, 90–94
  club scene, 95–97
  commodity value/exchange of, 84–85, 89–90
  historical aspects, 85–87
  identity formation, 95–96
  marginalization of, 84
  "northerness" of, 87–88
  place–identity relationship in, 94–97
  rarity/exclusivity of, 88–89, 100*n*
  records, value of, 91–92
  regional base of, 91
  religious associations, 96
  respect for history/tradition in, 92–93
  sense of community in, 94–97, 96
  travel and, 94–95
  value of music in, 93–94

O

Opera, English, 187–188
Orpheus Charming the Animals (Savery), 310

P

Pacific Asia markets, 42
Pan-Africanism, 200
Parry, Sir Hubert, 178, 187–188, 213
Pastoral Music School, 180, 186
Performances, musical
  embodiment of place and, 285–286
  Liverpool Jews and, 273–276
  in Los Angeles underground movement, 225
  sites of, 6–7
  specificity of, 36
  value of, 35
Performers. *See also specific musical performers*
  specificity of, 36
  value of, 35
  "world artists" repertoire, 43–44
Piracy, 68
Place identity. *See also* Production of place
  absence, in Canadian music, 138–139
  geographical interventions and, 19–21
Poets, 179, 210
Politics, music and, 2, 8–9, 31
Popular music
  American influence on Europeans, 38–39
  British pop invasion, 39, 47
  consumers, 32
  experience of, 131
  global production/consumption, 14–15
  interpretation of, 32
  lesbian identification in, 141–142
  subversion of national identities and, 19–20
Production of place
  economic, 276–280
  embodiment and, 285–288
  migration/travel and, 284–285
  music in, 269–288
  status and, 283–284
  transformations in, 280–284
Psychedelic rock. *See* Acid rock
Publicity images, for gramophone marketing in India, 68–74
Publishers, music
  brass band movement and, 116–117
  in Britain, 202–203
Punk rock, 19–21

R

Radio
  programming, in Canada, 16, 136–137, 139, 140
  spatial relationships and, 129–131

Reception, musical. *See also* Listening
  space production for, 132
  technological mediation and, 132
Record companies, 10–11
Recorded music industry
  business cycles and, 37–38
  consumption and, 35
  world sales, 40
Reorganization, corporate, 42–43
Retailers, music, 14
Road songs, 22–23
Rock music
  acid/psychedelic. *See* Acid rock
  punk, 19–21
Royalties, music, 34, 202

S

Saheb, Bhaya, 62
Salvation Army bands, 123
San Francisco, California, 224–225, 226, 236
Sarasvatī, 70–72
Savery, Roelant *(Orpheus Charming the Animals)*, 310
Sax system, 110
Scottish songs
  contemporary writing strategies for, 162–167
  dialect/accent and, 152–153, 167–171
  language variations in, 152–154
  "National Songs," 158–162
  postmodern concerns, 151–152
  transglossic ballad, 155–158
Sex Pistols, 19, 20
Sharp, Cecil, 180
Social networks, musical meaning and, 200–201
Social order, sonoric landscape and, 295–299
The Song of Hiawatha (Coleridge-Taylor), 209
Sonoric landscape, 23–24
  contemplative listening and, 299–302
  defined, 291
  domestic privacy and, 306–308
  envelopment and, 305–306
  musical differences and, 302–305
  nature and, 315–317
  noise and, 308–311
  observations/assumptions, 292
  representation/embodiment of, 293–295
  social order and, 295–299
  surveillance/judgment and, 311–315
Sound-carrier markets, forecasts, 42
Space production
  Canadian radio programming and, 139–143
  electronic media and, 129–130, 129–131, 131–134
  listening and, 6, 129–131
  for reception, 132
Sports themes, 182, 183

Spring (Grimmer), 295–306, 308
Stanford, Charles Villiers, 208
Subcultural capital, 12
Subcultural identity, 84, 96
Subculture theory, 84, 103*n*
Subscription bands, 114

T

Techno-economic networks, 201
Teniers, David
  Kermis, 314–315
  Landscape with Shepherds, Swineherds, a Harvest, and a Genteel Couple at Music, 308–311
"This Land is Your Land" (Guthrie), 249–250, 255
Ṭhumrī, 66, 75, 76
Town bands, 114
Translation, of musical meaning, 206–207
Trombones, 108
Trumpets, 108–109

U

Underground culture. *See* Los Angeles
Universality, musical, 8–9

V

van Kessel, Jan *(Bird Concert)*, 315–317
van Thulden, Theodoor *(Wedding Feast)*, 312–314
Virtuoso composer/conductor, 204
Volunteer bands, 114–116

W

Waits, 114
"Watts aesthetic," 228
Watts riots, 227, 228
Wedding Feast (van Thulden), 312–314
Western music
  markets, 43
  misconceptions held by Indians, 61
Whitman, Walt, 179
Wigan Casino, 86, 87, 95, 97
Williams, Vaughan, 182–183, 186–187, 191
Women musicians, 63–64, 123, 127*n*
Working-class
  in Liverpool, 286
  Victorian brass bands and, 105, 106, 107, 125
World music
  corporate globalization and, 41–42, 49
  exploitation/appropriation in, 17–19
  use of term, 47